STUFF

STUFF

*Humanity's Epic Journey
from Naked Ape
to Nonstop Shopper*

CHIP COLWELL

HURST & COMPANY, LONDON

First published in the United Kingdom in 2023 by
C. Hurst & Co. (Publishers) Ltd.,
New Wing, Somerset House, Strand, London, WC2R 1LA
© Chip Colwell, 2023
All rights reserved.

The right of Chip Colwell to be identified as the author of this publication is asserted by him in accordance with the Copyright, Designs and Patents Act, 1988.

A Cataloguing-in-Publication data record for this book is available from the British Library.

ISBN: 9781805260493

Published by arrangement with Chicago University Press.

www.hurstpublishers.com

Printed in Great Britain by Bell and Bain Ltd, Glasgow

TO MINA AND AMEN.
BECAUSE YOUR LOVE MEANS
MORE THAN ANY THING.

CONTENTS

On the Origin of Things:
An Introduction
1

LEAP 1: MAKE TOOLS

1. First Things First 13
2. The Matter at Hand 38
3. Everything under the Sun 59

LEAP 2: MAKE MEANING

4. A Thing of Beauty 87
5. Articles of Faith 106
6. All Things to All People 127

LEAP 3: MAKE MORE

7. In the Thick of Things 155
8. A Material World 180
9. Too Much of a Good Thing 206

On the Future of Things:
A Conclusion
229

Acknowledgments 249
Key Terms and Concepts 251
Notes 255
References 271
Image Credits 307
Index 311

ON THE ORIGIN OF THINGS

AN INTRODUCTION

> That's the whole meaning of life: trying to find a place for your stuff.
> GEORGE CARLIN

Some years ago, I was visiting family in Seattle when my sister casually asked me a question. A question that, as an archaeologist who makes his career studying the things humans have made and left behind, I felt I should have been able to answer.

"Why do we have so much stuff?" she asked.

My mouth opened to reply, but no words came. I stared awkwardly at my sister.

"I mean, where does it all come from?" she added.

My mind froze because the answer at first seemed so obvious—but also so obviously complex.

I looked around my sister's place. It was a nice American home. Framed pictures hung on the walls. Matching chairs encircled the dining table. Fat couches squatted next to a wood coffee table planted on a patterned rug slung across the floor. A guitar hung next to the fireplace, surrounded by bookshelves. A flat-screen TV hung on the wall. I could catch a glimpse of the kitchen, which I knew contained a stovetop oven, a sink and dishwasher, and cupboards overflowing with plates, silverware, Tupperware, and canned and fresh food. It was easy to guess all the stuff in the other spaces—the bedrooms, bathrooms, closets. Then I thought about the house itself, made of thousands of nails, bolts, screws, knobs, latches, along with all the metal, stone, wood, and plastics for the roof, walls, plumbing, electricity, and ventilation. Outside were patio furniture, tools for yardwork, the family cars, a boat, and a storage unit stuffed with more furniture, photo albums, and family heirlooms.

In that moment, as I sat there stumped, I was surrounded by perhaps 300,000 things—according to an especially enthusiastic estimate of the average American home.[1]

I knew why my sister had so much stuff. Some things were inherited. A few things were gifted. Most of it had been purchased, made in distant factories in China, Cambodia, and India. The simple answer was that she had so much stuff because she is an American consumer with enough resources and space to keep packing more and more stuff into her life.

Even as I began to offer this reply, I knew that my sister's question pointed to a deeper one about how humans have arrived at this moment. My sister's place—and my place, and likely yours too, whether in Swansea or Shanghai or Seattle—are spectacularly strange phenomena. In our planet's 4.5-billion-year history, no other organism has invented such a unique relationship with things.

In some ways, our species *Homo sapiens* is only a single iteration on a long evolutionary trend. The seeds of toolmaking are deeply buried in humanity's animal instincts. A dizzying array of creatures use the world's raw materials to survive. Octopuses off Indonesia turn broken coconut shells into homes. Elephants use branches to swat flies. Tuskfish swimming along Australia's Great Barrier Reef break apart clams using anvil stones. Crows, beavers, orangutans—the list goes on—all use tools.

And yet, while toolmaking is not unique to humans, humans have done something fantastically unique with the things they make. Humans make things to survive—houses and clothing—but we also make things because they give us pleasure, power, and pride. We make churches to worship God. We make art to express beauty. We make exuberantly expensive purses to display wealth. And we are constantly inventing ever more stuff. That *is* unique. After all, elephants make flyswatters. They don't make nuclear missiles and whoopie cushions and Italian villas.

What my sister was really asking was this: How did humans come to make the things that make us human? How did *Homo sapiens* also become *Homo stuffensis*, a stuffed species, defined and made by our things?

AN OVERSTUFFED WORLD

The holiday came and went, but that conversation stuck with me. In my life and my job, I found my sister's question playing like a catchy tune in a maddening loop in the back of my head.

I was then a curator at a natural history museum in Denver, Colorado. I shared responsibility for overseeing a collection of 100,000 human-made objects from around the world. With my new question acquired in Seattle, I became struck by how wondrously bizarre the museum's collection was. Whereas before I'd largely thought of each object's individual story—who made it, when, and in what cultural context—I now began to look across cultures and time periods. Only then did I begin to appreciate the collection's breathtaking unity and diversity. As I looked around the museum storeroom, it was an astonishing realization that the minds and hands of just one species invented everything from religious icons to shell money, stone knives to shotguns, coffins to drums. I was beginning to grasp that the museum collection was more than an array of distinct cultural notes. What story, I began to wonder, could all these objects tell if I were to listen to it as a symphony of human creativity played since the dawn of our kind?

As I became more fascinated by things after speaking with my sister, I also became more conflicted. I confess to a love-hate relationship with things. The love part comes with some particular objects: Vincent van Gogh's *Starry Night*, the turquoise ring my father has worn for decades, a table made by a carpenter friend, hand-hewed from blocks of glowing red cherry. Growing up, I lusted after the sensual curves of Lamborghinis. I prized my Air Jordan sneakers and (embarrassing to admit now) my Michael Jackson parachute pants (they really were cool then).

In high school, I had the luck to learn about archaeology and was hooked. Discovering ancient things was much of the fun. When I found my first arrowhead poking above the sand of the Sonoran Desert I whooped with joy. During college, I spent one summer in a cave in Belgium lying flat on my stomach scraping dirt with a dental pick; when I finally uncovered a stone tool that hadn't been seen in 75,000 years since a Neanderthal likely dropped it, a current of electricity rocketed up my spine. In my research with Native American tribes in the US Southwest, I have seen hundreds of ancient rock-art panels, yet my pulse still quickens when I come across those enigmatic images on stone made by unknown hands centuries or millennia ago.

But, as I've grown older, other things mean less and less. I don't care much about my car. I don't buy the latest tech gadgets. (My 2014 iPhone lasted me eight years.) My clothes fit in a handful of drawers. Junk drawers repel me. I crave a clutter-free home; I spend far more time trying to get rid of things than acquiring them. What I now love most about archaeological objects is what they say about the people who made them. In short, along with losing my hair, I've lost an interest in possessing things.

That minimalist instinct made me a strange kind of museum curator. Rather than collecting things, I spent much of my museum career returning sacred objects and ancestral remains to communities from where they were stolen or usurped. While I was often thrilled to see these things return to their place of origin, many of my colleagues were horrified to watch them go. Most curators are as loving and protective of their collections as a mother bear of her cubs. Consider that night in 2018 when Brazil's national museum of natural history caught fire and lit up Rio de Janeiro's dark sky. As some 20 million irreplaceable artifacts—the first dinosaur found in South America, Portuguese royal furniture, Indigenous ceremonial robes—were turning to ash and smoke, museum staff ran into the inferno to save what they could.

If I'm honest, I'm not so sure I would risk a burning building to save old stuff.

After years of running from this contradiction—*a museum curator who doesn't want more stuff!*—I finally realized that I would do better if I tried to understand it. Like an atheist fascinated by religious believers, I would study what I was not. I wanted to understand how our species went from naked ape to nonstop shopper. What happened over the millions of years that led our species from having nothing to needing everything?

I started searching for answers. I read. I found masses of tangled knowledge entwining history, psychology, archaeology, business, engineering, and philosophy. I considered the convergence of evolution and technology. I paused at the intersection of human ingenuity and imagination. I traveled. I visited an Italian cave with then the world's first known painted art, a Hong Kong skyscraper where a priestess channels the gods, and a mountain of trash so tall it rivals the Statue of Liberty and Big Ben. Yet I found no unified explanation, no theory that connected the dots across continents and generations.

This search was for my own good as much as anyone's. In the face of my minimalist disposition, I am aware of how I am constantly pulled back into the orbit of stuff. There is always some new need (a printer for my daughter's virtual schooling during the COVID-19 pandemic) or gift received (a letter opener from my parents for my 45th birthday) or thing needing replacement (running shoes to replace my old ones that have a huge hole in the left toe) that keeps finding its way into my life. Despite myself, I think Tesla cars are super cool. There is just an endless flow of things leaving and entering my life, as steady as the ocean's tides. Many days I have wondered: Is being with things simply being human?

In this, at least, I am not alone. By almost any measure, humanity today is trapped in a web of stuff, an endless cycle of consumption. Annual US spending on durable goods—products that do not wear out quickly, such as washing machines, jewelry, furniture—adjusted for inflation, has soared from about $100 billion in 1967 to more than $1.4 trillion in 2017.[2] The UK, France, Germany, and on, all saw similar increases. All that stuff goes into our big houses. Following World War II, the average American house was about 800 square feet; today, houses newly built in the US, but also Canada, Australia, and New Zealand, all hover around 2,000 square feet.[3] And the junk goes into storage. In 1993, new construction of self-storage facilities in the US was $100 million; in 2018, it was $5 billion, a 4,900 percent increase.[4] And a lot more of it ends up as waste. According to a World Bank report that surveyed 217 countries, in 2020 the world generated about two billion tons of trash; by 2050, that number will grow to 3.4 billion tons.[5] In more concrete terms: in three decades, the world will throw away the equivalent weight of more than 38,000 aircraft carriers every year. There is now even a multimillion-dollar industry, led by the Japanese organizing consultant Marie Kondo, simply instructing people how to "tidy up" all our junk.[6]

Our world is overstuffed.

THREE BIG LEAPS

I propose humanity has taken three big leaps—and lots of little steps in between—that have taken us on our journey with stuff for more than three million years, that carried us from the first known tool to Marie Kondo's empire of closet organizing.

The first step was to recognize that the natural materials of the world can be transformed into something different, bent to one's imagination and will. Today, it is obvious that a stone can become a spear, or that a hollowed-out log can serve as a canoe. But to our distant primate ancestors, they did not see the things of the world as a puzzle to put together to solve the challenge of survival. To most of our evolutionary kin, a rock was just a rock.

The discovery of tools seems to have happened this side of 4 million years ago—the first cut marks on bone from a stone tool date to 3.39 million years ago in Ethiopia, while the first stone tools date to 3.3 million years ago in Kenya—when rough stones were used to butcher animals. By 2.5 million years ago, ancestors in the *Homo* line advanced these rudimentary utensils into a more sophisticated technology. Called the Oldowan toolkit (for where these tools were first found, in the desert of Olduvai Gorge, Tanzania), it included knives and scrapers and other basic implements. From this tradition arrived the Acheulean hand ax. Shaped like a big, clumsy arrowhead, this stone ax was super versatile: it could chop and scrape, pry open and poke.

Make no mistake, this all-in-one tool was not merely a thing. It was the gate opening to a new evolutionary path. Biology and culture combined to give our ancestors bigger brains and more-efficient digestive systems, which increased their chances of survival. Some of the first human technologies were so good that they lasted for more than a million years. They laid the foundation for the development of hunter-gatherer societies and then the successive material revolutions that followed the Stone Age.

Each new tool created the possibility for the next. Stone implements allowed our ancestors to butcher animals efficiently, which led to the extraction of tough tendons. Tendons became thread. Thread led to needles. Needles led to clothing. Through such a cascade of inventions, our ancestors, those naked apes, eventually no longer had to be naked at all. Clothing, as just one example of a crucial material creation, then enabled our ancestors to infiltrate every corner of the globe, providing warmth in the cold and shade in the heat. Clothing also served as camouflage for hunting and hiding, wraps for wounds, backpacks for carrying babies or supplies—becoming still much more when used for dancing, rituals, and art.

Enter leap two: meaning. This moment arrived when tools became more than just gadgets to accomplish discrete tasks. Somewhere along the line, but definitely on this side of 50,000 years ago, our ancestors realized that tools held the capacity for something more.

In the fog of deep history, we do not know what form of meaning our ancestors invented first. It could have been religion—the belief that a stone tool was the representation of a hunting god. It could have been an early form of money—two Neanderthals trading a pound of food for a dozen beads. Or perhaps it was art, when one day a distant *Homo erectus* cousin sat by the ocean and carved a zigzag into a shell to represent the mesmerizing beauty of crashing waves.

Meaning began. Our ancestors came to realize that objects could contain something more than their utility. Things could be made into art, into belief, into money, and into memories. The insertion of meaning into objects ensured that things would be central not just to humanity's biological developments; things would come to have meanings that changed how people interacted and saw themselves and each other. The symbolic value of money and gifts created new economic and social networks. People's identities could literally be worn on their sleeves. Through this second leap, things would come to live at the very center of *Homo sapiens'* existence as social beings.

The third leap started some 500 years ago in the lead up to the First Industrial Revolution. Although the elite throughout history had always acquired vast wealth and surrounded themselves with abundance, the arrival of new manufacturing processes and energy sources changed everything for the rest of us.

With the invention of factories, industrialists could make consumable goods more cheaply and in massive numbers. In tandem, the shifting economic structures of society created new classes of people who could afford to consume those goods. Designers and marketers would eventually master new techniques to tap into our deep evolutionary desire to possess—and then invent a strategy to have things fall apart so that we would constantly need to buy more. Archaeologists have found hoards of treasure buried millennia ago. In the post–Industrial Age, however, hoarding would take on entirely new meanings, some with profoundly destructive effects. Leap 3 was the invention of abundance.

Which explains our predicament. The first tool changed our lineage's odds of survival, by altering our bodies and our imagination. It created the possibility of a wild three-million-plus-year ride that took the world from crude stone tools to, seemingly beyond all odds, violins and condoms and drones. Our nameless-ancestor inventor who realized a sharp stone could be a cutting tool unwittingly laid the foundation for our human story. Stuff empowered humans to remake Earth itself, to suit our own wondrous and terrible needs.

Given a world of endless consumerism and compulsive hoarding, an environment strained beyond its limit, we must ask where our next collective destination on this journey will be. Can humans live without stuff? If not, then what will it take to rearrange our connections to the material worlds we create? It is hard to imagine, and yet, as this book shows, we have been constantly changing our relationship with things since things were first invented. So why not welcome another change that reduces overconsumption and halts a world binging on stuff?

This next step might be humanity's most difficult yet. It might also be the most important.

RETHINK EVERY THING

This book, then, is a tour across millions of years to explain how humans have arrived at this moment — a world that both needs things and is suffering terribly because of them. Through the lens of archaeology, travels across the globe, and interviews with the people who study and manage material culture, this book tells the story of humanity's stuff.

This story is a big one, spanning eons and covering every place humans have come to call home. In this way, it joins other recent "big histories," such as Yuval Harari's blockbuster 2018 book, *Sapiens: A Brief History of Humankind*, and David Graeber and David Wengrow's magisterial 2021 *The Dawn of Everything: A New History of Humanity*. Like Harari, I frame our human story in three big successive moments. But like Graeber and Wengrow, I am skeptical that these moments were inevitable, that our world today is somehow the inexorable result of an evolutionary drive toward shopping malls and global supply chains. Instead, our material life, as it turns out, is the product of chances and choices, opportunities pursued and refused.

What this means is that our story is not only still being written, but it is a story that we are still writing together. Because this story is past and present as well as future, I do hope I am justified in asking that this book will find a place on your bookshelf. Another thing in your life, to help you rethink every thing.

LEAP 1

MAKE TOOLS

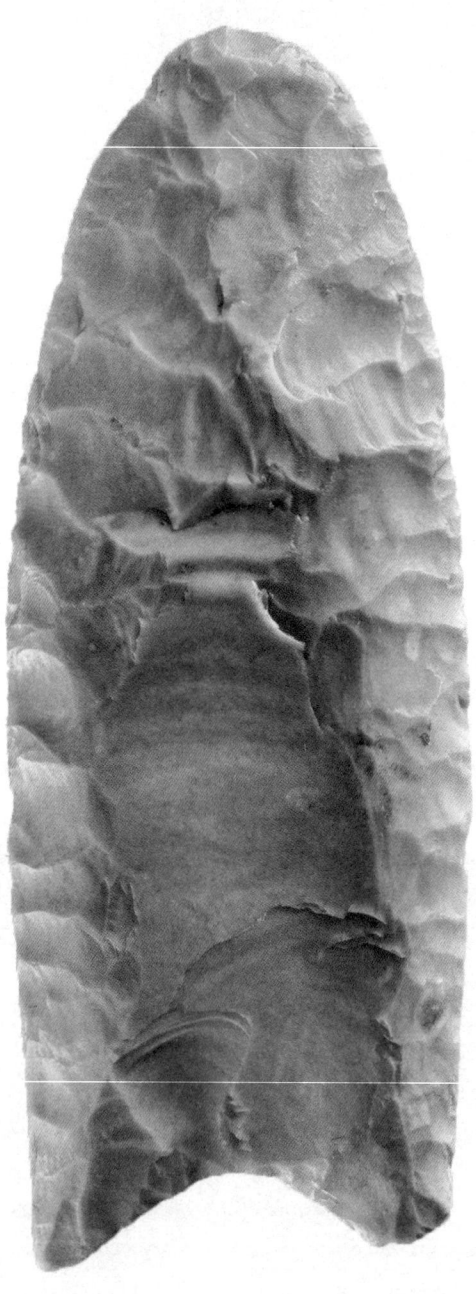

1. Clovis spearpoints are among the earliest stone technologies in the Americas.

1

FIRST THINGS FIRST

In the summer of 1960, a young woman landed on the shores of Lake Tanganyika, a long, thin expanse of still water surrounded by green and brown hills in the heart of Africa.[1] She had traveled from England to Nairobi and then hundreds of miles over dirt roads to pursue a novel research project: to observe the lives of chimpanzees to see what the great apes could reveal about human evolution.

Only 26 years old, brainy and quiet, Jane Goodall had not yet gone to college. She was accompanied by Vanne, her mother, since the British authorities would not allow a young woman to go into the Gombe Stream Chimpanzee Reserve alone. And yet, it was Goodall's observations walking one day alone that would change humanity's perspective on its relationship with things.

Her arrival at Lake Tanganyika coincided with a moment of dire chaos. The first town where she stayed, Kigoma, was filled with refugees. They were fleeing violence on the other side of the lake, in the Republic of the Congo, as the country struggled to find its footing following independence. After two weeks in Kigoma living on the grounds of the local prison and making thousands of Spam sandwiches for the refugees, the aspiring primatologist was finally able to make the last leg of her journey. Goodall, her mother, and a local man named Dominic Charles Bandora, who joined them to look after the camp and cook, left Kigoma in an aluminum boat with several weeks' provisions. They headed north, skirting the shore for a dozen miles to the reserve. The boat driver dropped them off and left. A British botanist who helped them make this trek later said that he was sure he would never see them again.

Deep in the forest, the group met up with two game wardens who took them in. The women set up an old army tent and unpacked. With daylight fast fading, Goodall started out for the hills to explore.

She savored the moment. This was her childhood dream realized. She had grown up in an old English manor house without electricity, becoming the kind of precocious girl who delighted in watching a chicken lay an egg. She devoured books on natural history. She created a museum in the glass conservatory, filling it with exotic bits of flowers and shells, and a human skeleton borrowed from her uncle who had acquired it in medical school.

Goodall developed into a woman who had no interest in the then traditional path of marriage and family. She set off for East Africa. In 1957, she met Louis Leakey. Leakey was a celebrated curator at the Coryndon Museum in Nairobi, famous for his discoveries of ancient fossils in East Africa. He was brilliant, pudgy, and gray haired; it has been said that he had a paradoxical tendency toward body odor and extramarital affairs. Leakey and Goodall's relationship was platonic, but the two bonded immediately over a mutual love of museum specimens, wild animals, and adventure. At first, Leakey asked Goodall to house-sit. Then he asked her to become his secretary. Then he invited her to join him on an archaeological expedition to Olduvai, a valley 500 miles southwest of Nairobi that Leakey was proving to be the birthplace of humankind.

Soon enough, Leakey had yet another scheme in mind for Goodall. To truly understand *Homo sapiens*' most ancient kin, he believed that an extended study of the living great apes in their natural habitat would offer incomparable scientific insight. Traveling to observe the animals would demand fortitude, mettle, and indifference to the criticisms that would likely come from the profession for this unproven method. Leakey hoped that Goodall would accept this audacious assignment. She did.

Leakey laid plans for her to go to the Gombe Stream Chimpanzee Reserve, which was then in the British protectorate of Tanganyika. (The reserve would become Gombe National Park in Tanzania.) Leakey struggled to finance the expedition, until finally a businessman from Illinois enamored with the burgeoning science of human origins provided money for six months of research.

The project did not start out especially well. The work was hard and tedious. Most depressingly, when the chimpanzees sensed Goodall's approach, they fled farther into the forest, out of sight. Still, Goodall was encouraged by her mother, who pointed out that she had already learned what the chimps ate, that they built nests at night and traveled in different group sizes.

The experience turned worse before it got better. Goodall's mother left five months in. The next week, a group of men wielding machetes arrived at Goodall's camp, to scare her off so they could turn the forest into farmland. But Goodall wasn't in camp, having gone off early that morning to search for chimpanzees. She went back to Kigoma for a while, until it was safe to return.

On the morning of Friday, November 4, 1960, Goodall started out from her camp, listening for the hoots and hollers of chimpanzees. She was unaccompanied; her local research partner was off running errands that day. Following the chimps' cries, she headed north and then up a high ridge. Through a thicket of trees, she happened to notice a tall tower of earth—a termite mound—and something black by it, which she first thought was the stump of a tree. It was a chimpanzee.

Swiftly, she dropped down and crept through the grass to hide behind a tree. The chimp was eating termites. She moved to get a better view. It was an adult male chimp, with a dark face, gently arched eyebrows, and an elegant gray beard framing his face. She wrote in her notebook: "very handsome."[2] Later she would name him David Graybeard.

She continued watching. Graybeard then did something odd. Goodall scribbled on: "Very deliberately he pulled a thick grass stalk towards him & broke off a piece about 18" long."[3] The chimp turned his back and climbed the hill. She couldn't make out what he did next. Then Graybeard left, going into the forest, returned for a moment, and then left for good. The researcher sensed she was onto something big.

Two days later, Goodall returned to the same termite mound. Again, she found Graybeard there, this time accompanied by another chimp, using straw to eat the termites. "I could see a little better the use of the piece of straw," she recorded in her notebook. "It was held in the left hand, poked into the ground, and then removed coated with termites. The straw was then raised to the mouth & insects picked off with the lips, along the length of the straw, starting in the middle. . . . He chewed each mouthful."[4]

Goodall realized this was a monumental discovery. It was then believed that while some animals used tools, only humans *made* them—the difference between a beaver using fallen logs for a den and a human sawing planks to build a house. Leakey's search in Olduvai was not only for ancient human fossil skeletons, but for the stone tools that defined them as being part of our human lineage. As early as

2. Bonobos, a closely related species to chimpanzees, use tools. Here, a bonobo at the San Diego Zoo uses a stick to fish for termites.

1791, the American polymath Benjamin Franklin was quoted as defining "Man" (embracing the gendered, and problematic, translation of *Homo*) as a "tool-making animal."[5] In 1831, the Scottish philosopher and writer Thomas Carlyle published a celebrated satirical essay that in part considered what makes humans unique. Carlyle described humans as naturally weak and useless, unable to carry loads or even defend themselves. But unlike other animals, humans can devise tools, and thus conquer the mountains and seas. "Nowhere do you find him without tools," Carlyle wrote; "without tools he is nothing, with tools he is all."[6]

Yet, others were not so convinced. In 1891, the Dutch physician and paleoanthropologist Eugène Dubois discovered in Java an ancient species with a big skull and upright posture—what we now know to be *Homo erectus* (upright human)—which shifted the field's emphasis to brain size and upright walking as the likely vanguard of human origins.[7] Additionally, there were other hints that tools were not the exclusive domain of *Homo sapiens*. In the early 20th century, chimps in lab settings had shown ingenuity in turning objects into tools, such as to retrieve out-of-reach food. And in 1950, Harry Beatty, an American adventurer, published an account of chimpanzees in the Liberia wilderness using stones as hammers and anvils to break open hard walnut shells. Six years later, Fred Merfield, an English hunter, saw chimpanzees in the wild use sticks and twigs to procure honey from a beehive.[8]

But these accounts were anecdotes, not field-based research.[9] And, by the time Leakey and his contemporaries were searching for fossils, the 20th century had given the world a new love of things. As Louis Leakey's son Richard, himself a paleoanthropologist, wrote, the question of what defines humanity took hold amid the material revolutions of his father's generation: "By the 1940s, the world was in thrall to the magic and power of technology."[10] When Goodall was sent to study chimpanzees, most archaeologists had turned back to "Man the Tool-Maker," as scholars of Goodall's time called it—the hypothesis that toolmaking uniquely steered humanity on its evolutionary course.[11]

Now Goodall's observations provided definitive proof that this hypothesis was wrong. Chimps made tools. Here they were purposefully cutting down straw to a particular length and stripping off leaves to make a kind of fishing rod for termites. The discovery would secure her funding to continue research in the years ahead. It would lead to her PhD at the University of Cambridge. Several years later, once published in the pages of *National Geographic* and shown in a 1965 documentary TV special, the discovery would rocket Goodall into the stratosphere of global scientist superstars.[12]

"Not only was he using the grass as a tool," Goodall later wrote about Graybeard, "he was, by modifying it to suit a special purpose, actually showing the crude beginnings of *tool-making*." The conclusion was clear: "Humans were not, after all, the only tool-making animals."[13]

BEHAVIORAL INNOVATION

Jane Goodall's breakthrough opened the eyes of researchers and the public to new possibilities. As Louis Leakey famously telegraphed her after she excitedly revealed the discovery to her mentor: "Now we must redefine tool, redefine Man, or accept chimpanzees as humans."[14] In fact, versions of all three happened. Some philosophers began searching for new ways to define humanity's distinctiveness.[15] (Language? Food sharing? Self-awareness? Opposable thumbs?) Scientists showed how closely related chimpanzees and humans truly are in our genes and behaviors. And other researchers revisited how "tools" are defined and which animals make them.

After all, if chimps made tools right under our noses, how many other species had been overlooked? Scholars were anxious to explore this question because they hoped it would offer new insights into the evolution of cognition, the emergence of creativity, and the genesis of humanity as biological and social beings. Precisely because tools could no longer be considered the exclusive domain of humans, they held the possibility of deep origins in the cavernous history of the animal mind. Much was at stake. Following Goodall, a new generation of scientists looked to the land, sea, and air for more species that made and used tools.

After decades of work, the list of toolmaking animals has proven to be paradoxically broad and limited. Tool use can be defined as an animal exerting control over an object to physically alter another object, or to mediate information between the tool user and their environment.[16] Of note, technology is a broader system of knowledge that can draw upon concepts of art, engineering, and science to materially connect life, society, and the environment. One widely referenced list, published in a 2010 article in the journal *Behaviour* by the anthropologists Vicki K. Bentley-Condit and E. O. Smith, catalogued 418 types of tool use across different animals.[17] These occurrences were not limited to a close circle of primate kin. A breathtaking array of animals make and use tools: insects, mollusks, crustaceans, fish, octopuses, birds, and mammals. Their tools are just as diverse as the animals who craft them. Objects are taken apart, added together, combined, reshaped. In this sense, tool use is very broad: from creeping critters to our primate cousins, tools are made in many ways and forms.

Not surprisingly, the 2010 list documents that food is a big motivation for tools (60 percent of the 418 instances). Red-tailed hawks bash snakes against boulders. Seagulls drop clams on rocks. Fire ants use sand to absorb honey so it can be transported home.

Yet, tools are made for more reasons than food. The list shows that 36 percent of the documented instances involve tool use for "physical maintenance"; for example, when a lion was observed using a thorn to remove a different thorn stuck in its paw. Other motivations include mate attraction (male African tree crickets cut holes in leaves to amplify their calls to females), nest construction (digger wasps gather pebbles to build tunnels), and predator defense (hermit crabs place sea anemones on their shells to ward off octopuses).[18] In a few cases, the motivation for tool use remains uncertain; for example, when an ornithologist in England watched a blackbird clear snow from the ground using a twig.[19] This list makes clear—with the exception of that curious British blackbird—the evolutionary benefits of tool use. Food. Shelter. Health. Defense. Sex. Tools help animals survive and reproduce.

Given the advantages of tools and their presence across radically different forms of life, it would be easy to assume that evolution would

3. A hermit crab dons a sea anemone as a tool for defense.

have led to many toolmakers.[20] In fact, tools are nature's unicorns, rare and elusive. While surely more instances will be discovered, it's striking that Bentley-Condit and Smith's catalogue proves a limited distribution: toolmakers are known in only 3 of 35 phyla and 7 of 107 classes in the animal kingdom.

Homo sapiens aren't the world's exclusive toolmaker. But *Homo sapiens* are in pretty exclusive toolmaking company.

Many people's first reaction to the list of toolmakers being so relatively short (given the world's 8.7 million known species) is that toolmaking depends on intelligence, and intelligence, this line of thinking would suggest, is a rare gift in nature.[21] A basic level of intelligence indeed seems necessary. A bacterium is unlikely to build a skyscraper anytime soon. However, while some smart animals make tools, other animals with limited cognitive capacities also make tools. The myrmicine ants who use leaves, mud, and sand to transport food to their nests are smart enough to make these tools, but they're not as smart—at least, in terms of measurable creativity, cognition, reasoning, problem-solving, and self-awareness—as octopuses or elephants or chimpanzees.[22]

This is not to say that intelligence is irrelevant beyond a minimal threshold. Intelligence matters a lot. But not for all toolmakers. Rather, intelligence is a primary driver for those animals that can be called "creative tool users."

Imagine a clear tube sitting on a laboratory table. At the bottom of the tube is a wiggling earthworm; a long stick stands beside the tube. A lab technician brings in a New Caledonian crow, a bird with luxurious black feathers and a thick beak that is a known toolmaker in the wild. These crows know how to shape sticks into hooks that they poke into trees to fish for insects—a method estimated to be 10 times more efficient than procuring insects without tools.[23] So, sooner or later in the lab, the crow will pick up the stick in its beak and fish out the worm for a snack. Next, the lab tech replaces the crow with its evolutionary cousin, a rook—a bird that does not use tools in nature. In the lab setting, though, the rook figures out the stick can be used as a fishing rod for the worm. Now imagine the lab tech replaces the rook with a pigeon—a bird that also does not use tools in nature. However, the pigeon, unlike the rook, no matter how much it deliberates, is very unlikely to realize on its own that the stick can be used to get to that tasty worm.[24]

This is the puzzle that Josep Call, the director of the Wolfgang Köhler Primate Research Center in Leipzig, Germany, has long worked to figure out. How is it that some species seem to be adept tool users in natural and experimental settings (like the New Caledonian crow), some only during lab experiments (the rook), and still others never at all (the pigeon)?

In a 2013 book chapter spelling out his research, Call is initially skeptical that intelligence can explain these differences.[25] He suggests that humans have largely assumed the importance of intelligence—the mental capacity for learning, reasoning, and understanding—because of our vanity and self-regard as master toolmakers: we're super toolmakers *and* we're super smart; thus, every toolmaker must be as smart as we are!

Call points out that while the list of tool users is now long, some tools require more complicated thinking than others. As an example,

Call compares the archerfish, which shoots water out of its mouth to gun down insects that hover above the river, with the orangutan that sees a deep tube with a peanut at the bottom and figures out that if it fills the tube with water, the peanut will float to the top. The archerfish is showing "behavioral specialization," whereas the orangutan is showing "behavioral innovation." The archerfish is shooting water because that's what archerfish do. The orangutan's solution to the peanut problem is showing its flexibility and adaptiveness. Unlike archerfish, which pretty much can *only* shoot water, orangutans and other creative tool users, Call explains, "are not only able to use old solutions to solve novel problems but also can generate new solutions for old problems."[26] Humans, orangutans, New Caledonian crows all are creative tool users.

Call continues to explain that animals who make tools through behavioral specialization—such as archerfish shooting water and ants carrying honey absorbed in sand—acquire this skill through learning. This kind of tool use is not so different from other behaviors, like a fear grin among macaques, which, once acquired by a species, are simply learned and repeated by successive generations.

This learning route to tools, however, is contrasted with animals that can also use *reasoning*. A pigeon can be trained to do complex tasks, but it struggles to connect disconnected fragments of information and spontaneously arrive at creative solutions.[27] As Call notes, an Egyptian vulture will use stones to crack open ostrich eggs; the vulture likely won't ascertain that the stones could also be used to hide food from its rivals. Like the pigeon's, the vulture's tool use is limited to behavioral specialization. On a continuum, the pigeon and vulture are clustered at one end, as they are missing some form of intelligence that a New Caledonian crow has.

In contrast, chimpanzees learn how to use tools like termite fishing rods from their mothers.[28] But they can also spontaneously and intentionally arrive at innovative solutions. In a lab setting with a scattering of boxes and a ripe banana hanging out of reach from the ceiling, chimpanzees have been documented to stack the boxes to make a ladder to reach the prize.[29]

4. In a 1927 experiment, chimpanzees made a structure of boxes to reach a banana attached to the ceiling, revealing their ability as "creative tool users."

All this suggests that tool use first arose as an evolutionary specialization that was learned. But then, for a select number of species that evolved to think in more intricate ways—to use reasoning—they were able to *creatively* innovate on these foundational tools. In other words, somewhere along an evolutionary branch of our sequoian ancestral tree, a relative of ours used its flowering intelligence to make a discovery that would forever change the planet: that the things of the world could be molded to our will.

LUCY'S TOOLKIT

In the summer of 2019, I sat at the National Museum of Ethiopia studying two fossils. Room 303 was well appointed with microscopes and computers, and cabinets topped with plastic replicas of ancient hominin skulls. The lab was filled with soft light from a bank of windows that opened to a canopy of trees and a busy street below. The chirping of birds mingled with the faint buzz of traffic.

My colleague, Zeray Alemseged, a biological anthropology professor at the University of Chicago, had brought out the two fossils he had discovered a decade earlier in Dikika, a land of barren eroded hills and washes in northeastern Ethiopia. Alemseged told me that when he first found the bone fragments, he didn't think much of them.

They looked ordinary. Both were about the length of my fingers, off white in hue and as smooth as ivory, like piano keys. Each had a few noticeable parallel marks, deep grooves cutting into the bone. "When I saw them," Alemseged said, "I didn't know what they were."

Alemseged and his colleagues analyzed the fossils. Eventually, they determined that the bones from two different animals—a rib from a buffalo-size animal, a leg bone from an impala-size one—bore the remnants of simple but revolutionary cut marks. A sharp stone had been used to butcher these animals 3.39 million years ago. The bones were evidence of the world's first stone-tool use.[30]

The 2010 discovery was so important because it pushed back the first sign of tool use by 800,000 years. Even more significant, it meant that the first stone-tool users were not from the genus *Homo*, our most immediate branch of the human family tree. Instead, they were further down evolution's tree trunk in the more distant hominin genus *Australopithecus*. (The word *hominin* refers to an individual belonging to extinct or modern human species, including all our ancestors in the genera *Homo, Australopithecus, Paranthropus, Ardipithecus, Orrorin,* and *Sahelanthropus*.)[31] Alemseged hypothesized that australopithecines—apelike creatures that walked upright, very much like the famous fossil discovered in 1974, called Lucy, or Dinknesh in Ethiopia, meaning "you are marvelous"—scavenged animals and butchered them with sharp rocks that happened to be lying around.[32] "Now, when we imagine Lucy walking around the East African landscape looking for food, we can for the first time imagine her with a stone tool in hand and looking for meat," said Shannon McPherron, Alemseged's collaborator, an archaeologist at the Max Planck Institute for Evolutionary Anthropology in Leipzig, when the discovery was published. "With stone tools in hand to quickly pull off flesh and break open bones, animal carcasses would have become a more attractive source for food. This type of behavior sent us down a path that later would lead to two of the defining features of our species—carnivory and tool manufacture and use."[33]

Not everyone accepted the idea that "Lucy's toolkit" had been unearthed.[34] Critics questioned whether stone tools really had made the grooves in the animal bones. Others thought two fragments of bone were not strong-enough evidence to make such an important claim. Still others asked where and what were the tools that could have made such marks.

Then in 2015, a team led by the archaeologist Sonia Harmand, working on the shore of Lake Turkana in northern Kenya at a site named Lomekwi 3, found more than 150 stone tools—identified by their shape and the wear on them—dating to 3.3 million years ago.[35] This discovery, combined with Alemseged's earlier one, convincingly demonstrated that stone tools were made more than three million years ago by Lucy's species *Australopithecus afarensis* or possibly an even more distant relative to us named *Kenyanthropus platyops*.

"With the cut marks from Dikika we had the victim" of the stone

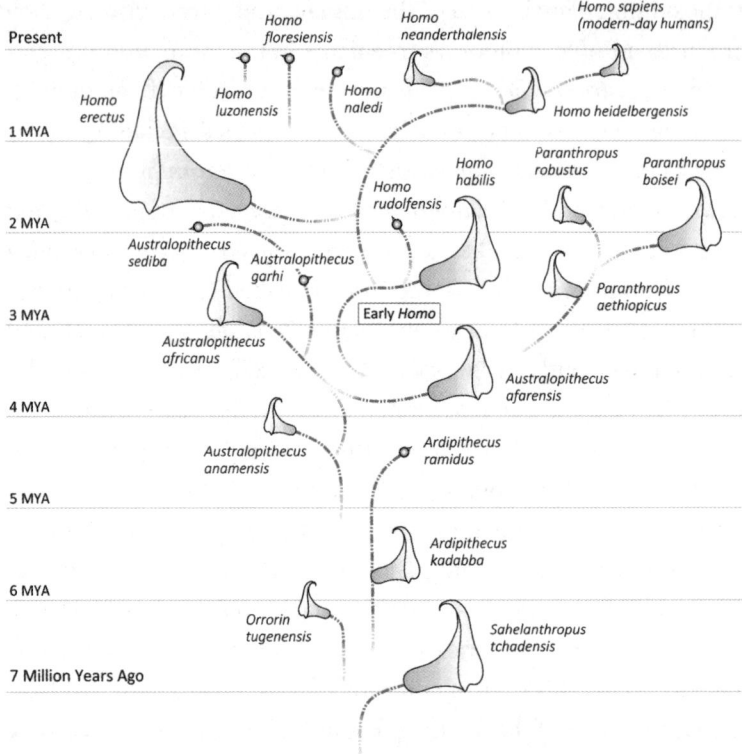

5. Our hominin family tree has many branches, buds, and flowers. The *Australopithecus* branch is Lucy's line, which seems to have first invented stone tools about 3.4 million years ago. Our most direct line, the *Homo* branch, broke off from other hominin species about 2.8 million years ago, and either inherited stone tools from *Australopithecus* or invented them independently.

tools, Alemseged told the press at the time. "Harmand's discovery gives us the smoking gun."[36]

Or, at least, the smoking stones.

While it's possible that even earlier tools made of plant material existed—for instance, digging tools made of sharpened wood would have been very useful for gathering root vegetables; or perhaps slings for carrying infants, leaving hands free for work—and that even older stone tools could be found, these recent discoveries show an incredible time depth to the invention of stone tools. They also show that the first tools (of any kind) preceded the *Homo* genus.[37] As Goodall discovered and as the list of toolmaking species reveals, tools were not a unique human invention. Nevertheless, these first stone tools, appearing by at least 3.3 million years ago, are vitally important because stone tools point to the beginning of our uniquely human love affair with things.

Sitting in Ethiopia in Alemseged's lab, I squinted at the two mute bone fragments. They were so simple—boring, actually. Broken bones with a few gashes. Yet, they distill one of the first big eureka moments of our lineage, no less important to humanity's history than the first wheel, first printing press, or first lightbulb. This was the first of everything.

THE FIRST CUT

High grass barely hides a family of lions devouring a buffalo-like animal along a riverbank. The prey lies prone on its back, not quite dead. Three lions pin the animal down with their massive claws. Their heads jerk as they rip off strips of muscle amid streams of dark blood.

At the river's edge, a troop of humanlike creatures hides among reeds. They watch and wait until the buffalo dies and then burst out toward the lions, screaming and fanning their arms. Some pick up round cobblestones and hurl them at the roaring lions. The battle wears on. As the sun sinks on the horizon, the lions finally grow weary and abandon their feast.

The hungry scavengers hover over the buffalo. Some struggle to tear off the slivers of meat left hanging from the lions' half-finished meal. Others imitate the lions, eating with their faces in the carcass. But one female pauses and looks down.

A cobble that had been thrown is lying on the ground, almost as if it had been waiting to be seen. The rock is half broken. One side is rounded; the other side has been fractured into a flat, sharp edge.

She picks it up—it fits just right in the hand—and lifts it to the dead buffalo. Then she moves the blade against the flesh, forming a deep groove. The first cut. Her fingers peel off a slice of velvety red tissue, and she slips it into her mouth.

This is what archaeologists do: we take the material evidence—the fractured traces of real events—and spin them into a story. Sitting in Alemseged's lab, this is what I imagined those two bones telling me. And while it's not a scientific account, it is based on what science tells us likely happened in those moments more than 3.3 million years ago.

As the researchers Gavin R. Hunt, Russell D. Gray, and Alex H. Taylor hypothesize, this scene would have been composed of three key elements.[38] First, our ancestor who made this discovery—let's call her Dinknesh—had a problem. Eating raw meat is hard; it requires strong jaws and sharp teeth. She needed a better way to eat. She looked down. She saw a sharp rock. But for her it wasn't just a sharp rock. She saw a sharp rock that could be a kind of knife—a blade for cutting. Instead of a world just filled with blank objects, now it had the possibility of holding things—a thing that calls attention to us because it is useful, because it holds the possibility of meaning.[39] This alone was a magnificent, mind-blowing realization. Consider that termites are found across central Africa, South America, and Southeast Asia. Yet few primates (and not even all chimps) have figured out what Graybeard and his clan have: that shaping blades of straw can be used to fish out those morsels.

What enabled Dinknesh to see the world so differently, to be an inventor? Perhaps there was some unknown preexisting behavioral specialization among Dinknesh's people. Maybe she learned to throw rocks as weapons to scare predators. Perhaps her people piled up stones to hide carcasses. It also seems probable that Dinknesh was playful when she was a kid. She would have climbed trees and run her fingers through streams. She would have watched insects hop from leaf to leaf. She would have picked up a broken rock and run her finger along its sharp edge. She then would have hoarded this information for use someday—a day years later, when she stood hungry before a carcass pondering how to get through its thick, tough skin to peel off strips of meat.[40]

So perhaps Dinknesh combined her species' behavioral specialization with her own insights, combining *learning with reasoning*. The first element was the brilliant insight that a stone can be used to cut.

Second was Dinknesh's ability to hold the rock and use it to achieve her goal. Dinknesh bent down to pick up the rock. She *could* bend down and pick it up. She *could* turn the rock over in her hand, line up the sharp edge to the carcass's skin and draw a line to cut. Creative tool use often requires considerable dexterity. Dinknesh not only needed the cognitive abilities to arrive at her idea but also the motor skills to execute it. The second element was *physical ability*.

Third, Dinknesh needed the focused attention, planning, decision-making, and mental flexibility to integrate information, visual processing, and still more cognitive abilities to move from the problem she faced to the solution she arrived at. She needed a good working memory. Dinknesh couldn't get too distracted from the problem she needed to solve. And then, once she finally broke through and discovered that a sharp stone could be a knife, the next time Dinknesh sat down before a carcass ready to eat, she needed to think, basically, "Now, how did I make that knife again?"

Later, as Dinknesh's evolutionary descendants added more steps to making stone tools, memory became even more important. There is a big difference between a red-tailed hawk that only must remember to bash a snake against a boulder to kill it, and an early human who has to bang two rocks together in some fashion to make a tool that makes dinner. The more creative and complex the tool, the more capacity is needed for mental gymnastics to address what researchers call the "problem-solution distance." One 2010 paper published in the academic journal *Current Anthropology*, by the German researcher Miriam Noël Haidle, mapped out how animals need to think about tools, and found that digger wasps, which use tools as a behavioral specialization to build tunnels, require far less working memory than behavioral innovators like chimpanzees.[41] The final element is a *working memory*.

Hunt and his colleagues believe that tools were not invented once in a single moment. Rather, toolmaking in the animal kingdom is the result of many "independent innovative events."[42] So, even the two bone fragments I was holding in Alemseged's lab were unlikely to be evidence of *the* first tools. Instead, the tools used by Dinknesh and all the species before and since were likely the product of many inventions many times, some fading away from use completely and others leading to new tools.

Yet even such events would have been spectacularly rare—a handful of moments across millions of species and millions of years. These moments would require a situation where (1) the material for a tool was available and helpful, (2) an individual could conceive of an object as a tool and physically use it, (3) the individual could be successful enough to remember to use the tool once again and (4) then, at some later time, the individual could be able to remember to use it yet again to start the process all over.[43] And even further, this behavior had to be so advantageous that it was learned across a group and passed down through the generations.

The invention of stone tools by Dinknesh, or whatever their names were, was the result of a string of moments so rare we could almost call them a beautiful accident. And while we can only imagine those mythic moments, we do know that those first stone tools, that first cut, changed everything.

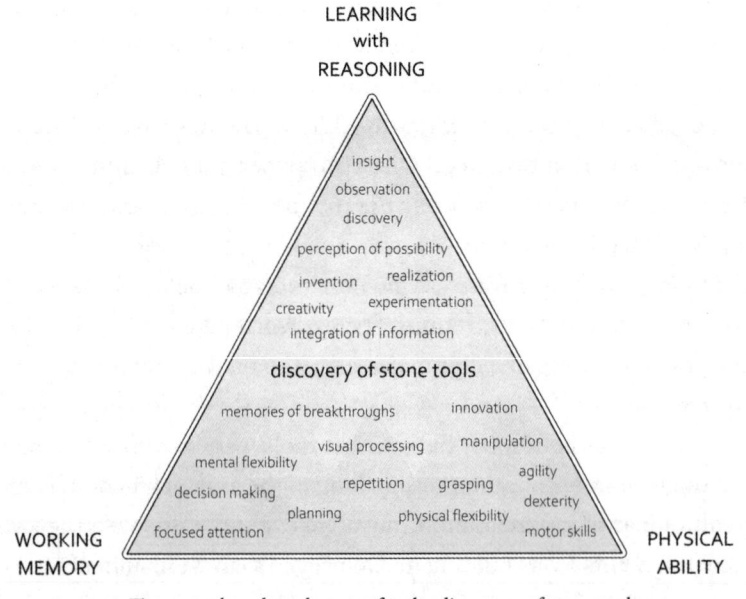

LEARNING
with
REASONING

insight
observation
discovery
perception of possibility
invention   realization
creativity   experimentation
integration of information
discovery of stone tools
memories of breakthroughs   innovation
visual processing   manipulation
mental flexibility   agility
repetition   grasping
decision making   dexterity
planning   physical flexibility
focused attention   motor skills

WORKING
MEMORY

PHYSICAL
ABILITY

6. There are three key elements for the discovery of stone tools.

HANDY MAN

On December 1, 1960, almost exactly a month after Jane Goodall telegraphed her discovery at the termite mound in the Gombe Stream Chimpanzee Reserve to Louis Leakey, the paleoanthropologist was scrambling up a hill accompanied by two colleagues from the Geological Survey of Tanganyika. Leakey arrived at the summit out of breath. He turned his gaze across Olduvai Gorge.

Located in what was then Tanganyika, now Tanzania, the gorge pierces the eastern edge of the Serengeti Plains—a land of undulating hills and scattered trees that is interrupted by low mountains and sudden columns of red earth. Leakey knew that, at the southern edge of the Great Rift Valley, where two tectonic plates diverged some 25 million years ago to create a series of basins, the Olduvai Gorge still held profound secrets. The conundrum was how to find them.

As he studied the landscape, Leakey noticed an area he had not yet explored—just beyond the excavations where the previous year his team had uncovered the remains of a 1.75-million-year-old skull of an early human species they named *Zinjanthropus boisei* (later named *Paranthropus boisei*).[44] Louis and Mary, his wife and fellow paleoanthropologist, believed that this new species existed historically between the primitive, stoutly built "ape men" of South Africa and more recent human species.[45] It was precisely the kind of find paleoanthropologists crave—a link that could connect two known points in the timeline of human evolution.

The discovery of *Zinjanthropus boisei* (Zinj for short) was a major achievement for Leakey. Born in 1903, he grew up in Kenya, the child of Anglican missionaries.[46] At age 16, he left Africa for England to attend public school and stayed to pursue archaeology and anthropology at the University of Cambridge. For his doctoral research, he hoped to find the most ancient *Homo* fossils in East Africa, a proposal his advisors considered silly. Up until then, the most important paleontological finds of human origins had been outside Africa. Nevertheless, Leakey persisted. His first expedition was in 1926. Five years later, his focus turned toward Olduvai, where he discovered ancient stone tools. In 1932, carried away, he claimed to have found ancient *Homo* fossils there but was quickly proven wrong. The humiliation stung—and lingered.

Leakey came to be known as a "showman" and a "maverick," either a "Renaissance man" or a "dilettante," depending on one's view.[47] He desperately craved the approval of Britain's academic establishment, but he pursued an eclectic range of topics—paleoanthropology, ethnography, rock art, animal behavior, experimental archaeology. In 1936, he married Mary Douglas Nicol, a young British woman with a passion for archaeology who became a renowned paleoanthropologist in her own right, even as Louis was often the one to take the limelight. The couple's first major discovery was not until 1948—made along with a team of Kenya excavators, including Heselon Mukiri, a childhood friend of Louis's who played a central role in their work of finding and reconstructing early human fossil remains—when they found the 18-million-year-old fossil of an ape known as *Proconsul*.[48] But it was their celebrated find in 1959 of *Zinjanthropus boisei* that made Leakey's dream real, 33 years after his first expedition, of decoding the cryptic story of human origins.

At last, Leakey felt he was tantalizingly close. In the summer of 1960, while Jane Goodall was preparing to leave for Gombe, a team that included Mukiri, as well as Louis and Mary's son Jonathan, found the fossil remains of a saber-toothed tiger just a hundred yards from the Zinj find in Olduvai Gorge. Encouraged to keep digging, the team discovered what was then the world's oldest hominin foot. Digging on, they found more hominin bones: a collarbone, several fingers, small skull fragments. Leakey was busy with administrative obligations that autumn, but he returned to Olduvai as often as he could.

On December 2, Louis Leakey was exploring the new area near the Zinj excavation of the previous year when he was struck by a "premonition that something important was about to turn up." He "half-jokingly" turned to his companions and said, "This is the sort of place where we'll find a skull."[49] Hominin skulls are among the most important elements in studying human evolution because in them lies such evidence as brain size, whether the individual walked upright, and what kinds of foods their teeth were made for.

Within moments of his half-joke, Leakey saw bones surfacing through the earth like primordial icebergs. He looked closer, wondering if the fossils were those of a tortoise shell. No, the fragments belonged to a hominin skull.

"I fell on my knees beside the spot," Leakey later recalled, "and... for a moment I could not speak coherently."[50]

The Leakey team went on to uncover a big-brained hominin that was noticeably less stout than *Zinjanthropus boisei*. The remains were humanlike.[51] This was the first *Homo* species known to date to walk on Earth, the first mile marker on evolution's highway from *Australopithecus* stretching toward us.

The team described the find as a new species, *Homo habilis*. Translated: "Handy man." "Handy" because Leakey and his collaborators believed it was this species—an even more direct line to modern humans than *Zinjanthropus boisei*—that was responsible for making the stone tools found at Olduvai.[52]

OLDOWAN

Louis Leakey had long made a career of overturning scientific interpretations of human evolution. In the early 1900s, most scholars believed the oldest stone technology in the world belonged to the Chellean culture, which dates to about 700,000 years ago and spanned Europe, Asia, and Africa. But in 1931, at Olduvai, Leakey had discovered tools that were older than Chellean technology.[53]

Leakey took to calling this even earlier stone technology "Oldowan," from the region, Olduvai. It involved a "toolkit" of three instruments. This was not to refer to anything like a box of tools that was carried around, but rather a term archaeologists have devised to describe the relationship between three stone tools. Ancient toolsmiths would take a nodule of rock (a "core"), then use another rock (a

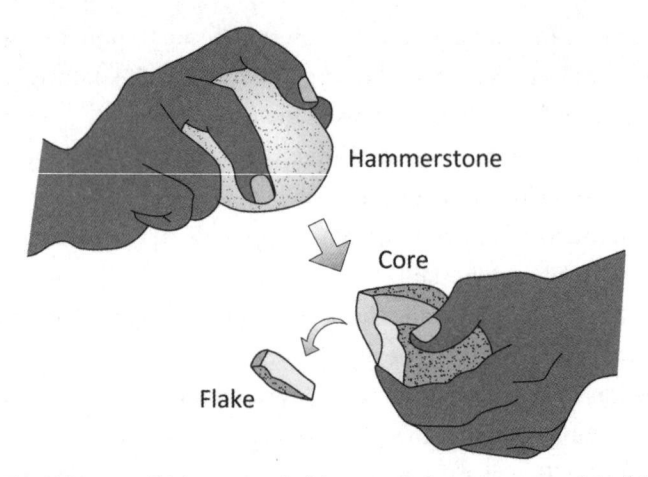

7. The Oldowan toolkit is composed of the core, the hammerstone, and the flake.

"hammerstone") to strike off a fragment (a "flake"). The flake would then be more finely shaped into the desired tool—the final product and goal of this process, although cores with sharp edges could also be used when needed, and hammerstones could, well, hammer.[54] For decades, it was unknown which species had actually made these tools.

Leakey's team found *Zinjanthropus boisei* in a layer of earth with tools that indicated a relationship between the species and Oldowan stone implements. But then, with the discovery of *Homo habilis* the next year in 1960, Leakey flip-flopped. Now, he said, it was *Homo habilis* who made the Oldowan tools. Leakey argued that only *Homo* species made tools, and since this new skull was *Homo habilis*, it therefore must have made the Oldowan technology.[55] Although not everyone was convinced, most scholars then thought that the Oldowan toolkit was the world's earliest ancestral human stone technology, at some 1.8 million years old.[56]

These successes in East Africa spurred even more research across the region, and then beyond, including through the training of Kenyan scholars such as Kamoya Kimeu and Isaiah Nengo.[57] Archaeologists kept finding tools that were even older.[58] They also found that Oldowan technology had spread from East Africa outward to North Africa and into Western Europe, the Mediterranean, and Asia. Oldowan tools persisted from 2.6 to 1.7 million years ago—a technological lifespan of nearly one million years.

Since the 1970s, the pace of fossil discoveries has accelerated, presenting new ways of thinking about and understanding these tools. Leakey's generation focused largely on creating categories (or types) and fitting the stone tools they found into them; they saw the Oldowan tools as the product of primitive intelligence. The generation that followed Leakey—who died in 1972—looked at the same Oldowan technology and saw more-sophisticated minds at work.[59] They viewed the Oldowan tools as choppers, scrapers, and awls, used for cutting, hammering, poking, and a host of other tasks. These were not rocks roughly and randomly bashed into each other; they were struck with a body and mind that could control how on each strike, the hammerstone's direction and strength would ripple through the core to create a particular shape.

In some ways, this technology was simple; yet it required innovation, planning, persistence, and imaginative leaps. In one study of Oldowan technology, an average of 18 flakes were found to have been removed from every core, indicating that the toolmakers were anticipating what series of strikes would lead to the desired tool.[60] Even the cores were selectively chosen and shaped, based on their properties; they were often carried a considerable distance from their source. By two million years ago, in part helped by climatic shifts that supported more game, *Homo habilis* was turning into a predator.[61]

Nonhuman animals such as chimpanzees in the wild are known to use more than one type of tool to solve a problem; for example, they could shape a piece of straw or a stick for extracting termites from their nest or honey enclosed in a hive.[62] But the Oldowan tools show a major leap in that two objects (a hammerstone and core) are combined that individually have little function but together can be used to create an entirely new tool. This process of "secondary tool use" requires an effective chain of action that shows how, by 2.6 million years ago, the ancestral *Homo* toolmakers had greater problem-solving ability than Lucy/Dinknesh's kind.

Of note, in one experiment in the 1990s, a bonobo in captivity named Kanzi was successfully taught to make stone tools based on Oldowan technology.[63] Some researchers believed that since Kanzi could not *precisely* replicate Oldowan tools, it showed how nonhuman great apes have lower biomechanical or cognitive capacity than the species that made these tools millions of years ago.[64] However, others have argued that the experiment was flawed because Kanzi's progress was hindered by an "impoverished learning environment."[65]

Still, the fact that Oldowan toolmakers showed real technical skill, selected and transported raw material, processed large game, and curated tools over time suggests to the prominent anthropologists Kathy D. Schick and Nicholas Toth, that these craftspeople were the first in our ancestral line to take on a humanlike relationship with things.[66] Based on the planning and behaviors evident in stone tools, Schick and Toth propose that it is possible the first *Homo* groups also invented skin or bark containers, carrying devices, digging tools, simple spears or throwing sticks, and wooden clubs. (This hypothesis is hard to test, since most of these organic materials would not survive the ages.) As significantly, tools would have both reflected and enabled new social behaviors. Oldowan toolmakers probably also shared food, divided labor based on sex, developed home ranges, maintained complex communication, and witnessed the birth of symbolic thinking. The arrival of more-complex tools, in other words, marks the arrival of more-complex behaviors that we would recognize as human.

Prior to Alemseged's discovery in 2010 in Ethiopia—and confirmed by the 2015 discovery of tool manufacture at least 3.3 million years ago at Lomekwi 3 in Kenya—scholars had long argued over whether stone tools arose gradually or were invented all at once. Including the Lomekwian pieces in the puzzle does make it seem that stone technology was likely created and used—experimented with—independently by different ancestral human groups across huge swathes of time and space.[67]

Each moment of invention might have come gradually or suddenly through profound inspiration—a whole family tinkered with tools for generations, or there might have been an australopithecine version of

Thomas Edison.[68] But they came, witnessed in the stone artifacts left behind. And there is another line of evidence: the bodies of the people who made these first tools.

The fossils I saw in Alemseged's lab document not only the birth of more-sophisticated technology, but the birth of our symbiotic relationship with stuff. In this ancient period, we begin to see how humans started to make tools. And then how tools started to make us.

2

THE MATTER AT HAND

After I returned from Ethiopia, I tried my hand at cooking Ethiopian food. I spent hours chopping piles of onions, dicing tomatoes, and slicing garlic, and reducing them over low heat to a thickened paste, which is the base of many Ethiopian dishes. I would then add in red lentils or vegetables or sour injera bread. I came to love most of all any dish with berbere, a dizzying mix of a dozen spices that embody how Ethiopia is perched at the crossroads of Africa, Europe, and Asia.

Following several months of cooking, I still hadn't tried one of Ethiopia's most treasured dishes: kitfo. A specialty of the Gurage people, *kitfo* means "finely chopped," a dish of spiced raw beef.[1] I lean toward vegetarianism, so I was not particularly attracted to learning the recipe. But it's a beloved dish. As early as 1841, James Barker, traveling through the Horn of Africa, noted that Ethiopia is "a nation who generally live[s] on raw meat."[2] In my experience visiting Ethiopian homes today, not much has changed in this regard. I needed to add kitfo to my repertoire. I called up my wife's friend Medi, who is from Ethiopia and makes a renowned kitfo.

Kitfo is hardly the only finely chopped raw meat dish in world cuisine.[3] France has steak tartare. Italians love beef carpaccio. Koreans have yukhoe, typically served as minced raw beef threaded with a garlicky sauce and topped with a raw egg. Many Lebanese love raw kibbeh nayyeh, a mixture of ground meat, onions, and bulger. Despite the diversity of these dishes, they all share one element in common: the raw meat is always cut up in some way—sliced, cubed, ground, chopped.

Raw meat presented a great puzzle to our distant predecessors. Meat provides abundant energy and nutrients for the body. But it takes very strong teeth and jaws to break down raw meat and make it edible. "Meat has a lot of nutrients, but it is also very elastic. You can think of it as being like a rubber band," the anthropologist Katherine D. Zink explained in 2016. "So the problem is that we can't break it down with our flat, low-cusped teeth."[4] For the earliest humans, there were only a few possible solutions. Cooking breaks down meat. But, according to many researchers, there's little evidence of controlled fires in hearths earlier than 400,000 years ago.[5] Fermenting also breaks down meat. Yet the earliest definitive evidence for fermenting doesn't appear in the archaeological record until 9,200 years ago, in Scandinavia, where trenches were dug likely to ferment large amounts of fish.[6] But cutting also breaks down meat. And sharp stone tools appear more than three million years ago.

To test how cutting meat and other tough food sources such as roots and tubers might have allowed our early ancestors to consume these high-energy foods, Zink conducted an experiment for her dissertation at Harvard University. She gathered some test subjects and fed them root vegetables and goat meat prepared four ways: raw, pounded, chopped, and roasted. She placed electrodes on the eaters' faces to measure the force their muscles required to chew and the effects of chewing on the muscles. As the subjects munched the dishes, each chew was also counted. For any food that couldn't be swallowed, she measured how much the half-eaten food was broken down.[7]

The experiment confirmed, as expected, that whole and pounded raw meat were largely unconsumable. "It's like chewing gum," Zink said.[8] At the opposite end of the spectrum, unsurprisingly, the roasted foods were easily consumed. However, the important discovery, published with her dissertation advisor, Daniel Lieberman, in *Nature* in 2016, was that chopped meat deployed nearly 32 percent less muscle force to chew than the average amount needed for unprocessed meat.[9]

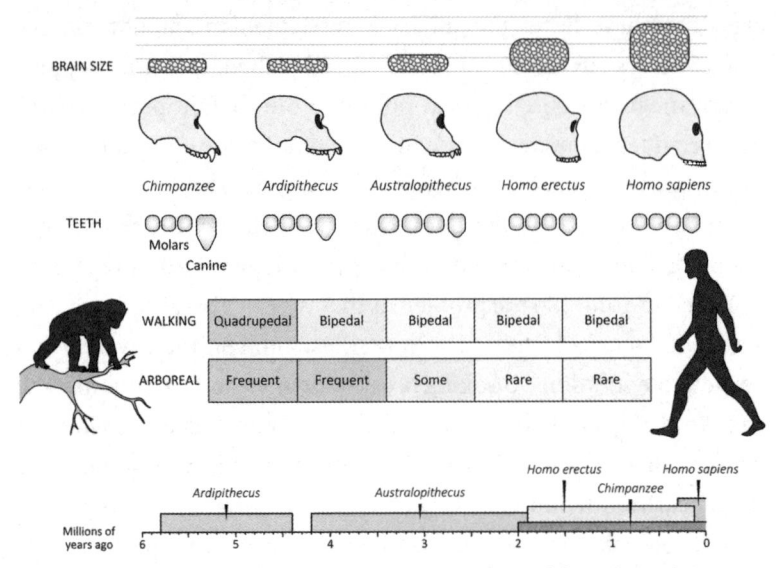

8. From chimpanzees to modern *Homo sapiens*, teeth have changed shape, along with other skeletal features and behaviors.

The experiment also showed how smaller bits of food are more efficiently digested because they are already broken down. The scientists estimated that an early hominin with a diet of chopped meat and vegetables—compared with a pure unprocessed diet—would have led to less than two million fewer chews (and with less force) each year, with meat tissue that would be nearly half as small and thus far more digestible. The experiment showed further that cutting up raw meat alone could have been enough to start changing the way our ancestors' bodies evolved. With a stone cutting tool, our ancestors could get by with less powerful and duller teeth, and their bodies could also extract more energy from the chopped foods they ate. In other words, the people who used stone tools didn't need such strong jaws and teeth.[10]

Evidence of just this shift to duller, less powerful teeth was demonstrated in Ledi-Geraru, Ethiopia. In 2015, the same team that found the oldest Oldowan tools published their discovery of the oldest fossil remains from the genus *Homo*: a lower left jaw with five teeth upwards of 2.8 million years old.[11] This fossil—combined with the find of the refined tools from the same region in a similar time period—

captured a fundamental change. The teeth on that 2.8-million-year-old ancestor are smaller than the species that preceded it. After some 600,000 years of living with stone tools, our ancestors' teeth were no longer as robust as they once were.

The Ledi-Geraru fossil shows when human culture and biology began to merge.

TECHNO-ORGANIC EVOLUTION

Before the invention of stone tools, our ancestors had access to a limited pantry. They could eat wild plants, insects, and animals small enough to catch easily, or leftover carcasses abandoned by predators. The hominin body was adapted to these foods.

When the first tools came along, they allowed hominins, in essence, to begin eating before food entered the body. Knives could cut up tubers and meat, saving the work of the teeth and the stomach. As Bill Schindler, an adventuring archaeologist who lives a re-created Paleolithic lifestyle (the time before humans settled down in villages and pursued agriculture full time) recently explained during an interview, "Beginning at three and a half million years ago, when we first struck two rocks together and produced a stone tool that led us to overcome our physical limitations, anything from that point forward we weren't designed to eat."[12] With stone tools and later technologies such as fire and fermentation, hominins could eat a wider array of food and process them more efficiently into energy—foods that hominin bodies weren't biologically equipped to process. As a result, something spectacular and strange happened: with the arrival of stone tools, the hominin body began to change.[13]

The anthropologists Kathy Schick and Nicholas Toth surmise that the very first ancestors to shape stones into tools were not dependent on them. Initially, the sharpened cobbles the hominins used were a minor addition to their survival strategies. As tools were deployed more regularly, the stone technology would have allowed their users to scavenge thick-skinned animals and maybe begin to hunt, to better protect themselves from predators, to dig up tubers, and to crack nuts. Over generations, the small advantages of tools started to add up until they multiplied into clear advantages for reproduction and survival. Finally, Schick and Toth argue, these early hominins "were at an evolutionary turning point" in which tools were not used as a mere specialization (like ants transporting honey in sand) but creatively used as a part of daily life—and so "became a recurrent facet of many of their activities and ultimately became *essential* to their adaptation."[14]

This moment was among the most important turning points in our planet's history—just as important as the realization that stones could be tools. At this moment, tools became caught up in evolutionary forces. The traits that made hominins more likely to use tools and reap the benefits led to biological changes. "For the first time in the evolution of life on the earth, a complex feedback loop between culture and biology began to emerge," Schick and Toth assert. "Due to the success of this synthetic addition to their biological repertoire (what we have called 'techno-organic evolution'), nature began to select for the innovative intelligence responsible for it."[15]

Put another way, the first stone technology our hominin ancestors invented started to alter the direction of biological evolution. Before stone tools, any hominin species that could benefit by eating larger animals or moving into a colder environment would have to wait for a natural shift—such as a random gene mutation that would lead to sharper teeth or more fur—that could facilitate new adaptations. Tools allowed for a "biocultural evolution" in which hominins could insert their will into natural selection.[16] Now hominins could make sharp stone tools in place of using sharp teeth; now they could stitch animal fur into clothing.

And yet, the forces of evolution never arrested. Hominin genes still replicated and randomly mutated, their genetic material flowing between different groups. The best-adapted individuals still produced the most offspring, who in turn carried those advantages to their offspring down the line. Consequently, with tools, hominin evolution became a dynamic loop—a mutual, interactive evolution of human culture and biology.[17]

BIG HEADED

Louis Leakey and his colleagues became convinced that *Homo habilis* was the first toolmaker on our ancestral lineage. And while the earliest stone tools Leakey found could have been used for a wide range of activities, it was long hypothesized they were used for food processing—most notably, meat. But as more ancient stone tools were recovered, researchers began to look at this technology and see that it likely would process not just meat but also bone marrow, a rich source of vitamins and fats.[18] For scavengers, meat would have presented numerous challenges. In contrast, there would be multiple advantages if the first toolmakers focused on bone marrow and the brain; marrow encased in bone preserves longer than exposed meat, and marrow is far easier to eat than raw meat. Still, even if many of the first tools were primarily used to extract what was inside bones, eventually everything of scavenged animals became part of the hominin diet.[19] Once sharpened tools become a steady part of the hominin repertoire, nothing of animals would have been wasted.

This shift mattered.

As more of an animal's entire carcass was incorporated into the early hominin diet, the nutritional benefits triggered novel changes in the hominin body. As Schick and Toth note, for most animals, brain size is constrained by how much energy their guts can extract from food.[20] The new sources of fats from marrow and other parts reframed the amount of energy our early ancestors could extract from the world around them. Once stone tools were used to extract and chop meat, technology allowed hominins to tap into yet another energy source. Tools, in essence, became "synthetic organs," supplementing the work of teeth and stomach.[21]

As a result, the hominin gut shrank and the extra energy went to our ancestors' most energy-hungry and advantageous organ: the brain.[22] The brain of an adult *Homo sapiens* is only 2 percent of body weight yet consumes 20 percent of the body's metabolic energy; the brain of a newborn human child consumes an astounding 60 percent of the body's fuel.[23]

The brain's size steadily increased as the hominin family tree sprouted new branches.[24] By the time Lucy and her *Australopithecus* kin showed up around 3.8 million years ago, they had a brain-case capacity of around 400 cubic centimeters (a little more than would fill a soda can). The first *Homo* species, *Homo habilis*, had a brain-case capacity of 600 cubic centimeters (about one and two-thirds soda cans).[25] By the time *Homo sapiens* are strolling around, the size of their brain case more than doubles, to about 1,400 cubic centimeters (nearly four soda cans) on average.[26] Fed by the new energy of fats and proteins from marrow, meats, and other new food sources, hominins' brain size likely changed over the millennia as they adapted to climatic conditions and ecological resources. Bigger brains further helped hominins better negotiate social competition—navigating relationships within their groups and with non-kin.[27]

Archaeologists have long focused on brain size because the fossil

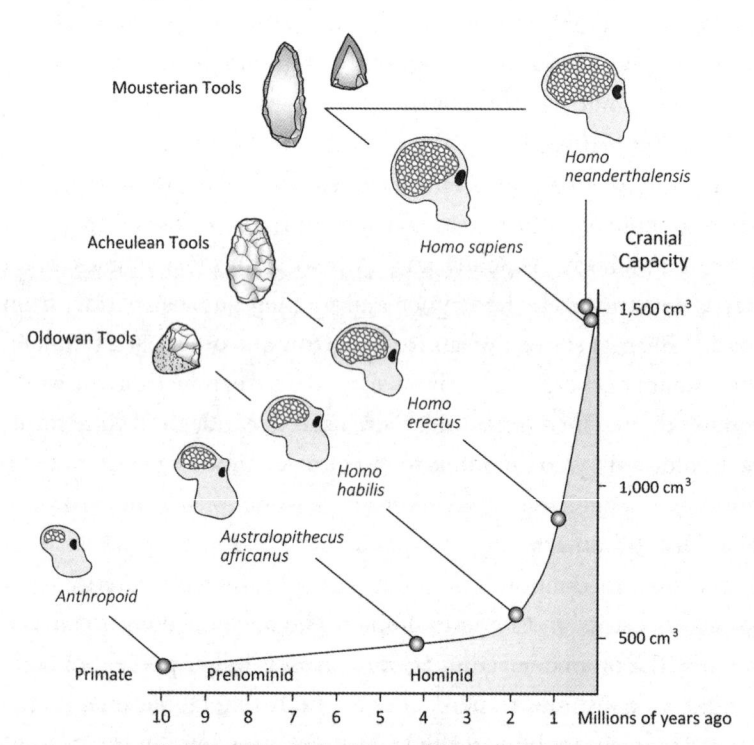

9. Hominin brain size has increased dramatically over millions of years, in tandem with advancing stone technologies.

record contains skulls, whose capacity can be easily measured. But does size matter?

Not necessarily—at least not if brain size is assumed to be correlated with intelligence.[28] Consider that a cow's brain is about 200 times bigger than a rat's brain but not apparently much smarter for it. For many years, researchers thought, then, that what matters for intelligence is not absolute brain size, but an animal's *relative* brain size—relative to its body mass. When scientists completed the various measurements of mammals, they found that this pattern holds quite well. Humans have big brains for our body size, dolphins somewhat less, chimpanzees less still, and rats and rabbits at the bottom.

However, not long ago, the neuroscientist Suzana Herculano-Houzel demonstrated that what matters most for intelligence is the number of neurons that can be packed into a brain. When she looked at the primate brain, she found that the number of neurons keeps pace with the mass of the brain. The brain of a macaque has 10 times more neurons than a marmoset's brain and is 11 times larger. The brain of a human has 134 times more neurons than a marmoset's brain and is about 190 times larger.

In short, not only did the primate brain grow in size relative to its body over millions of years, even more important, the number of neurons in those brains kept pace. The hominin brain seems to have done this more efficiently than other species' brains, by reorganizing the nerve cells that transmit information. As a result, hominin brains grew bigger *and* smarter.[29]

The feedback loop continued as bigger and smarter brains led to the ability to create better tools, which in turn provided more energy for bigger and smarter brains. To create and use Oldowan tools requires a sophisticated coordination between the brain's visual cortex (to process size, shape, etc.), motor cortex (to control hand and arm movement), and parietal cortex (to communicate between the other two spheres).[30] One study even suggested that humans have evolved to have "tool-specific" regions in their brains.[31] In this research, scientists used an MRI scanner to analyze the brains of subjects as they looked at images of tools that require active manipulation (e.g., scissors), animals, and graspable objects (e.g., candles). They discerned that several areas in the brain activated when looking at tools, compared with images of animals or graspable objects.

Intelligence was central not just in the stone technology's development but also in its advancement. In one experimental study, a team of researchers tested how much manipulation is required in making simple flaked-stone technology versus the more intricate hand-ax technology that appeared around two million years ago. They found that the two required equal manipulative complexity. Given that both technologies require the same manual abilities, the source for changes must have lain elsewhere. Changes to the early hominin brain were responsible for the technical advance from flaked-stone cutting tools to sophisticated hand axes.[32]

In another study that compared how the brain responds when learning Oldowan techniques and the hand-ax technology that followed it, researchers found different areas of the brain activated for hand axes, suggesting that better cognitive control was needed to create the more complex stone technology.[33] Poetically, the higher-order areas of the cerebral cortex that light up when making the more advanced hand-ax tools is the same area that is engaged when trained pianists play the piano.[34] The tools that got more calories to feed brighter brains in turn led to ever-better tools.[35]

THE DAY LUCY DIED

One day, some 3.2 million years ago, Lucy climbed a tree. Perhaps she did it to harvest fruit that hung seductively from its branches. Perhaps she dashed up the trunk and hid among the leaves to save her life—a predator snapping at her feet. (At just three and a half feet tall and weighing only 60 pounds, Lucy had a lot to fear.) Or perhaps the sun was setting at the edge of the savanna and she ascended a tree, tired after a long day, to make a nest and settle in for the night, like chimpanzees today. While it is unclear why Lucy climbed the tree, what is clear—or at least as clear as things can be looking across millions of years—is that on this day, she fell from a tree's heights to her death.

In 2007, Lucy went on tour in the United States, leaving her home at the National Museum of Ethiopia. It was hoped the fossil would become a blockbuster museum exhibit. Instead, Lucy primarily attracted controversy. Many scientists objected to the tour, saying the risk of damage while transporting the fragile australopithecine was too great. The Smithsonian refused to exhibit her remains.[36] Richard Leakey denounced the exhibit as a "form of prostitution" for selling heritage and a "gross exploitation of the ancestors of humanity."[37]

After Lucy's first exhibition, at the Houston Museum of Natural Science, she was taken to the University of Texas at Austin for further study.[38] There she was placed in a CT scanner. Using the machine to take photo "slices" of the bones, the team collected 35,000 images of Lucy's skeleton.[39] The famed australopithecine — named in English after the Beatles song that played on a loop the night archaeologists celebrated her discovery in 1974 — was undergoing a kind of Paleolithic autopsy.

The research, directed by the anthropologist John Kappelman, led to a startling discovery. Kappelman and his colleagues were intrigued by unhealed fractures in Lucy's right shoulder. Investigating further, they found more breaks along the arm that suggested Lucy extended her right hand as she slammed into the ground. "If a person falls and they reach out their arms to break that fall, if the fall is high enough energy, what that does is drive the elements of the shoulder against each other," Kappelman explained in an interview. "If the force is high enough, the scapula acts like an anvil and fractures the head of the humerus. That break forms a unique signature on the bone."[40] Published in *Nature* in 2016, the hypothesis of a dramatic fall was important because it suggested not only the cause of Lucy's death, but evidence her species sometimes perched in the canopy of trees.[41]

Lucy likely did not fall because of a poor grip. While australopithecines walked upright, their long arms and curved fingers were like those of chimpanzees — well suited to climbing tree trunks and hanging from branches. However, subsequent hominin species' hands did begin to change dramatically, becoming more humanlike. A key question is whether these alterations took place, as Schick and Toth wrote,

10. A reconstruction of an *Australopithecus afarensis* stands before a real *Homo sapiens*.

to adapt "to the more precise and powerful demands of stone tool manufacture and use."[42]

In a 2015 *Science* article, Matthew Skinner, a biological anthropologist at the University of Kent, and his colleagues studied the hand bones of different hominins—work led by Tracy Kivell, a paleoanthropologist also at Kent.[43] They focused on the five major bones that spread across our palms like a fan. They argued that the internal structure of these bones reflects certain kinds of behaviors. Swinging among branches and walking on knuckles lead to one type of bone structure, chipping stones to make cutting tools another. When they studied the structure of a species called *Australopithecus africanus*, they found that these evolutionary cousins of Lucy's were tree swingers who also pinched small objects—in other words, having hands that were well adapted to being in trees but also to making stone tools.

However, in a reply to Skinner and his colleagues, Sergio Almécija, now at the American Museum of Natural History in New York, and his colleagues argued that the technical analysis was flawed. Moreover, they pointed out evidence that hominin species living six million years ago had developed precise grasping abilities—millions of years before stone-tool technology emerged.[44] While some (including Charles Darwin as far back as 1871) suggested that hands evolved in tandem with the shift from knuckle walking on all fours to walking on two feet, it is notable that upright walking now appears to have begun with the species known as *Ardipithecus ramidus*—one million years before stone tools.[45] Thus, Almécija and his colleagues concluded, "the eventual application of human-like hand structure to stone tool flaking and use was almost certainly an exaptation, not an adaptation."[46] They meant that the hand was not an adaptation for making stone tools. Rather, natural selection had changed the hominin hand for nontool reasons (e.g., refined to pick out lice from fur), which then just turned out to be super helpful for making tools.

While the debate continues about how and why hominin hands changed, it is striking that the hand *did* change to become more dexterous, with a grip both strong and precise.[47] Human hands are well suited to many of the tasks that our brains ask them to accomplish.

These changes in hominin hands accompanied other changes in the body that mutually reinforced each other and responded to increasing intelligence, cultural behaviors, and emerging technologies. Brain size, teeth, hands—all are part of the changing hominin body. This can be seen in hominin height and weight. Adult australopithecines could range from 43 to 59 inches tall, while *Homo sapiens* prior to about 12,000 years ago ranged from nearly 59 to 74 inches, so in some cases nearly twice the size of their predecessors.[48] Just as stone tools enabled the acquisition of more food for the brain, they also provided more energy for the whole body.

Of note, brains can grow only so big. The scientists Karin Isler and Carel P. van Schaik proposed in *Current Anthropology* that there would have been a "gray ceiling," limiting how large the brains of our ancestors could grow. Even after considering that a newborn's head can't be larger than the mother's birth canal, a child with an extra-large brain would also take too long to physically develop once born—such a child would be defenseless for a long time and require too much care.[49] An increasingly large brain could lead a species to extinction. The hypothesis suggests there is one primary way around the gray ceiling: cooperation—meaning that a group could care for a child's

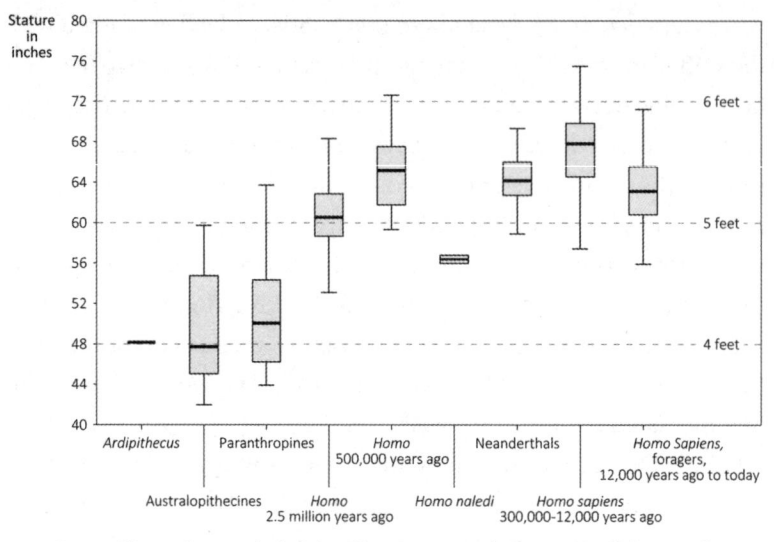

[Chart: Box plot showing stature in inches for various hominin species: Ardipithecus, Australopithecines, Paranthropines, Homo 2.5 million years ago, Homo 500,000 years ago, Homo naledi, Neanderthals, Homo sapiens 300,000–12,000 years ago, Homo Sapiens foragers 12,000 years ago to today. Reference lines at 4 feet, 5 feet, and 6 feet.]

11. Over millions of years, the height of hominins varied. One major shift upward occurred around 500,000 years ago, when evolutionary forces seemed to mostly select for taller people (with several notable exceptions being species such as *Homo naledi*). Then another major shift occurred about 12,000 years ago, as foraging *Homo sapiens* occupied nearly every space on Earth, including smaller-bodied adaptations to islands and forests.

longer development by sharing in different responsibilities and tasks for survival. Schaik showed this ceiling was about 650 cubic centimeters (just under two soda cans), right at the upper limits of *Homo habilis*'s brain size. This suggests the species that came after *Homo habilis* cooperated around defense, hunting, food sharing, and parenting.

A cascade of more changes followed. As Schick and Toth wrote, "Increased body size usually has a number of other biological consequences: reduced metabolic rate, longer gestation time, longer life span, more mobility and larger day and annual ranges, longer periods of suckling, maturation, and learning, fewer offspring, increased social interaction, wider diet breadth, and the ability to exploit larger prey species in hunting."[50]

It was new foods and new ways of processing food, enabled by stone hammers and knives, that led to these significant biological and behavioral changes—bigger brains and better cooperation to accommodate longer childhood development. Hominins became a product of the tools they made.

EXTENSION OF MY BODY

In the emerald countryside of Wales sits a manor named Nantclwyd Hall.[51] Built 400 years ago, the luxurious two-story brick sanctuary is painted peach and capped with a gently sloping slate-gray roof. Surrounding it are acres of neatly geometric gardens, adorned with ornate temples and whimsical structures that stand like stone jewels amid long fields of trimmed grass.

One December evening in 1873, Nantclwyd Hall hosted a garden party. While staying at the manor, Major Walter C. Wingfield, an inventor and soldier who had served in India and then China during the Second Opium War, used the occasion to introduce a new game to his fellow guests. He called it *sphairistike*, roughly translated from ancient Greek for "the art of playing ball."[52]

Inspired by a ball game played indoors by aristocrats for centuries, Wingfield's innovation was to move the game outside and replace the leather ball with a bouncing rubber one. The game was a hit. Within months, Wingfield had patented sphairistike. He began a business, published two books to promote the game, and sold playing sets. Presented in a handsome long wooden box, a typical set included written instructions, a long net, court markers, a rubber ball, pegs and tape to mark the court, and four lopsided rackets (better to hit the low bouncing ball).[53] In the first year, Wingfield sold a thousand sets that quickly spread across the British Empire and beyond. Just three years later, in 1877, the first tournament of champions for lawn tennis, as the sport became known, was held at Wimbledon.

Although the major's game of tennis is rarely recognized as a product of hominin evolution, the ability to strike a bouncing ball with a racket is evidence of an ancient symbiosis between human and tool. Consider what happens when you pick up a tennis racket the first time. At that moment, the racket is just a thing. An external object in the world. Next, a ball is tossed in your direction to strike. Perhaps you use both hands, keeping your feet firmly planted, and swing at the wrong angle, with the racket's face parallel to the ground. You miss. But a coach gives you some instruction and then tosses another ball your way. Now you turn your body to the side, step forward, grip the racket at the right angle, and swing to the ball with the racket's wide face perpendicular to the ground. The racket releases a fulfilling *thwock!* The ball sails over the net.

With more practice, each swing becomes more "natural," each ball hit more precisely as your hand feels ever more at home wrapped around the grip. As the literary scholar Steven Conner has noted in *A Philosophy of Sport*, one possible origin for the word *racket* is *rachette*, Middle French for the palm of the hand.[54] This etymology suggests how the racket becomes a part of the hand itself. "If I wish the racket to become me," Conner writes, "I must first become it."[55] Or, as one of the greatest living tennis players, Roger Federer, once said, "I love my racket and it's the extension of my arm and it does all the magic for me."[56]

One study has shown how Federer's sense of bodily extension is not magic but an acutely human experience. In 2017, researchers at the University of Genoa tested how tennis players perceived the space around their bodies when holding rackets.[57] They had subjects hold their own tennis racket as well as one they had never used before, and

12. Lawn tennis grew rapidly in popularity in Victorian England and beyond.

then respond to a tiny electrical current to their hand and a sound that was played by a speaker positioned at either the hand or the end of the racket. When subjects were holding their own racket, they reacted much more quickly to the far current/sound. This suggests that the subjects had embodied their own rackets more fully than the unfamiliar one, even if they weren't playing tennis.

Such an experience is not limited to tennis rackets but includes every tool humans create and master: brooms, rakes, spoons, fishing rods, needles, saws, eyeglasses, pencils, paintbrushes, saxophones, computer mouses, prosthetics, wheelchairs, and far more.[58] We are all having this experience every day of our lives.

How does this happen? One theory observes how humans, when we are infants, are great explorers, touching and feeling everything, building our sense of what belongs where. These explorations trace the topographies of our bodies and our relationship with things, how our bodies interact with the spaces and objects surrounding us. This theory posits that in the neocortex of a human child's brain, a "somatosensory map"—an atlas of the body known through the senses—is forming that tells them where skin ends and the world begins.[59] Unlike most maps, though, this one is not fixed but changes constantly and rapidly as we use things and then leave them behind.

Sometimes we rewrite the map from necessity.[60] As an infant grows into an adolescent, the mind is endlessly adjusting to the body's development (or trying to, if you've ever seen a stumbling toddler or gangly teenager). Through trial and error, and practice and repetition, with tools we can purposefully rewrite the map. The map is more than a metaphor. When a violinist practices six hours a day, they can increase the relative size of the area in their neocortex that corresponds to their fingers.[61]

Another theory is that of "radical embodiment," in which objects become part of a whole, unconscious, and dynamic system.[62] When a person rides a bike, there is a beautiful unison where the person and bike become part of the person-bike machine. But a bike that has a flat tire, no handlebars, and a broken chain becomes just a bike, and its rider becomes just a person. The same experience unfolds when a driver steps in and out of a car. "Not only do I incorporate the internal space of the car, such that pushing the brakes becomes as 'natural' a way of stopping to me as halting in my stride, but I incorporate the external space of the car; its power, velocity, and acceleration," the sociologist Nick Crossley writes. "When I park, overtake, or pull onto a roundabout, for example, I 'know without thinking' how big the car is and how fast it will accelerate. I feel its size and speed as surely as that of my own body, moving only into those spaces in which I will fit and have the time to reach. I do not think about the car. I think as the car, from the point of view of the car."[63]

Another example is the person without sight who uses a cane. By tapping and touching, the sightless person does not feel the cane per se but the objects—the curb, the doorway—that are felt through the tool, in the same way sighted people experience these objects through their eyes. And so, in this line of thinking, embodiment occurs when there is a convergence between the tool and its user: the two become one.[64]

The underlying neural networks for these abilities evolved with the rise of mammals millions of years ago.[65] After primates broke off into their own evolutionary branch, their sensorimotor systems became more elaborate than those of many other mammals.[66] These changes happened long before Lucy's folks picked up a stone and cut with it. The timing of these changes in the brain suggests to the neuroscientist Alison L. Barth that human "brains were built by ancient evolutionary processes that did not anticipate that we would pick up objects in our environment to extend our physical abilities."[67]

Aligning with Barth's arguments, some paleoanthropologists have suggested that our ancestor hominins had relatively well-developed and integrated visuospatial and sensorimotor systems.[68] That means that long before hominin brains started exponentially growing in size and hominin hands started making stone tools, the basic brain architecture for making somatosensory maps was already in place. Once tools were invented, our brains hijacked areas intended for other purposes to help us experience the magic of stretching our bodies into the world through tennis rackets, cars, bikes, and canes.

The assimilation of tools into our bodies is fundamentally an

Transparent Cover

Opaque Cover

Unstimulated Hand

Stimulated Hand

Rubber Hand

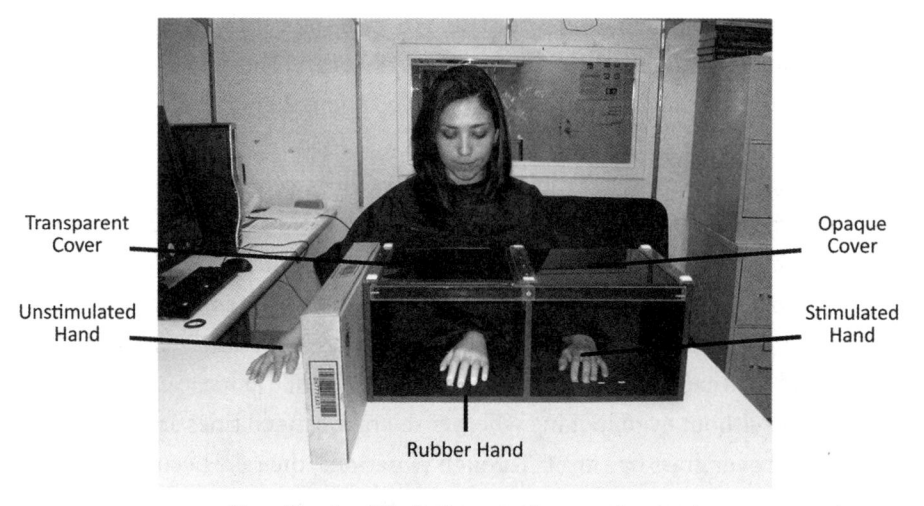

13. The rubber-hand illusion has a simple setup where a subject can "feel" the fake hand has become their real one.

inward, immersive experience. This can be seen in the rubber-hand illusion. For this experiment, a subject sits at a table, with a large mirror set perpendicular to their body. Their real hand is set behind the mirror out of sight; a fake rubber hand extends outward in sight. A researcher then gently strokes the real fingers behind the mirror while also visibly stroking the rubber hand. After several minutes, the subject's mind combines the visual information with the touching sensation and will come to feel that the rubber hand is actually their real hand. Just how real this sensation can be is demonstrated by when the researcher takes a nearby hammer and strikes the rubber hand; the subject often screams in pain because of the mind's perceived link to the rubber hand. This points to how the map of our body is fluid, fundamentally shaped by physical experience as well as how the mind sees the body.[69]

But the assimilation of tools into our bodies also works the other way: tools extend and project us out into the world, doing what our bodies otherwise could not accomplish. Imagine a concert violinist who enjoys a sushi lunch, maneuvering a pair of chopsticks; then they practice all afternoon, dancing their bow across the violin's strings; and then they leave their studio and pull a car out of the garage, swiftly backing up, anticipating what angle to turn the vehicle so that the side mirrors won't strike the adjacent parked cars. The chopsticks extended their fingers by five inches. The bow lengthened their arm by 29 inches. The car extended their body to 14 feet. As the person expertly maneuvered each tool, their mind, without a conscious thought, allowed their body to grow—all to better eat, create music, and transport itself—and then shrink back to its naked, tool-less size.

Finally, we can do this because the body's experiences and the mind's perceptions work together to quickly interpret the signals from the tools we use. When autumn comes and you rake fallen leaves, you know without even looking whether the rake's metal tines are being pulled over grass or gravel. Through vibrations, the rake becomes an ersatz hand. In one study, research subjects tapped objects with a rod while both brain activity and rod vibrations were measured. Researchers found that the rod, on average, vibrated for about 100 milliseconds. But the somatosensory cortex often reacted within 20 milliseconds. In other words, well before the rod even stopped vibrating, the body's touch sensors had already sent signals about the tool to the brain.[70]

Another study—one looking at how professional athletes in China embody their equipment—made similar findings, though it measured this in experience rather than milliseconds. "The tennis racket is an extension of my arm and hand," a 24-year-old player told researchers. "Judging from the [ball's] vibration [as it strikes the racket], I know the ball's power and spin, and then I can return it."[71]

HOMO FABER

We shape our buildings; thereafter they shape us.

WINSTON CHURCHILL

One evening, our friend Medi came over and showed me how to make kitfo. On to the counter, she placed a tub of niter kebe, Ethiopian clarified butter with herbs and spices, and a bag of mitmita, a delicious mix of dried chili, green cardamom, cumin seeds, black pepper, dried ginger, dried garlic, cloves, cinnamon, and coarse salt—all blended together into a warm fire orange. To the pile, she added a package of finely ground beef sirloin.

With all the ingredients ready, Medi heated the butter in one pot. She opened the package with the beef and emptied it into a pan. With her fingers, Medi started to break up and knead the beef. Studying the dish, I was struck by the triangle between the meat, the tool that ground it down, and my body—all entwined in an epic story that had started millions of years ago. With the invention of stone cutting tools, our ancient ancestors underwent a series of changes that transformed them from animals who made tools to animals who depended on tools. In some cases, our bodies evolved in response to these new tools; in other cases, our bodies changed alongside tools. Eventually, for hominins, the tools were not a supplement to survival but necessary. Seeing the beef tender and easily broken apart, I imagined how a knife was really a kind of tooth, a "synthetic organ," getting a head start on digestion. Further, thinking of the feeling of a knife meeting a hard cutting board, made me acutely aware how a knife could also be a kind of extension of me out into the world. A simple evening of cooking was a culmination of millions of years of evolution: a complete symbiosis between people and stuff.

Benjamin Franklin and Thomas Carlyle were right that humanity is uniquely defined by tools, but they were wrong in the way they imagined it. They meant that what makes *Homo sapiens* special is that we alone are toolmakers. We are not. But what is special is the role tools have played in generating our species. These tools, I realized, as Medi finished the dish by simply blending the butter, spices, and meat, made a dish like kitfo—but also us—possible.

As the philosopher Don Ihde and the archaeologist Lambros Malafouris argued in a 2019 article, in the end, *Homo sapiens* is really *Homo faber*—a species of makers. "We become constituted through making and using technologies that shape our minds and extend our bodies," Ihde and Malafouris wrote. "We make things which in turn make us."[72] To a degree more than any other animal, things make us in the process of our becoming.

This evolutionary history was not unidirectional, progressive, or preordained. Multiple hominin species experimented with tools. Many likely failed; some succeeded. Collectively, over the last 3.3 million years, tools have helped particular human species flourish, filling more niches around the world, from grass savannas to Ice Age caves to tropical rainforests. From *Homo erectus* to *Homo florensis*, our ancestral cousins found ways to survive from Africa to Asia, tools in hand—though eventually there would be just one species left, a species that would make more things than any other *Homo* species that ever touched Earth.

3

EVERYTHING UNDER THE SUN

On the morning of September 18, 1991, Helmut and Erika Simon set out to ascend Similaun, a diamond-shaped peak that rises into the clouds of the Italian-Austrian Alps.[1] The hike was not easy. The weather was unseasonably warm. Glaciers blanketing the mountains were melting. Icy rivers raced downhill, carving small gullies, tunnels, and caves that dropped into blackness and the unknown.

The Simons were on vacation from Nuremberg, Germany. They threaded their way across the fields of melting ice and crevasses until eventually they stood at the top of Similaun, triumphantly looking down on the world from a height of nearly 12,000 feet. As they happily descended, daylight began to fade. They wouldn't be able to make it back to their hotel in Vernagt, Italy, before nightfall, so they found their way to a rustic stone-and-wood lodge set high up among the peaks.

The next day broke clear and beautiful. The Simons decided to squeeze in another hike. With some new friends they had met at the lodge, the couple started out for Finail Peak. The trail took them through a barren landscape, far above the tree line. Patches of liquifying snow were spread across a broken patch of sharp fragmented stone, colored charcoal and ash. By noon, the group reached the blustery summit and then headed back down. Soon after their descent began, the new friends said their goodbyes to Helmut and Erika and took off in a different direction.

The Simons looked for the trail that would take them back to the lodge. They were skirting a trench when Helmut looked down into a pool of thawing snow. He saw a strange shape. His first reaction was anger, thinking it was a piece of trash marring the magnificent landscape. As Helmut's mind caught up to what his eyes were seeing, Erika cried out, "Look, it's a person!"

Just feet away from them was the head and upper back of a human being suspended in the slushy water. Face down, the remains were dried out, the person's skin leathered—smooth, hairless, orange.

The Simons returned to the lodge and reported their discovery to the caretaker, Markus Pirpamer. He called the police in both Italy and Austria, not knowing on which side of the border the corpse had been found. Markus then went to investigate, joined by the lodge's cook. After an hour's hike, they found the body and began inspecting the area for clues when Markus noticed an object lying nearby. He picked it up and admired the long, smooth handle that turned a sharp 90 degrees like a perfect L. Wrapped at the end was a fine, symmetrical metal blade. It was an ax, but unlike any Markus had ever seen. He noticed other things too—fur and sticks and boards and a birchbark tube of some sort stuffed with hay—all camouflaged in the mud. A half hour passed. The two men returned to the lodge.

The next day, a helicopter flew out to the site, where Anton Koler, an Austrian inspector, met Markus. They began using a jackhammer to loosen the glacier's grip on the man. Storm clouds were moving in. The men worked hard, often submerged in the icy water pulling at the body with bits of dried flesh breaking off. After all their effort, the person was only half excavated and the air compressor was empty. They went home.

Word spread at the lodge about the find, including to Reinhold Messner, a world-famous mountain climber who happened to be traveling through the region. He couldn't resist checking out the man. With his companions, Messner tried to pry the body loose, pulling at it and using one of the sticks lying around to hack at the ice by the person's legs. The body stayed stubbornly locked in place. But based on the artifacts and the preserved condition of the body, Messner began

14. A mysterious ax head and handle were found in the Alps.

to suspect that this person had been hidden under the glacier for a long time.

Several days later, another Austrian government helicopter arrived to extricate the body from the ice, but the crew had not brought a shovel, to save weight on the flight. The inspectors borrowed a ski pole and an ice pick from a passing hiker to hack at the ice. After much more yanking and pulling, the glacier finally let go. The person was stiff as a board and now completely naked. Most of the leather clothing had been shorn off in the ad hoc excavations. The men scoured the area for more evidence. They found a grass mat, a whittled branch, and a knife made of stone. The helicopter flew off with the strange body and mysterious things.

On a cool, crisp late summer morning in 2019, I visited the South Tyrol Museum of Archaeology, in Bolzano, Italy. The museum, set along a cobblestone street with high-end clothing stores, opened in 1998 in an old bank—a fitting location for an archaeological treasure. After passing through security, we met our guide for the day, Nico Aldegani. A trained archaeologist, Aldegani had a stylish beard, and his long hair was pulled back in a hipster bun. He exuded energy and enthusiasm.

We started a tour of the exhibit hall. Aldegani began narrating the Simons' discovery of the man eroding from the glacier. He then turned to the scientific excavation of the site in 1992, which led to a bitter dispute between Austria and Italy over control of the remains and artifacts. Eventually, it was resolved when the site was shown to be just 101 yards within the Italian border, and an international team began a collaborative phase of research.

After a few exhibit panels, we stopped before a dramatic silver metal wall that stood like a vault. A small window was framed at its center. I stepped up on a platform and pressed a button. A muted blue light flashed on, revealing a stark white refrigerated room.

On a glass table lay Ötzi, the iceman from the glacier. His spotted ochre skin looked glassy, a result of the room kept humid to preserve the body. His left arm was tucked tight under his chin, across his chest. Naked and tonsured, preserved and decayed, with only a thin rind of muscle and skin wrapped around a skeleton, Ötzi looked to me half alien, half human.

The exhibit went on to reveal Ötzi's amazing story. Arguably, he is among the most well-studied bodies in history. Ötzi lived about 5,300 years ago. He stood five-foot-two and was a wiry 110 pounds. He had 61 tattoos pecked into his skin. He suffered from several ailments, including bad teeth, arthritis, parasites, and broken ribs and a broken nose that had healed. He was lactose intolerant and had plaque in his coronaries. His lungs were coated in soot from a lifetime of living around open fires. He was about 45 years old when he met his end.

We continued on, for the main reason I'd come to the museum: to see Ötzi's stuff. As Aldegani said, "The man comes alive with his artifacts."

Although some of what Ötzi carried had been destroyed in the initial struggle to remove his body, archaeologists have recovered many of his belongings and reconstructed others. Ötzi was clothed from head to toe, wearing a bearskin hat with a chin strap, goatskin leggings lined with deer fur for warmth, a sheep- and goatskin coat, a loincloth, a belt with a sewn-on pouch, and shoes made with bearskin for the soles (for strength) and deerskin for the uppers (waterproofed through tanning techniques with oils), and stuffed with grasses. He was well dressed. "It was fashion for sure," Aldegani joked, "because it was found in Italy."

With him, Ötzi carried a longbow and 14 arrows in a quiver, two birchbark containers (with one carrying fire), tinder fungus, a scraper, a boring tool, a bone awl, a retouching tool to make stone flakes, a stone flake, a stone dagger with an ash-wood handle and sheath made from the fibers of tree bark, a mysterious stone disk hung from strips of leather, and a copper ax. He carried all this—and likely more that was lost to time—in a backpack made with an upside-down U-shaped frame with slats and netting. All told, Ötzi carried 400 things, made from stones, minerals, 21 plant species, and the remains of a variety of wild and domesticated animals.[2] "It's a lot of things," Aldegani said. He estimates that all of it would have weighed more than half of Ötzi's own weight.

Because so much organic material typically degrades at an archaeological site, Ötzi offers a stunning view into the material world more than 5,000 years ago. He shows how far our ancestors had traveled from those first few stone tools Lucy's species had invented millions of years ago. Everything that Ötzi possessed are things recognizable to us today—things not very different from what you likely are wearing right now (underwear, shoes) or have at home (matches, knives).

15. The 2017 film *Iceman* meticulously re-created Ötzi's clothing and equipment.

At some point between the rough stone tools Lucy's kind used and the iceman's overflowing backpack came the foundation for every thing in our modern world.

THE FOUNDATION

The basic tools in the iceman's toolkit—the scraper and flaked-stone cutting tool—were invented millions of years ago; they do not look that different from the technology found at Ledi-Geraru in Ethiopia. However, Ötzi's arrowheads and dagger are the culmination of vast technological leaps across continents and countless generations of ancestral human species.

Unlike the simple tools that can be manufactured by striking two rocks against each other, the arrowheads and dagger were made through a complicated series of steps that require striking a hammerstone precisely against the "core" and then using, in Ötzi's case, a wooden handle with a fire-hardened antler tip embedded in the end—a tool that looks like a thick pencil—to press into the stone's edges to shape and sharpen them. A 2018 study found that Ötzi likely sharpened the scraper and other tools just hours before his death.[3]

A long line can be drawn from Ötzi's stone tools all the way back to Lucy. After the initial discovery of stone technology, by at least 3.3 million years ago, came long periods of stasis interrupted by moments of dramatic change. Each new form of stone technology was radical and advanced, but then, as it was replaced—looking back from later years—the earlier version seems mundane and simple.

That Lucy's species realized sharpened stones could be used as tools was a profound discovery. These tools lasted almost a million years without much change. But then came the Oldowan toolkit, around 2.6 million years ago, and this combination of tools—used to make more refined tools—was a game changer. More attention was given to flaking off finer pieces of stone that could be used to cut and scrape, while the cores could be used for chopping as well as for hammering. The Oldowan technology lasted nearly another million years.

At 1.8 million years ago, another revolution unfolded. The emergent species *Homo erectus*—an intelligent and durable ancestral human species living from about 1.9 million to 110,000 years ago—ushered in a new technology that archaeologists call the Acheulean. The Acheulean technology is defined by "large cutting tools"—hefty cleavers and axes of a standardized form. These axes were produced through more-complex techniques that required reducing a core or a flake from both sides. The typical result was an elegant tear-shaped stone tool that could fit in the hand to slice and chop, pick and pound.[4] The tools were made across Africa, Asia, and Europe for more than 1.5 million years.[5]

The arrival of the Acheulean hand ax documents new cognitive leaps in our ancestral species. The fact that this technology required more-complex steps to produce, as well as its symmetry and relatively standardized appearance, all point to the genesis of mathematics, symbolic thinking, and language among *Homo erectus*. These connections are still hotly debated among researchers. Some see Acheulean tools

16. An Acheulean hand ax discovered in Saudi Arabia, dating to about 1.8 million years ago, reveals the symmetry and beauty of these early tools.

merely as the result of geometrical constraints in making a triangular tool; others see its features as merely functional.[6] Some researchers point out that there was not one uniform "tradition" of the tool around the world.[7] It is hard even to say if the celebrated symmetry of the Acheulean hand ax was the intended final form, or if it was merely the product of reworking the tool from each side over time as it was used and resharpened to complete tasks.[8]

Part of the problem with this debate is that there is no widely accepted view of what Acheulean tools did. They have the versatility of a Swiss Army knife, and likely would have been used primarily to butcher animals. However, they also could have been used to dig tubers and roots, and to chop down trees, and they could have been thrown as weapons. Some scientists have controversially suggested that they were like dating profiles—that is, meant to attract sexual partners, symbolic demonstrations of intellectual prowess for potential mates.[9]

Acheulean tools may not mark the arrival of superintelligence, but this innovative way of engineering stone was complex and required toolmakers to systematically strip off flakes from both sides of a raw chunk of rock. The technology was good enough to last about 1.5 million years.

While there is little evidence that *Homo erectus* and its later cousin *Homo heidelbergensis* (a species that lived 700,000 to 200,000 years ago in Europe, Africa, and possibly Asia) had little more than stone tools at their disposal, we begin to see around their time the first signs of a new kind of material world. At a 400,000-year-old site called Terra Amata in France, archaeologists found the world's first known shelters: oval structures, likely made by bending pliable saplings, positioning them into postholes, and securing them with rocks at the base.[10] *Homo heidelbergensis* engineered some of these huts to be 25 feet long. Some contained rock-lined hearths with blackened bones—evidence of the earliest cooking.

Not far away in Germany, archaeologists found three long spears carved from spruce that date to 400,000 years ago.[11] And in Zambia, archaeologists excavated more than 300 fragments of yellow, red, and

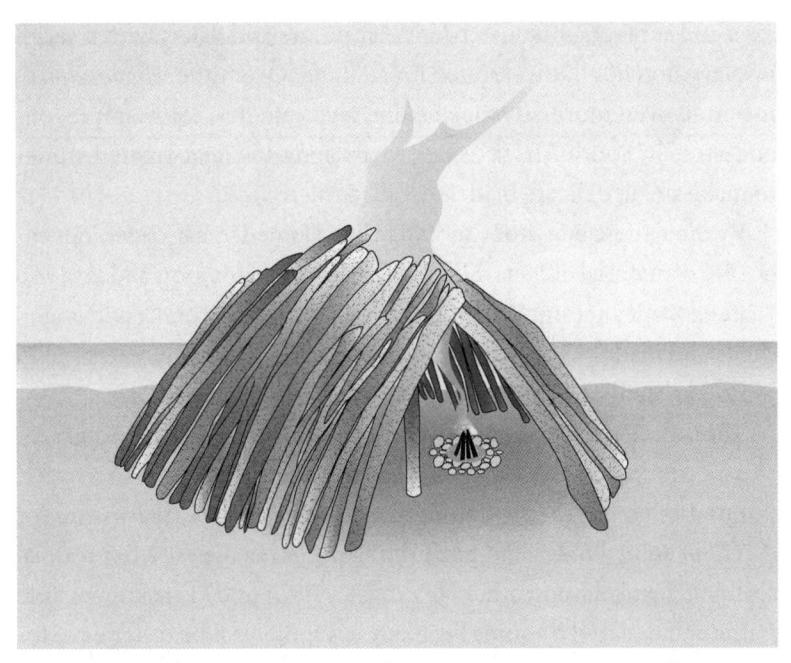

17. What the Terra Amata huts, from 400,000 years ago, might have looked like.

purple pigments and grinding tools that are 400,000 to 350,000 years old, pointing to the origins of paint, possibly applied to people's bodies for rituals or as social symbols.[12] In this same time frame, a *Homo erectus* artisan living in Germany etched a series of parallel marks into an elephant tibia, pointing to the possibility of art.[13] A cave site in Austria dating to 300,000 years ago yielded a bone point and a wolf incisor each with a hole at their root, seemingly used as pendants for personal ornamentation.[14] Houses, paint, sculpture, body ornaments—our distant hominin ancestors were starting to make our material world.

By 400,000 years ago, *Homo neanderthalensis* appears in the fossil record, followed by *Homo sapiens* about 100,000 years later. During this period, yet more-sophisticated stone tools were invented: what archaeologists dub the Mousterian tradition. These tools required that the core be more carefully prepared to increase control over the flake's size, shape, and thickness. The resulting tools are more diverse than those produced by the Acheulean technique and appear to have been made to be far more specialized for particular functions—not only axes and scrapers, but also triangular points and flakes with a series of sharp notches like a serrated bread knife. Over time, *Homo sapiens* invented even more-advanced stone technologies; for example, our ancestors in South Africa 71,000 years ago used heat-treated stones to make small, delicate bladelets called microliths.[15]

By then, these new stone tools had been joined by a broadening repertoire of material objects. Somewhere between 160,000 and 120,000 years ago, our ancestors in the Near East collected naturally perforated shells and made string to join them together.[16] By 82,000 years ago in Morocco, shell was worked into beads and strung together.[17]

The oldest arrows tipped with stone points were used in South Africa 64,000 years ago.[18] Recovered in the same cave were two slender, pointed bone fragments dating to 61,000 years ago, likely used for stitching animal hides and performing other needlework to produce clothing, blankets, and other coverings.[19] The world's first known flute (although debated by some) is likely a fragment of bear bone perforated with two holes, recovered in Slovenia and thought to have been played by Neanderthals 50,000 years ago.[20] Beads, arrows, needles, flutes—the modern material world was coming into focus.

18. The world's earliest known flute may be this fragment of bone from a cave bear, dating to about 50,000 years ago, found in Slovenia.

About 43,000 years ago, *Homo sapiens* was ushering in a new stone-tool tradition in Europe, called Aurignacian, which produced long, fine blades and tools made from a prepared core. These early modern humans also made fine blades, animal bones with incised patterns, bone needles and awls, and burins for incising stone and wood. A still wider array of things was invented, such as the oldest known figurative sculpture (a lion man, from 40,000 years ago in Germany),[21] fiber (woven flax, dating to 34,000 years ago in the Republic of Georgia),[22] fishhooks (at nearly 23,000 years ago in Japan),[23] mammoth bones covered in ochre, which could be drumsticks and rattles (dating to 22,000 years ago in the Ukraine),[24] and fired clay pottery (at 20,000 years ago in China).[25]

While there will always be new discoveries pointing to earlier times in different places, this list makes it abundantly clear that by the time *Homo sapiens* become the last surviving *Homo* species on Earth, about 40,000 years ago, our ancestors were establishing a material world that is entirely familiar to us thousands of generations later. Housing, clothing, visual art, musical instruments, and tools for hunting, fishing, and gathering—all these categories were firmly in place well before the Ice Age ended 12,000 years ago. This is the world Ötzi inherited, and the world we inherited from Ötzi. There is a direct historical path our ancestors walked from the 400,000-year-old Terra Amata hut to the Palace of Versailles.

But this description does not fully capture the *how* of our modern material world. For that, we must understand how our human ancestors and we today have made every thing through an endless series of small and large changes to these basic themes—the ability to elaborate on the cultural advances made over time, and the consequences of a new form of settled human life centered around domesticated animals and agriculture.

COMPLETE THE CHAIN

On December 7, 1877, an ambitious young inventor and his associate traveled from their laboratory in Menlo Park, New Jersey, to New York

City, to visit the offices of *Scientific American*, then the United States' leading magazine of technology and scientific achievement. The inventor placed a small metal device on the editor's desk. Once the staff had assembled, he turned a crank.[26]

"Good morning," a scratchy voice piped out of the device. "How are you doing? How do you like the phonograph?"

The group stood in collective awe.

For the first time in history, a voice had been transported across space and time. The magazine literally stopped the presses to report Thomas Edison's invention of a talking machine. "Speech has become," *Scientific American* proclaimed, "immortal."[27]

The machine so astonished listeners that some of them fainted when they first heard it. Others called it witchcraft or evil, the voice of the devil. Yet, the invention's ingenuity could not be denied. One newspaper announced, "The phonograph is regarded as the greatest triumph of inventive genius which has been attained even in this inventive age."[28] When Edison played it at the White House for President Rutherford B. Hayes, a celebration followed into the night. The National Academy of Sciences declared to Edison, "These other men are only inventors—You, sir, are a discoverer!" Edison was launched into worldwide fame, soon to be known as the "Wizard of Menlo Park."[29]

The story of the phonograph raises a fundamental question about stuff: How are things invented? This question is the heart of our modern material world, because without new ideas, there can't be more things. Once Lucy's kin moved our ancient ancestors from behavioral specialists to creative behavioral innovators, hominins became the world's great inventors. But how did these moments unfold once stone tools were born into the world? How are new technologies developed?

In his 2009 book, *The Nature of Technology*, the economist W. Brian Arthur proposes an explanation of the origin of new things—the advent of "novel technology" that applies a new principle to a problem at hand. He believes, whether an inventor is creating the first stone tool, phonograph, or space shuttle, that all these inventions share a basic process. Arthur's theory sees human inventions as beautifully and

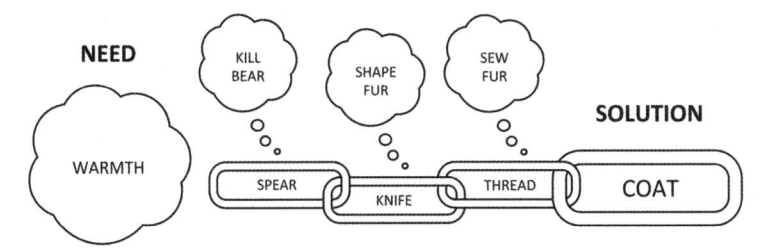

19. The chain to create a novel technology like a coat to solve for the problem of warmth would require multiple sublinks.

endlessly connected. He writes that an invention "consists in linking a need with some effect to satisfactorily achieve that need." For example, a coat keeps a person warm on a cold day. To conceptualize the linkage between the necessity of warmth and a coat, Arthur uses the metaphor of a chain: at one end is the need (warmth); at the other end is the solution (the coat). The inventor links these two points, either starting with the need and looking for solutions, or starting with a tool that can be applied to a new problem. While some needs can be easily and directly linked, most solutions require sublinks or even sub-sublinks. A simple coat, for example, could require three sublinks: a spear to kill a bear for its fur and tendons, a knife to cut the fur into shape, and thread to sew the tendons into the coat. In turn, each of these tools—spear, knife, thread—would require their own links to be invented. The novel invention, in Arthur's terms, only arises once all these links have been made and the chain—evidenced by the finished coat—is fully in place and functional.[30]

Looking across the history of human technology, Arthur sees how solutions have been found in different ways. Sometimes inventors borrow a principle from an unrelated area of knowledge and apply it in new ways (tendons used for hafting a stone point to a spear can also be used as thread to sew a winter coat). In other cases, inventors combine concepts. The spark for solutions can come from an incident, accident, or observation. Sometimes solutions are arrived at by methodically working through sublinks until the chain is complete. The key point of Arthur's theory is that every novel invention arrives from some experience or previous invention. Nothing comes out of thin air. Arthur argues, "At the heart of invention lies appropriation, some sort of mental borrowing that comes in the form of a half-conscious suggestion."[31]

This theory certainly describes the phonograph. As early as the ninth century, Persian inventors created the first mechanical instruments, including a water-powered organ that played music from interchangeable cylinders with raised pins.[32] A thousand years later, the French inventor Édouard-Léon Scott de Martinville created his phonautograph, etched sound waves, produced by a voice speaking into a tube, onto a soot-stained cylinder; however, there was then no way to play the recording to reproduce the sound. Edison, inspired by Alexander Graham Bell's 1876 telephone, experimented with ways to record voices. In the *Scientific American* article announcing Edison's discovery, six other inventors are mentioned who were also working on voice machines.[33]

Once the idea (or ideas) of a solution is imagined, an invention depends on the ability to make the technology. De Martinville could imagine the phonograph but didn't have tools to invent it. Edison did. "At [the invention's] heart lies the act of seeing a suitable solution in action—seeing a suitable principle that will do the job," Arthur concludes. "The rest, allowing some high degree of exaggeration, is standard engineering."[34]

On November 29, 1877, Edison sketched his idea for a voice-recording machine, which closely resembled de Martinville's device, except instead of a strip of paper covered in soot, he imagined a spiral-grooved brass cylinder wrapped with a thin piece of tinfoil. In Edison's machine a spring-held stylus similar to that of a record player (styluses date at least to the Romans, 2,000 years ago) ran over the tinfoil (used in scientific experiments since at least the 1760s), making indentations of the sound vibrations produced by speaking into a funnel.[35] When the stylus was reset at the beginning of the cylinder and drawn over the imprinted tinfoil, it reproduced the vibrations, reproducing the spoken sound.

This is not to say that invention is routine. On the contrary—when

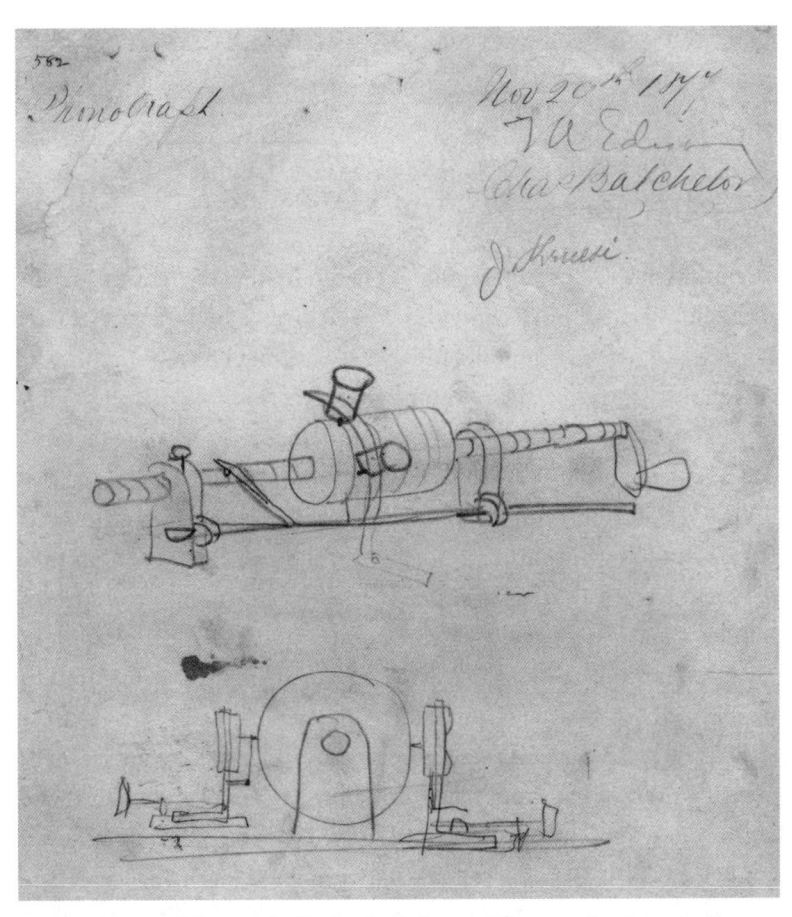

20. Thomas Edison made this sketch of what would become the phonograph.

Edison tried his talking machine in his lab for the first time, he was just as astonished as anyone to hear his own voice say, "Mary had a little lamb."[36] Novel inventions require creative acts that make fantastic "mental associations," as Arthur describes them, that draw links between the need or problem and the potential tools that can complete the chain.

The discovery of a novel technology still requires an inventor's profound vision: of seeing a problem, seeing that it is solvable, seeing possible solutions, seeing the actual solution, and seeing how to build the solution. From Lucy's kin to Thomas Edison, every human who created a novel technology accomplished a dazzling feat of engineering and imagination, even though they only built upon the material world they were born into.

ENDLESS ITERATION

Technologies are ceaselessly being taken in new directions. As the tech philosopher Tom Chatfield writes, "Alone among species (at least until the crows have put in a million years more effort) humans can consciously improve and combine their creations over time.... It is through this process of recursive iteration that tools became technologies; and technology a world-altering force."[37]

The endless iteration of technology that has obsessed our hominin family has led us in three important directions. First, recombining different parts into new "composite tools" leads to important possibilities. Chatfield gives the example of the Gutenberg printing press, invented around 1440, which was combined from parts inspired by paper from 6th-century China, movable metal alphabet pieces from 13th-century Korea, and ancient European wine-making presses. The printing press was a composite tool, both familiar (in its parts) and entirely new (as a whole). In the same way, Edison's phonograph was made from springs, rods, screws, plates, pulleys, a wax cylinder, and stylus parts that all had been invented decades, even millennia earlier. The only thing new about the Gutenberg press and the phonograph was how their parts were put together. Every novel technology, like any newborn, is the material product of its parents and yet radically unique.

Chatfield points out that the phenomenon of combination explains how the number of things in the world increases exponentially over time. Three different parts can be combined in six different ways. Adding just one more part produces 24 different combinations. And 10 different parts can be combined a mind-staggering 3,628,800 possible ways.

Not only does the invention of each new part vastly increase the number of possible composite tools, but each new tool can be used to create more tools. An ax can be used to cut down a tree that is made into a spear, which then takes down a bear whose fur can be used for a coat. The proliferation of stuff is turtles all the way down. Infinite regress.

A second point is that the more sublinks and the more parts that are needed for a composite tool, the greater the "problem-solution distance." As discussed in chapter 1, Miriam Noël Haidle has explained how our first hominin ancestors, to make tools, needed a better working memory than their predecessors. This was necessary to sustain their focus on both the problem they were solving and the solution they found. Composite tools require ever more working memory because there are ever more steps involved. Haidle has summarized experimental research showing that even the relatively simple 400,000-year-old spears found in Germany would take about five hours to construct. The process would involve steps from harvesting a branch to stripping off the bark to smoothing its surface to straightening the wood to sharpening the tip.[38]

Compare the phonograph. Once Edison had the idea mapped out, his shop crew turned out a prototype in 30 hours.[39] But Edison's laboratory had a fully stocked workshop. And the 30 hours does not count the thousands of hours that were needed to produce the specific parts—a simple screw was made of metal mined from Earth, transported to a factory, smelted down into a long spool of wire, fed into a screw-cutting machine, and shipped to New Jersey. Whereas our very first toolmaking ancestor likely had just minutes of working memory to make a tool, today, a NASA space shuttle involves the work of thousands of people to put together 2.5 million parts over five years, so that scientists can explore planetary questions that may take a lifetime to answer.[40] Over millions of years, endless iterations became ever more possible as humans extended problem-solution distances.

A third point is the slow progression of invention as an intergenerational project. The improvement and recombination of things requires cooperation over centuries, millennia, or sometimes a million years, in the case of the first stone technologies. While many species that use tools as a behavioral specialization are driven by biological instinct, behavioral innovators learn how to use tools through culture—a process of learning. For example, research on wild bottlenose dolphins off the coast of western Australia suggests that their use of sponges as foraging tools (a sponge is broken off the seafloor and then placed on the nose to probe into the seafloor for fish) is not a behavior that comes from DNA but rather from cultural transmission through the female line, with the mother teaching her female offspring.[41]

But while animals like bottlenose dolphins have the capacity for cultural transmission, this process would become a hallmark of our species.[42] Thomas Edison's brilliance came from his own genius, but also from his grasp of chemistry and physics, his access to engineering instruments, and the knowledge and toolkits amassed over thousands of years before he walked into the offices of *Scientific American* in the winter of 1877.

It is this cultural transmission that makes "cumulative culture" possible.[43] Cumulative culture, as defined by the ecologist Robert Boyd and the zoologist Peter J. Richerson, is the technological accumulation of "changes over many generations, resulting in culturally transmitted behaviors that no single human individual could invent on his own."[44] The overwhelming evidence for this process is the archaeological record that starts with rough stone tools by at least 3.3 million years ago, and goes to modern landfills with castoffs of millions of different technologies.

The psychologist Michael Tomasello has called this the "ratchet effect," meaning that a tool is created and then many generations later is modified, and then generations later is modified again.[45] Tools are always being ratcheted up, "improved" over time; this is how we go from the phonograph in 1877 to the gramophone disk in 1887 to reel-to-reel players in the 1930s to the vinyl record in 1948 to the cassette tape in 1963 to the CD in 1982 to the MP3 file in 1989 to the myriad digital technologies of the new millennium.[46]

Tomasello and his colleagues have argued that the ratchet effect is unique to humans.[47] Nonhuman animals like chimpanzees that use cultural transmission tend to learn individually, be product-oriented, and make tools that fit their behavioral repertoire. For humans, social

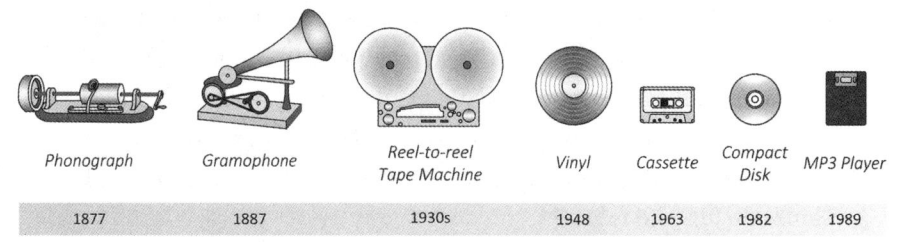

Phonograph	Gramophone	Reel-to-reel Tape Machine	Vinyl	Cassette	Compact Disk	MP3 Player
1877	1887	1930s	1948	1963	1982	1989

21. The evolution of music-playing devices demonstrates the "ratchet effect," in which a technology is constantly being modified and improved upon.

learning is more process-oriented, and our unique ability to cooperate leads to strong social motivations for active teaching and learning—and improvement.

In a recent article, the primatologist Carel P. van Schaik and his colleagues Gauri R. Pradhan and Claudio Tennie look at a wide range of evidence to conclude that hominin cumulative culture unfolded in three distinct surges.[48] The first took place around 500,000 years ago. They believe this change came with verbal teaching as hominin groups more proactively cooperated, particularly in raising children. The second happened around 75,000 years ago and may be tied to an increasing impulse towards curiosity and seeking novelty. The third seismic shift, as we'll see, arrived on the precipice of 12,000 years ago—one that reshaped human life on Earth, shaped Ötzi's life, and has continued on ever since.

SETTLING DOWN

The Neolithic Revolution, the New Stone Age, began around 12,000 years ago in the Fertile Crescent, a region stretching from the Nile River in Egypt up the eastern coast of the Mediterranean through Turkey and arching through Jordan, Iraq, and Iran.[49] This was the beginning of the material world that would be most recognizable to Ötzi, and to us today. Due to a favorable, warming global climate, or to resource scarcity, or to the beginning of organized religion that brought people to one location, hunter-gatherer tribes in the Fertile Crescent surrendered their nomadic way of life to settle down. They began to plant seeds such as emmer wheat, einkorn wheat, and barley, and then tended the crops to harvest, picking the most desirable seeds to sow again the next year. As plants required more time for their care, many early agriculturalists had less time and opportunity to hunt; they began to domesticate wild animals—at first, sheep and goats, for milk, skins and fur, and meat.[50]

This initial transition might have been difficult, and even less productive than foraging; farmers must work longer, harder hours with poorer health outcomes than foragers.[51] Significantly, this transition was seemingly often a process of experimentation—not an easy and rational change, like the choice to flick on a light switch. Many groups continued a foraging or hunter-gatherer nomadic lifestyle. Yet, agriculture likely pulled some Neolithic peoples to it because land could be more easily established and protected (a nascent modern notion of private property) than procuring scattered resources across a big territory, particularly in the face of climate shifts that were then occurring.[52] Those who primarily domesticated plants and animals began to live year-round in the same place, decade after decade, for the first time in human history.[53]

One of the first villages where this transition can be documented is Tell Abu Hureyra, situated in modern Syria along the Euphrates River.[54] Within several thousand years, the sedentary lifestyle spread across the region. Large towns blossomed, such as Çatalhöyük in eastern Turkey, with 8,000 people at its height. In the remains of Çatalhöyük, archaeologists have recovered a rich material life, including a range of objects for art and religion.

The Neolithic Revolution was not limited to the Fertile Crescent; it became a global phenomenon, independently invented. Around 10,000 years ago in China, people domesticated Asian millet and rice. Nearly 9,000 years ago in Mexico, people began domesticating squash and corn. Some 6,500 years ago in Sudan, sorghum was domesticated; then 4,500 years ago in Mali, African millet and rice followed. These crops fostered the transitions toward sedentary lifestyles around the globe.[55] The new stability, food surpluses, and social organization afforded by agriculture eventually gave rise to the Great Pyramids in Egypt, the vast palaces of Teotihuacán in Mexico, the sprawling temples of Angkor Wat in Cambodia.

The transition to settled life led to a dramatic increase in stuff. Nomads, by definition, are mobile. Being on-the-move meant that foragers could possess only what they could carry or build from materials immediately at hand. After dogs were domesticated between 40,000 and 20,000 years ago, and then later horses and camels and other beasts of burden, domesticated animals could help carry possessions.[56] But, they could only carry so much. Once people began to settle in one place, however, the need to transport all our belongings ceased to be a limiting factor. Anyone who has lived in a house for a long time knows how easily things accumulate.

A settled life was often far more precarious than a nomadic one. A single flood could destroy an entire year's food supply, leaving farmers with no way to feed their families. A war required people to stand firm and defend their homes. A disease could ravage a city, leaving survivors nowhere to run. Settled life required new technologies to help navigate these vulnerabilities. Agriculture and pastoralism led to new tools to pursue these activities full time. Hoes, plows, shovels, spades, and sickles were needed to grow and harvest grains; new threshing and grinding tools were needed to process them; and new cooking equipment was needed to prepare them. Keeping livestock required fences and pens, shearing scissors and ropes. Living in one spot, permanently, also entailed inventing new kinds of structures. People desired robust abodes that would last lifetimes. Wells, cisterns, and canals were invented to irrigate croplands. Dams and dikes were needed to retain water or ward off flooding. Having only one home meant it had to be protected, prompting better weapons. A town like Çatalhöyük 8,000 years ago was filled with pottery, baskets, obsidian-tipped weapons, murals, ritually painted leopard and bull skulls, clay and stone figurines, bone tools and ornaments, and stone axes, maces, grinding stones, and pendants.[57]

With settled life, communities created new forms of cooperation and social organization. Jobs could become more specialized—the division of labor—with one person tending crops, another raising animals, another making pottery. Each job spurred the creation of more-specialized tools. Because people did not move around much, trade became crucial: vast networks of roads, horsedrawn carts, and seafaring ships were devised. Religious life grew more formal, with the rise of priestly castes and things to facilitate belief, such as altars and temples. Many societies would become hierarchical, with formal governments that disseminated laws to control the citizenry and create social orders of their design. Government and religious authorities would require methods for keeping records of taxes and tributes, royal lineages and histories, mathematical theories and astronomical observances—the birth of writing can be traced to 5,500 years ago in Iraq, 5,200 years ago in Egypt, 3,300 years ago in China, and 3,000 years ago in Central America.[58]

Yet another vital technological leap centered on the discovery of metallurgy. From the beginning of the Neolithic, people across the Fertile Crescent collected pure copper and pounded it into decorative objects. Archaeologists have recovered copper beads at Çatalhöyük.[59] However, around 7,000 years ago, toolmakers across Iran and southern Europe seem to have independently realized that raw copper threaded through stone could be extracted by melting it. A thousand years later, artisans combined melted tin with copper to make bronze, a much stronger, synthetic metal. The technology quickly spread across the eastern Mediterranean, Africa, and Europe through trade networks.[60] Hard metals opened new possibilities, first in the creation of agricultural tools, domestic items, and weapons—and then across the millennia to build railroads, ocean liners, and jumbo jets.

All these new activities and things led to urbanization.[61] As more people came together, towns, rather than having a natural limit, continued to grow and grow until they became cities. Once permanent villages and farming areas were established, with the right climatic and social conditions, these communities could quickly scale up by intensifying resource extraction to become large population centers. Demographers estimate that the world's population little more than doubled from 50,000 years ago to 10,000 years ago; but from 10,000 to 2,000 years ago, the global population exploded from 5 million to

300 million.[62] In some cases, urbanization resulted in economic and political centralization, in which people were convinced or forced to settle in cities by religious, political, or military authorities. In other situations, cities materialized organically, with citizens pulled in by new opportunities or fashions, or pushed out of their rural homes by drought or war. Many of the first cities were designed as sacred centers, evidenced by their orientation in certain directions or the placement of churches, temples, or shrines. Cities encouraged social hierarchies, establishing substantial and profound material differences between the haves and the have-nots.

And cities themselves created crises that needed to be materially addressed. Plumbing, sewerage systems, garbage disposal, streets, streetlights, communal spaces, and more all descended from urbanization. Urbanization, with people living in such close proximity, sometimes with domesticated animals, also brought new relationships with animals and parasites, rodents and bacteria.[63] New diseases arose, prompting the need for medical specialists and hospitals and new tools to treat the sick.

Tying all these elements together—settled life, new forms of labor and inequality, and much more stuff—is an easily overlooked feature of the Neolithic Revolution: storage. Storing food and tools was a very old human practice before the rise of agriculture and animal husbandry, especially in places with long and cold winters where food was scarce or where raw materials for tools in a given environment were hard to come by. However, storage became essential with sedentism, with farming especially. Farming required the long-term storage of seeds and harvests, which in turn would have to last a year or more while the next crop was being raised. Storage was necessary to have enough to eat during down months (or years, in the case of extended droughts) while also having seeds to keep planting. But storage implied the possibility of something much more: surplus. While foragers or hunters might have a sudden bounty—an especially good year for strawberries, or an entire herd of bison driven off a cliff—without storage, such abundance was fleeting. On the other hand, farmers in the good times could keep years of food just sitting in a cold, dark storage room, and herders could have massive amounts of food grazing in their fields (since living animals were themselves a form of surplus).

The fact that settled people could potentially have a surplus—more food than they needed—created the possibility of debt. This is because lenders could provide seed or young animals with the promise that they would receive a portion of the surplus later on. Such an agreement created debt for the farmer or herder.[64] In a society where people are equal, then there is a "balanced reciprocity," where the creditor waits until the debt can be fully repaid.[65] However, debt also created the possibilities for inequality because the debtor was obliged to the creditor until the debt was paid. In these conditions, social hierarchies emerged, as creditors could force debtors into their service. In this way, debt could be foremost about control over people.[66] This was an important change in human relations because now surplus—the abundance of stuff—was not merely about survival but about power.

Most of the world today follows a direct path from the Neolithic Revolution. What emerged on the threshold of 12,000 years ago—cities, specialized jobs, stratified societies, and surplus—became the foundational stuff of the modern world. This, too, was the world Ötzi inherited. Ötzi lived in a village of tall wooden homes below the Alps where his people grew cereal grains, processed cheese from domesticated goats and cattle, and hunted wild deer and ibex. His people dressed in coats and pants and underwear. They carried lanterns and had backpacks. Just like us, Ötzi had many things. That might even be what got him killed.

THE ICEMAN'S MURDER

Only in 2001 did researchers identify a flint arrowhead lodged in Ötzi's left shoulder. Suddenly, Ötzi's other known injuries began to make more sense.

Scholars now believe that a few days before he died, Ötzi endured a struggle that left a serious cut in his right hand. It was an early summer day when he fled to the safety of the mountains. He lasted a few days, even eating a hearty meal of ibex or red deer and einkorn wheat several hours before pursuers caught up with him and shot him with an arrow from about 90 feet away. Ötzi also had a bad head wound that might have come from falling after being shot or during the earlier hand-to-hand combat. But it was the arrow from the back that shattered Ötzi's scapula and pierced an artery; he bled to death within minutes. Ötzi died lying against a boulder, to be covered by snow and time, until the day two hikers from Germany stumbled upon his remains.

Why was the iceman killed?

A hint is in the things Ötzi possessed. Of course, Ötzi could have been killed because he was a bad man. He might have been in the wrong place at the wrong time. But he also could have been killed because of his things. Not in the sense of being robbed (after all, he was found with so much), but because his things represented all the reasons people can be killed—envy, religion, wealth, politics, identity. Things have functions: they serve particular goals and needs. But for humans, things are much more. Things create us as social beings.

Ötzi's finely made striped coat of alternating furs is a thing of beauty. The twine hung with a stone is likely a religious object. His copper ax had great value. His bearskin hat might have represented Ötzi's position as a tribal leader—clothing that embodied his identity.

In other words, Ötzi not only had a lot of things. He had things filled with meaning.

LEAP 2

MAKE MEANING

22. This statue embodies the bodhisattva of compassion, Guanyin.

4

A THING OF BEAUTY

About 90,000 years ago, a group of Neanderthals came upon a small cave set above a forested valley in what is now northern Italy.[1] There they sheltered from the freezing cold in winter and torrents of rain in the spring. There they lit fires and shared meals, loved and fought, slept and dreamt. For 50,000 years, generations of Neanderthals made this cave their home. Then, one day, for reasons that will never be fully known, the Neanderthals left and never returned. Before long, their species would go extinct.

Almost immediately, *Homo sapiens* moved in. In most ways, the cave's new tenants continued to use the space as their Neanderthal cousins had. The humans were hunters and gatherers too, and needed shelter and safety. They also made the cave their refuge, taking comfort in the small alcove that sat above a winding creek.

And yet, the cave would witness new behaviors. While Neanderthals left behind a few ornamental beads, humans left behind hundreds. While the Neanderthals wore the whole furs and skins of animals, humans crafted needles and thread to sew clothing. Some nameless human inventor then created something else without precedent in the cave's history and with little precedent in the history of the world: a thing of beauty.

By 30,000 years ago, the humans had abandoned the cave. Over the millennia that followed, landslides and earthquakes buried the cave until it was completely concealed with soil, rocks, and trees. Yet eventually, the forces of erosion took hold, and the hill's slow striptease began.

Water and wind released small clues of the region's Ice Age inhabitants. In the late 1800s, passersby noticed strange stone tools and fragments of bones poking out from the face of the hillside. Word got around; curiosity seekers and collectors came to gather the relics. After World War II, road construction bit into the hill and even more artifacts poured out. Now the archaeologists arrived. They confirmed that Grotta di Fumane was a place where Neanderthals had once lived, but they left without taking their research further. The site was close to being forgotten once again.

In the late 1980s, artifacts from the site made their way into the hands of two archaeology professors, Alberto Broglio and Mauro Cremaschi, and their graduate student Marco Peresani. They visited the cave and started an excavation. More than 30 years later, Peresani is still digging. "It's a dream for us," he told me when I visited him at the cave not long ago. "When we started in '88, we didn't think it would be so perfectly preserved."

Almost a decade after the excavations began, the team unearthed one of its most important finds without even knowing it: they uncovered several stone fragments with two spots of ochre, a red mineral used as paint. But the spots were small, and the stone was covered with a layer of white calcium carbonate. Shoulders were shrugged and the fragments were placed in storage.

Then, in 1999, the team found a second stone piece painted with ochre. "I said to my professor," Peresani recounted, "'Hey, how about those stone fragments we found a few years ago?'"

The first fragment was brought out of storage. A conservator removed the carbonate. Beneath the film of white was the painted image of a humanlike figure.

It was startling in its careful lines and intentional depiction of a body with two legs spread out and arms dangling like a lopsided, upside-down U. What might be an erect penis extends from the pelvis. The rounded head is framed by two large, flat horns.

A THING OF BEAUTY

23. The archaeologist Marco Peresani holds a reproduction of one of the world's oldest pieces of art, a half-human, half-bison figure from Fumane Cave in Italy, dating to between 32,000 and 36,500 years ago.

Up to that point, humanity's oldest known cave paintings were located in Grotte Chauvet in southern France, dated to 32,000 years ago. The Fumane team dated their stone to 32,000 to 36,500 years ago. This mysterious silhouette in red became the world's oldest painted art.

CHAPTER FOUR

THE LONG REVOLUTION

Deep in our evolutionary past, the tools humans made began to have more than a functional purpose. An ancestor realized that a stone knife could do more than just chop up meat, that an ax could do more than just fell a tree. Things could be an outward expression of what a person felt, experienced, and believed. Hopes did not have to stay hidden in the heart. All of this could be translated and communicated, permanently and clearly, manifested in the world through things.

The emergence of meaning matters in our human story because it marks when objects began to do more than just serve our biological needs—when a thing conveys a message, when it signifies something more than itself. This shift points to when things began to sway us, inspire us. This is when things truly began to organize us as *social* beings. With meaning, the human relationship to our things did not merely take a new turn. It transported us to a new dimension—a new future. With meaning, stuff's second great leap was underway.

It is an unsolvable mystery when exactly things began to have meaning. However, the archaeological record holds hints and whispers that we can use to reconstruct parts of this history.

The search for the world's first art has been a central actor in this drama. This is partly because art could have been the first type of meaning imbued in objects. And it is partly because art is a traceable material act that archaeologists can find and study—and argue over.

And there has been a lot of arguing. Much of the debate centers on how to define art as such. Must it be aesthetically driven? Do a few parallel lines carved into stone equal art? Or is art more clearly representational—a lion painted on a cave wall? Additional quarreling arises because archaeologists are constantly finding new evidence—something that challenges the orthodoxy, something that pushes forward new hypotheses, something older or in some surprising new place.

Despite disagreements over theories and specific finds, for the last several decades archaeologists and anthropologists have developed a clearer picture of how "art," as we know it, began. The birth of visual art was a revolution of human cognition and behavior—but it was a *long* revolution, I argue, that ultimately links three unique abilities: an animal instinct for beauty, the desire for self-expression, and the invention of symbolic thinking.

AESTHETIC INSTINCTS

In a way, the revolution began even before the *Homo* line broke off from other primates about 2.5 million years ago. An aesthetic sense—that is, having a sense of the beautiful—would seem to be a beginning point for art, and yet new research shows that it is an entrenched animal instinct.

Experimental studies prove that nonhuman animals can perceive and differentiate between different artistic styles. In Tokyo, psychologists at Keio University trained pigeons to distinguish paintings by Claude Monet from those made by Pablo Picasso.[2] These scholars showed in another study that goldfish could regularly distinguish between the music of Bach and Stravinsky.[3]

"It's scientifically demonstrable that animals have an aesthetic capacity," the ornithologist Richard Prum, author of *The Evolution of Beauty* (2017), once said in an interview. "What I mean by that is that they can perceive objects, they can evaluate whether or not they like them, and then act on that. That in-and-of-itself makes for an aesthetic experience."[4] This points to aesthetics as an experience of preference, of one's pleasure.

The fact that nonhuman animals seem to share what could be called an aesthetic instinct suggests an underlying evolutionary process. In other words, aesthetics could be about sex. In the language of biologists, aesthetics have improved the "fitness" (the ability to find a mate and produce offspring) of artists, by so visibly demonstrating their intelligence and insight. As the psychologist George Miller has suggested, humans first started decorating rocks, like a peacock flashes its tail, to grab the attention of potential mates.[5]

And yet, even if there is an evolutionary basis for aesthetics in hominins, it is unclear how far it goes.[6] For instance, if the human aesthetic sensibility is driven solely by evolution, then there should be a genetic basis for art, but no one has found an art gene yet. And, even as humans share a deep capacity for aesthetics with many in the animal kingdom, what the human line did with that capacity is unique.

In his 2014 book *The Aesthetic Brain: How We Evolved to Desire Beauty and Enjoy Art*, the evolutionary psychologist Anjan Chatterjee explain how humans might have taken a basic instinct and turned it into an advantage that went beyond biology. Chatterjee uses as a metaphor, or parallel process, the domestication of a bird in Japan several centuries ago. There, people captured the white-rumped munia, a type of finch, for its rich plumage of chocolate brown and ivory white. In the wild, the bird had a lovely song. However, once in captivity—once its basic needs of food and freedom from predators were satisfied—its songs became even more dramatic and varied, a grand series of melodic squeaks and chirps.

This is Chatterjee's idea: art, like the white-rumped munia's song, may initially have had some evolutionary advantages that drew humans toward aesthetics, which people then took to a new level—the elevation of scribbles on a shell to Frida Kahlo's sumptuous oil paintings. Only when some people were freed up (domesticated, in a sense) to no longer worry about where every meal was coming from, artistic practices expanded. Art may have originally had adaptive roots, Chatterjee argues, but over the millennia, it outlived its adaptive purpose.

It is also possible that early humans expanded their aesthetic possibilities because of the very things that enabled their success: stone tools.

As we saw in chapter 2, stone tools changed early hominin bodies and brains, providing key evolutionary advantages. It is not outlandish, then, to consider how these early toolmakers began to look at their tools differently, through the aesthetic lens they likely would have already possessed buried among their instincts.

Some scholars have suggested that Acheulean hand axes—the large tear-drop-shaped tools that *Homo erectus* made over the course of a million years—may have been hominins' first purpose-made aesthetic objects. The hand ax's precise use remains somewhat of an enigma, but it could have been used for chopping trees and cutting, or possibly wielded as a weapon. Yet some of these stones show no sign of wear, even though making them took a lot of work. So why make them? Perhaps to make something beautiful. As the *New York Times* critic Jason Farago put it, very ancient tools such as Acheulean hand axes show an aesthetic sense of proportion and balance. "Someone a little like us invested extra time and effort," he wrote, "to enact these shapes on hard stone."[7]

"In size and shape it would not have been a useful butchery implement, and is worked on to a degree out of proportion to any likely use," the philosopher Gregory Currie has similarly argued. "While it may be too much to call it an 'early work of art,' it is at least suggestive of an aesthetic sensibility."[8]

While few scholars would accept the argument that ancient stone tools are fully formed art, they do seem to point to the beginning of something beautiful.

EXPRESS YOURSELF

In 1887, Eugène Dubois left a prestigious academic post at the University of Amsterdam on what many people said was a fool's errand.[9] As a medical student, Dubois had been profoundly inspired by Charles Darwin's exciting new theory of evolution. He became obsessed with finding the "missing link" between modern humans and apes. Dubois pinpointed Southeast Asia as a place to search for this fossil evidence but failed to find a funder to support an expedition there. To pursue his dream, Dubois surrendered his professorship for an eight-year term as a military doctor at the edge of the Dutch Empire, in what is now Indonesia.

Dubois's search cost him dearly. His son died from tropical fever. He himself suffered from malaria. He narrowly escaped a tiger. During one expedition, the ceiling of a cave nearly killed him as it came crashing down. He spent more than two fruitless years searching on the island of Sumatra. When he moved on to Java, though, Dubois finally struck archaeological gold. At Trinil, along the Solo River, his workers uncovered a fossil skullcap (the top part of the head), a tooth, and an upper leg bone that proved the existence of a previously unknown humanlike species.

In 1894, Dubois published his discovery: *Pithecanthropus erectus*, "upright ape-man." But sadly, few scholars accepted his claims, hypothesizing that the remains belonged to an ape or to a primitive human, or amounted to a medley of animal and human parts. Dubois's marriage soured, and he accepted an obscure academic appointment. An anatomist named Gustav Schwalbe started a successful speaking tour on "Java Man," usurping Dubois's discovery. And yet, although Dubois did not find the accepted "missing link" he was searching for, he was right to maintain for the rest of his life that he'd made an incredible discovery.

Throughout the 20th century, archaeologists found extensive evidence of a highly successful species that had spread across Africa, Europe, and the far reaches of Asia. Dubois was the first to identify the species, since renamed *Homo erectus*, that researchers now believe was an ancient human cousin who likely used fire and hunted. Bones have been found that show healed wounds—evidence that *H. erectus* cared for the sick and the injured. They also made sophisticated stone tools such as the Acheulean hand ax. Perhaps they were also the first hominin species to bring the aesthetic instinct closer into the realm of decorative art.

At Trinil, Dubois collected piles of freshwater mussel shells, the leftovers from *Homo erectus* meals. These shells were taken to a natural history museum in the Netherlands. There they sat for decades. In 2007, Stephen Munro, then an archaeology student, was photographing the shells when he noticed a strange pattern on one of them. Holding the shell up in slanted light revealed a distinct zigzag pattern. Sand grains in the shell dated it to half a million years ago.[10]

From the first publication of this discovery in 2014, debate has centered on what to call the geometric shapes. Some saw "art." Others saw something different.

Even Josephine Joordens, a biologist at Leiden University who collaborated with Munro and others to first publish the discovery,

24. A *Homo erectus* etched a zigzag pattern into a mussel shell some 500,000 years ago. (The shell's main carving area is highlighted in black for clarity.)

equivocated. "If you don't know the intention of the person who made it," she said, "it's impossible to call it art."[11]

It's awfully hard to determine if a few scratches are intentional aesthetic expression. Sometimes a scratch is just a scratch. However, sometimes a scratch is made to reach an artistic itch.

"But on the other hand, it is an ancient drawing," Joordens added. "It is a way of expressing yourself."[12]

Joordens is right to be reluctant to call the engraved shells "art"—a modern concept. After all, maybe the patterns are something very different—a map or a story. But it is reasonable to consider the lines more than arbitrary, and so, in a simple and profound sense, a form of self-expression. An engraved shell is more than just an engagement with something beautiful—the aesthetic instinct—but possibly an assertion of a personality onto the object itself. This ancient *Homo erectus* carver picked up a shell and inscribed a distinct pattern. Whether it was a doodle or an intentional design, the result was an object marked by that person's mind. As the neuroscientist David Edelman has said, "Regardless of intent, the very process of rendering a geometric form would seem to indicate the workings of a mind no longer tethered solely to the here and now, but capable of a uniquely abstract form of conscious 'wandering.'"[13]

Gillian M. Morriss-Kay, an anatomist, has observed that the kinds of creative acts *Homo erectus* was capable of required "a seminal evolutionary change in the neural structures underpinning perception."[14] She theorizes that this change came about because of the convergence of innovative physiological, conceptual, and evolutionary processes.

Some of the first designs people created perhaps came not from the outside world, but from people's psychological experiences. Here, Morriss-Kay observes the prevalence of zigzags among the first known artistic expressions. In addition to the 500,000-year-old *Homo erectus* engraved shell, there are the zigzags in a 77,000-year-old cave painting in South Africa and a 54,000-year-old decorated stone from the Near East. Zigzags can be seen through our own internal visual experience—for example, migraines, seizures, and hallucinations produce flashes and zigzag patterns in a person's visual field.[15] These internally produced patterns might have been the inspiration for the first stumbling efforts at self-expression.

Archaeologists have discerned other indications of early forms of self-expression. One example is ochre, a mineral (the same one used to paint the figure found at Grotta di Fumane) typically colored a rich red or yellow. Researchers have found ochre at sites in Africa and Europe dating to hundreds of thousands of years ago. Some ochre fragments have been shaped as objects themselves, while others seem to belong in toolkits meant to process the mineral into paint. The exact uses are unknown, but hominins could have painted their bodies because they offered pleasing form and color (not unlike birds wanting mates with brighter feathers), or body painting could have been more functional, such as for camouflage during hunts. The extension, then, from painting bodies to painting objects and cave walls is not hard to imagine. At Blombos Cave in South Africa, researchers have found more than a dozen pieces of ochre, dating upwards of 100,000 years ago, all engraved with zigzags.[16]

More evidence of self-expression has accrued. At Grotte du Renne in France, archaeologists have uncovered teeth from foxes and other

A THING OF BEAUTY

25. A block of ochre mineral was engraved with zigzags, about 100,000 years ago, in South Africa.

animals that Neanderthals made into jewelry, seemingly to be strung into necklaces.[17] Archaeologists have also recovered carved and painted shells dating to 115,000 years ago in Spain[18] and an eagle-talon necklace dating to 130,000 years ago in Croatia.[19]

What do all these things reveal? They reveal that once our ancestors combined the aesthetic instinct with self-expression and applied these to the objects that made up their world, they were then just a few brush strokes away from inventing art.

SYMBOLIC THINKING

Amid the lush jade-hued hills of southwestern France, an amateur archaeologist and nobleman named Paul Hurault made the first discovery of Stone Age art—art created more than 10,000 years ago.[20] One day in 1864 while working at Laugerie-Basse, an ancient archaeological site in the Dordogne region, Hurault drew from the dirt a three-inch piece of glossy-brown mammoth ivory.

Studying it closely, he saw that it resembled a nude woman. The fragment lacked a head or arms, but it was carved with a hint of breasts, long legs, full, rounded hips, and a groove for the vulva, marking it as female. Hurault immediately interpreted the sculpture as art, naming it *Venus impudique* (immodest Venus), in contrast to a type of classical Greek statues called *Venus pudica*, in which nude female figures modestly cover themselves with their hands. (The term *Venus* is loaded

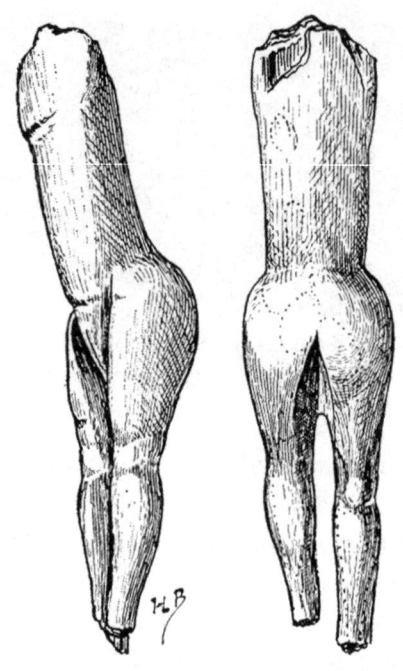

26. The first "Venus" figure was found in France in 1864, dubbed the *Venus impudique*.

and misleading because it overly focuses our gaze on these figures' sexual implications. But the term has stuck.[21]) Hurault did not know it at the time, but the little statue was about 40,000 years old.

Scientists were primed for this discovery. Leading up to Hurault's find, scholars had been slowly coming to understand that humanity extended far back into unknown time—a heretical idea then, when the Bible's chronology and concept of the animal kingdom was viewed by many in Western culture as definitive. But, by the mid-1800s, stone tools that were recovered alongside extinct animals, combined with mounting geological knowledge, proved there had been an ancient Ice Age, then thought to stretch back beyond 10,000 years.

Hurault's contemporaries had also found hints of an earlier world that contained beautiful things. In 1833, in Switzerland, archaeologists exploring a quarry found two antlers: one seemingly carved to represent a plant, the other a bird. Nine years later, a French priest found an antler fashioned into a horse's head. Although scientific methods to date these finds were not yet established, based on the geological context and artistic uniqueness, they were thought to date to a very ancient Ice Age, what came to be known as the Paleolithic, dating from about 2 million to 10,000 years ago. The evidence of Paleolithic art mounted with more discoveries buried in caves, rock shelters, and quarries across Europe. In 1867, Paleolithic pieces were grandly displayed at the Exposition Universelle in Paris, a world's fair.

In the decades that followed, collectors, explorers, archaeologists, and everyday people found more and more ancient artifacts dating back thousands of years.[22] Since Hurault's discovery, more than 200 "Venus" figurines have been found from Europe to Siberia.[23] Adding to these three-dimensional works was the discovery of engraved and painted walls in caves. In 1880, a Spanish nobleman named Marcelino Sanz de Sautuola published his analysis of the Altamira Cave's dense murals of animal figures and handprints.[24] In 1940, four French teenagers stumbled upon a cave in the Dordogne:[25] Lascaux Cave holds some of the world's most sumptuous images of the last Ice Age: 2,000 figures of humans, animals, and abstract signs. Many believe the works depict hunting scenes that either record histories of hunts or were produced as magic to empower the hunts to come.[26]

It is unclear exactly how our ancestors expanded their capacity from self-expression to symbolic thinking. Yet, these image makers were not just early artists but also early philosophers. Through representational art, these ancestors realized there was a relationship between a thing in the world, a symbol of that thing, and the concept of that thing. The depiction of a mammoth painted on a cave wall could represent a *real* mammoth in the real world and also the *concept* of a mammoth.[27] In other words, these ancient images seem to track the invention of symbolism.

However, once people had transposed internal patterns to the external world—via body painting with ochre, and then transposing it further to engraved or painted shells, stones, and cave walls—they would have been primed to see artistic expression in the natural world. As toolmakers, they had the technical knowledge that natural objects could be shaped through hammering, carving, and etching. They also had the conceptual means to study planes and angles, to use the basic principles of reverse engineering—to envision the process of working a stone until it arrived at the desired object.

Take the Berekhat Ram artifact, a figurine from the Near East made between 280,000 and 250,000 years ago, in the time of both *Homo neanderthalensis* and modern *Homo sapiens*. Many could say the stone happens to naturally resemble a voluptuous woman in the same way a passing cloud can look like a lamb. However, close analysis by the archaeologists Francesco d'Errico and April Nowell in 2000 conclusively demonstrated by examining the raw material, microscopic analyses, and experimental reproduction that the stone was shaped by tools—although only subtly—seemingly to emphasize the rock's natural features to suggest a humanlike form.[28] Worked just a bit, the stone became the representation of a woman.

Morriss-Kay believes different *Homo* lines experimented with this emerging practice of making representational sculptures and

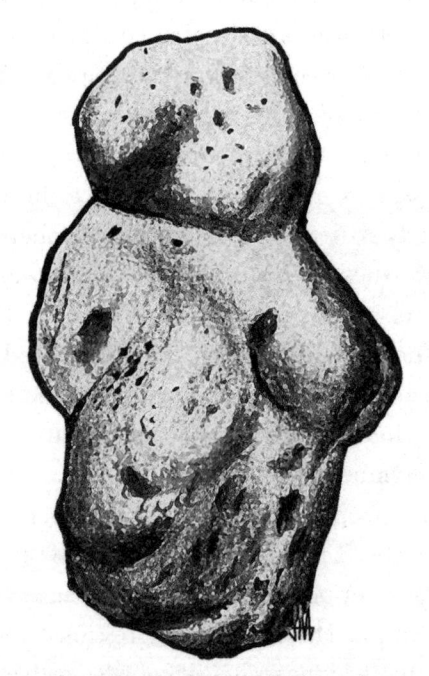

27. The Berekhat Ram subtly modifies a stone that naturally resembles a voluptuous woman.

paintings over thousands of years, some embracing it, others allowing it to fall away. Thanks to the discovery in a Spanish cave of a 66,000-year-old ladderlike image and three hand stencils painted in red, we now know that even Neanderthals got in on the game.[29] (In just the last decade, several panels around the world have surpassed Fumane as the world's oldest painted art.) Neanderthals, despite long-held biases against our evolutionary kin as brutish and dumb, engaged in a range of symbolic behaviors, from carving bones to engraving patterns on cave walls to making jewelry.[30] The ancients who surged forward in artistic achievement would have been, Morriss-Kay writes, "rare, highly gifted individuals."[31]

Morriss-Kay argues that the first Paleolithic painters and sculptors, through a combination of cognitive changes in their brain's neurological structures and the cultural inheritance of artistic traditions, ushered in the "blank canvas" stage: the ability to imagine an image or hold a concept in the "mind's eye" and then express it through a block of stone or a blank cave wall.

The "mind's eye" could envision real things—objects that existed in the world—as well as things that were purely imaginary. Consider the figure at Fumane in Italy. Marco Peresani interprets the figure as half man, half bison, "an entity between animal world and human world," he told me. Strikingly, this fits with some of the other earliest known art in Europe. At Chauvet in France, there is a painted figure that looks half human, half rhinoceros. In 1939, the shattered fragments of a mammoth ivory statue of a half man, half lion were found in the recesses of a cave in southern Germany. And in 2019 in Indonesia, archaeologists discovered a cave wall painted 44,000 years ago that includes humanlike figures featuring animal parts[32]—one has a beak, another a tail.

What these discoveries exhibit, then, is a new way of imagining the world. "It is one thing to represent a horse," said the archaeologist Randall White in 2000 when the Fumane rock art was first published, "but another thing to represent something that is a figment of the collective imagination, something that doesn't exist in reality."[33]

By the late Paleolithic, on this side of 50,000 years ago, we can see the full flowering of meaning among *Homo sapiens*. When things can have symbolic meanings that are fully real or entirely imagined, the number of meanings they can contain becomes almost limitless.

A BRAIDED STREAM

The search for the first artwork reminds me of a game I played as a child when my family went on road trips.

I grew up in Tucson, in the heart of Arizona's Sonoran Desert. When we were coming home from a trip, the game was to spot the first saguaro cactus. I can still recall how I studied the landscape with every ounce of focus. Yet, somehow, almost magically, the view would always just suddenly go from a world with no saguaro to one populated with the towering cacti, their arms twisting skyward.

Now I realize that I never won the game because I was always searching for that first lonely sentinel — standing alone before the forest of saguaro. Instead, I should have been looking at all the hints that foreshadowed them: the change in elevation, the arrival of sand and rock, the appearance of other cacti. The saguaro forest does not appear all at once. It takes shape in the context of everything around it.

This is how finding the first art feels to me. We look back so intently. But despite all our efforts, the ancient record just seems to go from no art to art nearly all at once. One reason is that most objects made of wood, feathers, and animal skins do not survive the ravages of time. It's probable that the world's first art shattered, burned to ash, rotted away, or was gnawed to pieces by a wolf. And since scholars can't agree on what art *is* — zigzags or *The Starry Night*? — everyone is looking for something different. Further, the claim to the oldest anything will always be topped by the next discovery. No archaeologist can know what is buried just beyond the edge of their trowel.

This is why the history of art is always being written on a chalkboard. Each new discovery revises the chronology and will in turn be superseded soon enough. (A case in point: only a week after finishing the first draft of this chapter, I had to revise it because the magazine *Nature* published the paper on the 44,000-year-old art panel in Indonesia.)[34]

The problem is that archaeologists and the public are such willing players in the "first-of-anything game." Obsessed with finding that *first* carved rock, those *first* scratches, the *first* painting, when in reality, history is written and rewritten. Far better to focus on the *process* of the development of meaning, from the expansion of an aesthetic instinct, to self-expression, to symbolism. The anthropologists Marc Kissel and Agustín Fuentes make the case that although those early art-like artifacts are ambiguous in intent, we have to acknowledge that something different and special was happening in our evolutionary lineage.[35] They have compiled a list of all the possible objects that point to the origin of meaning.[36] The stone figurine Berekhat Ram, for example, features, as does an engraving that *Homo erectus* made between 370,000 and 230,000 years ago in what is now Germany. Ochre in the Czech Republic and Sudan also made the list, plus an engraved stone in South Africa and an engraved bone in China, all dating from 200,000 to 120,000 years ago.

Kissel and Fuentes suggest by their list that any one of these objects by itself might not be convincing evidence of the origins of meaning making. But when we add up these early pieces along with the use of wood and bone for tools, and the collection of exotic materials including ochre—as well as other "modern" behaviors, such as interring the dead (documented in burials), music (seen in the flute), complex social organization (with evidence of large social groups that included care for the sick and the elderly), and more—we can more clearly see when our distant hominin cousins were up to something new.

The anthropologists point out that all these things do not arrive together at once, in sync. For instance, *Homo erectus* in Indonesia engraved a shell 500,000 years ago. *Homo naledi* in South Africa might have buried their dead 250,000 years ago. *Homo sapiens* in the Near East began to bury the dead 115,000 years ago.[37] Neanderthals, too, in France, likely buried their dead 60,000 years ago.[38] These are very different species in very different times, separated by thousands of miles, engaged in symbolic behaviors.

The conclusion: these practices and capacities of meaning making arrived in waves. What happened, Kissel and Fuentes believe, was not

28. In 2014, archaeologists found an engraving in Gorham's Cave, Gibraltar, likely made by Neanderthals sometime before 39,000 years ago.

a sudden flood of firsts, but a "braided stream of human evolution." Different *Homo* species tested out different meaning-making practices at different moments. Many failed. Some endured.

Kissel and Fuentes's viewpoint is convincing because it draws our attention to a long-expanding process that began with those stone tools that enabled humanity's first great leap in our history of stuff. Several million years ago, stone tools were merely tools, instruments without symbolic meaning. Yet those instruments changed our ancient ancestors biologically, feeding bigger brains, providing an edge for survival, enabling new kinds of social relations and cooperation for defense, hunting, food sharing, and parenting.

Somewhere along the line, some of the stone tools became something more. As far back as the Acheulean hand axes beginning 1.76 million years ago in Kenya, a *Homo erectus* toolmaker felt the flicker of a creative spark, as Fuentes calls it.[39] While we do not know what fueled the spark, there was something in the *Homo* line that enabled it to catch fire in different times and places. *Homo erectus* carving zigzags on a shell in Indonesia. *Homo heidelbergensis* grinding colorful pigments in Zambia. *Homo neanderthalensis* crafting an eagle-talon necklace in Croatia. The emergence of objects with meaning had the possibility of changing the genus *Homo*'s evolutionary trajectory.

Kissel and Fuentes estimate on the basis of their list of artifacts that, by 400,000–300,000 years ago, the evolutionary stage was set for meaning making in the genus *Homo*. When anatomically modern humans appeared as a distinct branch on the evolutionary tree about 300,000 years ago, they did not yet engage in every "modern" behavior (such as burials, control of fire, and symbolism). Art and all those other behaviors arrived only in the ensuing millennia, in different moments and places, as various *Homo* species experimented with ways to create meanings through objects.

Only on this side of 50,000 years ago does art — the congruence of the aesthetic instinct, self-expression, and symbolism — become a centerpiece of humans' meaning-making activities. A figurine. An engraved hashmark on a cave wall. The silhouette of a half human, half bison painted in red on a stone.

Shortly after 30,000 years ago, *Homo sapiens* was the only *Homo* species left on Earth. By then, our ancestors were making art everywhere. By then, the world was filling up with beautiful things.

5

ARTICLES OF FAITH

Deep in the heart of Hong Kong is a serene, tree-lined alleyway filled with abandoned wooden and ceramic gods. On each side of the alley are uneven platforms and shelters, like oversize doll houses, made of cement and crimson bricks. The alley harbors a shrine of hundreds of statues tightly packed together and interspersed with offerings of flowers and incense. The statues are Buddhist and Daoist gods: Monkey God, Earth God, Warrior God. The Big-Tummy Buddha and the Twin Immortals for Peaceful Relations. But most are a Buddhist bodhisattva named Guanyin.

Guanyin's origin story begins thousands of years ago in India, where a prince was on his way to reaching Nirvana, the ultimate salvation from the endless cycles of suffering, passion, hatred, and delusion.[1] But at the last moment, he refrained, electing instead to become a bodhisattva, a kind of near god. He would listen to the sufferings of all and try to help them. By AD 250, Guanyin was a popular deity across China, as stories widely circulated about the miracles—escaping death, curing illnesses, striking it rich—effected merely by uttering the bodhisattva's name.[2] By about AD 1100, Guanyin in China had morphed into a female, a mother figure, not unlike the Virgin Mary.[3] Over the centuries, she was worshipped in many configurations, becoming one of the most popular Buddhist personages, serving believers from Mongolia to Malaysia, India to Japan.

In the blistering hot summer of 2018, I went to Hong Kong to study Guanyin, in collaboration with local scholars.[4] Martin Tse, a researcher at the University of Hong Kong, served as my guide, teacher, and translator. In his 20s, with thick glasses and tussled black hair, Tse was keenly attentive, gentle, and jovial, containing endless reserves of energy. In just two weeks, we conducted nearly 60 interviews at more than 30 temples, monasteries, and shrines. It was Tse who brought me to the alley of abandoned gods.

We approached a middle-aged woman, Ms. Yu, who ran a traditional medicine shop next to the shrine. We chatted as she burned small piles of medicinal herbs on banana leaves, the wisps of smoke creeping over patients' arms and legs to heal arthritis and other ailments. She explained that the Guanyin statues in the alley had been deserted by their owners, who had converted to Christianity or moved to a senior living facility with no relative to adopt the statue. Ms. Yu insisted that the statues should be adopted and cared for by someone new. "You should each take one."

Martin and I huddled nervously. From our interviews we understood Guanyin's power and the responsibilities the statues entail. We would have to maintain a spread of fresh offerings, burn incense, and pray daily. If treated well, Guanyin would bless and protect us. At first, I thought it would be good firsthand research to adopt a statue; I could then place it in the Denver museum where I worked. But there were also tales of ghosts and misfortune, a naked danger lurking beneath the surface of these statues' benevolence. Should we each really take the responsibility for one?

Tse and I walked around the shrine, looking at the statues not as researchers but prospective collectors. I stopped when I saw a Guanyin statue of a woman sitting with a slender gold vessel in her left hand; her right hand was gracefully raised upright in a pose for meditation. The statue glowed pearl white, her face and flowing robes painted in flashes of pastels. She was beautiful. But she was coated in grime and bird droppings. Above her left eye was a bright red gash, as if she had been struck. I felt a vague urge to rescue her.

I paused to consider how strangely attracted I was to the statues. I then considered how strange it was that *Buddhists* are attracted to

29. Abandoned Guanyin statues sit in a Hong Kong alleyway; the one on the far right, front row, called to the author.

these statues. Buddhists are essentially anti-materialistic. Their beliefs start with the truth of human suffering, which happens in great part due to attachment. We suffer because of attachments to our bodies, our opinions about the world, and the objects we desire. Material goods, Buddhists argue, are only a chimera of happiness and fulfillment. Buddhism offers a path to enter a realm beyond the world of things. And yet, here I was desiring—feeling attachment for—a material thing born of Buddhist beliefs.

After Tse and I had each picked a statue, we looked up and saw a woman glowering at us at the end of the alley. She was sitting in a small hut that sheltered a special altar at the base of a tree. We went to meet her. Ms. Lee was 70 years old and sturdy, with lively eyes and a raspy voice. She explained that she was the shrine's keeper. We would have been wise to consult her first, she said, before taking the statues. Nevertheless, we were right to be talking to her now. Ms. Lee took the two statues from us and placed them before an altar.

She asked our names and began mumbling a chant. Uttering my name under her breath, Ms. Lee lit three sticks of incense. She took out a pair of wooden dice, each shaped like a crescent moon. The dice are a sacred instrument used to pose questions to those in realms beyond our own. Each roll would reveal Guanyin's answer, which only Ms. Lee could hear.

"Do you want to go to the US with Chip?" Ms. Lee asked the Guanyin I had picked.

She rolled the dice.

"Yes," Ms. Lee muttered—Guanyin's answer.

She rolled again to confirm.

Yes, definitely. Guanyin wanted to go.

"Now," Ms. Lee asked Guanyin, "will you protect Chip?"

It was an ominous question. I held my breath.

Ms. Lee threw the dice.

FLOWERS FOR THE DEAD

On the other side of the world from Hong Kong, about 30 miles northwest of Johannesburg, South Africa, Rising Star Cave drops into the blackness of the earth. By 2013, the popular cave system had been well mapped for years. But in the fall of that year, two spelunkers, Rick Hunter and Steven Tucker, hoped to discover some of the cavern's hidden corners.[5]

They traveled far into the musty cave before squeezing through one narrow passage, traversing a void, and then climbing a serrated boulder. Behind this, they found a narrow passage that dropped further down. Tucker cautiously lowered himself and called Hunter to follow. The slender men, who barely fit through the tight space, landed in a contorted slate-gray chamber about 30 feet long and less than 9 feet wide. They saw bones everywhere.

Archaeologists would later determine that the bones belonged to a humanlike ancestor who lived about 250,000 years ago and constituted a previously unknown branch of our evolutionary tree. The newly discovered hominin, named *Homo naledi*, would have stood in adulthood nearly five feet tall and weighed about a hundred pounds. The species was a peculiar mix of humanesque and more ancient features. Its arms, wrists, and fingers would have been primed for hanging

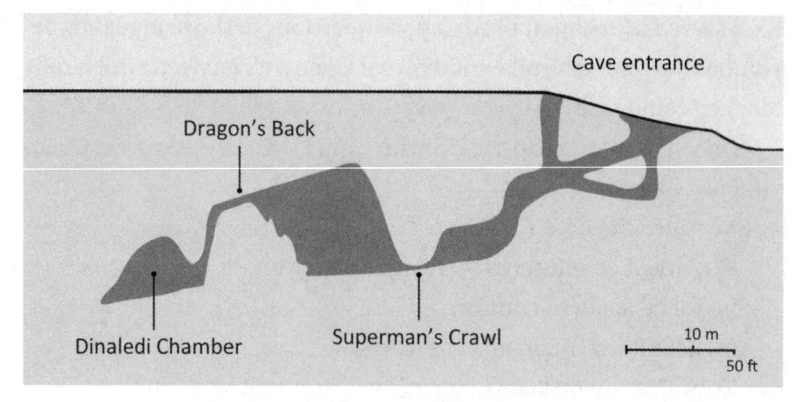

30. The Dinaledi Chamber in the Rising Star Cave system in South Africa might be the world's oldest known burial site.

and climbing, but it had a pelvis for standing upright and feet nearly indistinguishable from ours. Our species, *Homo sapiens*, lived at least 300,000 years ago in northern Africa. And so, our ancient *Homo sapiens* ancestors perhaps even saw and interacted with their *Homo naledi* relatives.

The mystery surrounding the find was not only about the new species' novelty. Just as surprising and strange was its location, so hidden within Rising Star Cave. The team of scholars who studied the remains concluded that the bones could not have been brought there by a predator or floodwaters. There was no indication *Homo naledi* lived in the cave. The bodies, some 15 of them, had been carried into the fissure and intentionally left there. Hunter and Tucker had discovered the world's oldest known gravesite.[6]

Not every archaeologist is buying the burial theory at Rising Star Cave. It's possible that *Homo naledi* isolated the dead in caves to remove the danger of spreading disease, or for other unknown reasons. What is at stake with this debate is not just the historical question of what happened in Rising Star Cave, but the larger evolutionary question of when our ancestors first conceived of worlds beyond their immediate reality—and then acted on those beliefs in material ways. In other words, the birth of religion.

The controversy surrounding whether Rising Star Cave is a grave is unsurprising. Claims for the earliest graves have always been controversial. As early as 1908, archaeologists found in southern France a 50,000-year-old skeleton of a Neanderthal who, they claimed, had been deliberately buried—to the dismay of many, who could not accept the idea of nonhumans engaged in such a definitively human activity.[7] The controversy of Neanderthal burials continued into the 1950s, when a team of US archaeologists uncovered skeletal remains of eight adult and two infant Neanderthals at Shanidar, a cave in northern Iraq. After analyzing their find, the scientists concluded that the pollen left in one of the 60,000-year-old graves came from flowers buried with the body. "Someone in the last Ice Age," wrote Ralph Solecki, an archaeologist at Columbia University who helped lead the excavations, "must have ranged the mountainside in the mournful task of collecting flowers for the dead."[8]

Although some continue to dispute these findings, it seems possible that Neanderthals did prepare the bodies of their dead, at least sometimes.[9] And so, while human burials were not commonplace until some 30,000 years ago, it does seem that the first inklings of religion go so deep into our evolutionary past that they were shared by our pre-*Homo sapiens* relatives—which could be shaped by broader mammalian practices, given some ritualistic behaviors around the dead seen in chimpanzees, elephants, dolphins, and other animals.[10]

One school of thought would suggest that the dawn of religious belief has been functional in hominin evolution.[11] The fact that every known human society today engages in some form of religious practice suggests to scientists its evolutionary benefits and fundamental social purpose. However, other evolutionary scholars think it more likely that religion originated as a byproduct of other processes or emerged for one adaptation and has stuck around—not unlike Anjan Chatterjee's idea, seen in the last chapter, about how modern human art is an elaboration on a much earlier adaptive purpose.

Whatever the source, faraway in our past, religious *belief* became known through religious *expression*—through things. This is weird. By definition, religious belief is nonmaterial. Religion most basically turns on faith and feeling, worship and community. Beliefs in the moral purpose of our lives, an afterlife, and superhuman beings all exist as *ideas*.

And yet, the belief in a life after death contributed to the development of burials and coffins, to tombs and pyramids. (Although not exclusively, since even most atheists honor the dead with burials as a gesture of respect and love.) The belief in gods led to statues, altars, offerings, and temples. This is so striking because a spiritual life does not require a material component. But in practice, believers use stuff to nurture their spirituality, conduct rituals, and build community.

Threaded through every known religion the world has ever seen are the objects that advance those beliefs. Every religion has a material component. Judaism has the Torah, yarmulke, and menorah. Christianity has the Bible and crosses. Islam has the Qur'an and Mohammed's sacred swords, shirts, and beard. Hinduism has bells, the shankha (a conch shell trumpet), the kamandalu (a pot), and the diya (an oil lamp). Native American religious practices, as diverse as the Hopi Tribe and Lakota Nations, often include eagle-feather fans, drums, and headdresses.

My adoption of that beautiful, lost Guanyin statue sparked a key question about the history of stuff: Why does religion need things?

SUPERNATURAL FEELINGS

In the shadow of skyscrapers and amid streams of shoppers and rushing cars sat Hung Hom Guanyin Temple in Hong Kong, like a vision from the past, as if this one parcel of land magically stood still in time. I was told that the building had survived a Japanese bombardment during World War II while everything around it was obliterated. Modern Hong Kong was built anew, engulfing the historic temple.

The gray-brick structure stood slightly back from the bustling street, rising two stories high. The slanting tile roof was adorned with dragons, lions, and phoenixes in faded green and blue glazes. Across Kun Yam Street were vegetarian restaurants and vendors hawking Buddhist paraphernalia — piles of incense, shelves stuffed with figurines — under bright red signs.

Martin Tse and I entered the temple through a curtain of smoke. Hanging in rows from the roof were enormous burning spirals of incense. A man below them was using a blowtorch to light one coil after another. Dozens of Hong Kongers milled about, praying and chanting. A Daoist priest circled the room, striking a drum. A Buddhist monk with a shaved head rushed by, covering his mouth with the end of his saffron robe.

At the far end of the room, centered on a massive altar, stood a giant statue of Guanyin made immediate and concrete. However, believers don't see Guanyin as material or historical, but supernatural and present. They believe Guanyin exists between our realm and Nirvana, waiting to help humans in need. Tse and I heard stories during our interviews across Hong Kong of sterile women becoming pregnant, criminals turning into upright citizens, the ill miraculously cured—all when people prayed to Guanyin.

Where and when such beliefs emerged in the human story is yet another mystery. Of course, believers believe that their experiences happen because they are real. Others would suggest that higher powers have given humans insights into the supernatural through natural mechanisms, such as evolution.[12]

In any case, the development of spirituality does seem lodged in the human past. Jane Goodall has observed how chimpanzees dance around waterfalls and stare mesmerized at the flowing water. She interprets this as a feeling of awe and wonder. Noting the range of emotions humans and chimpanzees share, Goodall concludes about our primate cousins, "Why wouldn't they also have feelings of some kind of spirituality, which is really being amazed at things outside yourself?"[13] If Goodall is correct about chimpanzees' experiences, then this may mean that the seeds of spirituality were planted more than six million years ago, when the chimpanzee and human lines diverged.

In his landmark 1993 book, *Faces in the Clouds: A New Theory of Religion*, the anthropologist Stewart Guthrie argued that spirituality is derived from the evolutionary benefits of our animal survival instincts.[14] Imagine you are Dinknesh or some other ancient hominin. You are out in the wild searching for dinner. Suddenly, next to you, a bush shakes. You freeze. Is there some carnivore about to attack? Or is it nothing, just the breeze? Guthrie suggested that our instinct is to believe there is something lurking in the bush. The reason is that there are obvious benefits and few risks to assuming there's something behind the bush—and there are huge risks and almost no benefits in assuming there's nothing behind there at all. If you assume nothing is in the bush but are wrong, then you could become a tiger's dinner. If you assume something is in the bush but are wrong, then you've merely been spooked.

This "better safe than sorry" instinct means that humans are always scanning the world through a lens that gives "agency" (the capacity to act or exert power) to things.[15] A bush shakes because something is in it, even when we can't see what that is. From this, things are given the possibility of being alive. Once this sense has been enabled, humans project their own feelings and forms onto nonhuman things in the world—a process called anthropomorphism.

This hypothesis raises a provocative question: What if religious *objects* arose before religious *beliefs*? That is, what if our ancient ancestors first saw the things in the world as alive, and then began to shape theories—spirits, gods—to explain them? To answer this question about religious objects, we might first turn back to art objects.

In 2018, Derek Hodgson and Paul Pettitt published a paper in the *Cambridge Archaeological Journal* pointing to studies in neuroscience showing that people who are conditioned to recognize a specific object, such as a face or animal, will then see it in ambiguous patterns. We are attuned, for example, to see faces in the clouds. Not unlike Guthrie, Hodgson and Pettitt hypothesized that Neanderthal hunters who had conditioned themselves to find camouflaged animals lurking everywhere perhaps saw outlines of those same animals in the flickering light of their torches in the dark chambers they inhabited. Studying 64,000-year-old images and sculptures at El Castillo Cave in Spain, the archaeologists came to believe that Neanderthals saw the crags and varicolored walls come "alive" with the images that filled their world. For example, a stalagmite with a rounded top and dark mottled patterns maybe wasn't merely a rock rising from the cave's floor to these Ice Age people but was interpreted as a bear rising to its feet.[16]

The hypothesis creates a chicken-and-egg conundrum for art. While some assume that early people turned abstract ideas of beauty and aesthetics into the kind of material expressions we call "art," Hodgson and Pettitt's 2018 article suggests that, instead, people saw natural shapes in caves *first* and *then* interpreted them as representations of their world. In a strange way, the objects that would become art might have existed before humans and their evolutionary relatives conceived of the idea of art.

Similarly, should we rethink our assumptions about religion and its objects? Could religious objects exist *prior* to beliefs—in some way, the material bringing creed into existence—when early humans recognized patterns in things and projected agency onto them?

With this question in mind, it is striking to consider the world's oldest known religious site. In 2006, the archaeologist Sheila Coulson and her team explored a small range of hills in Botswana's Kalahari Desert. There they found a massive boulder that naturally resembles the head of a python. Inspecting the stone closer, they discovered hundreds

31. A massive naturally shaped boulder was worshipped about 70,000 years ago in the Kalahari.

of human-made indentations that give the appearance of snakeskin. Nearby, they documented rock paintings and carvings at the mouth of a cave, and thousands of stone-tool fragments. The researchers dated the site to 70,000 years ago. The place is still sacred among the region's Indigenous people, the San, who worship the python.[17]

It seems more than a coincidence that among the first known religious sites is a rock *naturally* shaped like a python's head. It is possible that 70,000 years ago people came to envision the snake as a spirit being or a godlike animal, and then noticed that the rock resembled the python and began to worship around the boulder. But it is equally plausible that these people *first* noticed the massive rock that looked like a python and *then*—because of this striking reflection of an animate being frozen into inanimate stone—began to consider the python a holy creature.

In some ways, we can even see this process with Guanyin statues. Of course, the first Guanyin statues 2,000 years ago were not born out of nature like a stalagmite. Their carvers and patrons were Buddhists who combined their new dogma with a sculptural tradition that had been invented in the Middle East. They adeptly employed objects to broadcast their faith. Scholars have noted that Buddhism spread across Asia first as a "material movement" of statues and ritual objects that so impressed people they became believers even before they had a full grasp of Buddhist doctrine.[18] And so, Guanyin statues were not initially embraced because people wanted to express their beliefs; they were made and viewed and adored, and *then* people came to believe in the Buddhist cannon. The *stuff* of Buddhism helped transform nonbelievers into believers. Religious things can precede religious belief—meaning that we can desire and use things we later categorize as "religious" before we grasp and accept the beliefs behind us.

Statues in particular seem to have a unique power to not merely represent something but actually come alive. This makes sense: if hominins imagine a stalagmite is a bear, then a sculpture of a bear, with its distinct shape and figure, requires fewer imaginative leaps. The view that statues are alive was prevalent in Greek mythology; for example, there is the story of Pygmalion, who sculpted his ideal woman into an ivory statue and fell in love with it. In the Old Testament, the idol of the golden calf must be destroyed not because it merely represents a false god, but because its followers treated it as a god. Among the Zuni, in New Mexico, priests carve two Keepers of the Sky from wood and then literally breathe life into them.[19] In Brazil, Xingú Indians hold a ceremony to remember the deceased where they carve and decorate logs, which are then possessed by the spirits of their loved ones.[20] In New Guinea, the Abelam make large wooden figures of spirits that they feed and entertain in exchange for blessings.[21]

The belief that Guanyin sculptures do not merely represent Guanyin, but in fact give her concrete and living form, helps explain why followers are so reluctant to toss away unwanted statues. Statues and other religious objects help proselytize faith while also embodying it. It's why that alleyway was filled with gods. And it is why Guanyin statues can be dangerous, even for an unsuspecting anthropologist who picks one up to take back to his museum.

DESTINY STICKS

Amid the clamor at Hung Hom Guanyin Temple, I noted a woman on her knees before an altar. She was shaking what appeared to be a canister of pencils. Martin Tse quietly explained to me that these are destiny sticks, a ritual tool to see into the future.

Tse encouraged me to join her, and soon enough I was on my knees before a statue of Guanyin shaking a canister of sticks. My arms pumped as I considered what question I should ask Guanyin, who knew what future awaited me.

Ms. Lee had said Guanyin wanted to go to America, and that yes, she would protect me. But I ruminated on how some of the most meaningful work I had undertaken as a curator involved *returning* sacred objects to where they're from—objects that belong in places where they can be worshipped, not in the sterile, dark storehouse of a museum. I shook the canister harder.

I looked around the temple, the epitome of a religion's need for things. Past the entrance, where temple employees sold a cornucopia of incense and paper lotus flowers to burn, were a series of altars. The first was a massive red table, ornately carved with gold highlights, with tall stalks of yellow and purple lilies in vases, and large bronze and stone incense vessels packed with burning sticks of incense and red candles. Behind the table were three towering, carved-wood altars encircled by immense bouquets of flowers, lights, oil lamps, pineapples, bananas, apples, and forests of smoldering incense. Each altar presented a Buddhist statue. I saw how everything—from the Guanyin statue towering over me to the destiny sticks in my hands—allowed me not just to passively observe the power of Guanyin but to participate in it.

In this temple, I saw, too, how the objects were spurring people toward particular kinds of actions. Most notably, the presence of the large statues prompted worshippers to clasp their hands and offer prayers, just as my possession of a grime-covered Guanyin statue prompted me to kneel on the floor shaking a canister of sticks. It is in this way that humans make objects, but objects shape our behaviors and beliefs in particular directions. In fact, some objects are made expressly to get people to act.[22] As the French philosopher Bruno Latour has written, a speed bump, for example, a material thing, forces the driver of a car to slow down.[23] Objects—especially religious objects that dictate life and death—exert real power over us.[24]

A stick finally plinked against the gray stone tiles. I carried it to the desk at the temple's entrance, where a worker examined the stick's number and then gave me a slip of yellow paper that matched its number. My fortune.

Tse and I took the paper across the room to the fortune teller. He was in his 40s, wearing a faded red uniform. Tse greeted him, calling him *shifu*, meaning "teacher" or "master." He looked up, bored. I handed over the paper fortune. He ignored me, speaking in Cantonese to Tse, who translated.

"What are you asking?" Tse said to me, meaning the question I asked while shaking the destiny sticks.

"I was asking—I just received a Guanyin statue, and whether it's a good idea to take her home with me."

The shifu and Tse talked and talked.

Finally, Tse turned to me. "Don't bring it home," he said. "Because there might be dirty things inside the statue."

I thought of the statue's red wound, eerily like blood, gashed above her left eye. The shifu studied the paper more closely, now serious, and gave his final opinion.

"There might be serious consequences if you insist on bringing it home," Tse translated. "You might have a lot of trouble, many troubles. And the worst scenario is that it sucks up your magnetic field—and brings you away."

I looked at Tse, uncertain.

"He means killing you," Tse clarified.

HILL OF THE NAVEL

As Tse and I left the temple, we passed the fortune teller again. Seeing my strained expression, he stopped us to offer a solution. He could ritually cleanse the statue and make it safe to take to the museum. He named a steep price, about $100 US for the ceremony. Martin and I deliberated. We thought the fee for the ritual was likely exorbitant, a rate set for a worried foreigner. Since we had only one day left of interviews, we wondered if we should cancel them and return the statue where we got it. No, we decided. Instead, the next day we would carry the statue with us and hopefully find someone else who could help. Across Hong Kong were dozens of temples, monasteries, and organizations dedicated to sustaining the Buddhist and Daoist faiths.

The community of believers is another hallmark of religion. Religious practice is built through shared commitments, behaviors, and faith. At some point in hominin history, the interpretations of the supernatural could be shared through language and the birth of symbolism, which could give members of a community the means of shared concepts. First through painted images and sculptures as well as rituals such as burials, communities began to form practices that delineated beliefs about the cosmic order. Then, these sacred objects and places coalesced into the dawn of organized religion.

32. This carving stood at Göbekli Tepe, in Turkey, the world's oldest temple.

Around 11,000 years ago, on a treeless hill overlooking a stark brown plain in southeastern Turkey, a group of hunter-gatherers built the world's first known temple.[25] They hewed massive stones into standing pillars and placed them in circles. Some stones reached 16 feet high and weighed 10 tons. Some pillars were left smooth and blank. Others were wreathed in carved beasts—vultures, lions, foxes, and scorpions. No residential dwellings surrounded the site, suggesting its purpose was religious. Göbekli Tepe (hill of the navel), as the site is known, was made some 300 human generations before Stonehenge and the first Egyptian pyramid. The temple is the earliest known building and gathering place erected expressly for rituals and religious expressions—pilgrimages and feasts and burials.

The need for community appears as deeply rooted as spirituality itself. While our nearest living primate kin have long been observed caring for their own family units, several years ago, researchers observed a group of wild bonobos sharing a meal with a different group of bonobos who were near strangers.[26] This points to an instinct that prompts primates to connect with those beyond our immediate circle. Behaviors such as food sharing suggests the origins of cooperation and empathy—the foundation of religious life.[27]

More than 20 years ago, Robin Dunbar, an evolutionary psychologist, made an important discovery by mapping the size of animals' social networks. He found that the larger the brain, the larger the network. He found that most humans have roughly the same size network: about 5 intimate friends, 50 good friends, 150 friends, and 1,500 people we can recognize by name.[28] Dunbar hypothesizes that religion—particularly with its endorphin-inducing activities, such as singing and rituals—is a central means of "engineering social cohesion" that has allowed humanity to evolve with these expansive networks.[29] We can also look to research by the anthropologists Christopher Manoharan and Dimitris Xygalatas, who studied a Sufi Muslim ritual in Turkey called the *dhikr*, a collective trance. By using heart rate monitors on participants, they showed how the heart rates of individuals aligned during the ritual, converging to a shared beat.[30]

About a thousand years after Göbekli Tepe was created, agriculture took hold across Mesopotamia. Settled farmers needed to find ways to live together. If your neighbors upset you, you couldn't just move over to the next valley. Farming was a precarious lifestyle: if crops failed, it was hard to simply move on to a new place. Too much rain, too little rain; too much sun, too little sun; too few good bugs, too many bad ones. Farming was and is a stressful way to live. Rituals reduce stress in humans. For example, a 2011 study by psychologists at Tel Aviv University looked at the repetitive behavior of basketball players, OCD

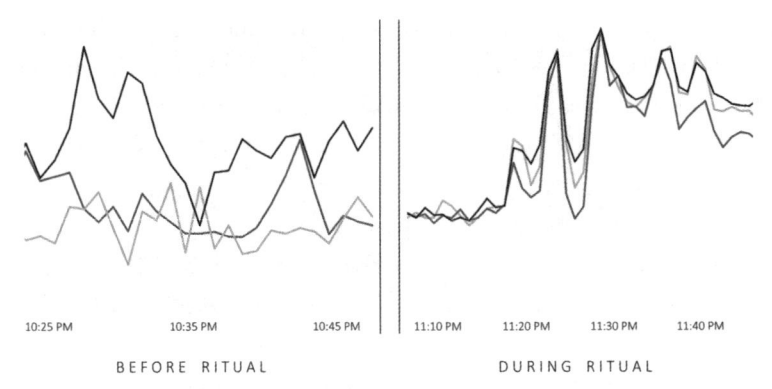

BEFORE RITUAL   DURING RITUAL

33. Wearable sensors documented how the heartbeats of three participants in the *dhikr*, a Sufi Muslim ritual, aligned once the dancing began.

patients, and captive animals. They discovered that the groups all used ritualistic-like behavior as a way to manage the stress caused by uncontrollable or unpredictable circumstances. Religion was a means to bring both communities and stress under control.

It is no coincidence that, following Göbekli Tepe, archaeologists see organized religion arise in tandem with agriculture across the globe. In the Yellow River region of northeastern China, Yangshao agriculturalists 7,000 years ago developed elaborate fertility rituals dependent on pottery, jade dragons, and goddess temples.[31] In Peru, around 5,500 years ago, the first monumental buildings in the Americas were erected in Peru at the same time that corn agriculture caught on.[32] In England, 5,000 years ago, Neolithic farmers erected Stonehenge.[33]

Some 250,000 years after *Homo naledi* perhaps buried their dead, the world would have religion in every corner, practiced by every human society. Those first burials not only laid the foundation for the world's astoundingly diverse religious beliefs, but also the creation of all the stuff that would sustain them. Religion produced shared experiences, shared stories, community—created and sustained by temples and offerings and statues.

So, on my final day in Hong Kong, I placed Guanyin in my grimy backpack to ask the Buddhist and Daoist community what I should do with the possessed statue. Hoisting Guanyin onto my back, I realized that the bodhisattva was heavier than she looked.

We arrived at the Chi Lin Nunnery, a cluster of buildings and shrines nested in an immaculate park. We met three Buddhist scholars who led the visit and talked about the Guanyin statues that were made for the nunnery. We settled into an office for tea and conversation.

During a lull, Tse asked for my backpack and pulled out the statue. I explained the quandary. There followed a pregnant pause.

And then the scholars burst into warm laughter.

"Doesn't matter," Tse translated for the first scholar. "Don't listen. Take it home, as long as you nicely treat it and don't put it in the garbage."

"It's not a Buddhist temple," said the second scholar of Hung Hom. "There they ask for money!"

"So, I won't die?" I asked.

"All of us will die," the third scholar said. "But not because of Guanyin."

A MONA LISA SMILE

After we said farewell to the three scholars, I told Tse that I still didn't feel right taking the Guanyin to the museum. It seemed somehow disrespectful to discount the shifu at Hung Hom Guanyin Temple who had insisted the sculpture be cleansed. Tse considered the options—which were few, since I flew back to the US in the morning. Then he remembered a nearby temple.

We took a taxi to an apartment building off a quiet alley, entered, and rocketed up dozens of floors in a tiny elevator. At the top, we knocked on the door to Sin Chai Buddhist-Daoist Hall.

We were welcomed into a bright, frenzied room with banks of windows that peered across the roofs of skyscrapers. This place of worship was really Daoist, separate physically and philosophically from the immaculate Chi Lin Nunnery. The hall was frenzied, with piles of books and papers, cups, electronics, vases, and, on the walls, old calendars and paintings. The perfume of sandalwood incense pervaded everything. At the far end of the room was a shrine with Guanyin wearing a gold shawl.

The spirit writer, Master Caihao, invited us to sit down. She was a medium who channeled the gods and other beings beyond our realm by transcribing their messages on a table of sand with a dowel. She was in her 60s and supremely confident. This was her domain. Several assistants in matching dark-blue outfits surrounded her; one was her daughter, Caigao, who spoke good English and assisted Tse with translation.

I was asked to tell my story. I related the events that led us to adopting the Guanyin statue from the alleyway shrine. Before I could even get to the destiny sticks, the spirit writer interrupted. She said there was trouble because "there are strong spirits inside Guanyin." She advised that the statue be cleansed. I agreed to the ceremony.

34. The Guanyin statue adopted by the author is ritually cleaned.

Master Caihao's cleansing was a literal cleaning. Her assistants brought out water and rubbing alcohol. Master Caihao scrubbed every part, pausing only when she saw the red gash across the face. The assistant asked me to kneel before the altar with my hands in prayer. The spirit writer sprinkled alcohol on my head, and then water on my face. We burned incense and Master Caihao spoke with the spirit world.

As the ceremony unfolded, I began to grasp that the adopted statue was simply a way for Master Caihao and all the Guanyin followers I met in Hong Kong to make their beliefs understood. They believe in bodhisattvas, beings beyond this world. Guanyin herself is supposed to be everywhere, yet nowhere too. Without the statues, no one would even know what she looks like.

The statue, then, becomes a material witness. Guanyin followers take this abstract idea—a being existing in another realm who has absolute compassion for all—and turn it into the touchable. Each statue makes the immaterial material. The red gash on the Guanyin I picked is the evidence that turns the ghost into something real. In essence, the tangible Guanyin statue becomes the vehicle for intangible belief.

As the anthropologist Roy A. Rappaport wrote in *Ritual and Religion in the Making of Humanity* (1999), when something "signified is incorporeal, like worthiness or influence, its representation may have to be material if it is to be taken seriously. Claims to rank and honor are empty unless made substantial."[34] Rappaport pointed out how ceremonial events like potlatches—great ceremonial feasts where huge amounts of things, ranging from clothing to boats, are gifted to guests—on the Northwest Coast of the US and Canada don't just *symbolize* wealth, they *demonstrate* it. Similarly, Guanyin statues do not just symbolize Guanyin's existence, they prove it. As Agustín Fuentes has argued, one of the biggest moments in human history was when our ancestors "broke the boundaries of the material and the visible so the realm of pure imagination could be made tangible."[35]

And so, it is precisely because religion trades in the immaterial that it needs the material. A religious object is like a weathervane—pointing to the invisible winds of belief. I think of *Homo naledi* conceiving of death 250,000 years ago; the burial in Rising Star Cave was perhaps a way for them to demarcate, physically and concretely, that there is something beyond their known world. As the cleansing ceremony continued, I thought of the Paleolithic bear sculpture, the python rock in the Kalahari, and Göbekli Tepe rising on the plains of Turkey, and it seemed to me likely that they all arose from the impulse to imagine the unimaginable. With things, the supernatural is natural, rituals can be performed, communities can be held together. Guanyin and all other religious objects make concrete what otherwise can only be known by faith. This is why religion needs things most of all.

When the ritual was done, we all sat back down in a circle. Master Caihao explained that a male ghost possessed the statue. The red gash was where he entered. He did not want to go to the United States; he was going to bring trouble. But now, with the ritual, he agreed to stay put in the hall's shrine.

"Good thing you brought her here, because we saved that male spirit," said Caigao, the spirit writer's daughter. She added that I would have died within months without the cleansing.

Master Caihao turned cheerful. She said that we should end with a Disaster Mitigation Ceremony, which would involve more incense and prayers. I was invited to "donate" a modest amount of money to the hall. Master Caihao instructed me to refrain from eating beef and carp—because of these animals' associations with Guanyin—and told me to burn incense before the statue once I had her installed at the Denver Museum of Nature & Science.

"I promise to not eat cow or carp," I dutifully declared, "and to do an offering when I return."

"Don't promise *me*," Master Caihao answered. "Promise Guanyin. She will know."

Finally, the medium talked to Guanyin herself, to make sure the bodhisattva wanted to come to the United States with me. Master Caihao sat back down. Guanyin was happy to go home with me.

"See?" Master Caihao said, tapping my knee. "Guanyin is smiling now."

I looked at the statue, and, well, to me, it was a statue. It was twinkling clean but otherwise the same. Still, I had to admit that I hadn't noticed before the faint Mona Lisa smile at the edge of Guanyin's lips.

6

ALL THINGS TO ALL PEOPLE

Jesse H. Bratley did not set out to oppress Native Americans. He was born in 1867, the child of hardworking farmers who tried and mostly failed to homestead on the Kansas frontier.[1] Jesse spent his childhood laboring on the family farm and attending school for only three months a year. As a young man without any advantage, he worked by turns as a janitor, accountant, and traveling salesman. Then, by chance, in 1893, Bratley saw an advertisement to become a teacher at US government schools on Indian reservations. He applied and was soon on his way to a ramshackle schoolhouse along Puget Sound in Washington, to teach children of the S'Klallam Tribe.

Through a research project about Bratley while a curator at the Denver Museum of Nature & Science, I learned, however, that he bore no real love for Native Americans. "I thought them too dirty to be people," he confessed late in life. "In fact, I despised them."

But he embraced a steady paycheck and the adventure of living among people so different from himself. Over the next 10 years, he thrived as a teacher at Indian schools in Washington, South Dakota, Oklahoma, and Arizona. He became so fascinated by the cultures he encountered that he took 1,000 photographs of Native people and their homelands and collected more than 900 kilograms of cultural objects. He came to dream of one day opening a museum about Native Americans.

Bratley's work was not only to teach children but to transform them. The US government's goal was to turn Native Americans away from "savagery" toward "civilization" (defined by the period's Victorian White, Christian norms). By the close of the 19th century, the government hoped to rid the country of Native Americans by forcibly assimilating them. As Richard Henry Pratt, the period's leading Indian boarding school proponent, famously argued in 1892, "All the Indian there is in the race should be dead. Kill the Indian in him, and save the man."[2]

Native children were thus removed from their families and communities and taken to boarding schools to undergo rigorous intellectual, spiritual, and bodily reprogramming. Teachers instructed students in reading, writing, music, drawing, history, and arithmetic, all to redevelop "the child's aesthetic sense."[3] Boys were taught farming, carpentry, and blacksmithing. Girls were taught cooking, cleaning, and sewing. Even games and toys were regulated. Children's Native languages were strictly forbidden. They were forced to worship the Christian God.

Every element of children's "Indianness" was to be erased. Every pupil was to receive a new identity. As required by the US government, Bratley worked to change the children's appearance and manner. "Each year we had a class to enter school," Bratley recalled in his unpublished autobiography. "We had to cut the little boys' hair, take off their Indian camp clothes, bathe them and dress them up in school clothes."[4]

This approach had been perfected by Pratt. In the 1870s, Richard Henry Pratt was a jailor at Fort Marion, Florida, a prison for Native Americans who resisted the US government.[5] To assimilate Native prisoners, he organized a compulsory educational program, which included forcing the Native men to wear US Army uniforms. When Pratt later founded the Carlisle Indian Industrial School in Pennsylvania, the boys wore military uniforms and the girls donned "proper" Victorian dresses. By the late 1800s, almost every Indian school had a dress code that did not allow any traditional Native clothing.

Pratt and his contemporaries hit upon an anthropological discovery, put to perverse ends. Clothing, they realized, is far more than

35. In the late 1800s, Jesse Bratley took this photograph of children lined up in uniforms and Victorian dress in front of the Cantonment Indian Boarding School in Oklahoma.

shelter for our bodies; it does far more than protect our skin from the elements. Clothes are symbols that shape us.

You *feel* different when you're in a swimming suit compared with your Sunday best. The Indian school uniform was a symbol of cleanliness, order, and conformity; through wearing these clothes, the children *became* something else. As Asa Daklugie, a Chiricahua Apache, recalled of the day in 1886 he entered Carlisle, after being taken from New Mexico and imprisoned at Fort Marion, Florida: "We'd lost our hair and we'd lost our clothes; with the two we'd lost our identity as Indians."[6]

Dress codes are coded with meaning.

The tragedy of the Indian boarding school experience shows how humans have given things—the objects we make, use, wear, exchange—meanings far beyond their mere utility. And beauty and belief are only two meanings; there are many more. Humans, for better and for worse, over the millennia have learned to empower objects with economic value, the ability to shape our social relationships, to remember and forget, and to make, and sometimes to exterminate identities.

MONEY IS NO OBJECT

Chief Swift Bear was a Sicangu Lakota, born in 1820. When he was young, his people trapped and hunted furs in Canada, then traveled hundreds of miles south to barter them in Mexico. Later, his people hunted and traded along the Missouri River. They were also farmers; Swift Bear was the leader of the Corn Band. Swift Bear was also a renowned warrior. As the US government became a more powerful force in his lands, Swift Bear tried to bring in tribes hostile to the government. He traveled to Washington, DC, seeking treaties that would bring peace. He even sent his daughter, Maud, as part of the first class to Carlisle Indian School in Pennsylvania.[7]

During his time on the Rosebud Sioux reservation, Jesse Bratley purchased a rare artifact from Chief Swift Bear—a winter count. Winter counts are the history books of the Great Plains tribes. They are written as a series of painted symbols on a cloth sheet or buffalo hide. Each winter, the keeper of the winter count would decide on the year's most important event and draw a symbol to record what transpired. Winter counts can be passed between generations, and hence document decades of continuous history. Swift Bear's winter count begins in 1800 with the image of a man in a hat, symbolizing the first time a White man lived among the Lakota.[8]

Among the last entries on the Swift Bear winter count is for the years 1896 through 1897, with a Native man drawn in profile, a red disk above his head. In the narrative Bratley purchased with this winter count, Swift Bear said this symbolized the effort to collect pledges of money from tribal members. This money was to be used in a Fourth of July celebration, "at which time the agent allowed the Indians to indulge in old Indian ceremonies and dance some of which they were told that they would never be allowed to practice again."[9] How strange this moment must have been for Swift Bear, a child raised in the barter economy of the fur trade, now needing coins and cash to purchase the goods needed to host traditional ceremonies. He must have wondered: Where did money come from, and why was it so important?

One rainy afternoon in the fall of 2019, I visited an unexceptional high rise in Lower Manhattan. I took an elevator up to a luxurious wood-paneled hallway, where I stood before a large glass door with black bars across it. A security guard buzzed me into an antechamber, where I signed in and waited for the guard to open the next door: a massive silver door, like a bank vault, with a giant seal of the American Numismatic Society.

Inside was a gallery furnished with a series of glass cases. I found the start of the exhibit, eagerly seeking out the tiny coins I had come to New York to see. I found them labeled numbers 8, 9, and 10—examples of an invention that became the foundation for everything in our world.

With the arrival of agriculture about 12,000 years ago came the arrival of settled life. Villages turned into towns, then cities. Urban centers fostered specialization. Whereas in the Paleolithic most hunter-gatherers would make their own tools and clothes, their own shelters and medicines, with city life many of these tasks were divided into discrete jobs. Farmers, architects, carpenters, government administrators, physicians, and priests all came to have specialized roles. This form of social organization required a way for people in one occupation to secure everything they needed to live—a farmer who needs medicine, and a physician who needs food.

While no doubt our earliest ancestors occasionally traded with neighboring groups as needed, trade became an essential part of many societies in the wake of the Neolithic Revolution. In the classic version of economic theory, these new forms of trade created a problem: simply trading item-for-item was not always practical. What was the farmer to do when they went to a physician with a bushel of wheat to help their sick child, but the physician didn't need wheat, but rather needed their roof fixed? The solution, for many societies, was money.

In an alternate version of these events, the anthropologist David Graeber posits that there's simply no evidence that this is what happened. He theorizes that people, before money, lived in enmeshed social networks: the physician would help the farmer because the farmer was a neighbor and needed assistance, and if in turn the physician needed some wheat, the farmer would provide it. Money, Graeber argued, was not about simple exchange. Rather, it was about power. By creating money, those in power could control economic relationships, including getting some members of society into debt, so that they could hold extra power over them.[10]

Whichever is true, it is notable that money emerged in many societies that were constructing new forms of hierarchy. At the height of the Aztec Empire in Mexico, for example, about 600 years ago, the most common form of money was cacao beans. These hard pods, which produce chocolate, were traded as a commodity, as food. But they were also used to determine the value of other commodities—such as copper, jade, cotton, feathers—and also to facilitate purchases.[11] As the anthropologist Jack Weatherford explained: "The seller who wanted to exchange a nopal (cactus) worth five cacao beans for an ear of corn worth six cacao beans, for instance, would turn over the nopal and then add one cacao bean to even out the trade."[12]

Over the millennia, such currencies proliferated around the world. Salt was used in China, North Africa, and the Mediterranean. Reindeer were used in Siberia, water buffalo in Borneo, and oxen among the ancient Greeks. Shell was used among many Native tribes on the east and west coasts of North America.

While commodity money has the advantage of being usable—you could eat your cacao, salt, or reindeer if you needed to—it could be difficult to store and trade across vast distances. It could also be difficult to reduce or grow into larger pieces, or to trade more than once. (It's hard to trade precisely an eighth of a reindeer—or a million reindeer.) Various metals were already prized in many societies—iron for its strength, gold for its purity. In ancient Sudan, people turned iron hoes into money; in China, they used bronze hoes and knives; in West Africa, copper rings; in Burma, lead became a currency.[13]

By 5,000 years ago, people in the Middle East were using ingots of gold and silver to exchange goods such as wheat, olive oil, and beer. The value of huge quantities of these commodities could be calculated with the weight of pieces of metal. This system facilitated vast trade networks that linked Asia, Africa, and Europe.[14] However, this new solution was imperfect because there was no standard value that merchants could use—and they still had to weigh a pile of metal for each transaction. Gold and silver were then rare enough that the ingots were useful for the merchant class to trade large quantities of things, but not for most people, for everyday use, to buy dinner or a new shovel.

A little more than 2,500 years ago, a people now known as Lydians, who lived in Turkey, took money in a new direction.[15] Known for their luxurious perfumes and cosmetics, which were traded throughout the ancient world, Lydians were otherwise unrenowned, a small city-state in a sea of striving empires. But around 640 BC, Lydian kings began to solve the limitations of ingots by minting the first coins of electrum, a natural mix of silver and gold. The three I saw on display at the American Numismatic Society in New York, labeled 8, 9, and 10, were modest: three bright lumps of yellow-hued metal, flattened with a vague outline of a design, smaller than a US dime.

Yet these small objects changed the trajectory of the world. These coins were assigned a set value, rather than valued based on their weight. They were small denominations, easy to use for everyday exchanges, and small enough to fit in a purse. They were made in standardized sizes, easy to count. They were stamped with an emblem that guaranteed authenticity, easy to trust. The Lydians' invention of the coin enabled the birth of retail and global commercial trade.

About a century after the Lydians invented the coin, they fell to the

36. The Lydian electrum (front and back) was the world's first modern coinage.

Persians. But their invention spread throughout the Mediterranean and took particular hold in the Greek states, which grew to be based on commerce, enabled by the ease, standardization, and durability of coinage.[16] The use of money altered the nature of markets, allowing transactions that required less trust between seller and buyer and were vastly scalable. "Money became the nexus connecting humans in many more social relationships, no matter how distant or how transitory, than had previously been possible," Jack Weatherford wrote. "Money connected humans in a more extensive and more efficient way than any other known medium."[17] Money came to measure one's work (income), one's contribution to the state (taxes), and one's beliefs in a god (tithes). "With the rapid monetarization of value," Weatherford concluded, "virtually everything could be expressed in terms of a common denominator—money."[18]

Today, every national, state-run monetary system can be linked to this origin story. Although economic systems continue to evolve—as when governments abandoned the gold standard, and with the creation of virtual currencies—these are still elaborations on the Lydian invention, those first coins which I saw on display in New York.

Chief Swift Bear and his people raised enough money to host their Fourth of July celebration in 1897. "Indians from several reservations were visitors during the first week of July," the winter count records. "The Indians followed the old custom of arranging their tipis in a circular fashion, making a circle nearly three miles across. It was a sight worth beholding."[19] Jesse Bratley took two pictures of the event. He wrote on the back of one photograph that 6,000 people attended, and he prematurely proclaimed it to be the tribe's "last, largest celebration." Swift Bear was grateful that the money he'd helped raise had led to this event. Yet he likely was also keenly aware of the power behind this new form of exchange: The US government. Americans had taken his land, his way of life, and his traditions. They even took his daughter. Maud, primed for assimilation at Carlisle Indian School, contracted tuberculosis just months after arriving and died.[20] What choice did Swift Bear have but to accept the latest form of American power—money—and do what he could to use it to survive?

THE GIFT

But not everything humans make is bought and sold.

Gifts, for example, are a type of material exchange humans created that eludes narrow economic purpose. We don't haggle over a birthday or holiday gift; it's just given. However, gifts still have tremendous value—they have a meaning—that we cannot fully escape.

At the Lakotas' July 4 celebration in 1897, for instance, one of Jesse Bratley's photographs is of a gathering of dozens of women sitting in a circle. In the middle is a huge pile of bolts of cloth, food, trunks, and scores of metal pots, tubs, and cups.[21] This is what, in part, Swift Bear's collected money went toward: a giveaway. Giveaways are part of every Lakota ceremony, an act of generosity and mutual support, respect and honor.[22] Still today, Lakota families planning to host a ceremony may take up to two years of saving so they can provide the food, goods, and cash to those attending.[23] Such gifting is widespread among Native peoples. However, perhaps no ceremony centered on giving away—rather than receiving—is more definitive of these practices than the potlach. But like the Lakota ceremonies, the potlatch has been assailed, barely surviving the age of colonialism.

Just before Christmas in 1921, Dan Cranmer, a member of the Kwakwa̱ka̱'wakw Nation and clan leader, held the biggest potlatch ever seen along Canada's west coast. On the emerald-hued Village Island in Alert Bay, some 100 miles northwest of Vancouver, scores of Native people gathered to give away things. A man named Billy Asu handed out $2,000 worth of blankets. Sam Charlie gave away a canoe. Sam Poulgash gave away jewelry. More canoes, and even gas boats and a pool table, were gifted. Piles of cash and 400 sacks of flour were distributed to those in attendance. Within a month of the celebration, the Canadian government accused the participants of violating Section 149 of the Indian Contract Act, which outlawed potlatches. Forty-nine individuals were convicted. Some served months in prison. But 23 received suspended sentences by agreeing to sell their ceremonial regalia, mostly ritual masks. These materials ended up in museums in Ottawa, Toronto, and New York City.[24]

37. Goods sit on display, waiting to be given away at a potlatch at Yalis (Alert Bay) at the turn of the twentieth century.

The Canadian government had outlawed potlatches in 1884 for the same reason it created residential schools, like those in the United States, for Native children: to extinguish Native culture. Although irregularly enforced, the ban aspired to put a stop to Native language, customs, and beliefs and assimilate Native peoples into 19th-century Victorian society. The potlatch perhaps was the target of special focus because its premise is so different from Western norms of accumulating wealth. The purpose of the potlatch is extravagant generosity. At the potlatch, honor and prestige are earned not by hoarding the most things but giving the most away.

The word *potlatch* in English is derived from the Nootkan phrase *p'atshił'*, and is similar in Kwakwa̱ka̱'wakw: *'pasa*, both meaning "to give."[25] The potlatch is a centuries-old ceremony, a pillar of the coastal cultures that stretch from central Alaska through western Canada to southern Washington. The potlatch is an extravagant party and feast with near-constant singing, dancing, speechifying, and eating. Years can be spent preparing for a potlatch, which can last a single day or many days. It can be held for many reasons, including marriages, memorials, naming babies, raising carved poles and clan houses, passing on a family's rights and privileges, and restoring one's reputation after a public humiliation. The potlatch serves to connect the living to the ancestors, reaffirm social bonds, and present clan regalia—such as blankets, clothing, staffs, daggers, copper shields, and canoes—to the community. As the Kwakwa̱ka̱'wakw chief Robert Joseph once said of his people, "The potlatch gives definition to our world."[26]

In a famous 1925 essay by the French anthropologist Marcel Mauss, titled "The Gift," he argues that the potlatch is unique for its complexity and centrality to a cultural group, but that across many societies, gift-giving is a powerful force that binds people together—even serving as a mortar that cements the bricks of human communities.[27]

Examining gift practices around the globe, Mauss argued that they involve three obligations: to give, to receive, to reciprocate. He observed that when a person gives a gift, they demonstrate generosity and thus they deserve respect. In turn, a person is required to accept gifts to demonstrate their respect for the giver, which itself reflects the receiver's generosity. And finally, a person is required to return a gift, which demonstrates that one is equal to or better (if the gift is better) than the original giver. Of course, once the original giver receives a gift back, the chain starts all over again, to be repeated endlessly. This infinite cycle of debt and return creates a web of social relationships.[28]

In this way, gift-giving is actually a system driven by morality—

expectations of appropriate and fair behavior. The unseen dynamic in a gift given and received is a moral bond that forms in the exchange. A person's honor and prestige are bound up in gifts. The act of giving and receiving gifts becomes a public demonstration of a person's moral standing and lays the foundation of a community's social relations. A gift can reaffirm ancestral connections. It can elevate or lower a person's social standing. It can bring people closer together or tear them apart. Exchanging gifts has the power to rearrange human relationships.

These general principles seem nearly universal. Scholars have searched for "pure gifts"—those given with no expectation of anything in return. Such gifts are hard to find. One example is donating blood;[29] however, even most blood donors have the reasonable expectation that they would receive blood if medically needed one day.

The idea of gifting is broad and cross-cultural, even for those of us who don't partake in potlatches. On the surface, for many of us, gifts may *feel* like they're freely given and received, but they create invisible bonds and obligations. A person who only accepts birthday and holiday gifts and never gives anything in return will not be a person with many friends or loving family members. When someone buys us a drink, we can anticipate feeling obliged to later return the favor. When someone invites us to dinner, we feel obliged to bring something, anticipating the need for reciprocity. The nature of the gift spurs us into action. Gifts are relationships wrapped in material form.

Canada's legal prohibition of potlatches continued until 1951, when Section 149 was removed. In some places, potlatches successfully continued out of sight of government authorities during the ban. But, in other places, the prohibition succeeded in breaking apart the tradition and hence the cultures and social relations that they held together. "Even though the ban was lifted in the '50s, it still took years for people to get over that," said Barb Cranmer, the granddaughter of Dan Cranmer, in 2006. "It took people a long time to feel comfortable about standing up and saying, 'This is who we are.'"[30]

Efforts to reclaim the forcibly sold regalia began in the 1950s. Twenty years later, the items began to be returned to the U'mista Cultural Centre, a museum in Alert Bay built for their care. The return of these things and the revival of potlatches has led to a slow renaissance among many Native communities.

"Our culture is a living culture," Barb Cranmer continued. "Recently, a relative of mine held a potlatch and he went back to the early teachings of our people. In that particular family they hadn't had a potlatch in more than eighty years. He worked hard and learned the songs and all. Well, there was something there, there was spirit in that big house and it was really powerful."[31]

In other words, through the potlatch, these communities have been rediscovering the power of the gift.

WEAVING GENERATIONS

For Lakota winter counts to work as records of history, they must be passed between the generations. Without passing from one knowledge keeper to another, they are merely biographical—one person's record of what happened. But, by passing the winter count itself, and by passing along the story behind each symbol, the object becomes a form of collective memory. In this way, objects weave together generations, binding their stories together.

Perhaps among the most remarkable—and tragic—objects of memory I have ever seen is a simple pillowcase, passed to her daughter by a woman named Rose. In 1852, Rose stepped up to auction block in South Carolina to be sold. We can only guess at the terror she felt, the unknowns of what would lie ahead, the forms of physical and spiritual suffering she endured. Her terror must have only been exponentially heightened by the fact that her nine-year-old daughter, Ashley, was also being purchased that day. Like the millions of people stolen from Africa and taken to the Americas where for generations they would be forcibly enslaved, Rose was powerless to prevent the fracturing of her life and family and soul. Most of those millions remain nameless, lost in the world of slavery that explicitly sought to make them anonymous, mere chattel in the grinding machinery of the cotton trade. But we do know Rose's name, that she existed, and that she loved her daughter, because of a gift she gave.

Not long after the National Museum of African American History and Culture opened in 2016, I had the chance to visit the stunning building, covered in intricately patterned metalwork, in Washington, DC. There, I traveled through time, to Africa's illustrious past, to the horrors of the transatlantic slave trade, to the battle for racial justice, to the immense contributions of African Americans in the arts and sciences. It was all so moving, but of everything I saw that day, the object that would haunt me was a tattered pillowcase.

I would have to read more to learn the full force of this object. But I did understand that much of its power lay in the fact of its survival: how an object as ephemeral as a pillowcase was passed among enslaved peoples and their descendants as an heirloom. Working with the collection Jesse Bratley made, I was primed to consider the special role heirlooms play in people's lives. Many of the items Bratley obtained—dolls, clothing, pottery, and more—would have been heirlooms among the tribes they were gathered from, if Bratley had not purchased them. And, fascinatingly, when I met some of Bratley's descendants, they saw the collection of Native objects now as their own inheritance, their own set of heirlooms.

The pillowcase was made from rough cotton, in a distorted rectangle. Faded and patched, the sack has several worn holes, frayed ends. In graceful cursive needlework, a message had been embroidered on the pillowcase seven decades after Rose was sold. It reads:

> My great grandmother Rose
> mother of Ashley gave her this sack when
> she was sold at age 9 in South Carolina
> it held a tattered dress 3 handfulls of
> pecans a braid of Roses hair. Told her
> It be filled with my Love always
> she never saw her again
> Ashley is my grandmother
> Ruth Middleton
> 1921

> My great grandmother Rose
> mother of Ashley gave her this sack when
> she was sold at age 9 in South Carolina
> it held a tattered dress 3 handfulls of
> pecans a braid of Roses hair. Told her
> It be filled with my Love always
> she never saw her again
> Ashley is my grandmother
> Ruth Middleton
> 1921

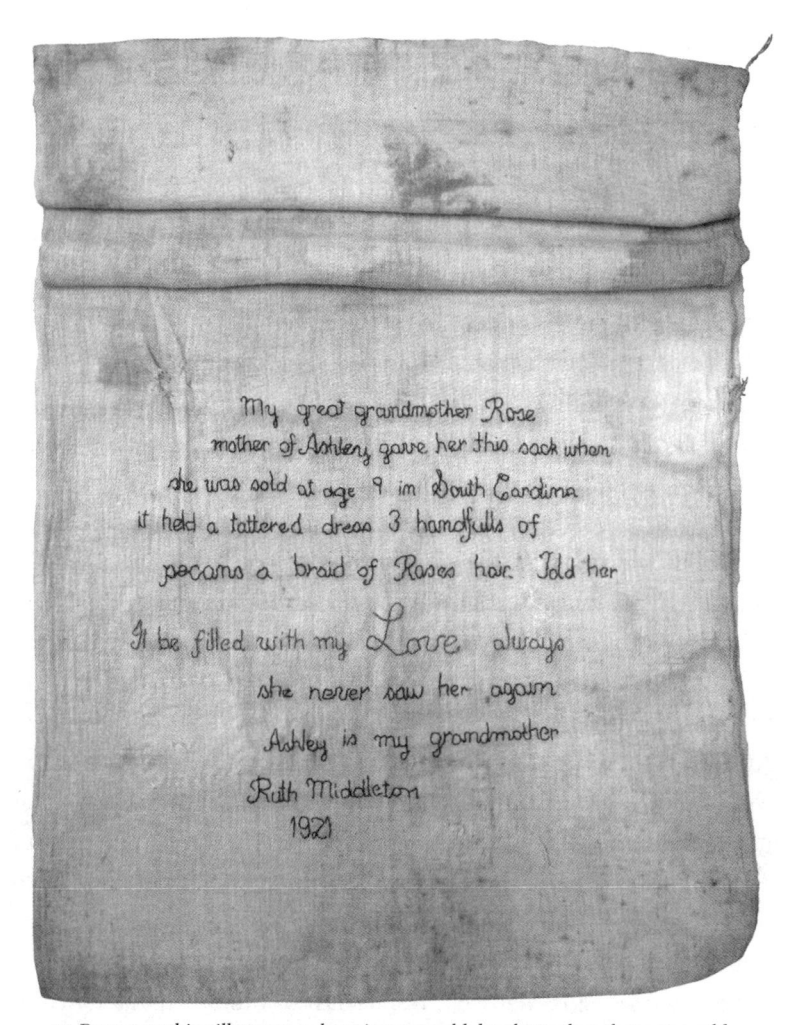

38. Rose gave this pillowcase to her nine-year-old daughter when they were sold.

As the Harvard University historian Tiya Miles reveals in her meticulously researched and heartrending book *All That She Carried: The Journey of Ashley's Sack, a Black Family Keepsake* (2021), this pillowcase was cherished by Ashley and then passed down through the family — an object of memory, a vehicle for Rose's love.[32]

Although few of us have such a profound and rare keepsake, many can understand the power of objects that come from loved ones. These things need not be extraordinary or monetarily valuable. In some ways, the more everyday they are, the more they may stand out to those who inherit them. For example, an online exhibit created by the *New York Times* during the COVID-19 pandemic shared a group of meaningful objects left behind by those who had perished from the virus.[33] The 50-plus objects were mundane: a cast-iron skillet that reminded a daughter of her mother's cooking, battered ice skates that reminded a son of his father's frugality, a small zebra figurine that reminded a friend of what had comforted her lost companion.

Margaret Gibson, a sociologist at Griffith University in Australia, would not be surprised by this collection. She writes: "Death reconstructs our experiences of personal and household objects in particular ways; there is the strangeness of realizing that *things* have outlived *persons*, and, in this regard, the materiality of things is shown to be more permanent than the materiality of the body."[34] It is through things, and the stories they tell, that we remember those who have gone before.

Things gather even greater force when they pass between generations as heirlooms. As Tiya Miles has pointed out, each of these seem "to have absorbed into its fibers the intangible essence of a past time."[35] Even in today's overstuffed world, people continue to find space for inherited items. A 2020 survey found that more than 40 percent of Americans hold an heirloom more than 50 years old.[36] A 2013 poll in the UK also found that about 40 percent of the respondents hold antiques, jewelry, or silverware heirlooms.[37]

The archaeologist Katina T. Lillios has hypothesized that in world history, the importance of heirlooms first became apparent with the emergence of chiefdoms.[38] A chiefdom is a kin-based form of political organization where a single leader inherits control over a large community. Chiefdoms appear at different times around the globe: in northern Europe more than 4,000 years ago, in the Andes of Peru 1,500 years ago, and 1,200 years ago on the Hawaiian Islands.[39]

Unlike egalitarian societies where leadership is achieved through demonstrated wisdom, bravery, or success, a chief's position is ascribed—inherited—and thus must be legitimized to maintain power. Lillios suggests that heirlooms became a key tool for chiefs to connect themselves to ancestral lineages, to tangibly show relationships across time. By surveying a range of societies, Lillios demonstrates how, because heirlooms are not equally shared or available to all, a single individual could draw from the object's power to evoke ancestral authority. Lillios found that heirlooms are central to chiefdoms: coats spun from flax among the Māori of Aotearoa (New Zealand), gold chains and pendants among the Yoruba of West Africa, and lace among the rulers of the Austro-Hungarian Empire. Lillios concludes that heirlooms become more than mere commodities when they come to be associated with a mythic past, historical ancestors, and a collective rather than individual history. Heirlooms are needed in chiefdoms to authenticate a chief's inherited rank. Heirlooms weave generations together.[40]

Lillios's argument explains how heirlooms came to play a pivotal role in the development of human societies, but how do specific objects become objects of memory? How exactly does a pillowcase become an heirloom?

Although there are different theories, a useful one appears in the 1890 anthropological classic, *The Golden Bough: A Study in Magic and Religion* by Sir James George Frazer. In his thick tome, the Scottish anthropologist describes "contagious magic," which assumes "that things which have once been in contact with each other are always in contact." As an example, Frazer discusses the cross-cultural view that the parts of our bodies we shed—hair, teeth—continue to carry our essence.[41] A particularly widespread example is the umbilical cord, which can be subject to rituals, buried, or burned.[42]

The belief in contagious magic extends beyond the body to the objects that we come into contact with. Research shows that one reason that objects collected from famous people are so powerful is they seem to literally connect us—through the thing itself—to the celebrity.[43] Possessing a real Picasso is also far better than a perfect digitized copy because it bears the artist's touch, providing "an almost magical sense of the artist's essence."[44] The pink suit that Jackie Kennedy wore on the day her husband was assassinated in Dallas, Texas, is now enshrined in a museum—a double dose of contagious magic, with the suit stained in President John Kennedy's blood, and bearing the aura of the First Lady's despair and stoicism that day, immured by the media in photographs.[45]

Heirlooms are also the result of contagious magic. They are objects that persist across time and distance without losing their human connection. This is how even a worn pillowcase can transmit love across generations.

EXTENSION OF MY SELF

> Every artist dips his brush in his own soul,
> and paints his own nature into his pictures.
> HENRY WARD BEECHER

Heirlooms are a form of memory. They anchor us to the past, and hence give us a history. They do this because we humans attach ourselves to objects: objects are an expression of who we are.

In chapter 2, we explored the revolutions that allow us to extend ourselves into physical space through things—we sense the edge of our car's bumper as we park, or the texture of the ground under a rake. Another revolution is how objects extend our sense of self, our identities, out into the world.

Consider how Jesse Bratley used the Native objects he collected. While hoping to one day open a museum, in the meantime he used many of the items to decorate his home. In one family portrait that Bratley composed, sometime while on the Rosebud Reservation in South Dakota between 1895 and 1899, Bratley, his wife, and their toddler son pose themselves in the corner of a room. Behind them is a plain wood bookcase filled with tomes on Native American history and culture. Hanging on the wall is a traditional Native smoking pipe and large beaded bag with long fringe. There is also a gorgeous traditional bag with a beaded floral design, hung over a portrait of President Abraham Lincoln. More Native objects and small photos of Native people sit on the bookcase. Bratley sits contentedly reading an open newspaper in a rocking chair.

39. Jesse, Della, and Homer Bratley pose in their home's "Indian corner" while living at Lower Cut Meat Creek Day School, on the Rosebud Reservation, sometime between 1895 and 1899.

This scene depicts what was then called an "Indian corner," a Victorian decorative trend for the home; such scenes were "dense, dazzling domestic displays" of Indian objects.[46] The aesthetic was intended to present a jumble of Native American–inspired objects presented against simple furniture. These corners were part of a larger "Indian craze" at the end of the 1800s, in which people living in crowded, hectic urban cities in Europe and the US imagined a simpler world of

Native peoples more authentically connected to the peaceful harbors of nature. What stands out for Bratley in particular was his choice to turn a corner of his home into a shrine of Native material culture while at the same time his day job was to remove all signs of Native culture from the children he taught. I believe he made this decorative choice because—despite the contradiction—his entire life was wrapped up in Native peoples. With his "Indian corner" of Native objects set amid modern furniture, Bratley could make sense of his life and have a measure of control over the two worlds he was trying to bring together, the "savage" and the "civilized," as he saw it. In other words, this corner of Bratley's house was not merely part of the house. It was as if the building and everything it contained was somehow . . . *him*.

In his seminal 1988 article, "Possessions and the Extended Self," published in the *Journal of Consumer Research*, Russell W. Belk argued that humans become attached to things through "incorporation processes." This begins in infancy, as children realize they are distinct from their environment and the things around them. They come to understand that the things in the world can be put to their use. This realization comes to full fruition as young people seek to build their character and belong to different groups. From toys to clothes, young people use things not only to *reflect* their identities but also to *develop* them. For example, wearing a dress in Western society can reflect a gendered feeling of being female, and then how others treat the person in the dress furthers that sense of femaleness.[47]

Belk cites evidence that it is a universal human experience to make things a part of our selves. The psychologists Mihaly Csikszentmihalyi and Eugene Halton believe we do this because humans—somewhere on our evolutionary journey—came to be uniquely able to summon "mobile attention."[48] This is the ability to direct our attention to realize a goal. We can select a rock, then knock it about to sharpen it, so that we can have a spearpoint to kill a mammoth. Our attention can be focused through different processes. The philosopher Jean-Paul Sartre argued that humans come to see an object as part of the self in three ways.[49] First, when we *create* objects, they are incorporated into our sense of self—in other words, making a piece of pottery feels like the expression of an inner person. Second, when we *appropriate* or control objects for our own personal use, they become part of us; for example, purchasing a coveted watch and wearing it feels like an extension of one's taste. Third, objects become part of ourselves when we *come to know* them—when you stand before a Picasso painting and ponder it, an attachment to self grows.

Put another way, the self and objects synthesize through the relationships of making and possessing things, pursuing activities with things, and being in the world with things. In this way, Belk says, "possessions are all-important to knowing who we are. People seek, express, confirm, and ascertain a sense of being through what they have."[50] Things are a vehicle for our identities.

The objects we own and use become "signals" of these identities, at both the group and the individual level. The impact of these signals will depend on the degree to which they are shared in a community: carrying an extraordinarily expensive Louis Vuitton purse will convey wealth, while an inherited antique purse from a grandmother may not signal to others much at all, even if beloved by its wearer.

The beginning of an attachment between a person and an object, according to the behavioral scientists S. Christian Wheeler and Christopher J. Bechler, varies widely in quality. If a person loves things, then an initial attachment can be strong. If a person sees something they want but does not own it, the initial attachment may be weak. However formed, from this initial attachment grows a "connotative link"—a thing's identity associations.[51] We seek out the things that advance our identities (for instance, purchasing a new luxury sports car if you're a wealthy, young urbanite), and avoid those things that detract from our identities (for instance, purchasing a used beat-up truck if you're a wealthy, young urbanite).

These connotations can play with our minds in subtle ways. Several studies have found that some consumers who used a Victoria's Secret shopping bag felt more feminine, glamorous, and beautiful, and that some who used a pen with an MIT logo perceived themselves to be more intelligent, harder working, and a leader.[52] Through such mechanisms, people can use things for affirming their self-view or for advancing the self they would like to become.

Csikszentmihalyi and Halton suggest that of all objects, the home and its contents are the most powerful expressions of self. Why? For many of us, the things inside our home are the things that can be curated, that are under our control. "Thus household objects constitute an ecology of signs," the authors write, "that reflects as well as *shapes* the pattern of the owner's self."[53]

Thanks to these theories, we can see how Bratley's Indian corner was about far more than interior design. "We are the sum of our possessions," Belk concludes.[54] Things are the "extended self."

A BEADED BLANKET STRIP

Lice are a surprising source of information about the world's first clothing. A 2011 study looked at the genetic history of when clothing lice (a parasite adapted to living among clothes) diverged from body and hair lice. They determined that clothing lice appeared as early as 170,000 years ago.[55] This indirect method of dating clothing was supported with a newly reported discovery in 2021. In a Moroccan cave, archaeologists recovered direct evidence of the world's oldest clothing: the remains of sand foxes, golden jackals, and wildcats with distinctive cut marks suggesting they were skinned, along with 62 bone tools uniquely suited to processing and tanning hides, dating to upwards of 120,000 years ago.[56]

The invention of clothing likely helped hominins as they spread from Africa and adapted to living in the Northern Hemisphere's colder climates. One study estimated that Neanderthals living in cold winter temperatures in Europe would have covered up to 80 percent of their bodies in "non-tailored clothing"—probably the fur of a single animal draped around the body like a cloak.[57]

While Neanderthals seem to have shared some of the initial technologies for making clothing—such as rib fragments used to soften hides—our direct ancestors created more-sophisticated clothes, perhaps due to their leaner bodies, which couldn't stay as naturally warm in the winter.[58] Unlike the simple capes of their Neanderthal cousins, our most direct ancestors tailored clothing trimmed at the neck and sleeves with the fur of rabbits, foxes, or wolverines.[59] The adaptation of making better clothes helped modern humans survive in ever harsher conditions. *Homo sapiens* continued to adapt new technologies to the need for clothing: as early as 30,000 years ago in the foothills of the Caucasus Mountains, humans spun wild flax into yarn to weave into garments.[60]

In *Climate, Clothing, and Agriculture in Prehistory: Linking Evidence, Causes, and Effects* (2019), the archaeologist Ian Gilligan distinguishes the first "simple clothing" from subsequent "complex clothing" perfected by *Homo sapiens*. Complex clothes fit snugly around the body, incorporate separate pieces that encircle the limbs, and can be composed of multiple layers. Gilligan argues that the invention of complex clothing had important effects. The drive for clothing spurred the creation of specific technologies to process, cut, and sew hides (and later fabric)—scrapers, blades, awls, and eyed needles—all of which appear just under 40,000 years ago. Clothing, then, enabled our human ancestors to travel vast distances, enduring harsh weather and making some of the most uninhabitable regions of the globe, such as the Arctic Circle, habitable.[61]

Gilligan goes even further to argue that the genesis of clothing is closely tied to climate changes and eventually to the arrival of agriculture. Drawing on historic examples, Gilligan shows that in many temperate environments, nudity prevailed; only when the climate grew cooler did clothing appear. As the last Ice Age ended 12,000 years ago, globally the climate grew hotter and wetter. By then, many human communities used clothing, but with the changing weather, porous fabrics made of wool and cotton were preferred over animal skins, which trap heat and moisture. Gilligan posits that it was this desire for clothing that pushed our ancestors toward settled farm life—where people could harvest the plant and animal material for their desired clothing—even more than the need to cultivate plants and herd animals for food.[62]

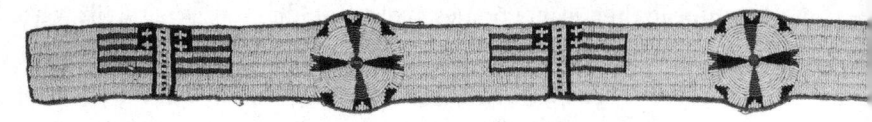

40. By incorporating the US flag into a traditional beaded blanket strip—and using the symbol for the morning star for stars on the flag—this object points to the resistance of Lakota artisans.

Whether or not clothing was a prime motivation, it was certainly a key product of the Agricultural Revolution. In the millennia that followed, we find forms of clothing indistinguishable from what we wear today: pants, dresses, skirts, sunglasses, sandals, shoes. Consider Ötzi the Iceman's outfit of 5,000 years ago: coat, leggings, belt, cap, and underwear—pieces that are likely in your own closet or dresser.

This story of firsts and function is important for understanding the invention of clothing, but it is only one part of the story. The other major part is the meaning that clothing came to have. As discussed in chapter 4, by 50,000 years ago, symbolic thinking had fully flowered for *Homo sapiens*, immediately preceding the creation of complex clothing. The painting of cave walls and bodies as artistic expressions likely would have transferred quickly to clothing, itself a kind of second skin. These clothing designs, like decorated caves and bodies, may have been simply pleasing or functional (e.g., for camouflage), but also would have taken on the weight of symbolism. Ötzi's bearskin cap would have kept him warm, but since it noticeably wasn't deer-, goat-, or sheepskin like his other clothes, it may also have signaled his power.

Because clothing does have power. In one historical example, we can see how Spanish colonialists viewed clothing in their despotic rule over the Americas. Spanish conquistadors and explorers frequently took note of Native clothing, body decorations, and nudity—particularly the latter, which they associated with savagery and the fall of Eden—and duly outlawed it.[63] As the Spanish settled their colonies, they became ever more dependent on clothing to monitor their caste system, meaning that particular classes had to wear particular clothing. This was necessary because as people became intermixed, their physical attributes like skin color or hair texture were often an imperfect guide to their caste, so colonists depended on clothes to demarcate people's place in the hierarchy. However, clothes are changeable. By wearing the clothes of a different caste, a person could *become* a person of that caste. The historian Rebecca Earle offers the example of a priest in Mexico City in the late 1600s who complained, "When an Amerindian put on a cloak, shoes and stockings, and grew his hair, he quickly became a *mestizo*, 'and in a few days a Spaniard.'"[64]

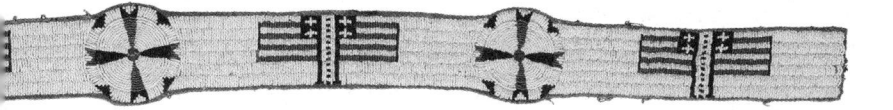

The US government inherited the colonial obsession with Native American clothing as evidence of savagery that needed to be stamped out. The school uniforms issued by Jesse Bratley and other teachers at Indian boarding schools had multiple purposes: to foster a disciplined atmosphere, displace traditional clothing, erase individual identities, and instill Victorian norms, aesthetics, and values.[65] In other words, for Native American children, clothing was a site of oppression.

However, Native Americans did not stand idly by, as the US government sought to destroy their way of life. They, too, understood the symbolic power of clothing.

In fact, some of the objects that Bratley collected during his time as an Indian school teacher reflect Native defiance. In the collection is a beaded strip, applied to a blanket, collected on the Rosebud Reservation in the late 1800s.[66] At first glance, the strip seems to embrace American patriotism: it features US flags laid across a white background. Closer inspection reveals that the stars on the flags are crosses—the Lakota symbol for the morning star, a vitally important celestial body. The beaded blanket strip was a clever way to pass muster with US officials (who would object to the US flag?) while perpetuating the Lakota tradition of decorated blankets and religious imagery.

Objects are far more than their functions. They take on multiple meanings, becoming sites for power—whether it is turning ochre into a painting, a ceramic sculpture into a goddess, electrum into money, 400 sacks of flour into gifts, a pillowcase into an heirloom, or a beaded blanket strip into a site of subversive pride. The appeal and necessity of these meanings held such sway that humans want them constantly to affirm our place in the world, to make us who we are. Because meaning is such a powerful force for humans, meaning laid the foundation for the next great leap: the insatiable desire for more and more and more.

LEAP 3

MAKE MORE

41. An iPhone embodies humanity's third leap with stuff.

7

IN THE THICK OF THINGS

Jedediah Strutt was born in 1726 on a farm amid the gentle green rolling hills of Derbyshire, England.[1] It was said that he was born ambitious, though his ambition would take years to blossom. As a young man, Strutt was apprenticed to a wheelwright for seven years, then became a journeyman, working short stints for whoever would employ him. Nearing the age of 30, he inherited a farm and married a longtime acquaintance, Elizabeth Woollat.

Strutt's new brother-in-law, William Woollat, was a hosier. For a time, William had been unsuccessful in developing a knitting frame to make ribbed stockings. Strutt took up the challenge to help refine the device. The two perfected the machine, which could produce stockings with textured lines 20 times faster than human hands. Their creation received a patent in 1759 and became a hit. Strutt was on his way.

Nearly a decade later, Strutt and a business partner were introduced to Richard Arkwright, who had invented an automated system for spinning yarn or thread that was powered by yoked horses. Strutt recommended that it be powered by water. Drawing on a long history that began with the ancient Greeks and Egyptians, simple waterwheels had long been used to power large stones that turned to grind grains such as wheat, and later for making paper and sawing wood. The new mechanism similarly used the natural force of falling water to turn a wheel, which turned a central axis, which spun levers and gears to power the Arkwright machine. Through a series of levers

42. The Arkwright machine helped launch the Industrial Revolution.

and rollers, the machine drew out cotton into long strands, twisted it tight, then neatly wrapped it around spools. This was essentially the same process as spinning by hand, but done automatically and continuously, and could simultaneously spin dozens of spools instead of just one at a time. Soon, Arkwright added other automated machines for the whole process, taking raw cotton and transforming it into strong, high-quality threads and yarns. Together, Arkwright and Strutt built Cromford Mill, the world's first water-powered cotton mill.

A remarkable innovation, the mill transformed the slow work of hand-spinning thread into a manufacturing system that could produce vast amounts of thread and yarn, far faster and with far less human labor than anyone could have imagined. Soon, cotton mills were sprouting all over Derbyshire. In 1777, Strutt constructed his own mill in Belper. Strutt's family inherited the work. His son, William, joined his father at Belper. There, William befriended Samuel Slater.

Samuel Slater was born in 1768 in Belper.[2] When he entered his teen years, Slater became an apprentice at a Strutt mill. Over the next eight years, he mastered how to operate the Arkwright machinery. He then planned a secret escape to the United States.

At the time, Great Britain had a near monopoly on water-powered textile mills. To control the industry, the government ruled it illegal to export mill equipment and for textile workers to emigrate. As a contemporary of Slater's wrote, "The king has frequently made proclamation against any tradesmen leaving the kingdom, and called on his officers for their most vigilant watch against it."[3] Still, Slater saw enough opportunity across the Atlantic that he was willing to risk arrest.

Entrepreneurs in the United States were desperate to start their own water-powered textile mills. This desire was fed by both the chance to make fortunes and a perceived patriotic duty for the new country, which won its independence from England in 1783, to establish its own independent industries. But attempts to make water-powered machines outside Great Britain were thwarted by technical challenges; mobs of craftsmen who, fearing for their livelihood, attacked inventors; and England's restrictions on patents and exports.

In 1789, after months of travel, Slater finally arrived in New York City. Through various introductions, he learned that two men, Smith Brown and William Almy, had been struggling to start up a water-powered mill just outside Providence, Rhode Island. Within a week, Slater was invited to join the failing venture. Slater arrived at the nascent factory and was not encouraged. As Brown later recalled, "When Samuel saw the old machines, he felt down-hearted, with disappointment—and shook his head, and said 'these will not do; they are good for nothing in their present condition, nor can they be made to answer.'"[4]

Slater, Brown, and Almy promptly set to work. Slater did not have any drawings or diagrams of the Arkwright or other machines; he had to build them entirely from memory. He was particularly stuck on the carding machine: giant metal rollers covered with leather and inserted with pins that gently combed fibers into neat, parallel lines. At last, the men progressed, creating the carding, drawing, roving, and spinning machines. After a year of work, the factory opened with 12 children as its employees, just before Christmas 1790.

The Industrial Revolution had arrived in America.

THE WEALTH OF NATIONS

The Industrial Age is what has made our modern world of things—creating our modes of production and enabling our habits of consumption.[5] Most deeply in time, the revolution could not have transpired without the invention of tools 3.3 million years ago, and without the full flowering of meaning some 50,000 years ago. But more immediately, the Industrial Age commenced because of events like Jedediah Strutt's investment in the Arkwright machine and Samuel Slater's mill outside Providence—events that launched the Industrial Revolutions in Europe and North America and then the rest of the world. Some have argued that there is a direct line from those first textile machines to rice cookers and radios, cars and computers—the millions and millions of goods that line store shelves, populate online search engines, and find their way into our offices, schools, homes, and hearts. The invention of industrial production leads to the next leap in the story of stuff, opening up an entirely new human relationship with things: a world of material abundance.

This revolution happened two ways, gradually and then suddenly. The successes of Strutt and Slater unfolded within years, but the social, political, and economic architecture for the Industrial Revolution was built over centuries.

Initially, the biggest limiting factor to abundance was scarcity. If there are only a handful of things to possess, then it is difficult to grow rich. For millions of years, our hominin ancestors apparently lived with very few goods. Initially limited by intelligence and need, only gradually did tools like spears enter the hominin repertoire, enhancing survival and the growing reliance on things. Even then, few of our ancestors before the last Ice Age were surrounded by a wealth of things.

For comparison, anthropologists have observed how small-scale hunter-gatherer societies, today and historically, tend not to have material abundance because they move frequently. As anyone who has moved knows, it's a lot of work to cart around a ton of stuff. This is not to say, though, that people in those nomadic societies don't sometimes dream of being materially rich. Archaeological evidence from such cultures suggests a long history of material inequalities.[6] People almost everywhere *want* to garner prestige and power through things.[7] But hunter-gatherer societies are largely dependent on natural scarcity and abundance; a mammoth hunter had no way of creating more mammoths during a slow year. A hunter-gatherer's affluence came not with accumulating a lot of stuff, but rather simply meeting the basic demands of survival and needing little more.[8]

Starting around 12,000 years ago, as humans settled down and began to revolutionize their material worlds—inventing money and monuments—there became more to possess.[9] The development of agriculture and pastoralism at the close of the last Ice Age, while still hugely dependent on natural events, conspired to give sedentary people a greater degree of control over accumulating wealth. Not only did these activities require more material goods (such as farming equipment), but in many places their development also led to new social hierarchies, job specializations, and urbanization. The abundance that could result from these new forms of social organization, however, was not always distributed equally. Under agriculture's rule, in many places, small, elite classes of people developed vastly more material abundance than their subjects, as the anthropologists David Graeber and David Wengrow wrote in their 2021 bestseller, *The Dawn of Everything*. Although the evidence suggests hunter-gatherer societies have long held complex notions of ownership and private property, inequality could be further driven by some elites claiming—and being able to politically defend—exclusive rights to otherwise collective resources, such as land and minerals.[10] Pharaohs, emperors, kings, khans, sultans, popes, and tsars had realized how to extract power from the domestication of plants and animals, the mining of ore, and the material abundance these forms of production created. Graeber and Wengrow observe how, in places such as 18th-century Europe, "power over possessions could be directly translated into power over other human beings."[11]

The archaeologist Michael E. Smith and his colleagues have recently argued that the two key mechanisms for the origins of inequality are the invention of relatively *permanent forms* of wealth (e.g., money) that have *economic defensibility* (i.e., the benefits of defending something are more than the costs of defending them).[12] They point to evidence that suggests inequality is correlated with both living in one place and group size—the lifestyle that followed from agriculture and pastoralism. In sedentary societies, wealth tends to be passed from generation to generation, which allows wealth to accrue. And the defense of resources is tied to group size: the bigger the group, the easier it is to defend accumulated wealth from rivals. Inequality is the result of what we call asymmetrical abundance.

Some preagricultural societies built material abundance—and possibly inequality—such as hunters and gatherers in Russia 30,000 years ago.[13] But at the end of the last Ice Age, abundance became possible in a new way. For many around the world, it meant more than just feasting on a great hunt or gorging on the summer bounty of wild blueberries. Of course, in many places, societies decided that gathering and hunting (and maybe dabbling in agriculture) was just fine—choosing not to go down the road of more stuff, as Graeber and Wengrow convincingly show.[14] But with settled life, in many societies, abundance could become the unequal search for permanent forms of wealth that could be protected and passed along to one's kin.

Even so, few achieved true abundance. This was due to the constant threat of loss through warfare and natural disasters. But there were other pressures on individual abundance. In small-scale societies, it is easy to monitor fairness by seeing who possesses how much. While this is less true for larger groups, Smith and his coauthors point to how, as people come to live in larger communities, they become more interdependent, and thus they actually need *more* social cooperation, which, in some cases, can promote increased material equality, such as public lands or forms of social security.

For thousands of years, an additional limiting factor was technolog-

IN THE THICK OF THINGS   161

ical: there simply was no way to produce a lot, quickly and cheaply. Even where people created such technology, there rarely was the perfect social and political infrastructure to support the wide distribution of goods. Yet, around the world, the first inklings of the possibilities of industrial-level material abundance were seen: in Mesopotamia 5,000 years ago, the Persian Empire 2,500 years ago, South Asia's Maurya Empire 2,300 years ago, the ancient Maya 1,700 years ago, China's Song dynasty 1,000 years ago, the West African Kingdom of Mali 700 years ago, the Inca 600 years ago, and Southeast Asia's Toungoo Empire 500 years ago. In all these cultures were small, elite groups who lived in luxury, even if that luxury was modest by today's standards.

In this way, 700 years ago, when Europe began to transition from the Middle Ages to the Renaissance with its dramatic shifts in culture, art, politics, and religion, its people were, at first, experiencing the kinds of changes common in many places, even if the details were different. In Europe, one major transformation concerned the power of the Roman Catholic Church. With a new embrace of classical education and the study of ancient Greek and Roman humanistic

43. The French scholar Charles Chipiez painted this reconstruction of the opulent palace of the Persian ruler Darius I, as it stood about 2,500 years ago in what is now Iran, based on archaeological and architectural research.

philosophy, many Europeans began to reshape their lives based on more secular principles. A challenge to the church's nearly thousand-year hold on every aspect of life eventually led to the Protestant Reformation, with a focus on personal spirituality. As a result of questioning the church's power and authority, business loans, long frowned upon by the church, were now accepted, and secular authorities—including merchants, and eventually industrialists—stepped into the political class. Additionally, the Roman Catholic Church's authority over natural law was challenged by new scientific inquiry. Mathematics, astronomy, physics, and knowledge about the human body advanced as scientists sought to unlock the secrets of the universe. The resulting knowledge would feed into the Industrial Revolution—joined by millennia of scientific developments in Africa, East Asia, and the Middle East—by applying principles in engineering and practical scientific instruments to new manufacturing processes.

The European Renaissance also launched a new ethos of global exploration—and world domination. The Roman Catholic Church, kings and queens, and a rising merchant class invested in colonizing Asia, Africa, and the Americas. Different European powers competed to control as much land and as many people as possible, each trying to secure abundance and dominance. These colonialist explorations resulted in new access to raw materials, new markets for consumer goods, expanded labor pools (especially in the form of enslaved people), and a new affluence for upper classes.[15]

By the early 1700s, the "Enlightenment" was in full swing, marking a period of increasing dependence on rationality and science. In England, more people were living in cities, and a movement began to increase agricultural production, since there were less people working the land. The successful efforts to expand agricultural outputs reinforced the use of a scientific approach to problem-solving. Yet even as markets and production increased, nearly everything was still produced by hand, often through "cottage industries": small groups of workers operating on a small scale. Almost all mechanized labor, such as milling grain, was powered by animals—an ancient tradition finally interrupted by the water-powered cotton mill.[16]

By the late 18th century, cotton mills were employing hundreds of workers, producing massive amounts of product for distant markets; the need for more and better roads, waterways, and modes of transportation joined the list of civic and engineering goals. In 1776, Adam Smith published *An Inquiry into the Nature and Causes of the Wealth of Nations*, inveighing against government regulation and advocating for a system of free trade. With the birth of the Industrial Age—the convergence of novel, science-driven technology with a thriving merchant class bolstered by upper-class investors, a secular political structure that supported commerce, and expanded transportation networks—Smith's book was not a theoretical argument but a prescription for a new world.

NO END TO MACHINERY

In the spring of 1811, authorities in Nottinghamshire sensed the locals were unhappy.[17] They were in the throes of an economic depression caused by the Napoleonic Wars. Food, especially bread, was scarce. And skilled workers were losing their jobs to the machines stationed in mills across the region, by then the center of England's textile industry. Nottinghamshire authorities started employing the unemployed to sweep the streets, in the hope of staving off unrest.

But on March 11, the street sweepers threw down their brooms. They assembled in the central marketplace and were joined by large crowds, gathering like storm clouds rolling in from the countryside. A string of orators gave fierce speeches demanding better wages and more work. Frantic authorities called in the military, who successfully dispersed the crowds.

When darkness fell, the protestors reassembled. They traveled southwest, to the village of Arnold, which had no military presence. The protestors entered the unprotected mills and smashed nearly 60 machine frames for making stockings. In the next several weeks, the nightly attacks continued, destroying 200 more machines. It took the establishment of local militias and police to finally quiet the rioters.

These riots were not spontaneous. They had been orchestrated by a secret organization made up of skilled craftsmen whose livelihoods the mills threatened. Inspired by a mythic, Robin Hood–like figure given the name Ned Ludd, the Luddites planned sensational operations to garner attention—roving towns at night to infiltrate mills. Sentinels kept watch as their comrades smashed machines with massive sledgehammers, then slipped back into the darkness.

While the new machines bore the brunt of the Luddites' wrath, the real targets were the mill owners. Luddites were not aiming to stop factories but rather to draw attention to the mills' grim labor practices and low-quality goods. They wanted to replicate the apprentice system that had stood in England for centuries, with skilled workers operating the mills and earning enough to care for their families.[18]

The British government had long proven its regard for machinery over people. The 1788 Protection of Stocking Frames, etc. Act established severe penalties for destroying equipment. The 1799 Combination Act prevented the formation of unions or collective bargaining for better pay and work conditions.

After months of calm, in November 1811, the Luddites reignited the riots. By the end of the year, the violence had spread to nearby Leicestershire and Derbyshire. Thousands of troops were stationed at mills. In Belper, gun loopholes were added to mills for defense. Spies tried to infiltrate the Luddites. But the organization was decentralized, without leaders—there was only the fictional General Ludd, Ned's nom de guerre—and its members were sworn to secrecy. The Luddites were also widely supported by locals whose lives were undone by the factories. In 1812, with little sign of the riots abating, the British Parliament passed the Frame-Breaking Act, making "machine-breaking" punishable by death. The following year, 17 men were convicted and hanged.[19]

The truth is the Luddite movement was behind the times. The Industrial Revolution was well on the way to living up to its promise. A range of technologies had already remade how people worked, traveled, communicated. The Watt steam engine, first sold commercially in 1776, had initially been used to pump water into cities; it was also used to pump water out of mines so they could go farther under-

44. The 1804 steam engine hauled a train and laid the foundation for the future of global transportation networks.

ground. By 1804 its applications had expanded, and the first steam railway trip proceeded nearly 10 miles at 2.4 mph, carrying 10 tons of ore, 5 wagons, and 70 men.[20]

In 1810, the Englishman Peter Durand introduced sealed tin cans for preserving and transporting food. The first permanent photograph was made in 1826 by the French inventor Joseph Nicéphore Niépce. In 1828, the Scottish inventor James Beaumont Neilson developed the hot-blast technique for efficiently making iron, turning iron into a key material of industrialization. An American invented the first typewriter in 1829. The first electrical generator, the Faraday disk, was introduced in 1831. The electrical telegraph was demonstrated in 1837 in London. In 1839, the American inventor Charles Goodyear received a patent for the vulcanization of rubber—curing rubber with sulfur and lead, to make it more stable for mass production. In 1856, the Englishman Henry Bessemer took out a patent for a new process—though a process known in East Asia for a thousand years—that removed impurities from iron by oxidation, resulting in the mass production of cheap and durable steel that became the backbone of railroads, bridges, buildings, and ships.

All these inventions and more reshaped how people could live and work. According to the Harvard economist David S. Landes, the Industrial Revolution revolved around three fundamental kinds of "replacements." First, tireless and precise mechanical devices replaced human labor (e.g., the Arkwright machine replaced the hand-spinning of yarn). Second, inanimate replaced animate sources of power, creating an almost unlimited supply of energy (e.g., water replaced horses). Third, minerals replaced organic raw materials, opening the door to more-abundant and more-powerful sources of materials (e.g., rock oil replaced whale oil).[21]

These shifts entailed not just what materials were used and what could be made; they also radically changed the *amount* of stuff produced. With new sources of power—water, steam, electricity—the industrial production process could move more swiftly and exactly, day and night, year-round. All but the engineers were low-skilled workers who could be supervised in the confines of a factory. The manufacturing process could then be honed to maximize production. Once a factory model maximized its efficiencies, it could be reproduced exactly next door, then in the next town over, then on the other side of the world. As companies grew, they established "economies of scale," with cheaper input costs and increasing product outputs. Far more stuff could be made far more quickly.

While the benefits of the industrial system flowed to mill owners and investors, for workers, the changes were often dehumanizing. No longer valued for their individual creativity and manual skill honed over a lifetime, workers were now just a cog in the Arkwright machine. The new technologies greatly advanced the colonial and imperial dreams of European nobility born during the Renaissance, as they ransacked Africa, Asia, and the Americas.[22] Everyone else's fate was less certain.

In an 1829 essay, "Signs of the Times," the famed Scottish philosopher and writer Thomas Carlyle warned that the Industrial Revolution was not ushering in a heroic or moral age but "the Mechanical Age"— turning things *and* people into machines. "It is the Age of Machinery, in every outward and inward sense of that word," he wrote. "Nothing is now done directly, or by hand; all is by rule and calculated contrivance."[23] He continued:

> For the simplest operation, some helps and accompaniments, some cunning abbreviating process is in readiness. Our old modes of exertion are all discredited, and thrown aside. On every hand, the living artisan is driven from his workshop, to make room for a speedier, inanimate one. The shuttle drops from the fingers of the weaver, and falls into iron fingers that ply it faster. The sailor furls his sail, and lays down his oar; and bids a strong, unwearied servant, on vaporous wings, bear him through the waters. . . . There is no end to machinery.[24]

Carlyle observed how industrial systems "indicate a mighty change in our whole manner of existence." Repetitive and thoughtless habits were changing the very nature of people. It was people who were becoming the machines. This was true for all the classes, as even the poor were sucked into a system that could make more goods abundant and cheaper. "Men are grown mechanical in head and in heart, as well as in hand," Carlyle concluded, resulting in a "mechanical character." Humanity had entered a new phase of being mindlessly tied to things.[25]

The belief that people were turning mechanical in every way—their work, habits, expectations, social relations—concerned not just philosophers like Carlyle but the craftspeople who joined the Luddite cause. Yet, critics of the emerging industrial system did not win the day. By 1816, the Luddite protests had faded; the secret order vanished. It took years for the British government to concede a few points, repealing the Combination Acts in 1824 and passing the Factory Act of 1833, which prohibited the employment of children younger than nine years old and regulated the number of work hours for older children.

In the end, the power of things was too great. Little could stop the economic and social machinery driving the Industrial Revolution, a new boundless collective human enterprise for overabundance.

CHAPTER SEVEN

CATALYST INVENTIONS

Give me a place to stand, and a lever long enough,
and I can raise the world.

ARCHIMEDES

On September 20, 1881, the London *Times* published an advertisement for a new theater that would soon open. A week later, another advertisement announced that the opening would be postponed by several days. Yet another deferral followed. On October 6, an ad explained that the delay was "unavoidably postponed . . . in order to complete the very complicated work and experiment connected with the application of electric light to the stage. These works have occupied a much longer time than was expected. Mr. Carte trusts that the novelty of the undertaking will be an excuse for the delay."[26]

Three years earlier, Richard D'Oyly Carte had purchased a parcel of land by the river Thames that was occupied by burned ruins and heaping piles of rubbish.[27] Carte was then 34 years old, charismatic and fashionable but slippery, often involved in sketchy schemes. After several failed ventures, he started the D'Oyly Carte Opera Company to pioneer a new form of English light opera, what would become a way station on the path from high Italian opera to the 20th-century musical. He began by commissioning operas from William Gilbert and Arthur Sullivan. The team won over English and American audiences with their first two efforts: *The Sorcerer* and *HMS Pinafore*. Now Carte wanted his own theater. He bought the dump by the Thames and called it the Savoy.

To add novelty and drama to the theater he was building, Carte invested in a new technology: the incandescent lightbulb. He ordered the construction of a steam-powered electric generator, and nearly 1,200 Swan incandescent lamps. Technical challenges continued to delay the opening until October 10, when the auditorium was illuminated with electric lights. It was an impressive but incomplete feat. Carte imagined his theater would be the first building in the world lit entirely by incandescent lights. And even with just the auditorium

45. The Savoy Theater in 1881 used electric lights to great fanfare.

strung with lights, the generator often broke down, plunging the room into sudden darkness. Carte's contractors struggled to adjust. A December issue of the *Journal of Gas Lighting* pessimistically declared, "Altogether the electric lighting of the Savoy Theater is not yet a success, and we shall be surprised if the experience of its enterprising proprietor does not, for a long time to come, discourage similar attempts elsewhere."[28]

Finally, on December 28, the Savoy opened its doors, and 1,292 people rushed to their seats. The entire theater, the auditorium, passageways, rooms, and stage—every corner glowed with incandescence. Unlike gas lighting, which heated rooms to uncomfortable temperatures, often set buildings on fire, emitted suffocating fumes, and left rooms in flickering half-darkness, the new bulbs radiated a steady, bright, warm, clean, safe light.[29]

At the close of the performance, Carte stepped onto the Savoy's stage before the hushed crowd. He held up a lit Swan lamp, wrapped in cotton gauze, in one hand; in the other hand, he raised a hammer. He smashed the light to pieces. If this were a gas lamp, the cotton would have caught fire. Carte triumphantly held up the cotton like a matador's cape to prove that it was still perfectly white. Not only were the lights beautiful, but they were also entirely safe. The audience erupted into applause.

Within a year, five continuous miles of streets in London were electrically lighted, as were railway stations, the British Museum Reading Room, the Old Masters Exhibition of the Royal Academy, a chapel, and the Crystal Palace exhibition hall in Hyde Park.[30] When Carte opened the Savoy Hotel next to his theater, in 1889, he installed a bedazzling array of lights that illuminated the entrances, courtyards, dining room, sitting areas, offices, and bedrooms.[31] The bedrooms were fitted with a portable electric lamp, strung with a 12-foot cord.[32] On the roof was a giant board with the hotel's name, spelled out in 600 lightbulbs.[33] The stage had been set for incandescent light's ascendance.

The story of lighting the Savoy incorporates key features of the so-called Second Industrial Revolution, which lasted from the 1870s to World War II: steam, electricity, and light in equal measures of wonder and perseverance.[34]

The practical lightbulb, to illuminate every building and street, was so breathtaking to people because it answered the call first made in the yawning valleys of human history, in which fire was harnessed to keep humans warm and safe in the dangerous dark night. The Second Industrial Revolution was about new inventions, but also new innovations—improving upon previous ideas. The incandescent lightbulb, for example, was first developed in the early 1800s when the English scientist Humphry Davy passed an electric current between two carbon rods; then advanced in the 1840s when it was discovered that placing the bulb in a vacuum made the light last longer; then advanced in the 1850s by passing the light through a gas within a tube; then advanced further in 1879 when Thomas Edison created the first practical incandescent lamp by attaching copper lines to a bulb with a thin filament, which could burn for hours.[35]

It was this kind of iteration—discussed in chapter 3—that was not only a hallmark of humanity's creative approach to making things but especially defined the Second Industrial Revolution. The industrialists and inventors of this age embodied the ancient Greek polymath Archimedes's pronouncement that, given the right tools, humans could improve upon everything and raise the world itself.

Significantly, the practical incandescent lightbulb was not just a great invention but fits a category of things in the Industrial Age that we can call a *catalyst invention*—an invention that precipitates an acceleration of other innovations without itself being affected (at least, for a time).

The demand for incandescent lighting led to an increased demand for electricity. The first large-scale power station opened at Niagara Falls in 1895, powering Buffalo, New York, 20 miles away. Soon dozens, then hundreds of stations had been built—commercial electricity becoming a catalyst invention. Large power stations required thousands of parts, but more important, its product came to power a vast number of nonlighting tasks: vacuums, refrigeration, washing machines, ovens, irons, boilers, grinders, grills, kettles, fans, and heaters.[36] In factories, electricity fueled a new generation of tools, shafts, and belts to make more things. Electricity drove streetcars, streetlights, and subways, and would make skyscrapers possible by powering air and water pumps, coolers and heaters, elevators, and more lights. Not only did millions of incandescent bulbs come to be made, but the bulb sparked immeasurable other new inventions that rushed across the land in a biblical-like flood of things.

The first and second phases of the Industrial Revolution were full of catalyst inventions. The water mill led the way, followed by the mass production of iron and then steel. More catalysts came with "machining tools" (industrial tools for cutting, boring, and grinding rigid materials), factory-scale papermaking, petroleum refining, and synthesizing chemicals. Prior to commercial electricity, the revolution had been powered by the catalyst invention of steam power.[37] Widely adopted in the late 1700s mainly for mining, coal-fed steam engines were gradually invented to be more compact, efficient, and self-contained. They could sit in a building's basement or power an entire ship. The steam engine fundamentally changed transportation, and enabled factories to produce far more things that were used in people's everyday lives.[38] By the eve of the Second Industrial Revolution in the 1870s, steam power had largely replaced waterpower in every industry.

But, given time, every catalyst invention is overtaken by the next. By the start of World War I in 1914, commercial electricity had replaced steam power in most manufacturing tools and machines.[39] Factories powered by steam had to be organized around a central shaft that powered gears and belts; with electricity, individual stations could be set up by the needs of each step in the manufacturing process. "Steam-powered factories had to be arranged on the logic of the driveshaft," the economist Tim Harford has written. "Electricity meant you could organize factories on the logic of a production line."[40] Most famously, Henry Ford reimagined mass production for the Model T. In 1913, he installed the first moving assembly line, arranging workers at individual stations based on the logic of the engineering process, maximizing the efficiency of the 32,000 machine tools used in production. Then, moving vehicles on conveyor belts to workers ready in their places, Ford's factory reduced the time to produce one Model T from 12 hours to under 2 hours.[41]

THE AGE OF PLASTIC

When the biplane reached 2,500 feet, Adeline Gray climbed out of the cockpit. The wind ripped around Gray's body as she gripped the vertical struts that bridged the two wings. She stepped farther out onto the plane's wings. For a moment, she studied the lush grassland below. She found her target: a group of 50 US Army officials standing at the edge of Brainard Field in Hartford, set along a gentle bend on the Connecticut River. Gray took a breath and let go, falling to the earth.[42]

On that summer day in 1942, the United States was already in crisis.[43] Having entered World War II, the country desperately needed to expand its industrial capacity to support soldiers in Europe and the Pacific. Silk, for example, was needed to make parachutes, but the global conflict had disrupted supply chains. In the 1930s, the US had consumed four-fifths of the world's silk, with 90 percent of it arriving from Japan—now an archenemy. The US Army frantically sought a replacement material.

46. Adeline Gray was the first person to jump from a plane using a nylon parachute.

For millions of years, humans had to make things from whatever nature produced: wood and stone, ores and minerals, animal fats, bones, skins, and sinew. But with the Industrial Revolution, chemists began to create brand-new substances made from scratch—substances that nature had never engineered.

Some of the first inventors in this area turned to plastics. Plastics describe a range of materials that are made from polymers: long, repetitive molecules, strung together. "You take a simple organic molecule and you react it with itself again and again and again," Andrea Sella, a chemistry professor at University College London, once explained. "A little bit like a bicycle chain, you attach one link, and you click on the next one and the next one and the next one, almost ad infinitum."[44] In fact, polymers are found in nature. Most woods contain an abundance of cellulose, a polymer, which makes it so pliable. Natural rubber is another example.[45]

For millennia, however, these materials remained largely unchanged from their natural state when crafted into objects. This history changed course in 1855 when Alexander Parkes, an English inventor, received a patent for a material that combined chloroform and castor oil. The result was a malleable liquid that hardened into a desired shape: buttons, jewelry, pens, brush handles. The first human-made plastic had been created—though Parkesine never became commercially viable.[46]

In 1869, two brothers, John and Isaiah, of Albany, New York, sought to win a $10,000 prize to find a substitute for ivory, as elephant populations had dwindled from overhunting. The Hyatts invented celluloid, as they named it, by combining cellulose from cotton fiber with camphor under heat and discovered a plastic similar to Parkesine that could easily be colored and molded: a replacement for ivory, horn, linen, and tortoiseshell, which were used for a wide range of domestic and industrial items.[47]

The story of plastics took one of its biggest leaps in 1907, when Leo Baekeland created the first fully synthetic plastic—combining a waste product of coal tar with formaldehyde. It had no natural molecules at all.[48] This was the first time that humans were entirely unconstrained by what nature produces. Now people could manufacture their own materials in any place and time—to both creative and destructive effects.

Bakelite was invented for electrical insulation, which it did well, but it could also be molded into nearly any shape and size, opening an infinite vista for manufacturers. And Bakelite could be molded more easily, cheaply, and quickly than celluloid—it was used to make everything from bracelets to telephones to pencil sharpeners to clocks to lamps to radios to dice to gun handles. Within several decades, more synthetic plastics followed: polystyrene for insulation, vinyl for raincoats, plexiglass for windows.

In 1920, the DuPont Fiber Company was formed. Its researchers set out to discover artificial fibers similar to rayon, which was another new and profitable synthetic material.[49] Using a "pure science" approach—focusing on fundamental principles rather than on trial and error to solve a problem—in 1928, the company hired Wallace H. Carothers, a lecturer in organic chemistry at Harvard University. After years of research led by Carothers, in 1938, DuPont began construction in Delaware of the first production facility to manufacture their new material: nylon. Although it had a range of potential uses, DuPont honed in on a single market: ladies' stockings. During its first week on the market in 1940, more than four million stockings were sold.[50] By the end of the year, another 60 million pairs were rolled onto women's legs.[51]

When the US entered World War II, manufacturers pivoted to find ways to support—and profit from—the war effort. DuPont partnered with the Pioneer Parachute Company, which had its roots in silk mills founded in 1838 in Manchester, Connecticut. The scientists and engineers developed a strong yet elastic parachute from nylon. They tested the new parachute on dummy payloads but would need a test subject to prove that it could safely deposit a person from a plane to the ground.

Growing up in Connecticut, Adeline Gray was fascinated by parachutes. "I used to take an umbrella and jump off the hayloft holding it over my head like a parachute," she once said. "But I ruined many umbrellas."[52] At 19 years old, she began parachuting. She also earned her pilot's license. She was hired by Pioneer and DuPont to pack parachutes. When they needed a test subject to prove the artificial material could be controlled just as well as silk, Gray eagerly accepted the opportunity. When she safely arrived on the ground from the plane in 1942, the army officials in attendance were convinced. Production began. By the end of the year, Pioneer was the world's largest producer of synthetic parachutes. Nylon use was soon expanded to make glider tow ropes, aircraft fuel tanks, flak jackets, shoelaces, mosquito netting, and hammocks. When 13,000 Allied paratroopers leapt to take France in 1944 on D-Day, they carried parachutes and other gear made from nylon.[53] Nylon became "the fiber that won the war."[54]

During World War II, plastic production in the United States soared by 300 percent from prewar levels, as the material was used in nearly every machine of war. At the end of the war, plastic manufacturers suddenly needed to pivot back to a domestic market. As one plastics executive noted about the consumer market: "Virtually nothing was made from plastic and anything could be."[55] Industrial designers reimagined an Age of Plastic.

In plastics, designers had found a cheap material that was a byproduct of oil refining, more malleable than steel or wood, and was entirely novel to consumers who saw it as a symbol of freedom and a future carefree world. The most famous example was DuPont's Tupperware—food-storage containers made from polyethylene that had previously been used to insulate cables and radar devices.[56] Polyethylene quickly spread to other kitchenware and to toys and packaging. In the coming years, plastic became the ultimate catalyst invention, augmenting or replacing countless catalyst inventions before it. As the science writer Susan Freinkel wrote in her 2011 book, *Plastic: A Toxic Love Story*:

> In product after product, market after market, plastics challenged traditional material and won, taking the place of steel in cars, paper and glass in packaging, and wood in furniture. . . . By 1979, production of plastics exceeded that of steel. In an astonishingly brief period, plastic

had become the skeleton, the connective tissue, and the slippery skin of modern life.[57]

Billions of tons of nylon fiber and resin have been produced globally.[58]

Understanding plastics is essential to understanding the exponential growth of things after World War II. However, plastics is just one material in the broader global movement toward industrialization. After the war, many parts of Europe were in ruins, and much of the rest of the world was still under the yoke of Europe's colonial exploits. But with the world in tatters, Europe began to rebuild while many of its colonies won their independence. Economic development became a collective global agenda, with institutions such as the World Bank financing massive infrastructure projects, and both capitalists and communists vying for influence by propping up industrial expansion. The end of World War II pushed the Third Industrial Revolution into full throttle.

By 1950, the United States, Europe, and the USSR dominated global industry, although raw materials and large-scale manufacturing were being developed on every continent.[59] Drawing on a long tradition of

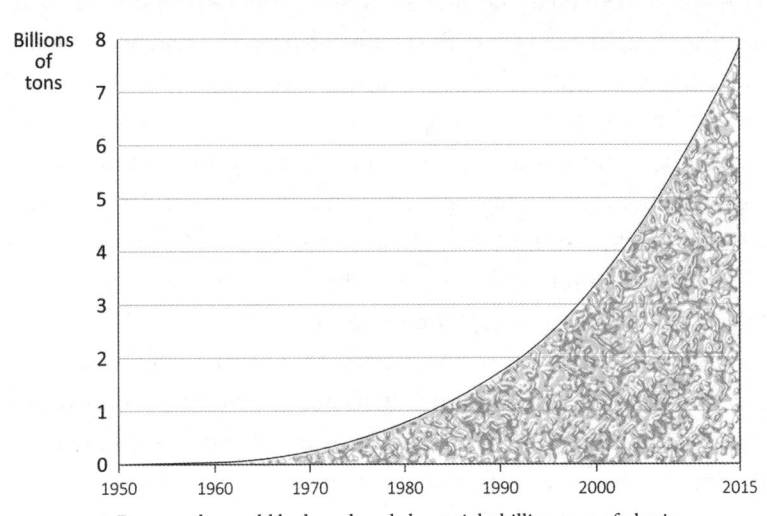

Cumulative global plastics production, 1950 to 2015

47. By 2015, the world had produced about eight billion tons of plastic.

invention, they continued to bring revelatory products to market.[60] Gradually the vast global trade networks, integrated banking systems, regional military and political alliances, cheap labor, and infrastructure investments resulted in economic expansion elsewhere. Due to automated manufacturing, which required low-skilled labor, and materials such as plastics that could be produced anywhere, countries such as Japan, Israel, India, the Philippines, China, and Brazil, rose to industrial power—and then, through the development of formal education systems, contributed their own industrial inventions. The rising global industrial system not only provided a countless range of new products to line the shelves of stores, but would also generate a far-reaching transnational, even near-global culture of consumerism.

SLATER MILL'S GIFT SHOP

On a bitter cold morning in the fall of 2019, I arrived at Old Slater Mill National Historic Landmark, on the banks of the Blackstone River in Pawtucket, Rhode Island. Waiting for me was Keith Johnson, looking professorial in a corduroy jacket. Keith was to take me on a tour of the mill that had launched the American Industrial Revolution.

As we walked up to the old mill, Keith recounted the story of Samuel Slater's upbringing and his stealthy flight from England, pretending to be an agricultural worker, taking with him little more than the inner workings of the Arkwright machine hidden in his mind. The heart of the mill was a long, spacious room, with tall windows and wooden floors and ceiling. Spread around it were a handful of reconstructed machines: the Arkwright machine, joined by a Carver cotton gin, a throstle spinning frame, and others. The room was sparse and bright and clean. Standing by one machine was a mannequin of a small boy holding a ball of raw cotton, alerting visitors to the child labor that fueled the Industrial Revolution's first decades. We rang a massive bell that had been added to the building's crown. We went down to a functioning reconstruction of a massive waterwheel, powered by the slow eddies of the Blackstone River.

Like any museum tour, mine ended in the gift shop. Having been away from my family for a time, I thought I would get them something. There was a lot to choose from. Packed along the walls and shelves were lines of books, sweaters and shirts promoting the mill, yoga mats and water bottles, postcards and magnets, hats and towels, keychains and mugs, and bags and jewelry and candles and more.

The contrast gave me pause. The historical mill was nearly empty; the mill's gift shop was stuffed. How ironic that the mill itself should be so sparsely furnished when this very factory had led humanity to a world of sweaters, yoga mats, magnets, and plastic everything—everything that was in the gift shop.

Standing there, wondering which of these plastic souvenirs my wife and daughter might enjoy, I realized that factories and the things born from them are only half the story of abundance. What exactly was prompting me to buy something?

I realized that the other half of the Industrial Revolution's story is desire.

8

A MATERIAL WORLD

In the summer of 1946, ready to move on from war and its depravations, 30,000 American women lined up in Pittsburgh's East Liberty neighborhood. A rainstorm swept through, but the women didn't budge, holding newspapers over their heads and sharing umbrellas. Day turned to night. The women stayed put. The police arrived: women pushed them away and offered to kill any man who joined the line. Two women got into a fight, pulling hair and scratching each other's faces. Only when midnight arrived did the line dissolve, thousands of women returning home crestfallen. The shop selling nylon stockings had sold out.[1]

Since their invention, DuPont's nylon stockings had been among the hottest commodities in the United States. Women loved that they were difficult to stretch and tear—nylon, it's said, was inspired by the phrase *no run* spelled backward—and easy to clean.[2] Following Adeline Gray's parachute jump, nylon fabrics were diverted to the war effort. Some women resorted to rayon or cotton stockings, but all disliked how they sagged. Millions of women were left with bare legs.

During the war, a black market developed for nylon stockings, and already in 1942 there was a riot in Manchester, New Hampshire, when a department store announced it had 240 pairs.[3] The next year at a war bond rally, the famed American actress Betty Grable auctioned off a pair of her nylons for $40,000. In 1944, a DuPont representative pledged that as soon as Hitler had been defeated and nylon was no longer needed for parachutes and other materials, the company would produce nine pairs of stockings for all of the country's 40 million women.[4] When Hitler finally did fall, DuPont's production couldn't live up to the promise; stocking shortages continued to plague America's department stores.

In January 1946, some 25,000 ecstatically screaming women lined up outside Macy's in New York to purchase the store's first shipment of nylon stockings since the war had begun.[5] The next month, Macy's sold another shipment of stockings at a rate of 10,000 pairs an hour, until police turned back a mob of thousands. In April, police cancelled a nylon sale in San Francisco that attracted 15,000 women. "We want nylons!" the crowd chanted as they threw vegetables taken from a nearby market and broke a shop window.[6] In May, more than 5,000 children lined up in Brooklyn, snarling traffic for hours, to buy nylons in anticipation of Mother's Day.[7] More nylon riots erupted in Georgia, Michigan, and Washington, DC.[8]

The desire for things goes back to the first stone cutting tool. After all, if the tool were not desired, it would not have been created, used, and passed between generations of australopithecines. Similarly, the first sculptures, weavings, houses, and clothes were made precisely because they were craved, coveted because of their function or for the wonder, beauty, or meaning they inspired. In short, things are made because they are desired.

People have likely wanted to have things easily and accessibly, to have as many of them as possible, since the beginning of things. For millions of years, material affluence was limited by just a few types of things that hominins had invented. Once more kinds of things arrived—particularly with farming and urbanization—for thousands of years, humans were limited by small classes of consumers with disposable income, the scale of production in manufacturing, and the problems of storage, transportation, and networked distribution. The First Industrial Revolution began to temper these limitations. By the Third Industrial Revolution, essentially all these technical and practical limitations had been overcome.

Even still, postwar industrialists faced a fundamental problem:

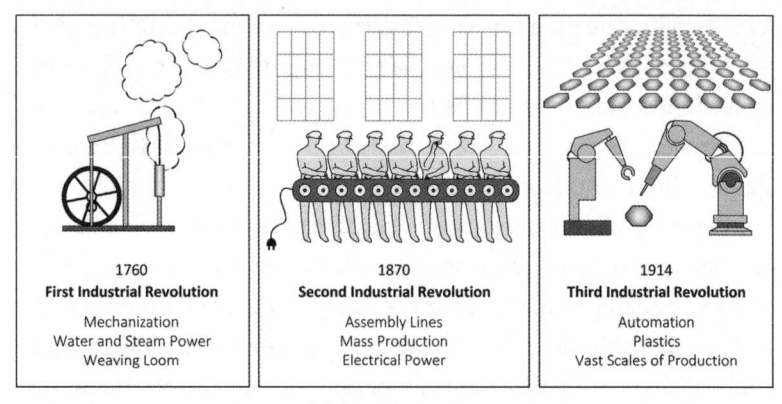

1760	**1870**	**1914**
First Industrial Revolution	**Second Industrial Revolution**	**Third Industrial Revolution**
Mechanization	Assembly Lines	Automation
Water and Steam Power	Mass Production	Plastics
Weaving Loom	Electrical Power	Vast Scales of Production

48. Many historians divide the Industrial Revolution into three parts, each starting in 1760, 1870, and 1914 with the onset of World War I. Note that the dates and features of each shift vary by historian, and some place us today in a Fourth Industrial Revolution, driven by computer technology, artificial intelligence, and big data.

although they could manufacture far more, far faster, and distribute things farther than ever before, production was only half the equation. The other half was consumption. Supply needed demand.

Those who had something to sell needed people who wanted to buy. Yet, once people had their basic needs met, what would prompt them to want more? Industrialists would need to create material abundance as well as help foster an ideology of abundance and a society of consumers who valued not things that lasted but the chance to buy more things. They needed tens of thousands of women willing to wait in long lines for hours in the rain and into the night, to curse and fight and riot over disposable pairs of $1 nylons.

BRANDED PROPOSITION

I left New York City's Hell's Kitchen in a taxi on a bright, cool autumn day in 2019, heading due west through the Lincoln Tunnel, thick with traffic, and into New Jersey. Skyscrapers surrendered to suburban strip malls and big-box stores. An hour later, I arrived at a set of large industrial, red-brick buildings encircled by a high barbed-wire fence. I called Lenny DeGraaf, and he soon appeared in his crisp olive uniform. DeGraaf opened the gates to the Thomas Edison National Historical Park.

In 1887, Edison opened this laboratory in West Orange, New Jersey. By then Edison was an international celebrity—renowned for advancing the telegraph, lighting, and electricity—and could have coasted to a comfortable retirement. Instead, he wanted to keep inventing. He stocked the lab with thousands of materials and tools and hired a team to help develop more trailblazing technologies. Edison and his crew's inventions were an unquestioned success. By the end of Edison's life, his experiments would lead to more than a thousand patents. Yet, Edison would learn that creating things and selling things were altogether different.

DeGraaf, a National Park Service archivist, and I sat down in a quiet office. He was warm and welcoming, with fantastic knowledge about everything Edison.

"He's a key figure in the late 19th, early 20th century," DeGraaf started our conversation, "in the emergence of the mass consumer market." He explained that for centuries, most markets were local or regional at best. However, by the late 1800s, railroads, steamers, and telegraphs linked vast distances, creating the possibility of national—and then global—markets for consumer goods. "But it wasn't obvious to everyone when this strategy emerges," DeGraaf added, "that you could actually make money by making things in high volume and selling them at low unit prices."

This was the problem facing Edison with the phonograph. He had come up with a revolutionary invention. In that historical moment, a voice-recording machine was "astonishing to people," DeGraaf said. "Prior to that, the spoken word was ephemeral—it just disappeared." But Edison was in some ways a better magician than businessman; it would take him longer to figure out how to make money from the phonograph than it took him to invent it. As DeGraaf explained, "The phonograph doesn't transition from that technological, scientific marvel to a widely used commercial product for some 15 years."

Edison's 1877 version of the phonograph was not a practical instrument; the tinfoil was delicate; the thing was difficult to operate; the sound quality was poor; the recording was impossible to store for a long period of time. So, in 1878, one of Edison's business partners decided to sell not the machine, but the experience of it. He launched an exhibition business, charging people to hear the phonograph. For a time, this was profitable. Then the novelty wore off. "What's the next thing?" people asked. Edison moved on to electric lights.

A decade later, prompted by the development of Alexander Graham Bell's competing graphophone and Emile Berliner's gramophone, Edison revisited his experiments on the phonograph in his new West Orange Laboratory in New Jersey. In 1887, Ezra T. Gilliland, Edison's friend and a partner, recorded that the "plan [was] to make a small compact instrument suitable for office use."[9] The next year, after a series of improvements, an investor purchased the rights to sell the phonograph. The goal was to capitalize on the expanding American market for office equipment, which had more than doubled between 1879 and 1889.[10]

The venture failed. The Edison phonograph was simply not designed well enough to work as a dictation machine in an office: The cylinder cracked and got stuck. Wax shavings from the cylinder clogged the machine's moving parts. The machine was heavy, clumsy, and complicated to operate. The phonograph's batteries were so erratic as to be nearly unusable.

The phonograph seemed destined to fall to the silent depths of history, until an unexpected turn. In 1889, while businesses were returning scores of failed phonographs, Louis Glass of the Pacific Phonograph Company invented an attachment that allowed patrons to listen to a prerecorded musical cylinder upon inserting a nickel—a jukebox. The new machine was tested in San Francisco's Palais Royal Saloon. It was an instant hit. By the summer of 1891, there were more than 1,200 coin-operated phonographs across the United States.[11]

Edison quickly pivoted and created his own music studio, but then gave it up over complaints about quality. In stepped the Columbia Phonograph Company—the seed of Columbia Records—which produced recordings across a range of musical genres. Other recording

49. An advertisement for the phonograph in 1899 points to its most celebrated use: playing music.

companies soon followed.[12] People started to buy phonographs and musical cylinders for themselves. The phonograph had finally found its market: not the drone of men dictating, but the melody of banjos and violins and arias. By the start of the new century, the phonograph could be found in homes around the globe, laying the foundation for the multibillion-dollar modern music industry.[13]

The phonograph is a perfect example of how inventors and investors of the Second Industrial Revolution were learning that it was not enough to make something spectacular, or to assume they knew how best things could be used. They would have to invest much more energy in selling.

Pundits such as Ronald A. Fullerton have observed that modern marketing did not arrive suddenly but slowly over 500 years.[14] Its origin can be linked to the rise of capitalism and colonialism in early modern Europe, with the extraction of new resources from Asia, Africa, and the Americas. A rising merchant class promoted luxury goods to the nobility and to a growing middle class in cities.[15] They did this through a structure of warehouses, wholesale trade, fixed retail shops, written advertisements, and traveling salespeople—the backbone of modern enterprise.

Between the mid-1700s and early 1800s, the First Industrial Revolution advanced these marketing practices. Railroads and shipping expanded markets geographically, while more people were concentrated in urban centers. Increasingly, businesses had to decide who their customers were and design products to appeal to them. In London, the first advertising agency opened in 1786, and there the modern department store flourished in the mid-1800s. This was joined by department stores in Sydney, Paris, Cape Town, New York, Montreal, and beyond, which created crammed marketplaces that dazzled customers with a cornucopia of endless modern goods.[16] Businesses intentionally sparked the "propulsive power of envy," as the Australian historian Kerryn Higgs has written.[17] Initially, the new fashions and luxury items offered with every new season were targeted to the upper classes, as it was feared that the "unleashing of the acquisitive instincts" in the lower ones would trigger aspirations to upward mobility.[18] But the economic potential of the masses eventually proved irresistible.

The mid to late 1800s was marked by the development of a marketing superstructure. Distribution networks expanded; factories accelerated outputs. As a result, Fullerton writes, "mass production required mass stimulation of demand."[19] Mail-order shopping thrived, laying the foundation for online shopping a century later.[20] Retail shopping moved from small family shopkeepers selling local goods to corporate-owned stores with flashy displays to entice customers, offering goods from around the world, with a singular drive for profit. The physical distance from the place of production to the place of consumption required sophisticated ways to find and sustain customers. No longer was someone spurred to buy something because their neighbor made it: a handmade table, a jar of jam, a knitted blanket. A fully modern approach to marketing developed: industrialists analyzed markets, designed products for specific segmented audiences, branded and packaged items for them, promoted items through advertising and direct sales, and created extensive wholesale-to-retail pipelines.

The kind of marketing that famously surfaced in the wake of World War II—the "mad men" of the TV show—accelerated and refined methods and strategies developed over centuries. As products became standardized (for example, one company's dish soap functioned just as well as any other), businesses had to work harder to distinguish themselves from competitors and convince consumers their product was singularly superior. Marketers became a professional class, essential to nearly every business, to develop products, decide prices, and plan distribution.[21]

In the 1950s, advertisers became especially adept at creating a "branded proposition" that convinced consumers of a product's performance and that also resonated emotionally.[22] Not only did a product need to outperform the one next to it on the shelf, but it also needed to speak to consumers, enhancing their sense of self and view of the world. Sophisticated survey, testing, and statistical measures were used to anticipate how customer segments would respond to particular ideas. For example, DuPont hired the sociologist John Dollard to analyze the scripts of *Cavalcade*, a television show it sponsored, to anticipate how it could sell certain products depending on each episode's themes and resonances for viewers.[23] They could now determine if a show set in a rural location could be used to sell agricultural products.

What changed after World War II, then, was the intensity of advertising and its application as a science. The first companies that excelled in branding, such as Kraft and Lipton, could charge more, sell more, and expect customer loyalty for a lifetime.

THE DEPENDENCE EFFECT

> Consumer sovereignty ... is now the highly contrived consumption of an infinite variety of goods and services.
>
> JOHN KENNETH GALBRAITH

By the end of 1946, DuPont faced a problem: after a year of production, nylon stocking manufacturers finally caught up to their orders. In part, what fueled the nylon riots in America was stockings' scarcity. Now there were plenty of nylon stockings available for any woman who wanted a pair (or nine pairs). Nylons were no longer selling themselves. DuPont was desperate enough to manufacture scarcity. When the stockings first went on sale in Britain after the Second World War—due to ongoing shortages and the need to attract tourists—retailers could sell them only to "foreign visitors," who had to show their passports upon purchase.[24]

Despite these challenges, in the end, DuPont was lucky. As Susannah Handley recounts in her 1999 book, *Nylon: The Story of a Fashion Revolution*, DuPont's marketers had a perfect item to sell. "The first completely synthetic fibre, nylon," Handley explains, "was a material without a past or an identity."[25] The advertising industry initially focused on convenience, performance, and economy as selling points. But, in a time when science was revered, marketers also dwelled on nylon as a "miracle" fiber that would contribute to a utopian future being created by chemists and engineers.

The housewife was the primary target of DuPont's advertising. With millions of men returning from war, it was thought that women needed to be "re-domesticated."[26] DuPont could help. The company's prewar slogan, "Better things, for better living—through chemistry," was revived with new vigor.[27] The idea was that the new inventions from DuPont were not just technological improvements, but improvements in living itself. Prospering—*happiness*—could be bought through things.

DuPont made this pitch through every available medium. The company opened showrooms and bought rivers of ads in print, radio, television, and film. From 1946 to 1972, DuPont published *Better Living*, where they "highlighted the durability, low cost, style, and freedom associated with its synthetic fabrics, most notably nylons."[28] The stories trickled down to other outlets and out into public life—for example, when a 1947 issue of *House Beautiful*, a popular women's magazine, was devoted to "Plastics: A Way to a Better More Carefree Life."[29] Companies such as DuPont were coming to realize that the most successful marketing did not merely *satisfy* needs but *created* them.

In *The Affluent Society*, published in 1958, the economist John Kenneth Galbraith looked at the relationship between production and consumption. Many of Galbraith's colleagues in the 1950s assumed that the production of goods reflected the wants of autonomous consumers; that, because humans are never fully satisfied, production will always grow. Galbraith believed this may be true for impoverished societies—those whose basic needs are not yet met. But something else was happening in affluent societies, he thought.[30]

Up to World War I, factories in Europe and North America were producing more kinds of products, and more of each kind, each year. By one estimate, US industrial production increased by more than 1,000 percent between 1860 and 1914.[31] Most people were having their basic needs met: food, water, clothing, shelter. A brief economic downturn in 1920 led companies to wonder if they were facing a crisis of overproduction. (They were.[32]) Perhaps people simply did not *need* to consume more. So, companies turned to manufacturing not just goods but also the *desire* for them. As Edward Bernays, a pioneer of the public relations industry, wrote in his 1928 book *Propaganda*,

> Mass production is profitable only if its rhythm can be maintained—that is if it can continue to sell its product in steady or increasing quantity. . . . Today supply must actively seek to create its corresponding demand. A single factory, potentially capable of supplying a whole continent with its particular product, cannot afford to wait until the public asks for its product; it must maintain constant touch, through advertising and propaganda, with the vast public in order to assure itself the continuous demand which alone will make its costly plant profitable.[33]

The economic growth of the 1920s was rudely cut short by the Great Depression—the perfect storm of financial speculation gone wrong, economic growth overly dependent on credit and consumer confidence, faulty economic policies, and national tariffs that backfired. But while the economic downturn was horrific for many individuals and businesses around the globe, they recovered as government interventions propped up and accelerated industrial production. When the United States entered World War II in 1941, industries were primed—as elsewhere, such as the United Kingdom and Germany—for increasing production further still. According to the economist Robert J. Gordon, the amount of industrial equipment produced in the United States between 1941 and 1945 was more than double what existed in the country in 1941, "and was more modern, and hence more productive, than the old equipment."[34] The industrial practices that flourished in the 1920s accelerated during the Great Depression, and were perfected during the war—notably, with the labor of women working in factories. This led to nearly exponential growth in many industries in the 1950s, when Galbraith was considering what prompted people to consume all these new goods.

Galbraith acknowledged that many consumption patterns arrive *passively*. People copy the behaviors of those around them. They tend to conform to social norms. People instinctively seek status through things.[35]

But consumption is also driven *purposefully*—through product

US Industrial Index 1800-1914

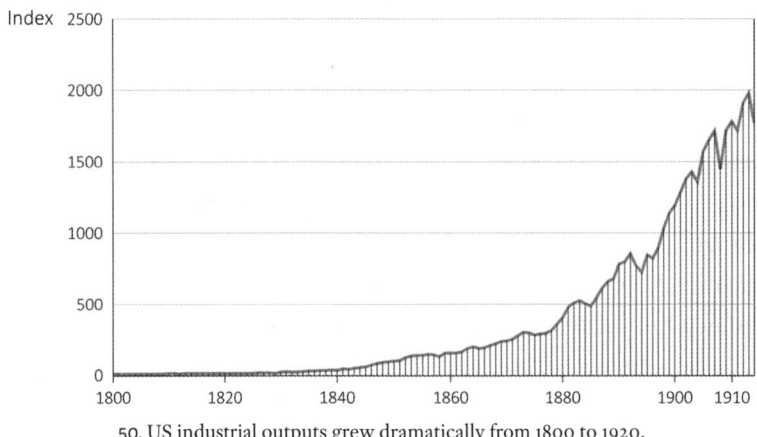

50. US industrial outputs grew dramatically from 1800 to 1920.

development and advertising. In the postwar industrial period, in many places there was a superabundance of goods. As a result, companies had to foster people's *wants*, the desire for things. While often targeted at basic human needs, such as transportation or friendship, companies strove to find ways to convince consumers that certain products could uniquely bring deeper gratification. A Ford Mustang would get a person from point A to B, but also make them cool and have more friends.

The more things an affluent society produces, the more it sets a value on things to advance a perceived high living standard. In 1950s America, for example, no longer was it enough to just have a home. Americans soon wanted bigger houses, with a bedroom for every person, a dining room *and* a living room with stylish carpeting, all equipped with a washing machine and a vacuum cleaner and a toaster, and a car (or two) in the driveway. Once consumers purchased all these things, they should have obtained a high living standard, their wants satisfied. But, of course, industrialists did not then stop producing new waffle irons and bathmats and everything else. So, the consumer (now theoretically satisfied) had to be convinced that in fact they were unsatisfied, and that just buying a bigger house, a better vacuum cleaner, the next model car would finally bring them happiness. As the American economist Hazel Kyrk—worrying over "underconsumption" and "oversaving"—argued in 1923, "A high standard of living must be dynamic, a progressive standard."[36]

Galbraith called this the "dependence effect," in which "production creates the wants it seeks to satisfy."[37] In other words, production precedes wants. The abundance of things drives the *desire* for more things—a never ending cycle of consumption. "The more wants are satisfied," Galbraith wrote, "the more new ones are born."[38] Galbraith likened this process to a mouse's wheel, always spinning without ever moving. The more things an affluent society produces, the more it must work to convince people to consume them.

The purposeful manufacturing of wants was the work of modern advertising. Galbraith described how, by the Third Industrial Revolution, it was regarded as "elementary" that there is a fundamental link between investing in producing goods and "synthesizing the desires for that production."[39] As early as the 1890s, industrialists and inventors began to grasp that their success lay in not merely selling their products' high points. Instead, they began to sell the idea that their products would lead people to a better life.[40] Business executives of Galbraith's time admitted as much: the DuPont vice president J. W. McCoy told his colleagues in 1949, "A satisfied people is a stagnant people, and business will have to work to ensure that people are never satisfied."[41]

Galbraith has remained an intellectual giant because so many of his explanations have been supported by new research through the years.[42] Advertisers cannot force people to buy things. But advertisers can prime or activate people to consume by convincing them that their needs can be satisfied with a specific product—a shampoo will make you beautiful. Furthermore, we know that consumption does not make people happier. For example, studies have shown that as a country increases its levels of income and consumption, self-reported levels of happiness do not increase over time. Similarly, at an individual level, research shows that after people rise past poverty, happiness does not follow over time.[43] Bruce Hood, a professor of psychology, has explained that modern consumption is a common human problem of "miswanting"—a misdirected belief that things will bring us what we truly need.[44]

Such miswanting is not a byproduct of modern consumption but a central feature of it. Companies have less to gain by actually making their consumers happy and much to gain by their discontentment. If you are happy with your looks and believe you are beautiful, you will be less motivated to buy the latest cosmetics or clothes. By keeping people insecure and unhappy, marketers motivate people to consume. As Charles Kettering, the general director of General Motors Research Laboratories, wrote in 1929, "If everyone were satisfied, no one would buy the new thing because no one would want it."[45] It's notable that Kettering's framing for the article, titled "Keep the Consumer Dissatisfied," is a friend's complaint that marketers had enticed him to buy a new car when the old car "ran like new" and he still had payments due on it. Still, the friend eventually traded in his "old" car and lost money on it.[46] That people often lose money on investments or go into debt to obtain prestige through things—fancy cars, bigger homes—only leads consumers to further despair, which, advertisers hope, people believe can be repaired by buying yet more things.

Consumption does increase production, which leads to more jobs and hence a rise in income in the short term for many workers. However, as workers' income increases, so does their desire to achieve a higher living standard and to emulate those better off. As a result, workers soon increase their own consumption. Many are thus liable to become indebted. With debt, workers are not able to save and invest. Inequalities widen. Additionally, as Galbraith pointed out, as societies grow into consumer societies, they tend to focus on building wealth in the private sector rather than investing in the public sector, prioritizing the rise of individual affluence over the health and well-being of all.[47]

CONSUMER SOCIETY

In early 1790, George Washington's secretary, Tobias Lear, wrote a letter to a Revolutionary soldier in Philadelphia. "The President wishes to get a carpet of the best Kind, for a Room 32 by 22. A Tea-Green ground with white or light flowers or spots would suit the furniture of the Room," Lear explained. "Carpeting would perhaps answer better than a Carpet—as the former would be made to fit the Room exactly." Lear was decorating Washington's new home at Mount Vernon. The president wanted wall-to-wall carpeting.[48]

In the late 1700s, carpets were a luxury in America. They were expensive, and the best had to be imported from Turkey or England. Most people made do with straw mats or cheap Scottish carpets in their homes. Carpeting had become such a symbol of wealth and power that when the US Senate chamber was opened in 1790, it included a monumental 22-by-40-foot hand-knotted carpet, woven through with patriotic symbols—a large eagle and 13 stars.[49] By the time George Washington moved to Mount Vernon, floors covered with carpeting signaled a wealthy and prominent homeowner.[50] Carpets were a form of *conspicuous consumption*, the term coined in 1899 by the Norwegian American economist and sociologist Thorstein Veblen, to describe the practice of buying expensive goods less to satisfy needs and more to display wealth.[51]

As textile mills flourished, the new technology was put toward manufacturing carpets. In 1834, US mills churned out a million woven

51. The large, elaborate 1790 carpet that covered part of the first US Senate floor was a sign of the new country's promise of exorbitant wealth.

square yards of carpet, which increased eightfold each year within several decades. Much of this carpeting served to decorate homes wall-to-wall, as a way to hide poor quality wooden floors as well as for insulation, dampening noise, and comfort. However, by the late 1800s, varnished hardwood flooring became trendy, with the idea that construction materials should not be hidden. The industry switched to creating accent rugs and carpets to add color and texture to rooms—becoming a decorative addendum in middle- and upper-class homes. By 1923, US mills were producing 83 million square yards' worth of carpets a year.[52]

The fortunes of the US carpeting industry shifted with the industrial boom of the years following World War II. DuPont's scientists developed bulked continuous filament nylon. The new fiber was as durable as wool and as inexpensive as cotton. The lustrous nylon yarn could take on any color and be produced with a perfectly even height. The new carpets, now affordable for everyone, offered the perfect solution to covering floors in America's postwar housing boom. As DuPont did for nylon stockings, the company launched a major campaign to promote the synthetic carpet's practicality while emphasizing its luxurious cachet.[53] The American journalist and social critic Vance Packard observed how such campaigns worked on the minds of consumers. He wrote in 1959 in *The Status Seekers*:

> They want to put some sizzle into their messages by stirring up our status consciousness.... Many of the products they are trying to sell have, in the past, been confined to a "quality market." The products have been the luxuries of the upper classes. The game is to *make them the necessities of all classes*. This is done by dangling the products before non-upper-class people as status symbols of a higher class. By striving to buy the product—say, wall-to-wall carpeting on installment—the consumer is made to feel he is upgrading himself socially.[54]

To this observation, the Australian historian Kerryn Higgs adds, "Though it is status that is being sold, it is endless material objects that are being consumed."[55] Tufted carpet sales of 6 million square yards in 1951 rocketed to 400 million square yards by 1968. Now practically anyone could be like George Washington and enjoy the symbol of wealth and opulence under their feet.

That carpet does not merely have practical functions, such as keeping a floor warm, but can be sold for its symbolic value speaks to the long history of meaning. As discussed in leap 2 of this book, symbolism is what makes art and religion and money and gifts—as well as wall-to-wall carpeting—possible. What profoundly caught hold of humanity's imagination in the 20th century, and what ultimately constituted the third leap, was the application of this symbolic thinking to the superabundance of stuff. Consumerism became a dominant behavior because it came to embody the values of liberty and democracy. In the early 20th century, we see the convergence of material affluence and the ideology of affluence.[56] We now had not only a world overflowing with stuff, but a belief that a world overflowing with stuff is good.

This convergence is the cultural world of a "consumer society," a society whose behaviors and beliefs pivot on mass consumption.[57] By purchasing goods, we construct our lifestyles and identities.[58] Underlying a consumer society is a capitalist embrace of constant expansion and profit as social progress. Advertising, as noted, plays a central role in constructing the images of the ideal life, but branded propositions are buttressed by our affection for technology and novelty. In a consumer society, consumption is a part of nearly every element of people's lives, particularly leisure time; shopping itself is considered an enjoyable pursuit. In one survey, Americans reported shopping as their second favorite leisure activity (after watching television, which itself promotes consumption through ads and product placement).[59] As early as 1955, the marketer Victor Lebow said: "Our enormously productive economy demands that we make consumption our way of life, that we convert the buying and use of goods into rituals, that we seek our spiritual satisfaction, our ego satisfaction, in consumption."[60]

Shopping is part of our emotional lives, how we express happiness or hope or anger—or even patriotism, as when President George W. Bush and other leaders encouraged Americans to go shopping and travel immediately after the catastrophes of 9/11.[61] Buying stuff is an

Global consumption expenditure, 1970 to 2018

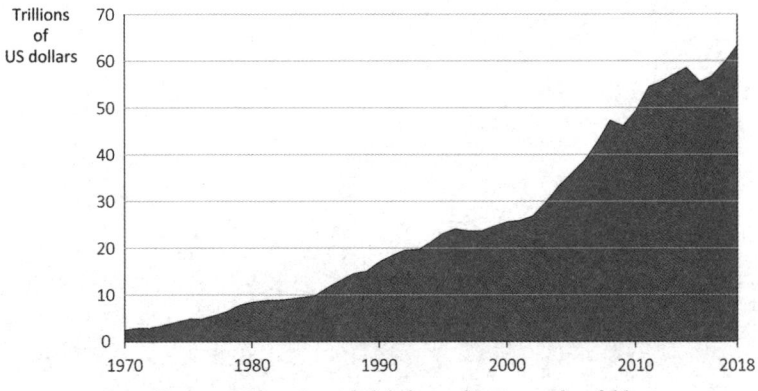

52. From 1970 to 2018, total global spending jumped 25-fold.

expression of friendship, personal ethics, and love. Consumption shapes our psyche through the stresses of trying to keep up.[62] The shopping mall is the emblem of the consumer society, but in this form of social organization, consumption appears at every opportunity—even in the most inappropriate places, such as the National September 11 Memorial & Museum in New York City located at Ground Zero, where nearly 3,000 people died.[63] In this world, consumption is how people define their affiliations and community, and also their individuality. With every new purchase, a consumer can signal their identity, class, and sense of self to the world.[64] Consumption is an active form of relationship building—among things, society, and the world.[65]

As consumers purchase things and come to see themselves inhabiting the ideals of the brands they wear and use, consumers themselves become a kind of commodity that markets the brand to those around them.[66] A consumer *society* (a group of people) is thus fundamentally shaped by consumer *culture* (a way of life). Over the last 500 years, a singular set of worldviews has become apparent around both the practices and ideas of consumption. As the historian William Leach puts it in his 1993 book, *Land of Desire*, "The cardinal features of this culture were acquisition and consumption as the means of achieving happiness; the cult of the new; the democratization of desire; and money value as the predominant measure of all value in society."[67] This is a

53. The National September 11 Memorial & Museum at the site of Ground Zero in New York allows visitors to mourn the dead—and buy some souvenirs.

totalizing set of worldviews, set in a complex web of meanings. As culture, consumerism is always on the move, always shifting with the capricious tides of values and taste. Even wall-to-wall carpeting can make a comeback.

Wall-to-wall carpeting expanded in the late 1700s, waned in the Victorian period, and surged again in the 1950s with the development of nylon fibers ready made for the carpets of the postwar housing boom. Wall-to-wall continued to be popular until the late 1990s, when it was again seen as overdone, passé. In the first two decades of the 2000s, in the United States, carpeting went from 60 percent of floor-covering sales—such as wood and tile—to 30 percent.[68]

Wall-to-wall seemed doomed until just the last few years. This change is largely due to "early adopters" who are embracing "grand-millennial décor"—millennials who favor the modern twists on traditional design, or "granny chic."[69] Residential carpet sales are up.[70] In a few years, global carpet and rug sales are projected to be more than $40 billion.[71]

PLANNED OBSOLESCENCE

After visiting Slater Mill, I took a short taxi ride to downtown Providence and the campus of the Rhode Island School of Design, one of the best art and design universities in the world. I made my way into a plain building and up to the sixth floor where I found a shared open space with a plethora of objects—clothes irons and vacuums and radios—that told the history of the Industrial Revolutions. There I met Matthew Bird, handsome and dressed in black, with a bass voice that exuded energy. Bird is a designer and professor at RISD. We sat down to talk. I had come to Bird to learn how consumer society is not *necessarily* wasteful. It is possible to imagine a form of consumption that is thoughtful and careful, making abundance that is sustainable. Instead, that modern wastefulness is planned by designers and learned by consumers.

"Earnest Elmo Calkins," Bird began. "Do you know who he is?"

"I don't," I admitted.

"Calkins ran an ad agency in the '20s," Bird explained. "And he wrote, in 1932, 'What Consumer Engineering Really Is.' It was the first written thing that laid out the trajectory of planned obsolescence as an intentional economic pathway."

After working as a copywriter for nearly a decade, in 1902, the pioneering adman formed the Calkins and Holden advertising agency. In 1905, Calkins and Holden published *Modern Advertising*, what many consider to be the first textbook in the field, while Calkins became known as the "Dean of Advertising Men."[72] In the 1920s, his firm operated at the cutting edge of the field, being the first, for example, to print packaging in color. "Partly because they could now technologically print in color," Bird said. "But he also realized that it had a crazy powerful emotional appeal. He understood the psychology of need and want and was well positioned to write about that." When Bird assigns Calkins's 1932 essay, he added, "it's the only time my students get really angry and come to me to say, 'We need to talk about this.'"

Calkins defines "consumer engineering" as a "business tool" to shape "a product to fit more exactly consumers' needs or tastes, but in its widest sense it includes any plan which stimulates the consumption of goods." He begins by summarizing the economic conditions of the Great Depression, how people stopped buying, "restrained by fear and misplaced thrift," which resulted in closed shops and shuttered factories.[73]

Calkins then explains how in the previous generation, manufacturers simply made goods and told the consumer, "Take it or leave it." But they learned that customers could be enticed by making things beautiful and cultivating a sense of taste. The next step for advertisers, he argues, was "obsoletism." This was to be done by changing styles. "Clothes go out of style and are replaced long before they are worn out," for example. But that is not enough. "That principle extends to other products—motor-cars, bathrooms, radios, foods, refrigerators, furniture. People are persuaded to abandon the old and buy the new to be up-to-date, to have the right and correct thing."[74]

Bird's students are often upset not merely at the cynical attempt to engineer people's consumption; it's Calkins's cavalier attitude to the consequences. Calkins rhetorically asks, does this strategy result in "sad waste"? "Not at all," he answers, arguing to the contrary that "wearing things out does not produce prosperity, but buying things does. . . . We have built up a complicated industrial machine and we must go on with it, or throw it into reverse and go backward."[75]

Calkins emphasizes the need for more things that turn from product to waste: "Goods fall into two classes, those we use, such as motor-cars or safety razors, and those we use *up*, such as toothpaste or soda biscuit[s]. Consumer engineering must see to it that we use *up* the kind of goods we now merely use." Calkins means that industry must make cars and razor blades disposable. He concludes by giving marching orders to his colleagues: "Would any change in the goods or the habits of people speed up their consumption? Can they be displaced by newer models? Can artificial obsolescence be created? Consumer engineering does not end until we can consume all we make." This is the ideology of abundance laid bare.[76]

Calkins has not been alone in his approach to obsoletism. For years, the bicycle industry changed the style of its products without any technological improvements. But the approach was first perfected in the early 1920s when Alfred P. Sloan Jr., then an executive at General Motors, proposed changing the outward appearance of GM cars, initially the Chevrolet, in order to get customers to buy the latest model. Henry Ford, GM's main competitor, was reluctant to make yearly models because he believed in design integrity and simplicity. GM pounced, changing the appearance of their cars without any substantive improvements. Its ad team worked each year to make not only Fords look outdated, but its own previous models too. GM did this to encourage Chevrolet owners to trade in their used cars for new ones, to trade *up*, as the Canadian social critic Giles Slade wrote, echoing Calkins, "to offer graduated product lines that encouraged customers to enter a new class of prestige and comfort each time they made a trade."[77] Within seven years, GM surpassed Ford in annual sales. Sloan called this strategy "dynamic obsolescence."

The practice spread across industries; the core idea adapted to different concerns. In 1932, Bernard London, an American realtor, tweaked the phrase *planned obsolescence* to argue that the government should legally impose obsolescence on personal items to stimulate the economy during the Great Depression.[78] London's phrasing gained prominence in 1954 when the American industrial designer Brooks Stevens gave a talk at an advertising conference titled "Planned Obsolescence," which he defined as "instilling in the buyer the desire to own something a little newer, a little better, a little sooner than is necessary."[79]

Soon after, industrial designers were put on the defensive, as the journalist Vance Packard's popular 1957 book, *The Hidden Persuaders*, attacked manufacturers for manipulating consumers and creating false wants.[80] Industry defenders acknowledged that "phony obsolescence," done as a gimmick, was wrong, but argued that if it was *planned*, then it could lead to real improvements and allow recently replaced items to find their way to secondary markets and thus become affordable to lower classes.[81]

Bird explained to me that industrial designers have discovered different types of planned obsolescence. The first is changing styles—"I

Shop With A Chevrolet

for Economical Transportation

CHEVROLET

Chevrolet Utility Coupé is proving a wonderful help to many housekeepers, more than paying its low cost of upkeep through economies of time, and money saved in cash-and-carry shopping.

Shopping that once employed a tiresome half day, can be accomplished with ease and pleasure in an hour with the Utility Coupé. The big rear compartment holds all the bundles and packages that would make up a week's supply.

Our Free Shopping List Pad can be had from the nearest Chevrolet dealer. Hang it in the kitchen. Check articles to be bought. Tear off top sheet when you go shopping. When one pad has been used up, any dealer will be glad to give you another.

The Chevrolet Utility Coupé is also a great favorite with women for social and general purposes. Every family needs a closed car of this type and quality.

Chevrolet Motor Company
Division of General Motors Corporation
Detroit, Michigan

Dealers and Service Stations everywhere. Get free list for your State from any Chevrolet dealer.

Applications will be considered from high-grade dealers only, for territory not adequately covered.

Prices f. o. b. Flint, Michigan
Superior 2-pass. Roadster . . . $510
Superior 5-pass. Touring . . . 525
Superior 2-pass. Utility Coupé . 680
Superior 4-pass. Sedanette . . 850
Superior 5-pass. Sedan . . . 860
Superior Commercial Chassis . . 425
Superior Light Delivery . . . 510
Utility Express Truck Chassis . . 575

54. The 1923 Chevrolet is often cited as an example of planned obsolescence because its restyled body covered a nine-year-old mechanical technology but was sold as new and "superior" (one model's actual name).

just don't like the way that looks anymore," as Bird described it—as Sloan did with automobiles. Changing styles is particularly a driver of the fashion and clothing industry. Known as "fast fashion," today about 80 million items of clothing are sold around the world each year.[82] A 2015 study of 2,000 British women age 16 and over found that the average "fashion buy" was worn just seven times, while 33 percent considered the item "old" after wearing them three times or fewer.[83]

But changing styles applies to many manufactured goods—especially personal use electronics that are status symbols. Packard called this "psychological obsolescence," which he defined as products that are "designed to become obsolete in the mind of the consumer, even sooner than the components used to make them will fail."[84]

"Another form of planned obsolescence would be technical," Bird told me. Most modern consumers will have experienced this form, even if they didn't know the name for it. Common practices include using cheap parts so that the item breaks easily (common for toys), preventing repairs (such as a digital watch that's sealed so users can't access the internal mechanism), making batteries fail early and/or difficult to replace, requiring continuous development without maintaining older systems (such as stopping updates to older operating systems or programs in electronics), and programming obsolescence (such as printer cartridges that are programmed to stop printing at a low level, even though they still contain more ink).

Many of these strategies have been around a long time. For example, in the 1920s, lightbulb manufacturers conspired to make them burn out after just a thousand hours, when the original incandescent lightbulb could shine for decades on end.[85] Some have even suspected that nylon stockings—made from material strong enough to make parachutes—over the years were engineered to run more easily and thus require more frequent replacement.[86] These strategies have been hugely successful. For example, surveys today show that when Americans' electronics break, they are more likely to buy a new one than even try to repair it.[87] While it could be argued that knowing goods will easily break or lose their value has stimulated technological advances, it's clear that engineering ingenuity could equally be focused on longevity—not how quickly a lightbulb could burn out but how long it could last.

Bird offered me a concrete example of how these strategies are often layered. He described how he'd just upgraded to a new, stylish Apple laptop, which came with a new plug. This plug is technologically better than the old one—able to go into four different ports and reversible in either direction. "They have improved it," Bird said emphatically. "What they haven't done is improve the transition to it. Because I should be able to use the old plugs I have for the next 20 years. There's no reason they couldn't make the computer cost $4 more and also have it receive the older technologies too. What Apple likes to do is force you to upgrade with them."

The reason, Bird suspects, is not that Apple can't include a transition but because it would make the laptop less sleek, less a Platonic ideal of what a computer should be. He suspects the designers don't want to do it merely because of style. "And that's the part I object to," Bird concluded. "I think that's stylistic obsolescence."

His only option was to buy a $75 adaptor. Or simply throw the old plug away.

THROWAWAY LIVING

A 1955 issue of *Life* presented a startling image of America's future. In the photo, a White, clean-cut young man and woman, and little girl, stand together with bright smiles next to a New York City trash can. Thrown up into the air are dozens of household items, falling like confetti.

"The objects flying through the air in this picture would take 40 hours to clean—except that no housewife need bother," the brief article accompanying the photo begins. "They are all meant to be thrown away after use."[88] The article inventories all the things that manufacturers have invented not to last, but to be thrown away after one use: vases and flowers, popcorn pans, frozen-food containers, napkins, baby diapers (partly credited for the United States' rising birth rates) and bibs, tablecloths, towels, plates, cups for beer and highballs, draperies, ashtrays, garbage bags, hot pads, mats, and even disposable duck decoys for hunters. A few more pictures follow, including a $1 plastic disposable feeding dish for a dog, a $2.98 pan with a foil lining that can be thrown away after a meal, and a barbeque grill for $0.79, complete with wire grill and asbestos shell.

This *Life* story encapsulates America's change to a consumer society, the embrace of both the abundance of things and the ideology of abundance. Perhaps inevitably, this vision for a consumer society led to the concept of throwaway living: constant, thoughtless consumption was enabled by things that were purchased to use only once or twice, and then be tossed. This mode of living must have been appealing because it embodied the values of choice, leisure, and freedom from labor. It was embraced as a way to improve anyone's life. As Earnest Elmo Calkins wrote, "The way to break the vicious deadlock of a low standard of living is to spend freely, and even waste creatively."[89]

Through the miracle of modern manufacturing, Americans—and everyone else in the world—could anticipate a better life: more stuff with less work. Today Americans throw out 20 billion disposable diapers a year.[90] About 40 billion plastic utensils are made globally each year.[91] In 2017, the world purchased 1 million plastic bottles *every minute*.[92] Fewer than 7 percent of those bottles were recycled, leaving most destined for landfills or dumped in our oceans. A scientific team at Ghent University in Belgium estimated that the average European shellfish consumer eats about 11,000 microplastics per year.[93] Since the 1950s, some eight billion tons of plastic have been produced globally[94]—more than one ton for every person on Earth today. That's the equivalent weight of more than 800,000 Eiffel Towers. Only about a third of that plastic is still in use. More than half has been trashed. Some 6 percent has been recycled.[95]

What is even more amazing than the throwaway living our world has created is that even with it, too many people are still living with too much. People are literally drowning in their stuff.

9

TOO MUCH OF A GOOD THING

On the morning of March 21, 1947, police in Harlem received a mysterious phone call. A man, falsely giving his name as Charles Smith, said there was a dead man at 2078 Fifth Avenue.[1]

A patrolman was sent to the address. He knocked. No one answered. He couldn't pry open the front door. A backup squad was called in. Using axes and crowbars, they finally opened a grill door covering a basement window but found the passage completely blocked by floor-to-ceiling stacks of neatly wrapped newspapers. They forced open the rear basement door and were confronted by a wall of junk. A cold rain fell on a crowd of 600 people, who had gathered at the footsteps of the infamous Collyer house.

The Collyer brothers were known in New York as the "Hermits of Harlem." Homer, the elder, was a lawyer, but being blind and stricken by severe arthritis, depended on Langley, a pianist and engineer by training. The well-heeled brothers grew up in the house and inherited it when their mother died in 1929. The year before her death, the family had stopped using gas and electricity. They already no longer used a telephone. In the years that followed, they refused to let anyone into the 12-room mansion. As their eccentricity gained notoriety, they were hounded by authorities—and thieves, who had heard rumors that the brothers had hidden millions in cash in the home.

When the fire department arrived that day in 1947, they set a ladder against the upper floor. The windows were all locked shut.

55. Inside the Collyer brothers' mansion, a breathtaking array of junk covered the entire floor and was piled up on every open space.

Finally, Detective John Loughery busted his way through a window and disappeared into the house. A few moments later, he returned to shout down.

"There's a DOA here!" Dead on arrival.

A medical examiner arrived and determined the deceased was Homer. The police began to search for Langley—a difficult proposition, since the front door was blocked by books and mounds of other stuff. In the basement, they tried to push past piles of rubbish that included thousands of used cans and bottles, and so much more that it boggled the mind. On the upper floors were narrow passageways among piles of newspapers and other debris—a broken sled, an automobile seat, Christmas cards, a folding car, piano parts, and two black hats. In the mansion's rear, they found cans rigged with wire, which would raise the alarm and pull down piles of junk on top of any unwanted visitor.

In the days that followed, police continued to search for Langley, believing he may have been hiding in a secret tunnel. Each day, thousands of onlookers gathered at the mansion as police cleared the junk—a litany of 20th-century consumption. One day's reported clearing included a rusted bicycle, a small radiator, a doll, a bag, a chair, a bedspring, a stove, a checkerboard, pianos, dressmaking forms, posters of pinup girls, 2,500 books, countless newspapers, letters and legal documents filling eight crates, toy cars, women's hats, curtain rings, lead pipes, and an opera program from 1914.[2]

The crowd struggled to make sense of the Collyer brothers' hoarding; the men were remembered fondly by many of their neighbors.[3] How was it, as one observer wrote, that "the lives of objects come to rule the lives of people; where any attempt to comprehend, distinguish, or manage possessions is outstripped by their proliferation beyond control?"[4] Was this some animal instinct gone awry? Did they have some singular psychological disorder? Or were they the victims of an emergent consumer society that asked its citizens to consume more and more and more?

From the vantage point of the 21st century, seeing our species' journey from scarcity to superabundance, it is striking that hoarding has become a central feature of the human experience. However, hoarding takes different forms; all acts of accumulation are not functionally, symbolically, and psychologically similar. Rather, "hoarding" exists on a continuum—as an animal instinct with clear purpose for survival, as a source of inequality and greed, as an expression of ownership, and, finally, as a psychological crisis. The point, then, is not to say that all types of stockpiling are equal, but that the accumulation of things (sometimes for good reasons, other times not) is a feature of humanity's relationship with things—and in its most extreme forms, of which many of us are a part, it is damaging to ourselves and our planet.

Finally, 18 days after the search began, Langley Collyer was found.[5] In one of the tunnels, he was wedged under a pile of junk, it seemed, asphyxiated by a crush of newspapers let loose by one of his booby traps. Authorities determined that Homer perished from starvation, unable to care for himself after his brother's sudden death. In the end, some 136,00 kilos of stuff were taken from the Collyer home.[6]

HOARDING SPECIES

The impulse to gather and accumulate is a deep animal instinct. A range of insect, mammal, and bird species are now known to hoard, making it clear that animals can be wise to welcome abundance when it arrives—and work to make abundance last by storing things for future use.

Squirrels are commonly recognized hoarders. They spend hours collecting food and stockpiling it every day.[7] Red squirrels, which evolved in evergreen forests, learned to survive lean months by protecting a territory and storing food in a big pile. Gray squirrels, which evolved in deciduous forests and facing more competition from other animals, bury their food in different locations (a behavior known as scatter hoarding), often carefully placing leaves and other cover over it.[8] Impressively, gray squirrels bunch their hoards by food type and can recall where all their stored food is based on smell and spatial location.

Other animals also depend on hoarding. The arctic fox, for example, which lives in the far north of North America, Greenland, Europe, and Asia, is a keen hunter of eggs. These foxes especially love snow goose eggs, during the brief time the birds nest in the north in the summer. Searching out unprotected nests, arctic foxes will raid an entire nest, first hiding eggs in a primary cache.[9] Once they have collected as many eggs as they can, the foxes will often move them to a secondary cache, where they can be stored up to a year, helping the foxes survive in scarce months.

Among the most spectacular displays of hoarding in the natural world is performed by the acorn woodpecker.[10] This bird, whose beautiful feather coat is midnight black with a snow-white belly and crimson crown, lives across the US West and down into southern Mexico. The woodpeckers are polyamorous, living in family groups of up to a dozen that maintain an acorn storage facility. Although acorn woodpeckers eat mostly insects, they gather acorns for winter when their preferred meal can be sparse. They find a tree or other large wooden surface, peck out round holes, gather acorns, and deposit them in the cavity. The acorns shrink as they dry, and so they must constantly be moved and rearranged. These "granaries" can have thousands of nooks. This strategy helps ensure that the acorns do not get moldy (as they would if piled up) and, because of their vertical arrangement off the ground, they are easier to defend from competitors. In one case, scientists weighed 485 pounds of acorns stored in the wood surface of a water tank in Arizona.

56. The acorn woodpecker's granary is among the most spectacular displays of hoarding in the natural world.

Hedgehogs, honeybees, ants, beetles, beavers, badgers, bears, blue jays, snowy owls, wildcats, possums, shrews, moles, mice, rats, hamsters, and still many other animals all hoard.[11] In nearly all cases, animals hoard food, either to save for later or, in a few cases, to allow the food to ripen—such as the tayra, a weasel in Central America, which picks green plantains, stores them, and then returns to eat them once they have turned yellow.[12] Such behaviors are assumed to be adaptations to the changing availability of food because of the seasons or other factors, giving certain animals an advantage even when food may be limited or unavailable. Food hoarding seems to have first evolved as a process for parents to provision their offspring.[13] The biologist Tom Waite has also suggested that hoarding is a way animals can demonstrate strength, vigor, and health to potential mates.[14]

Hoarding has benefits; it also has costs. Gathering items only to store them for later requires an immediate expenditure of energy with future benefits that may never be reaped. A red squirrel who is attacked by a coyote after an exhausting day of collecting seeds might do better eating as much as possible to have the strength to escape rather than saving up for the future. Also, many animals spend energy defending their caches. "Any creature that stores food faces myriad parasites and predators," Thomas D. Seeley, an animal behaviorist, once explained, "and every foe has a different set of tools for getting through the hoarder's defenses."[15] Honeybees, for example, must battle fungi and bacteria as well as ants and bears and people. Ultimately, biologists have theorized, hoarding is advantageous only when it leads to more successful offspring—and it's more advantageous to store foods than to raid the stored foods of others.[16]

In his seminal 1990 book, *Food Hoarding in Animals*, the biologist Stephen B. Vander Wall notes one type of animal with conspicuously little evidence for hoarding: the primate. A captive squirrel monkey was once observed hiding food. A green monkey once stored two golden apples—one being immediately taken by other monkeys, the other consumed as soon as they left the area. Some presume chimpanzees cache meat. But Vander Wall notes with puzzlement that given the *Homo sapiens* propensity for hoarding, one might assume it is an evolutionary trait that would be manifested in other living primate species.[17]

Perhaps more evidence will yet be found. But for now, strangely, it seems, humans either share some animal instinct for hoarding that has fallen out of evolutionary favor among other living primates—or our ancestral line uniquely adopted hoarding behavior.

NOT ENOUGH TO OWN

In Plato's renowned treatise, the *Republic*, written around 380 BC, he has his protagonist, Socrates, explore the relationship between justice and the good life. Through a long dialogue, Socrates and his interlocutors imagine the ideal city of justice, Kallipolis. Socrates envisions that the city will be protected by the guardians, a class of highly educated soldiers. Notably, the guardians live communally and do not own private property. Plato's point is that this is necessary to avoid divisiveness and ensure that the guardians work in the common interest.[18]

It is difficult to imagine the guardians of Kallipolis being hoarders. Their collective ownership is a way to foreclose inequality, so they focus not on personal obtainment but on everyone's pursuit of *eudaimonia*—human flourishing. Put the opposite way: overconsumption requires a belief in private ownership.

The world would have been put on a different material trajectory if Plato's views had taken hold. Instead, they were soon challenged by his student, Aristotle. Aristotle argued that a society does better when people attend to their own business. In contrast to being enslaved, Aristotle felt, to be free was to be one's own person, in control of oneself. Personal possessions were an extension of a person's freedom, so long as they were managed by the virtue of self-control.[19]

In the 13th century, Thomas Aquinas, the Italian philosopher and Catholic theologian, extended Aristotle's view in the context of the church. He wrote that private property was good as long as it amplified a person's moral duties, such as the rich person's duty to the poor. Subsequent European philosophers, however, such as Thomas Hobbes and David Hume, departed from the constraints of the Christian faith. They framed private property as a mere social construct. In nature, things are not owned. Rather, a society agrees what ownership is, which the state formalizes through laws.[20]

The English philosopher John Locke, writing in the late 1600s, was the perfect bridge between these viewpoints. Locke has been one of the most influential Western thinkers on property over the centuries. He began with the Christian concept of God giving the world to humankind. But, Locke puzzled, if the world is a gift to all people, then by what right can an individual claim some portion of the world as privately owned? Humans do this, he argued, by investing their own person, through labor, in things. As he famously wrote:

> Though the Earth . . . be common to all men, yet every man has a *property* in his own *person*. This no body has any right to but himself. The *labour* of his body, and the *work* of his hands, we may say, are properly his. Whatsoever then he removes out of the state that nature hath provided, and left it in, he hath mixed his *labour* with, and joined to it something that is his own, and thereby makes it his *property*. It being by him removed from the common state nature placed it in, it hath by this *labour* something annexed to it, that excludes the common right of other men.[21]

Western philosophers who followed debated these different stands. Immanuel Kant accepted the Lockean relationship between property and agency, but also acknowledged the social contract that many societies employ to decide who owns what and what is fair. Karl Marx focused less on individual attainment and more on the stages of a society in its relations to ownership. In its beginning stages, a society may embrace private property and the responsibilities that attend it, but eventually this will lead to a collectivist economy based on cooperative labor.

Of course, the concepts and terms of ownership have been developed far beyond the discourse of European philosophy. Cultural specifics define what is owned and what is not. And yet, the idea of ownership is nearly universal in the human experience, as are its broad categories. For example, many Native American societies similarly frame ownership, even though it has long been assumed that they hold only common rights to property—an assumption propagated as far back as Locke, with the implication that nomadic peoples did not own land because they did not work it.[22] The Hopi Tribe, in Arizona, for instance, traditionally holds that individuals can own things such as their house; that some things are collectively owned through the rights of villages and clans, such as farmlands; and that some religious

57. The Māori people of Aotearoa (New Zealand) hold sacred cloaks that are "inalienable possessions"; such an object transcends the individual who uses it.

things are "inalienable" — so sacred and tied to group identity that they are beyond ownership. These categories of private, collective, and inalienable are well embedded in my own mainstream American culture: I can own my house, but I'm only one of many owners of public US federal lands, and as an American I can't conceive of the sale of the original written and signed US constitution.

These concepts of ownership are the foundation for accumulating things. Only from the basis of control over things are people then free to pursue them. "It is not enough to own," as the psychologist Bruce Hood wrote, "but rather we pursue more stuff, because in doing so we are satisfying the urge to acquire."[23] In other words, the human concept of ownership is the foundation of human hoarding.

HUMAN HOARDS

In the fall of 2021, I drove from my home in Denver, to the University of Colorado, Boulder, to see a spectacular archaeological find. At the university's natural history museum, I met Douglas Bamforth, an archaeology professor.

Bamforth recounted how, in the summer of 2008, Brant Turney was running a landscaping crew not far from campus. Working on the front yard of Patrick Mahaffy, Turney put his shovel into the ground, and about 18 inches down struck a hole about the size of a shoebox. He inspected the strange void and pulled out a hidden treasure. Mahaffy was called and shown the discovery. He wasn't sure what to do, exactly, but ended up telephoning the university's department of anthropology. The next day, Bamforth went out to investigate.

Bamforth confirmed the find was a collection of 83 stone tools — one "core" for chipping off flakes, scores of flakes, one chopping tool, and eight finely made knives, flat and tear shaped, like big fallen leaves from a fantastical jungle tree. "I thought they were Indian artifacts from maybe 100 or 200 years ago," Mahaffy later said.[24] Mahaffy, collaborating with Bamforth, paid for a residue analysis on the stones. The results: on some of the tools was blood from sheep, bear, horse, and an extinct species of camel. The cache had likely laid buried for 13,000 years.[25]

Bamforth believes that the Paleoindian people who made the tools lived in small groups in the region. Most of the raw stone material came from what is now Colorado and next-door Wyoming. The cache was buried at the edge of a stream, placed in a sandy, coarse soil and covered by a dark, clay sediment. "It looks like someone gathered together some of their most spectacular tools and other ordinary scraps of potentially useful material," Bamforth theorizes, "and stuck them all into a small hole in the ground, fully expecting to come back at a later date and retrieve them."[26]

Because so much work can go into crafting tools, it is not surprising that toolmakers expend additional effort preserving them. Macaques in the wild reuse the tools they make.[27] Chimpanzees do too. One study by the biological anthropologists Crickette M. Sanz and David B. Morgan found that chimpanzees in the Republic of Congo reused wooden sticks for puncturing termite mounds more than half the time.[28] Similarly, in Guinea, scientists have observed chimpanzees reusing stone hammers and anvils—often several times, occasionally more than a dozen times—for cracking nuts.[29] The scientists interpret this as a near caching behavior, to reduce the amount of energy it takes to find the right raw materials (they are selective in the plants used) and to construct the tool.

Stone tools, which our most distant ancestors started creating more than three million years ago in East Africa, are uniquely suited objects for reuse. From the very first days of stone tools, it seems that our forebears realized that they are a kind of blank slate, open to nearly endless reuse. Studies of Oldowan tools, the technology that started about 2.6 million years ago, show that toolmakers were highly selective of the materials they quarried, transported across the landscape, used, and then reused—constantly sharpened by breaking off dulled edges.[30] Stone tools are never really "finished"; their potential for reuse is continual.[31] Initially, these tools could have been left in the open, waiting for their next use, as macaques and chimpanzees do.

But at some point, early hominins would have realized—perhaps even from watching food-hoarding animals—that they would do better to accumulate their tools when they had the chance, then store them for a later day. As our hominin ancestors invested more in a tool, the more energy and value expended on it, the more likely it would be protected. It is probable that hominins using the Oldowan technology applied the scatter hoarding strategy—*à la* the gray squirrel, to cache tools around a territory, ready for wherever an animal needed to be butchered or some tough roots needed to be processed.[32]

The hoard emerged as a human strategy. While it seems probable that our ancestral lineage long used hoards to hide tools and food, it is difficult to recover and study hoards. They are, by definition, often hidden, and even when a collection of items is found, archaeologists may be reluctant to label it as a hoard because the intent behind it can be hard to discern. Hoards become far more prominent in the archaeological record with the introduction of metals, in part because these are easier to find using metal detectors. Additionally, metal items—particularly in the form of weaponry and money—were highly valued items, transportable, and easy to hide. For many, the ground proved to be the safest bank.

Many hoards are presumed to result from people needing to hide their valuables when faced with a crisis, such as during riots or war. For instance, the Bredgar Hoard of 34 gold coins in Kent was likely buried when the Roman Empire invaded Britain in AD 43.[33] Archaeologists and metal detecting sleuths have found more than 1,200 hoards of coins in England alone. The Staffordshire Hoard is among the most famous.[34] Found by an amateur metal detectorist in 2009, the hoard is the largest ever recovered in England, comprising more than 600 gold and silver artifacts of religion and warfare. Archaeologists believe the hoard belonged to King Penda, who ruled Mercia, an Anglo-Saxon kingdom in central England, until his death in AD 665. They believe the hoard is loot taken from his enemies and then buried for safekeeping during this tumultuous period. In many cases, it's easy to imagine that the person hiding the valuables was hurt or killed before they could reclaim the buried treasure.

Still other hoards are thought to be ritual offerings—"votive hoards," left behind as gifts to unearthly powers. The archaeologist Richard Bradley has noted that hoards are known to have been deposited 20,000 years ago in southern Scandinavia. By 7,000 years ago, such offerings were commonly made throughout Europe, particularly in water—rivers and springs—and later at ceremonial sites and burial grounds made of huge, monumental stone. Bradley believes many of these offerings were related to fertility and food production.[35]

As the Roman Empire expanded, coins circulated more widely and became a common type of offering to the gods, in the belief that it was payment for their services. Similar practices have been noted around the world: the ancient Maya in Central America, Jains in India, and among Javanese in Southeast Asia.[36]

Throughout much of human history, this drive to accumulate has been tempered by scarcity. People had access to little, so they could accumulate little. After the Agricultural Revolution led to settled life, storage of large surpluses became possible, and necessary. As explored

58. In 10th-century England, Vikings buried hundreds of coins and other precious items, in what would become known as the Vale of York Hoard. Discovered in 2007, the hoard likely illustrates the practice of hiding wealth in uncertain times.

in chapter 3, debt became a feature of social relations, which in many cases led to social inequalities. These inequalities meant that some individuals could have access to more wealth than others. And nearly every human being who gained power garnered things—consider the palaces and treasuries of emperors and empresses, sultans, tsars, kings and queens. In a real sense, one can think of the wealth of the most powerful as both an act of *hoarding* and the possession of a *hoard*.

As civilizations made more stuff, covetous behaviors became more visible.[37] Hoards of valued objects found in China, the Middle East, India, and beyond, dating to thousands of years ago, all point to the ability of individuals to amass small fortunes and try to protect them. But while no doubt many aspired to have as much as they could, in many cultural contexts, the hoarder became reviled. One can hypothesize that such scorn led to the extravagant gifting rituals around the world, such as potlatches and giveaways. The scorn heaped on hoarders can be seen in myths around the world: in ancient Greece, dragons guarded treasures, as did griffins in ancient India and ants in Ethiopian tradition.

The Bible is filled with admonitions against greed, a prerequisite for some forms of hoarding (Ecclesiastes 5:10–11: "As goods increase, so do those who consume them. And what benefit are they to the owner except to feast his eyes on them?").[38] In AD 590, Pope Gregory I listed greed as one of the seven deadly sins, which were then elaborated in Dante's Inferno, where the fourth ring of hell is inhabited by hoarders and wasters.

For a number of centuries now, you do not have to be a conqueror to collect masses of things. Due to industrialization and the emergence of the consumer society, nearly everyone on Earth has access to markets that allow them to accumulate more than even some of the most powerful people in the ancient world. This is not to say that there is material equality today, but rather that for the first time in human history, hoarding is no longer a strategy of the elite; it has been democratized. In 2013, *Vanity Fair* ran a "pop quiz" that listed a string of items and then asked readers whether they belonged to King Tut's tomb or to the contemporary apartment of hoarders: "A large painting of pussywillows, a brown chair made from animal hide, stalks of live bamboo, a blue painted urn, dried bars of oats and grain, boxes of papyrus, a painting of a giant sun, woven wool fabric, another brown chair made of animal hide, skeletal remains of cat." The answer: they all belonged to two ordinary hoarders named Gordon and Gaye—demonstrating that, in some respects, the line between ancient king and modern accumulator can be razor thin.[39]

Building a collection—be it comic books or shoes—usually entails setting a goal and enjoying its pursuit, acquiring the most exemplary objects. In the collector, we can see the spectrum of our human relations to things. On one end is the most basic relationship: a desire to possess something of value. On the other end is the most fanatical desire unbound—when people become possessed by things. Today, the problem is that the distant human instinct to hoard food and tools, as well as the cultural behaviors that developed for small groups of the wealthiest, is not well suited to the Age of Plastic, built on the ideology of consumption.

DISPOSOPHOBIA

> They struck against each other, hapless souls,
> And then each wheeled around, with backward sweep,
> Crying: Why hoard ye? and, Why waste ye, fools?
>
> DANTE ALIGHIERI

While ancient hoards were gathered and collecting became a Victorian hobby, compulsive hoarding in domestic spaces appears to be a relatively new phenomenon.[40] An early mention occurs in 1842, in Nikolai Gogol's novel *Dead Souls*, which features a character named Plyushkin, who collects everything in his path:

> He walked about the streets of his village every day, looked under the little bridges and stiles, and whatever he came across—an old shoe sole, a woman's rag, an iron nail, a potsherd—he carried off and added to the pile . . . in the corner of the room.[41]

In *Bleak House*, first published serially in 1852, Charles Dickens describes a full-fledged hoarder, Krook, who owns a secondhand store and compulsively amasses bottles of every variety, rusted keys, rags, and discarded legal papers that he cannot even read, being illiterate.[42] In the 1893 story "The Adventure of the Musgrave Ritual," Sir Arthur Conan Doyle describes Sherlock Holmes as a kind of hoarder of "chemicals and criminal relics," and as having a "horror" of destroying the accumulated papers that were piled in every corner of his room.[43]

These fictional characters seem to point to a growing anxiety about how consumption was seeping into the lives and homes of everyday people in industrial societies. In one literary analysis, Nicole Lobdell argues that "hoarders appear with greater frequency in periodicals and literature of the nineteenth century than in any previous time period."[44] Although hoarding is deployed as a symbol of greed, regarding concerns about new domestic spaces and other worries of the age, Lobdell's analysis posits that such depictions are a product of the new superabundance of things and consumption:

> The rapid social, technological, and economic developments of the nineteenth century changed the relationships between people and things. The rise of mass manufacturing during the Industrial Revolution meant that nineteenth-century consumers found themselves in a new world of cheap, readily available material goods. Hoarding was no longer economically necessary for survival. . . . More than mere nineteenth-century curiosities, hoarders are evidence of an instinctual urge responding to constant availability where, before, there had only been scarcity.[45]

In turn, the historian Daniel Lord Smail has argued that scholars are still pondering what exactly "triggered the growing prevalence" of compulsive hoarding but suspects that humans have always had the capacity for it.[46] What has changed is that for tens of thousands of years, almost every society had little access to things of value and what was of value was reused and recycled until it was no more. Only in the Industrial Age did it become possible to so easily possess and discard so much.

While the greedy miser has long been reviled in many societies, in the 19th century, such behaviors became directly linked to hoarding. It was first described as a psychological condition by the famed philosopher William James in 1893: "The hoarding instinct prevails widely among animals as well as among men." He gave as an example a Massachusetts man who filled his house with newspapers from floor to ceiling, leaving only "a few narrow channels between them."[47] In Russia, this condition became known as Plyushkin symptom, and over the years has enjoyed any number of names, including the Collyer Brothers syndrome.[48] As hoarding became more recognized, it was also seen as increasingly problematic, implicating people in civil and criminal charges, allegations of animal cruelty, landlord disputes, and divorce and child-neglect cases.[49]

For some years, clinical psychologists categorized hoarding as an expression of obsessive-compulsive disorder. However, as the psychologists Scott O. Lilienfeld and Hal Arkowitz have discussed, research gradually showed that around 80 percent of people who hoard don't meet the OCD criteria.[50] Additionally, studies have indicated that hoarders are older, poorer, more prone to anxiety and mood disorders, and less likely to be aware of their affliction. Genetic studies and brain imaging also have shown different patterns for hoarders. In 2013, the fifth edition of the American Psychiatric Association's diagnostic and statistical manual (*DSM-5*) included for the first time "hoarding disorder," defined as "persistent difficulty discarding or parting with possessions, regardless of their actual value."[51]

An estimated 1 million people in Australia, 3 million people in the UK, and 19 million people in the US suffer from the disorder, with the numbers only rising.[52] But hoarding disorder is a global phenomenon affecting an estimated 2–5 percent of humanity.[53] A study of Japanese hoarders found the same underlying behaviors as elsewhere around the world, suggesting that the disorder is "a universal disease with consistent clinical symptoms."[54]

Two of the world's leading researchers on hoarding, the social worker Gail Steketee and the psychologist Randy O. Frost, have written how hoarders are just an extreme version, causing distress and disfunction, of what most of us have: an attachment to objects. After conducting detailed evaluations and studies of hoarders, Steketee and Frost have come to see how "the abnormality lies not in the nature of the attachments but in their intensity and extremely broad scope."[55] Surprisingly, their research shows that hoarders do not replace people with objects, but instead they use "possessions to make connections between people and to the world at large."[56] Hoarders experience an intense connection to things, where "every object is rich with detail."[57] We need to see things through the eyes of the person who holds them.[58]

In one telling example, Steketee and Frost worked with a hoarder named Irene, going through her mountains of stuff. They came across a scrap of paper with an unidentified phone number scrawled on it. Irene doesn't remember whose number it is; the psychologists set it on a pile to throw away. Irene resisted, then kept bringing it up, asking to save the scrap of paper, imagining the number holds some unknown importance. For hoarders, it is not that *nothing* has value, but that *everything* has value. Hoarders can't distinguish in the same ways as nonhoarders between things that are important and things that are unimportant.[59]

As a result, hoarders are prone to excessive acquisition because they see the value in everything. At the same time, they can't get rid of anything, because of its perceived value—a form of disposophobia. These behaviors are further driven by "fear of waste, the allure of opportunity, or the comfort and safety provided by objects."[60] After going through many hoards, Steketee and Frost have found that people with this disorder have trouble categorizing their things, trusting their decisions, and having confidence in their memory. Strangely, given the profound chaos and messiness of extreme hoards, interwoven into these issues is a tendency toward perfectionism. Hoarders want everything just so, and yet can't make that happen due to indecision and the safety blanket of things. Hoarding is like addictive gambling, an intense mix of pleasure and pain, comfort and torment.[61]

In 2009, the American reality television show *Hoarders* premiered. The series explores the tragedy of peoples' lives when their stuff

59. Modern hoarders can struggle with deep attachments to things, making it difficult to decide what to discard and what to keep.

overtakes them. More than a decade later, it is still running. The show has brought hoarding into popular consciousness while also, according to one study, increased the stigma attached to it.[62]

I suspect that the stigma appears because we are reeling in dread not from the strange, but from the familiar. A group of anthropologists studying American household goods argued that "we live in the most materially rich society in global history, with light-years more possessions per average family than any preceding society."[63] They found that in one of the smallest homes in their study, at nearly a thousand square feet, there were more than 2,000 visible items. In their study, 75 percent of homes had so much stuff in the garages that residents couldn't park their cars in them.[64] A 2015 survey found that 54 percent of Americans are overwhelmed by their clutter, and 78 percent have no idea how to declutter their lives.[65] Another study found that British homes have twice as much stuff as they did 30 years ago.[66] And while hoarders come in all varieties, we can reflect on how one California family that made the news was reported to the police for extreme hoarding, and eventually 8,000 pounds of "trash" were removed.[67] To compare, in the United States, the average weight of a household's goods when moving is 8,000 pounds.[68]

And what people do not keep, they absentmindedly throw away. As the journalist Edward Humes writes in *Garbology* (2012), the things and quantities that compulsive hoarders gather is "perfectly, horrifyingly normal." He points out, "It's just that most of us hoard it in landfills instead of living rooms, so we never see the truly epic quantities of stuff that we all discard."[69] What is largely different between hoarders and nonhoarders is more about the definition of their stuff as either trash or of value.

Consider this: if the Collyer brothers' mansion contained their accumulated lifetime of trash, then the amount removed equaled about 2,250 pounds per year. The average American today is not far behind, producing 1,800 pounds of solid waste a year—tires, furniture, newspapers, plastic cups, milk cartons, yard clippings.[70] The situation in the UK is somewhat better, at a thousand pounds per person a year. What separates people diagnosed with a hoarding disorder and those not is the emotional weight given to stuff and the compulsion to keep it all. But it's clear that many people today, whether hoarders or not, consume a ton of stuff. Most of us nonhoarders are just willing to throw it away, discarding things at the same rate we buy them. Either way, consumption is a problem. There's just the line between preserving and purging—not letting go and always remembering, or letting go and eagerly forgetting it all.

COLLYER BROTHERS PARK

On a beautiful late autumn day in 2019, I took the subway from my hotel in midtown Manhattan up to Harlem. A half hour later, I exited 125 Street Station and typed the address into my cellphone: 2078 Fifth Avenue.

After the Collyer brothers' death in 1947, their mansion was finally emptied with weeks of work. Only 150 items were worth auctioning; the rest was trashed.[71] The home was in such disrepair that it had to

60. The simplicity of Collyer Brothers Park in New York does not recall the chaos of the Collyer brothers' overstuffed mansion.

be demolished. The corner lot stood empty until 1958, when locals planted flowers.[72] In 1965, it officially became a park, and in 1998 was named in memory of Homer and Langley. In 2002, some petitioned to have it renamed, but authorities demurred. "Not all history is pretty," the parks commissioner explained, "and many New York children were admonished by their parents to clean their room 'or else you'll end up like the Collyer brothers.'"[73]

Collyer Brothers Park is a slender rectangle of land, the exact footprint of the mansion. Set against a towering beige apartment building, the park is enclosed by a pointed wrought-iron fence. I walked inside. Trimmed grass faded to packed dirt. Evergreen shrubs lined one side of the park; along the other side were well-tended potted plants. Some tall, graceful trees leaned over the sidewalk. Several benches were set at the park's end. I sat down to think.

Watching birds flit by, listening to the hum of the city, it struck me how sad that the Collyer brothers' pursuit of everything should turn to this: to nothing, a nearly empty space. But of course, this is the end for all of our stuff. When we die, our possessions are disconnected from us, resold or inherited for a time. Eventually every bit of it becomes waste. As an archaeologist, I am all too aware that everything, always, goes to ruin, an ever-receding trace of our time on Earth. But surely most everyone knows this. If you have ever cleaned out the house of a loved one or even just trawled a flea market, you know that fashion, value, and desire are fleeting. One person's cherished possession is another person's junk. We know this. Yet we live our lives as if we don't. As the psychologist Bruce Hood wrote,

> During our time on this planet, we fight for property, fence it off, covet it and feel that the goals of life come down to everything we can claim ownership over, only to die and return to dust and never know what becomes of the stuff we worked so hard to get. We spend our lives building sandcastles with turrets and moats to defend from intruders, only for them to be washed away by the waves of time.[74]

There in the shadow of the Collyer mansion, it struck me how we humans, at times, turn spaces of vast waste into parks — particularly the new movement to transform landfills into parks — as if the antidote to everything is nothing. It does make sense. Parks are mostly empty of stuff, but full of life. They are places to walk with a friend, hold a lover, play a game, or simply breathe.

As I sat in Collyer Brothers Park, I gazed up past the dancing leaves of the trees and into the glassy emptiness of the cobalt sky. Suddenly, my heart began to race. The question that had plagued me during this entire book project rushed to my mind.

I wondered: Can we live without stuff?

ON THE FUTURE OF THINGS

A CONCLUSION

One freezing cold morning, I drove past the outer edge of Denver, past Buckley Air Force Base, past the suburban neighborhoods huddled at the edge of the Great Plains. I saw rising from the prairie several low bumps, lifting from the horizon like icebergs. At first, I assumed they were natural hills. But barreling down the road toward them, I realized they were too angular to be natural. Arriving at their base, I saw they were encircled by barbed wire and knew I had reached my destination.

I pulled into the Denver Arapahoe Disposal Site, cutely known as DADS. I found the trailer where the tour was to start. I was part of a tour, arranged by a local reporter. Ten people gathered around our guide, Doc Nyiro, a DADS manager, middle age with the studious, geeky demeanor befitting an engineer. Nyiro began by telling us that DADS is open 24 hours a day, six days a week. Every day, 800 trucks arrive, culminating in around two million tons of refuse a year piled high. We watched the trucks pulling into the weigh station. "It just doesn't slow down," Nyiro said, "truck after truck."

Climbing into a van, Nyiro took us to an area where a new cell was being constructed: the foundation for a new mountain of trash. It was 25 acres and lined with clay and crushed glass to prevent the liquid that would gather as the garbage breaks down from leaking into the groundwater. Once completed, the cell will be filled with waste and reach 300 feet high within two years—each mountain of trash as high as the Statue of Liberty, Big Ben, or the Taj Mahal.

Once we saw how the cells start, Nyiro took us to an active landfill area. We joined the line of traffic, driving a steep, rough dirt road to the top of a hill. We parked at the top, and all got out of the van. I noted a scent vaguely like manure. We watched as a line of trucks stopped around us to empty out everything imaginable. "It looks like they just took all the contents of my apartment and dumped it here," a man on the tour said, not joking. The wind whipped trash into the air like snow as 100-ton tractors compressed couches and cookie boxes and everything in between into thick strata that contain the full record of modern life. The result: a dry tomb of waste that will endure for millennia. Standing there on the desolate hill, I imagined future archaeologists in the year AD 8000 prying open DADS, and like Howard Carter when he first gazed into King Tut's tomb, whispering in quiet awe, "Wonderful things!"

Nyiro moved on to an achingly small area of DADS dedicated to gathering recyclable and compostable materials. At the final stop, we visited an electricity plant, with old train motors powered by methane released from decomposing trash. The plant produces enough electricity to power 2,500 homes a year.

By the tour's end, I couldn't help but admire the landfill's efficiency, the engineering that goes into managing so much waste. DADS enables the endless cycle of consumption of my city to go on uninterrupted while reducing the chances of immediate environmental harm. But not every place has the resources to manage such monumental waste. Ghana, for instance, receives 1.5 billion tons of throwaway clothing from the United States each year.[1] The salvage market of America's low-quality "fast fashion" there is so overwhelmed that the bulk of garments end up in informal dumps, which, after seasonal rains, wash out millions of rotting, tangled pieces of clothing onto local beaches.

Yet, while grateful for the work of Nyiro and his colleagues, I felt nauseated. It is hard to stomach seeing what actually comes of our collective consumption—the waste that makes literal mountains, not to mention the waste of resources that are spent on dealing with it. Just this one dump was a perpetual-motion machine to manage a ceaseless flow of abandoned things, like trying to manage the ocean's tide.

A CONCLUSION   231

A feeling of dread took hold of me as I imagined not just DADS operating day and night for decades, but the thousands of other landfills around the world that, doomed like Sisyphus, cap off one mountain of waste only to start immediately on the next.

Mass consumption has brought numerous good things to the world. For many: jobs and financial wealth, physical safety and security. New ways of connecting, talking, and thinking. Easy travel to nearly anywhere in the world. Longer lives. Medicines that heal horrific diseases. Lights that keep the dark nights at bay. Music that can always play. Foods beyond the imagination of that first australopithecine who banged a rock into a cutting tool to feast on buffalo tartare.

But the costs have also been staggering. By almost every measure, extreme consumption is bad for people and the environment.[2] Obesity and economic inequality and the wars over nonrenewable resources have killed untold numbers. The steep increase in products in recent decades has accelerated pollutant emissions, deforestation, climate change. It has depleted water supplies and contributed to the rapid extinction of animals. There are vast "garbage patches" floating across the world's oceans, with infinite bits of microplastics working their way into food webs. Even if we accept the positives of mass consumption to date, we must acknowledge that the situation is unsustainable. Here is where the epic story of humanity's stuff has taken us, and left us:

1. The hominin invention of tools came from deep animal instincts.
2. Yet, through behavioral innovation, humanity began its own distinct trajectory with tools.
3. The minds and bodies of *Homo sapiens* have been fundamentally shaped by our use of things.
4. Many of the basic ideas and materials of our modern world are very old—in place as of 50,000 years ago.
5. The invention of one thing often entails the invention of other things to create it; humans are unique in their endless iteration of things.
6. The development of symbolic thinking transformed humanity's relationship with things, expanding the possibilities of what things could

do for the human imagination and human expression: art, religion, money, gifts, heirlooms, and much more.
7. The Industrial Revolutions created the possibility of extreme material abundance for billions of people around the world.
8. Abundance is not only about making more stuff, but is also an ideology of consumption.
9. Hoarding is an animal instinct that is often veiled in humans by what some consume and insist on keeping and what others consume and happily throw away.
10. Our world is overstuffed.

Our three-million-plus-year journey of stuff has led to this: a constant, insatiable desire for more stuff. If there is one trend in the business of being human that connects Olduvai Gorge to the modern shopping mall, it is the increasing dependence on stuff to mediate our lives—our desires and actions.[3] A desire that we know ultimately won't make us happy or better people. A desire that is a collective suicide, death by uninhabitable planet via stuff. And yet, we can't seem to stop ourselves.[4]

Or can we?

Perhaps we are on the cusp of stuff's fourth great leap.

STOP CONSUMING

The root of suffering is attachment.

THE BUDDHA

When Diogenes arrived in Athens, he saw a city in love with things.[5] After more than a century of clawing its way to power, Athens's economy and culture was booming. Surrounded by massive walls, classical Athens contained an array of buildings—temples and colonnades, theaters and stadiums. The most luxurious were filled with marble and bronze statues. The overflowing central marketplace, the agora, fed and clothed some 100,000 citizens with plentiful domestic goods such as fine ceramics and long-burning torches, and a cornucopia of exotic goods from lands near and far. Fine perfume. Perfect wine. The purest olive oil. Gleaming jewelry of every precious stone. The softest textiles for bedding. The most radiant art to garland the walls of homes, gorgeous statues to populate gardens. There were tradesmen selling refined clothing and sturdy shoes. Barbers and hairdressers made the rich beautiful with tonics and pomades.

Diogenes wanted none of it.

Born nearly 2,500 years ago in what is now Turkey, on the coast of the Black Sea, Diogenes fled his home after he (or possibly his father) defaced the local coinage.[6] He ended up before the Oracle at Delphi, who seemed to tell Diogenes that he must challenge the customs and values of the time. Diogenes arrived in Athens with an enslaved man named Manes, who promptly escaped. Diogenes shrugged, "If Manes can live without Diogenes, why not Diogenes without Manes?"[7] Diogenes proceeded to the temple of Cybele, where he moved into a large, discarded clay wine jar for a home.

A student of the ascetic philosopher Antisthenes, Diogenes resolved to shun all earthly pleasures, disdaining vanity and pretense. He lived as a beggar. He owned nothing but a wooden bowl until he saw a child drink water from his own cupped hands. Diogenes broke his bowl apart. "Fool that I am," he exclaimed, "to have been carrying superfluous baggage all this time!"[8] For Diogenes, true freedom could come only with freedom from things.

I took up a version of a Diogenesean challenge at the start of 2021. Having thought about the modern predicament of stuff for so long, I wanted to find a way to live with less. I was especially moved by John Kenneth Galbraith's argument that the crisis of the affluent society is not really due to limited resources or what to do with all our waste; the true crisis is the constant desire for more. "What of the appetite itself?" Galbraith asked in 1958 about consumerism, with echoes of Diogenes. "Surely this is the ultimate source of the problem. If it continues its geometric course, will it not one day have to be restrained?"[9]

At the start of 2021, my wife, our daughter, and I sat down for a family meeting to see if we could restrain our household's consumption.

I had been drawing inspiration from a range of so-called minimalists and wanted to give it a try. I had investigated Lauren Singer who lived a "zero-waste lifestyle" in Brooklyn, limiting her trash of eight years to so few items that they could fit in a single mason jar.[10] I'd read about a family of four in Los Angeles who had given up all plastics, even ordering a special toilet paper packaged without plastic wrap.[11] I had learned about Lara Joanna Jarvis, a mother of two in Hampshire, England, who didn't buy anything for a year and saved £25,000.[12]

"What could we do?" I said as I opened my laptop and pulled up a *Forbes* article (of all magazines) that provided a guide to a "no buy" year.[13] "How about this?" I asked.

My then nine-year-old daughter nodded in agreement. "I want to save the environment," she said. She didn't like all the boxes that things came in. "The environment matters because that's where animals live and the trees that are living too," she added. My wife eagerly subscribed to the idea. "And I want to be less consumerist," she said, "because sometimes you think you have joy out of things. But things don't bring joy." We were off to a good start.

Social commentators have noted a wide range of motivations for this strategic living: an aesthetic sense (when people like spaces with fewer things), sustainability (driven by concerns over the environment), thrift (saving money), mindfulness (wanting to be more intentional in one's life), and experience (when people are excited to try different lifestyles). So, for my daughter, the environment; for my wife, mindfulness. For me, I lean toward a minimalist aesthetic. But mainly I was exhausted by endless shopping and terrified by the possibility that our overconsumption was destroying the planet.

After a moment of silence, my wife reconsidered: "Okay, maybe a speaker that brings out music brings out joy."

She had a good point. Living without things is impossible. Even if Diogenes did not use a bowl to drink water, he still depended on a well to draw the water he drank. And things can give us experiences of joy. And things connect us to each other, our pasts, our identities. Even if we loathe some things for the destruction they bring, we love the things that make us who we are. After all, humans have long depended on our things. It is not easy to simply cut off a three-million-year-old relationship.

"What if," I improvised, "we don't do a *no-buy* year, but a *slow-buy* year? Besides necessities, we each only get to buy five things this year."

We considered this. I drafted a list of "approved items," not to be counted toward our five things: food, school and work items, health necessities, and car parts (if needed). We could accept gifts from others, though we'd discourage them. But if we purchased gifts to give, then it would count toward our five.

Everyone happily agreed.

But, after I closed my laptop, I began to think about all the things I wished I'd purchased before we arrived at this plan—another phone plug, a better automatic cat feeder, running shoes, sunglasses . . . maybe this was going to be more difficult than I'd imagined.

My family's effort was a version of minimalism, a growing movement in many consumerist societies to live with less.[14] Just as my family shifted to slow-buy, there exists a range of practices on the minimalist continuum. On one end are the extreme ascetics—people who dedicate their lives to abstaining from material satisfactions.[15] Diogenes is an exemplar. Many ascetic practices grow out of world religions. The Inca high priests of South America were expected to live an ascetic life: eat little, be chaste, and own few possessions.[16] Judaism includes a strain that carried over to Christian traditions. From Matthew 19:21: "Jesus answered, 'If you want to be perfect, go, sell your possessions and give to the poor, and you will have treasure in heaven. Then come, follow me.'"[17] St. Paul the Hermit and many others took up this charge, filling their lives almost exclusively with faith. Islam too, especially in the Sufi tradition, includes ascetics. Sects of Baha'i, Buddhism, and Hinduism all have strong ascetic practices. Some Buddhist priests, for example, are only allowed to possess eight personal items: three robes, a belt, a needle, a razor, a water strainer, and an alms bowl.[18]

Notably, in many traditions, asceticism is not really about *things*, but managing *desire*—as if these religious traditions anticipated and identified the heavy heart of our consumerist society. As Sri Baba Hari Dass, a yoga master and silent monk, wrote:

> The existence of [the] material world is only our desire. When humans wanted to run fast, they tamed a horse. When they wanted to go still faster, they made cars and trains. When they wanted to fly, they made aeroplanes. In the same way the material world is made by our desires. For those ascetics who are living in caves, there is no material world. A car is a heap of iron, tin and cloth for them.[19]

And yet, one does not have to be a Buddhist to grasp how attachment to the material world leads to our suffering. Asceticism is not limited to religion. Henry David Thoreau famously complained in 1854 that "men have become the tools of their tools."[20] He believed that material luxuries hinder rather than elevate humanity. Walking through Concord, Massachusetts, he was oppressed by the signs hung out to lure him into the dry goods store, jewelers' shop, barber, tailor, and shoemaker. He escaped these "dangers," he recounted, by walking briskly, keeping his thoughts on lofty topics, and suddenly bolting through the occasional hole in fences he passed.[21] For several years, he lived in a tiny cabin on the shore of Walden Pond.

Today's minimalism rarely goes to such extremes as those practiced by Diogenes or even Thoreau. The proposition is not to stop consuming but to consume less.

First are those who *refuse* to bring more stuff into their lives. A perfect example is the Jarvis family in Hampshire. Elizabeth Chai, a 40-year-old in Portland, Oregon, got rid of 2,020 possessions and didn't buy anything in 2020 except food, drink, and toiletries.[22] Others refuse to buy certain things, such as anything made of plastic, like the LA family. Others may give up single-use gadgets or fast fashion or things that just seem wasteful, such as paper plates.

Then there are individuals committed to the ethic of *reuse*, who throw away less and save items that would otherwise be tossed. In recent years, an app called Nextdoor has gained popularity: neighbors borrow tools, trade items, and give away things headed to the landfill. Nextdoor reports that it is used in 11 countries and in nearly one in three US households. Similarly, Buy Nothing, a social network group founded in 2013 and dedicated to the "gift economy" of sharing and loaning items that would otherwise be purchased or tossed, has a massively popular app.[23] Creative reuse is also central to Lauren Singer and others seeking a "zero-waste lifestyle," which requires reusing items (such as cloth grocery bags), borrowing others' items (such as wine glasses from a neighbor for a big party), and repurposing, or "upcycling," an item (such as turning wine corks into a countertop).

Finally, there are those who *reduce*, like my family's attempt at a slow-buy year. Some have reduced their possessions to just 100 things. The 2021 Netflix film *The Minimalists* challenges viewers to consider getting rid of one thing in the first month, two things in the second, three things in the third—and so on—selling, gifting, or trashing the items. Another version is the rise of a kind of "heirloom materialism," in which people try to purchase only items that will endure for many years—*planned perseverance* instead of planned obsolescence. Yet among the most famous examples of reduction minimalism is Marie Kondo's philosophy of "tidying up": fans are encouraged to declutter their homes, to keep only essentials and the things that mean the most to them.

My family's attempt to slow-buy for a year fell into this last category. My initial panic endured for a week. I kept coming across things that I "needed" to buy—sunglasses, a bouncy ball to play with my daughter after our favorite one got a hole, a new book, a gift for a friend who had a baby. Let it be said: I resisted all these temptations. I reminded myself to be grateful for what we had, and I found ways to make do. But then the COVID-19 pandemic hit, and suddenly, our small house became my office, gym, and vacation spot—the place where our family spent almost every moment of our lives. Hesitantly, we started house hunting.

By April, we had purchased a piano book for my daughter and a new bike for her too. A hole finally opened in the toe of one of my running shoes; I had no choice (I thought) but to buy a new pair. After all, my physical fitness depended on it. My wife bought two books as a gift to a friend.

Then things got dicey. Some permanent pens accidentally went into a load of wash with nearly all my clothes. Still, I resisted buying more clothes. But then, the next month, we saw a great house for us. We made an offer knowing—half accepting, half denying—that to make it our home, we'd have to buy a lot more than five things each.

When our "slow-buy year" was on the cusp of failure after just six months, I came across a harsh but hilarious screed against minimalism, written by Chelsea Fagan of *The Financial Diet* blog. Fagan levels multiple arguments against all forms of minimalism. She writes that it is classist, a fad for the rich, because people in real poverty don't have to worry about what not to buy, and because of how expensive "sustainable" and "heirloom" items often are. "'Stop wasting money on all that IKEA nonsense!'" Fagan imagined a minimalist saying. "'With this $4,000 dining table hand-whittled by a failed novelist in Scandinavia, you will never need another piece of furniture!'—which really just points to having enough disposable income to 'invest' in your wardrobe and surroundings." Furthermore, she derides the idea that a simple aesthetic and decluttering equals moral worth, a "fauxspiritualism." Every form of minimalism, Fagan concludes, "is just another form of conspicuous consumption, a way of saying to the world, 'Look at me! Look at all of the things I have refused to buy, and the incredibly expensive, sparse items I have deemed worthy instead!'"[24]

Others have pointed out that attacking consumption itself in order to solve the problems of overconsumption is unlikely to succeed. As we learned in the previous chapter, consumerism has become a symbol of liberty and democratic equality—in today's world, the idea goes, anyone can consume anything, and thus be turned into the person they want to be.[25] The symbolic glow of consumption cannot simply be turned off. Anti-consumer rhetoric thus becomes anti-freedom. And who doesn't want freedom?

Furthermore, people do love things. The anthropologist Daniel Miller spent 18 months studying how hundreds of people in South London interacted with their stuff. He found that people create relationships with the things around them, often just as profound as their relationships with people.[26] These relationships cannot simply be excised from consumers' lives. In a previous project, Miller studied shoppers in London and saw that many people do not see consumption as an act of hedonism but as necessary provisioning for themselves and their families.[27] The items brought into the household were a way of showing thought and concern about the needs of the people in it. In this way, shopping is a means to express care—an act of love. Anti-consumer logic, in a strange way, can be interpreted as anti-love. And who doesn't want love?

While these arguments against minimalism, particularly in its most extreme forms—struck me as worryingly true, I also reflected on how much, by at least trying it, I learned about myself, my family's needs, my relationship with things. When I asked my wife about these critiques, she explained how our slow-buy phase made her pause before each purchase, to ask herself if she really needed the item or if there was some other way to obtain it. She was less stressed during holidays and birthdays because she knew she didn't have to worry about what to buy. And it made her consider how just because a person has the ability to buy something doesn't mean she should. For her, minimalism isn't faux spiritualism, but a real contentment and reframing of what brings true joy.

I agreed, even as I worried that while minimalism can be an important approach for individuals, we still need bigger answers—answers that don't reframe just individual consumption but how our larger world of consumerism operates. I went looking for another possible answer.

START CIRCULAR ECONOMIES

In the early dawn of one summer day in 2008, Marcus Eriksen's raft, floating in the Pacific Ocean 60 miles west of Los Angeles, was sinking. Fifty-knot gusts churned the sea and threaded through the powerless vessel, pulling it apart. This should not have been a surprise. After all, the raft, named *Junk*, was constructed of a Cessna airplane fuselage sitting atop plyboard and strapped to 15,000 plastic bottles.[28]

Eriksen had been motivated by the plastics crisis eight years earlier, when he had visited Midway Atoll, a speck of flat land at the western edge of the Hawaiian archipelago. There lay hundreds of thousands of

Laysan albatross nests. Led by the biologist Heidi Auman, Eriksen's visit was focused on the amount of plastic that the birds ingest as food. Albatross parents feed their young the breathtaking range of plastics that litter the island and its waters—toothbrushes, utensils, wires, cigarette lighters—providing a false sense of satiety. Many of the birds die, of course, their rotting carcasses burst open to reveal stomachs overstuffed with plastics.

Eriksen is a man of action. He has the acute confidence that comes with having been a Marine during the Gulf War. He dedicated his life to bringing what he witnessed at Midway Atoll to those who were unaware of how humanity's love affair with plastic had become a horror show for our oceans. He earned a PhD in science communication from the University of Southern California, and in 2003 paddled 2,000 miles down the Mississippi River in a raft made of 232 two-liter plastic bottles, the *Bottle Rocket*, to bring attention to the waterway's pollution. Next Eriksen wanted to see where all the plastic from North America's rivers ends up.

He traveled to the Great Pacific Garbage Patch—a collection of human debris bigger than Peru trapped in a circular ocean current—guided by the man who is credited with discovering it, Captain Charlie Moore. There, Eriksen learned that the patch is less garbage and more a thick soup of fragmented plastics, as he would write, "a kaleidoscope of microplastics, like sprinkles on cupcakes."[29] This terrified him; he realized how nearly impossible it would be to clean up the tiny fragments infiltrating marine life. In 2014, after 24 expeditions, Eriksen and a team of scientists would be the first to estimate the total amount of plastics in the world's oceans: five trillion pieces, weighing more than 500 million pounds.[30]

The scale of this crisis mocks attempts like my family's to reduce the amount of waste—especially plastic—in the world. The US Environmental Protection Agency estimated that Americans threw out nearly 30 billion pounds of plastics in 2018, or about 89 pounds per person.[31] Even if I had somehow managed not to consume and throw away a single ounce of plastic that year, my actions would have reduced the country's total plastic waste by about .000000003 percent. When I finally did these calculations, the amount of energy and worry I'd spent on my slow-buy year seemed absurd.

This was the conundrum buzzing in my head when I sat down to interview Marcus Eriksen. He wore dark jeans and a black fleece sweater. He reminded me of my hardnosed high school baseball coach, but with glasses perched atop his salt-and-pepper hair, he had a professorial air. He sipped out of a reusable coffee cup, branded with a sticker from the 5 Gyres Institute, the nonprofit organization Eriksen cofounded with his wife, Anna Cummins.

Although Diogenes, Buddhist priests, and other ascetics point to the long history of the question of individual responsibility for what we consume, Eriksen emphasizes that our modern debate has been shaped by narratives created by some of the corporations most responsible for the crisis we find ourselves in. "Do you know about the 'crying Indian' commercial?" Eriksen asked. In 1971, a now famous commercial aired on US televisions in which an actor dressed in traditional Plains Indian clothing paddles a canoe in a pristine river, only for it to become more polluted; he then watches someone throw a bag out of a car window, fast-food wrappers scattering. A single tear trickles down the actor's cheek. A voiceover says, "People start pollution. People can stop it."[32]

"This commercial pointed to the individual consumer," Eriksen explained. "The product isn't polluting. The person is." We now know that this campaign was bankrolled by packaging and beverage corporations—the very businesses responsible for producing the waste featured in the commercial.[33] This ad campaign and its offshoots lasted for decades as a means for businesses to deflect responsibility from themselves onto the consumer. "For a long time, the industry owned the narrative," Eriksen added. "Today, it's changing."

Eriksen believes the primary responsibility for solving the environmental crisis belongs to businesses and governments. Those who produce materials, and those responsible for overseeing it, can act at the scale necessary for real change. "We're fooling ourselves if we think that individual actions are going to move the meter," Anna Cummins recently told the *Los Angeles Times*. "Every little bit helps, but public policy and corporations have to change."[34]

Eriksen believes the overall strategy must involve moving from a "linear economy" to a "circular economy."[35] This is a shift from a single-use, throwaway economy, as he wrote in 2017, to a model "with end-of-life design, recovery, and remanufacture systems that keep synthetic materials like plastic in a closed loop."[36] Ideally, synthetic materials are increasingly replaced by less environmentally harmful and less wasteful substitutes. Businesses can develop innovative packaging and delivery systems—for example, creating returnable and reusable boxes.[37] Governments can pass laws that ban certain materials or products, and moderate planned obsolescence—for example, a proposed US federal law, the Right to Repair Act, which would support far more gadgets being repaired instead of replaced.[38] France already passed a 2020 anti-waste bill that compelled makers of smartphones, washing machines, televisions, laptops, and lawnmowers to list their products on a "repairability index" to inform consumers.[39] Kenya, Rwanda, Uganda, and Tanzania have all banned single-use plastic bags, and Kenya recently outlawed all single-use plastics in national parks.[40] Legislation in Chile will ban all single-use food and beverage products by 2025.[41] "There is also the Zero Waste City Model," Eriksen said. "We especially see this movement in emerging markets that don't have space for landfills or funds for incinerators." This strategy involves creating a workforce built around waste sorting, recycling, and composting.

These ideas, while visionary, have received considerable criticism.[42] Some suggest that there is little evidence that industrial societies can make the switch from linear to circular and have the anticipated environmental benefits. From an engineering standpoint, some have suggested that it is impossible to build a truly closed-loop system.[43] In industrial production, there will always be times where new materials must be introduced into the system and waste products must exit it. Materials wear down. Machines leak. Some toxins are too dangerous to be recirculated. Additionally, when one study looked at circular *economies*—not just the industrial mechanisms to create closed-loop systems—there was a paradoxical increase in overall production. The reason is that precisely because circular production decreases per-unit production costs, there is an increase in demand for the cheaper stuff, which ultimately increases production and reduces the intended environmental benefits of a circular economy. In other cases, the savings in efficiencies are offset by consumer choices about what to do with those potential savings. For example, in recent years, there have been leaps forward in fuel efficiency in cars, but those savings in fuel have been offset by the increase in car size. The study found that steps can be taken to mitigate this "circular-economy rebound," but that they are incongruous with the goals of for-profit companies.[44]

Still others argue that the circular-economy idea merely reframes rather than rejects the corporate and capitalist assumptions that got us into this mess in the first place. Instead of challenging the goal of growth, circular economies create a new form of growth that is still in the hands of industrial corporations. Critics point to how the effort to build circular economies has been embraced by elite corporate players; the World Economic Forum in Davos created the Circulars Award, for instance. And the circular economy has become a featured political and industrial sustainability strategy in the European Union, China, African nations, and the United States. "But this vision ignores the fact that on a finite planet endless economic growth is not an option," critics wrote in 2017. "And it fails to see that solving our ecological crises means diluting the power of global corporations—not propping them up."[45]

The accusation is that the circular economy has become a corporate slogan that depoliticizes our environmental crisis by seeing the answer as a technical one to be solved by industry, rather than tackling an unjust economic system that gives power and benefits to a few at the cost of the many. The sociologist Alice Mah has even argued—reminiscent of the "crying Indian" campaign—that the plastics industry has coordinated their efforts to commandeer the circular-economy agenda, to ensure that public policies do not fundamentally challenge the dominance of plastics and seek the reduction of plastic production.[46] In this way, the plastics industry wants the public and policy-makers to see them as an essential part of the solution rather than being at the heart of the problem.

So, what is to be done?

BE A REAL LUDDITE

Here we are.

More than three million years, and three big leaps, later.

We and our ancestors have traveled from nothing to everything, from naked ape to nonstop shopper, from the simplest tools to the most complex machines, even ones that travel the solar system and beyond. We made these tools. These tools have made us. The proverb, perhaps meant to be a warning, is absolutely true, individually as much for our species: *the more stuff you own, the more your stuff owns you.* These tools have created our world—and threaten to wreck it.

The fourth leap will come, one way or another. The main question is when it will come and what form will it take. I can imagine the next leap being brought on by a global economic catastrophe, another world war, environmental collapse. But I can also imagine some radical new formulation of humanity's material culture—a political visionary, a mass movement led by the world's children, a sweeping shift in corporate culture and priorities. The fourth leap doesn't have to be born from disaster; it can arise from the opportunity to reimagine our relationship with stuff.

Although I've used "leaps" to describe humanity's changing relationship to stuff over three million–plus years, these shifts could also be described as revolutions, revelations, upheavals, cataclysms, transformations. Perhaps to some, "leap" implies a relentless movement forward, toward an inevitable end. But there is nothing in our story that is inevitable. "Leaps" are the turns, challenges, shifts, and choices humanity has faced and made. Given the alternating opportunities and crises that our materialism has created for our world for thousands of years, they are leaps forward, to the side, and then backward—or backward altogether.

I believe the fourth leap will not be easy or straightforward, but ultimately must entail both individual and collective solutions. On the individual level, I concede to critics such as Chelsea Fagan that we must ensure modern minimalism is not classist. But surely we need not trash all minimalist ideals because of the dangers of elitism. Were Diogenes, the Buddha, and Jesus conspicuous consumers? Certainly not. Yet they lived and preached as exemplars of how things are ultimately an illusion, a distraction from humanity's higher purposes—true happiness, escape from suffering, spiritual awakening. And while consumption is a powerful symbol of freedom for many, living without things is also a form of freedom, as Diogenes would say, because then a person is beholden to no corporation or set of expectations. Buddhists would add that we can only truly be free when we free ourselves of attachments. And when we acknowledge the harms of endless consumption to family, friends, communities, and the planet, then isn't it also a form of love to lessen those harms through less consumption? There are even strong arguments by moral philosophers that we do have an obligation to reduce our consumption and its associated waste because although our individual contributions to the environmental crisis may be infinitesimally small, our small sacrifices—buying less plastic, for example—do add up to meaningful change.[47] Such sacrifices also express our values, which can inspire others around us to do their part.

On the collective level, changes must be structural—new public policies, laws, international treaties, infrastructure, economic programs, investments. No doubt, the idea of the circular economy has practical limitations and may be usurped by commercial interests. But I find it naive to imagine that the world can simply do away with capitalism and the global economy in time to save our planet. In practice, the circular economy is not one approach but many—a wide array of practices within certain industries, a way of thinking about engineering problems, a set of guidelines and aspirations for governments and corporations.[48] Although this range of approaches in some measure fractures the movement into parts, it also means that we can look to these different experiments to see what works and what doesn't. This moment of emergency requires immediate action, and for now that must mean collaborating with the companies that make our modern world. This does not mean acquiescence, however. All of us must do our part to push those in power to create real and meaningful change, even as we must seek to make real and meaningful change in our own lives.

This I saw in Marcus Eriksen's story. Eriksen does not let individuals off the hook. He just doesn't expect us all to become the next Diogenes. "Plastic is cheap and easy—and you also find it everywhere," he said, pointing to the reality of our world filled with plastics in everything from food packaging to electronics to health industries. And this is true not just of plastics, but so many of the consumer goods that engulf us. Eriksen's viewpoint helped me feel a little less guilty about my slow-buy year lasting only six months. In the end, I'm probably like most people: busy and predisposed to convenience—and ultimately unable to live without things. We consumers are like water, I realized, always traveling the path of least resistance.

Still, we do have obligations, Eriksen emphasized. "The responsibility of the individual," he said, "is to put pressure on governments and corporations." We must use all available tools—voting, letter-writing campaigns, petitions, teach-ins, pray-ins, walkouts, boycotts, donations to action-oriented organizations—to put pressure on those in power. This argument was essentially made more than 50 years ago, when Barry Commoner published his 1971 book *The Closing Circle*, and wrote that action could be *of* the public but must be *by* the public.[49] He meant that individuals could change their lifestyles to be more environmentally minded, but that ultimately the environment was a public good and thus the public must take collective action to shape government policy.

Eriksen had been a member of a research team that, in 2013, discovered microbeads that came from cosmetics were infesting the Great Lakes of North America. The team then moved, he wrote, "from science to solution."[50] Eriksen contributed to the science and the advocacy. But many people were involved, from all walks of life. "We had filmmakers, engineers, alternative materials companies, ocean advocates, lawmakers," he told me. "So, you need to have an organized campaign, a team, and collaboration; it's powerful and it works." Just two years after the discovery, the Microbead-Free Waters Act became US federal law. Today, the work of cleanup is underway, as well as additional legislation that would ban other items, such as some types of toothpaste, that are also sources of microbeads.[51]

Ultimately, I took heart from Eriksen. If someone who has studied and wallowed in our plastic-filled world can be optimistic, I felt I should be too. If someone can brave the ocean in a plastic junk raft, surely others will follow in their courage to pursue a better world.

"You have to look at the long trajectory of humans," Eriksen said at the end of our interview. "We invented tools to *sustain* our existence. We just have to go back to where we began."

In the end, I wonder if the fourth leap might be for all of those embedded in consumer society to become real Luddites. Not "Luddite" in the sense of people who inveigh against technology. I mean Luddites with their original commitments, who protest technologies that alienate people: technologies divorced from social and environmental values. I am advocating for real Luddites who can look at our three-million-year relationship with stuff and see both its wonders and its terrors. These are the questions and actions real Luddites would consider from the story of our stuff:

1. Ask: What can we change in our individual habits of consumption?
2. Identify the moments when we are "miswanting" and suffering from "psychological obsolescence"—driven only by the *desire* for new things.
3. Reassess our gifting practices: Can we give and receive something other than stuff to represent our love and appreciation?
4. Prioritize buying more items built for *planned perseverance*.
5. Ask: What does real wealth mean? If the accumulation of stuff, which stuff? If it is more than stuff, what else should we pursue in our lives?
6. Be cognizant of our lust for control, power, or wealth expressed through stuff in lieu of real connections with other humans and the environment.
7. Ask: How can we all contribute to this next leap of being mindful of our stuff?

8. Ask: How can we change businesses driven by selling more and more stuff?
9. Work to hold our politicians accountable for real change.
10. Remember: Our legacy should be the positive changes we make in the world, not the stuff we leave behind when we're gone.

Can these lessons bring us to the verge of a fourth leap? I would hope that real Luddites can use the wisdom of the past and an understanding of our ancient and complex relationship with things to contribute to a movement that demands a moral system for technology. This would be a world in which tools are produced and consumed in ways that are fair and just, causing the least harm and the greatest good.

After more than three million years, our story with stuff goes on.

ACKNOWLEDGMENTS

As with any published book, an author is never working alone. But, for this book, which covered so much new ground for this author, I am especially grateful to the many people who offered their time, support, assistance, expertise, and productive criticisms.

I began this project while a curator at the Denver Museum of Nature & Science, which was hugely supportive, especially in material resources. I wrote a portion of the book while a resident at the Rockefeller Foundation Bellagio Center in Italy, which is an incomparably beautiful and wonderful place to think and write. Finally, I finished the manuscript while working for the Wenner-Gren Foundation, which was equally generous in its support. Special thank-yous go to Stephen E. Nash, Pilar Palaciá, Danilyn Rutherford, and Maugha Kenny.

For their time in allowing me to interview them for this book, I am exceedingly grateful to Zeray Alemseged, Nico Aldegani, Marco Peresani, Master Caihao, Medhanet Gelaw, Keith Johnson, Lenny DeGraaf, Matthew Bird, Doc Nyiro, and Marcus Eriksen. Further help on specific questions came from Daniel Berkowitz, Mark Aldenderfer, Michele Koons, Zach Barnett, and David Linden. Kaye Reed and Ato Gemechis helped provide access to facilities in Ethiopia. The research reported in Hong Kong would not have been possible without David A. Palmer and Martin Tse. Evan Colwell helped with math problems. I'm particularly indebted to Catherine Gilman for her meticulous and gorgeous drafting. Several people took the time to read portions of the manuscript in its draft form: Leslie Aiello, Metin Eren, Steve Woods, and Amen Sergew. Two anonymous peer reviewers added genuinely brilliant insights. I'm obliged to them all, while claiming full responsibility for any mangled facts and/or sentences.

Furthermore, this book would not have been possible without my agents Wendy Strothman and Lauren MacLeod of Aevitas Creative Management, and Andrew Gordon at David Higham Associates Limited. Thank you to the University of Chicago Press and C. Hurst & Co. for adding this book to your inimitable catalogues. I am thankful for these presses' outstanding staff members and editorial contractors, especially Elizabeth Ellingboe, Karen A. Levine, Adrienne Meyers, Dylan Joseph Montanari, Johanna Rosenbohm, and Lara Weisweiller-Wu. I am once again greatly indebted to Susan Bielstein for the liberal use of her digital red pen, which every time made every idea clearer, every sentence sharper, every story stronger.

Finally, I owe so much to my family—to my sister, who first inspired this book and her indefatigable encouragement; to my parents, for their unconditional support; to my brother, whose example I hope one day to fully realize; and most especially to my wife and our daughter, who teach me every day that life's greatest rewards are found in sharing a life together and not in things.

KEY TERMS AND CONCEPTS

ACHEULEAN TOOLS. A type of stone tool dating from about 1.7 million years ago to nearly 100,000 years ago, and found across Africa, Asia, and Europe. Known as "Large Cutting Tools," this technology is composed of hefty cleavers and axes of a standardized form. The elegant tear-shaped stone tools could fit in the hand to slice and chop, pick, and pound.

AESTHETIC SENSE. Having a sense of the beautiful.

AGE OF MACHINERY. Coined in an 1829 essay, "Signs of the Times," by the Scottish philosopher and writer Thomas Carlyle, the phrase was a warning that the Industrial Revolution was not ushering in a heroic or moral age but a "Mechanical Age" that was turning things *and* people into machines.

AGE OF PLASTIC. A period that describes the rise of industrial synthetic plastics, beginning in 1855 with the invention of Parkesine and continuing today.

ARKWRIGHT MACHINE. An automated machine, powered by a waterwheel, for spinning yarn or thread, patented in 1769, which helped launch the Industrial Revolution.

ART (VISUAL). Defined in this book as a revolution of human cognition and behavior that links three unique abilities: an animal instinct for beauty, the desire for self-expression, and the invention of symbolic thinking.

AUSTRALOPITHECINES. A group of apelike hominins that walked upright in southern, central, and eastern Africa from about 4.2 million to 2 million years ago.

BEHAVIORAL INNOVATION. The use of reasoning to connect disconnected fragments of information and spontaneously arrive at creative solutions: a necessary approach to problem-solving for the emergence of creative tool use by ancient hominins.

BEHAVIORAL SPECIALIZATION. A skill that is learned and repeated by successive generations.

BLANK-CANVAS STAGE. A period emerging about 50,000 years ago that describes the ability to creatively imagine a picture or hold a concept in the mind's eye and then express it through sculpture or painting.

BRANDED PROPOSITION. An approach to marketing that emerged in the 1950s in which advertisers convinced consumers of a product's performance and emotional resonance.

CATALYST INVENTION. An invention that precipitates an acceleration of other innovations without itself being affected (at least for a time).

CIRCULAR ECONOMY. A manufacturing model in which materials are kept in a closed loop, from their production and use to recycling and reuse.

COLONIALISM. An economic and ideological system that depends on the inequitable extraction of resources by one people over another.

COMPLEX CLOTHES. Clothing characterized as fitting snugly around the body, incorporating separate pieces that encircle the limbs, and/or composed of multiple layers.

COMPOSITE TOOL. A tool that is composed of multiple other tools, often combined in an innovative and unique way.

CONSUMER SOCIETY. A society whose behaviors and beliefs pivot on mass consumption.

CONTAGIOUS MAGIC. The perception that things that have been in contact with each other continue to have a relationship: for example, a famous person's hat, even after no longer worn, continues a connection with that famous person.

CUMULATIVE CULTURE. The accumulation of technology over multiple generations that results in tools that no single person could have created on their own.

DEPENDENCE EFFECT. Coined by the economist John Kenneth Galbraith in 1958, this describes an economic strategy deployed by manufacturers and marketers to artificially create demand for a product that is in surplus.

DINKNESH. Found in 1974 in Ethiopia, this is an ancestral hominin that belongs to the species *Australopithecus afarensis*. The name in Amharic means "you are marvelous." Also called Lucy in English.

GUANYIN. A bodhisattva in Buddhism and Daoism that is known as the goddess of compassion for her assistance to the ill, troubled, and desperate.

HAND AX. A tool invented by our early ancestors that could be held in the hand and used as an ax to cut and chop, pound and pry.

HOMININ. Any individual belonging to extinct or modern human species, including all our ancestors in the genera *Homo, Australopithecus, Paranthropus, Ardipithecus, Orrorin,* and *Sahelanthropus.*

HOMO ERECTUS. An intelligent and durable ancestral human species that lived from about 1.9 million to 110,000 years ago and spread eastbound from Africa across Asia. Their body proportions would have resembled modern humans. They are associated with the first hand-ax technology.

HOMO NALEDI. A humanlike ancestor who lived before 300,000 to nearly 200,000 years ago in southern Africa. They are perhaps the first hominin ancestor that intentionally disposed of their dead.

HOMO NEANDERTHALENSIS. See *Neanderthals.*

HOMO SAPIENS. Us. The entire human race, which emerged about 300,000 years ago in Africa and spread around the globe.

HUNTER-GATHERERS. A society based on the economy of hunting animals and gathering wild foods.

INCORPORATIVE PROCESS. The means by which humans become attached to things, which begins in infancy as children begin to distinguish themselves from the things of the world.

KEY TERMS AND CONCEPTS

INDUSTRIAL REVOLUTION. A period of transformative growth in technology, manufacturing, and production that dramatically shifted national and then global economies, living conditions, and social values. Beginning in the 1760s in England with the birth of modern textile factories, the movement spread throughout the globe, ultimately resulting in urbanization, the reorganization of human labor, mass transportation and communication, and much more. The era is often divided into different parts: the First (1760–1870), Second (1870–1914), and Third (1914–present) Industrial Revolutions. However, some scholars use different years as bookends; others include a fourth period that points to the changes brought by digital technologies, including artificial intelligence and "cyber-physical systems" such as robotics.

LOMEKWI 3. An archaeological site in Kenya, where the earliest known stone tools, dating to 3.3 million years ago, were excavated. The tools from this period are sometimes called *Lomekwian*.

LUCY. See *Dinknesh*.

LUDDITE. A member belonging to bands of English workers who joined a movement between 1811 and 1816 to destroy machinery in mills in order to protest the industrial developments that they believed were threatening their livelihood.

MINIMALISM. A modern lifestyle defined by those who refuse, reuse, or reduce consumption of manufactured things and their waste.

MOBILE ATTENTION. The human ability to direct our attention for a long period to realize a goal.

MOUSTERIAN TOOLS. A sophisticated stone-tool technology that is associated with Neanderthals in Europe and modern *Homo sapiens* in Africa and Asia, dating from roughly 200,000 to 30,000 years ago.

NEANDERTHALS. Our closest ancestral extinct hominin kin, Neanderthals lived across Europe to central Asia, from about 400,000 to 40,000 years ago. Neanderthals in many ways lived similarly to *Homo sapiens*, and even produced offspring with them.

NEOLITHIC REVOLUTION. Also known as the Agricultural Revolution, this period began around 12,000 years ago when some human groups shifted from nomadic foraging economies to settled communities based on agriculture and domesticated animals. These shifts began across northern Africa and the Middle East, but eventually independently unfolded around the world.

OLDOWAN TOOLKIT. Named for the Kenyan region of Olduvai, this is a technology that included three instruments: a nodule of rock (a "core"), another rock to strike the core (a "hammerstone"), and the resulting fragment (a "flake"). This technology dates from about 2.6 million to 1.7 million years ago, and has been found across Africa, Western Europe, the Mediterranean, and Asia.

PALEOLITHIC. An era dating from about 2.5 million to 12,000 years ago, prior to settled life with farming and domesticated animals, when early humans lived by hunting, gathering, and foraging.

PLANNED OBSOLESCENCE. A design and economic strategy in which consumer goods are intentionally designed to rapidly become obsolete and so require replacing.

POTLATCH. An intricate ceremony conducted by the coastal cultures of central Alaska, western Canada, and southern Washington. The potlatch is a ritual feast that includes singing, dancing, speechifying, eating, and extravagant gifting.

PROBLEM-SOLUTION DISTANCE. The amount of time, energy, and focus an animal is capable of expending to find a solution to a problem.

RADICAL EMBODIMENT. A theory that described how objects become part of a person's whole, unconscious, and dynamic bodily system.

RATCHET EFFECT. The process that describes how tools improve over time—how a tool is created, then modified and repeatedly modified again, over multiple generations.

SEDENTARY LIFESTYLE OR SOCIETY. An approach to living or a community that involves living permanently in one place. Sedentism is supposed to have emerged with the Neolithic Revolution.

STUFF. The things humans make, love, and loathe, which all of us need and too many of us have in excess.

SYMBOLISM. The practice of representing things by symbols. Symbolic thinking involves the ability to invest things with symbolic meanings.

TECHNO-ORGANIC EVOLUTION. A complex feedback loop between culture and biology, in which successful social behaviors drive, shape, or replace evolutionary forces—such as early tool use to butcher animals and process tubers, which allowed for hominin bodies to evolve with less-sharp teeth.

TOOL USE. Can be defined as an animal exerting control over an object to physically alter another object, or to mediate information between the tool user and their environment.

NOTES

ON THE ORIGIN OF THINGS

1. MacVean 2014.
2. Minter 2017.
3. Pinsker 2019.
4. Gardner 2019.
5. Kaza et al. 2020, 2–3.
6. Nilles 2019.

CHAPTER ONE

1. The following discussion on Jane Goodall is drawn from Goodall 2002, 2010a; and Peterson 2006.
2. Quoted in Peterson 2006, 209–10.
3. Quoted in Peterson 2006, 208.
4. Quoted in Peterson 2006, 209.
5. Quoted in Schick and Toth 1993, 16.
6. Carlyle 1885, 40.
7. Tattersall 2012, 4, 41, 74.
8. Peterson 2006, 207.
9. Goodall 1964.
10. R. Leakey 1994, 10.
11. Oakley 1956.
12. Peterson 2006, 274, 378.
13. Goodall 2010b, 6.
14. Peterson 2006, 212.
15. Hart and Sussman 2018.
16. St. Amant and Horton 2008, 1203.
17. Bentley-Condit and Smith 2010.

18. Mhatre et al. 2017; Rosenheim 1987; Brooks 1988.
19. Priddey 1977.
20. Osiurak 2020, 22.
21. Sweetlove 2011.
22. Fellers and Fellers 1976.
23. St Clair et al. 2018.
24. But see Epstein and Medalie 1983; and W. Davis 1950.
25. Call 2013.
26. Call 2013, 5.
27. Call 2013, 8.
28. Musgrave et al. 2016.
29. Köhler (1925) 2019.
30. McPherron et al. 2010; Alemseged 2021.
31. Blaxland 2020; Pontzer 2012.
32. Johanson and Wong 2009, 8–9.
33. Quoted in Jacob 2010.
34. Gibbons 2010.
35. Harmand et al. 2015.
36. Quoted in Balter 2015.
37. De la Torre 2019.
38. Hunt, Gray, and Taylor 2013.
39. Preucel 2021, 4.
40. Call 2013, 11.
41. Haidle 2010.
42. Hunt, Gray, and Taylor 2013, 92.
43. Hunt, Gray, and Taylor 2013, 103.
44. Wayman 2012b.
45. Lewin 2002.
46. Kaufman 1972.
47. Lewin 2002.
48. Broderick 2019a.
49. Quoted in Morell 2011, 208.
50. Quoted in Morell 2011, 208.
51. Corbey 2012.
52. L. S. B. Leakey, Tobias, and Napier 1964.
53. L. S. B. Leakey, Hopwood, and Reck 1931.
54. L. S. B. Leakey 1936.
55. L. S. B. Leakey, Tobias, and Napier 1964, 9.
56. Gibbons 2011, Toth and Schick 2006.
57. Broderick 2018, 2019b; Nordling 2021; Rowan et al. 2022.
58. Sahnouni et al. 2018; Titton et al. 2020; Barsky 2009; Chavaillon 1976; Kimbel et al. 1996; Roche et al. 1999; Braun et al. 2019.
59. Toth 1985.
60. McPherron 2013, 290.
61. Plummer 2004.

NOTES TO CHAPTER TWO

62. Haidle 2010, 161.
63. Schick et al. 1999.
64. Toth and Schick 2009, 298.
65. Eren, Lycett, and Tomonaga 2020.
66. Toth and Schick 2009, 299.
67. Lewis and Harmand 2016; de la Torre 2019.
68. SciNews 2015; de la Torre and Hirata 2015; Boesch and Boesch 1982.

CHAPTER TWO

1. Samuelsson 2020, 133.
2. Barker 1868, 25.
3. Dean 2013.
4. Quoted in Reuell 2016.
5. Sandgathe and Dibble 2016.
6. Boethius 2016.
7. K. D. Zink and Lieberman 2016.
8. Quoted in Zimmer 2016b.
9. K. D. Zink and Lieberman 2016.
10. Pontzer 2012.
11. Villmoare et al. 2015.
12. Schindler 2019, 0:16–0.30.
13. Taylor 2010.
14. Schick and Toth 1993, 183.
15. Schick and Toth 1993, 314.
16. Marks 2015, 129–55.
17. Jurmain et al. 2012, 7.
18. Kemeny 2019; Cowen 1981; de Heinzelin et al. 1999; J. C. Thompson et al. 2019. For an example of a specific site where tools were used to process bone marrow, see Blasco et al. 2019.
19. Pobiner 2013; Schindler 2019.
20. Schick and Toth 2003, 28.
21. Toth and Schick 2009, 299.
22. Aiello and Wheeler 1995; Wrangham 2010, 43; Zaraska 2016, 31.
23. Aiello, Bates, and Joffe 2001.
24. Bretas, Yamazaki, and Iriki 2020.
25. Balzeau et al. 2014.
26. McKee, Poirier, and McGraw 2016, 17.
27. Bailey and Geary 2009; Flinn, Geary, and Ward 2005.
28. This paragraph and the next are based on Fox 2018.
29. Seymour 2020.
30. Stout 2006.
31. Mruczek, von Loga, and Kastner 2013.
32. Faisal et al. 2010; see also Stout et al. 2015.
33. Hecht et al. 2015.

34. Putt et al. 2017.
35. K. R. Gibson 1993.
36. Py-Lieberman 2007.
37. Quoted in Doughton 2008.
38. Zimmer 2016a.
39. Marris 2016.
40. Quoted in Marris 2016.
41. Kappelman et al. 2016.
42. Schick and Toth 2003, 29.
43. Skinner et al. 2015.
44. Almécija, Wallace, et al. 2015; see also Almécija, Smaers, and Jungers 2015.
45. Wayman 2012a.
46. Almécija, Wallace, et al. 2015, 1101.
47. Marzke 2013, Kivell 2015.
48. Will, Pablos, and Stock 2017.
49. Isler and Schaik 2012.
50. Schick and Toth 2003, 29.
51. The following discussion is drawn from British Listed Buildings 2020.
52. BBC 2012; Kronenberger 1973; Sokolowski 2020.
53. Racquets 2020.
54. Conner 2011, 182.
55. Conner 2011, 182.
56. Quoted in Express Digest 2020.
57. Biggio et al. 2017.
58. Martel et al. 2016; Rognini et al. 2019; Carlson et al. 2010; Schettler, Raja, and Anderson 2019; Sposito et al. 2012.
59. N. P. Holmes and Spence 2004.
60. Barth 2018, 61.
61. Elbert et al. 1995.
62. Schettler, Raja, and Anderson 2019.
63. Crossley 2001, 102.
64. Gregory 1972; Merleau-Ponty (1945) 1962.
65. Kaas 2009.
66. Kaas 2004.
67. Barth 2018, 64.
68. Sherwood, Subiaul, and Zawidzki 2008.
69. Ehrsson, Spence, and Passingham 2004.
70. L. E. Miller et al. 2019.
71. L. Liu and Howe 2012, 176.
72. Ihde and Malafouris 2019.

CHAPTER THREE

1. This opening section is based on Fowler 2000.
2. Vidale et al. 2016.

3. Wierer et al. 2018.
4. Diez-Martín et al. 2015.
5. Key, Jarić, and Roberts 2021.
6. McPherron 2013, 194; Moore and Perston 2016.
7. Lycett and Gowlett 2008; Lycett, Schillinger, et al. 2016.
8. Davidson and Noble 1993.
9. Kohn and Mithen 1999.
10. Tattersall 2008, 74–75.
11. Kouwenhoven 1997. For a spear dating to the same period in England, see Allington-Jones 2015.
12. BBC 2000; Barham 2002.
13. Klein 2009, 408.
14. Bednarik 1995, 202–3.
15. K. S. Brown et al. 2012.
16. Mayer et al. 2020.
17. Bouzouggar et al. 2007.
18. Lombard and Phillipson 2010.
19. Backwell, d'Errico, and Wadley 2008.
20. Stringer 2012, 124.
21. Cook 2017.
22. Kvavadze et al. 2009.
23. Fujita et al. 2016.
24. Bahn and Vertut 1997, 85.
25. Wu et al. 2012.
26. Ramirez 2020, 152.
27. Beach 1877a.
28. Dewey and Ewer 1878.
29. Wills 2019, 107.
30. Arthur 2009; quotation on 109.
31. Arthur 2009, 115.
32. Moyer 2009.
33. Beach 1877b.
34. Arthur 2009, 121.
35. Michel 1967, 18; Nollet 1769.
36. Martland 2012, 3.
37. Chatfield 2020.
38. Haidle 2010, 162.
39. Library of Congress 2020.
40. Phys.org 2011, 2013.
41. Krützen et al. 2005.
42. Tennie, Premo, et al. 2017; Vale et al. 2017.
43. Mesoudi and Thornton 2018.
44. Boyd and Richerson 2005, 54.
45. Tomasello 1999, 5.
46. Rising Starr Middle School Chorus 2017.

47. Tennie, Call, and Tomasello 2009.
48. Schaik, Pradhan, and Tennie 2019.
49. Simmons 2011.
50. Balter 2014.
51. J. C. Scott 2018.
52. Bowles and Choi 2019.
53. Graeber and Wengrow 2021; Kelly 2019.
54. Fellman 1994.
55. Lu et al. 2009; Ranere et al. 2009.
56. Botigué et al. 2017.
57. Hodder and Marciniak 2015.
58. Clayton 2019.
59. Radivojević et al. 2017.
60. D. Berger et al. 2019.
61. Cowgill 2004.
62. Kaneda and Haub 2021.
63. Hassett 2017; Krause and Trappe 2021.
64. Green 2020.
65. Sahlins 1972, 194.
66. Graeber 2012.

CHAPTER FOUR

1. The following section is drawn from Benazzi et al. 2015, as well as my interview with Marco Peresani and the exhibits at the site when I visited in September 2019.
2. Watanabe, Sakamoto, and Wakita 1995.
3. Shinozuka, Ono, and Watanabe 2013.
4. Quoted in Furness 2017.
5. G. Miller 2000.
6. S. Davies 2013, 184.
7. Farago 2018.
8. Currie 2009, 1.
9. The following discussion on Eugène Dubois is drawn from Shipman 2002.
10. Joordens et al. 2015.
11. Quoted in Callaway 2014.
12. Quoted in Callaway 2014.
13. Quoted in Brahic 2014.
14. Morriss-Kay 2010.
15. Clottes and Lewis-Williams 1998.
16. Henshilwood, d'Errico, and Watts 2009.
17. Caron et al. 2011; Hublin et al. 1996.
18. Hoffmann, Angelucci, et al. 2018.
19. Radovčić et al. 2015.
20. Muskett 2018, 10.

21. Nowell and Chang 2014.
22. Bahn and Lorblanchet 2017; Curtis 2007.
23. Gotthardt 2019.
24. Ramos 1999.
25. Bataille 1955.
26. R. D. Guthrie 2005, 209–302.
27. Preucel 2006, 44–66.
28. D'Errico and Nowell 2000.
29. Hoffmann, Standish, et al. 2018.
30. B. Hardy 2022; Rodríguez-Vidal et al. 2014.
31. Morriss-Kay 2010, 158.
32. Aubert et al. 2019; see also Brumm et al. 2021.
33. Quoted in Balter 2000, 421.
34. Aubert et al. 2019.
35. Kissel and Fuentes 2018.
36. Kissel and Fuentes 2017.
37. Schwarcz et al. 1988.
38. Rendu et al. 2014.
39. Fuentes 2017.

CHAPTER FIVE

1. Yü 2001.
2. Harvey 1990, 125.
3. Tythacott 2011, 24.
4. Colwell 2022; Palmer, Tse, and Colwell 2019.
5. L. R. Berger et al. 2015; Mead 2017.
6. Hawks and Berger 2020, 58–60.
7. Than 2013.
8. Solecki 1971, 247.
9. Egeland et al. 2018; Sykes 2020, 283–14.
10. Van Leeuwen, Cronin, and Haun 2017.
11. Ambrosino 2019; Fuentes 2019.
12. Wright 2009.
13. Goodall 2011, 1:30–1:42.
14. S. Guthrie 1993.
15. Gell 1998.
16. Hodgson and Pettitt 2018a, 2018b.
17. Coulson, Staurset, and Walker 2011.
18. Horton 2007, 1; Karetzky 2014.
19. Ferguson and Eriacho 1990.
20. Schomburg-Scherff 2000, 192.
21. Schomburg-Scherff 2000, 192.
22. Hoskins 2013, 75.
23. Latour 1999, 189.

24. Bennett 2010; Chua and Elliott 2013; Harrison, Byrne, and Clarke 2013.
25. Curry 2008.
26. Fruth and Hohmann 2018.
27. De Waal 2014.
28. Zauzmer 2017.
29. Dunbar 2020.
30. Manoharan and Xygalatas 2019.
31. Shelach-Lavi 2015.
32. Hearn 2008.
33. Pearson 2013.
34. Rappaport 1999, 141.
35. Fuentes 2020.

CHAPTER SIX

1. The following discussion on Jesse Bratley is drawn from Montgomery and Colwell 2019 (quotations on 35, 42) unless otherwise noted.
2. Pratt 1973, 261.
3. Hailmann 1896, 343.
4. Bratley 1932, 108.
5. Pratt 2004.
6. Quoted in Ball, Henn, and Sánchez 1973, 144.
7. Sprague 2005, 49; Waggoner 2013, 469–70.
8. C. Greene and Thornton 2007. On Swift Bear's winter count, see Montgomery and Colwell 2019, 6–22.
9. Montgomery and Colwell 2019, 22.
10. Graeber 2012.
11. M. E. Smith 2013.
12. Weatherford 1997, 19.
13. G. Davies 2002.
14. Krmnicek 2019.
15. Maestro 1993, 17.
16. Seaford 2004.
17. Weatherford 1997, 35.
18. Weatherford 1997, 36.
19. Montgomery and Colwell 2019, 22.
20. Morin 2021.
21. Montgomery and Colwell 2019, 173.
22. Young Bear and Theisz 1994, 58.
23. Grobsmith 1981; Pickering 2000, 57–59.
24. Loo 1992.
25. Cranmer, Sanborn, and Logan 2006.
26. Joseph 2005, 10.
27. Mauss 1950.
28. Mauss 1950.

29. Titmuss 1997, 140.
30. Cranmer, Sanborn, and Logan 2006, 9.
31. Cranmer, Sanborn, and Logan 2006, 9.
32. T. Miles 2021.
33. Blum and Riyait 2021.
34. M. Gibson 2008, 1, emphasis in the original.
35. T. Miles 2021, 11.
36. SWNS 2020.
37. Express 2013.
38. Express 2013; Lillios 1999.
39. T. Earle 1997.
40. Lillios 1999.
41. Frazer 1922; quotation on 2.
42. Laferrière 1978, 48.
43. Newman, Diesendruck, and Bloom 2011.
44. Jacobs 2014.
45. Hallemann 2016.
46. Hutchinson 2009, 3.
47. Belk 1988; quotation on 139.
48. Csikszentmihalyi and Halton 1981, 4.
49. Sartre 1943.
50. Belk 1988, 146.
51. Wheeler and Bechler 2021, 6.
52. Park and John 2010.
53. Csikszentmihalyi and Halton 1981, 17.
54. Belk 1988, 139.
55. Toups et al. 2011.
56. Hallett et al. 2021.
57. Collard et al. 2016; Wales 2012, 793.
58. Hogenboom 2016.
59. Collard et al. 2016.
60. Kvavadze et al. 2009.
61. Gilligan 2019.
62. Gilligan 2019.
63. Levine 2008; Slack 2018.
64. R. Earle 2021.
65. Montgomery and Colwell 2019, 150.
66. Montgomery and Colwell 2019, 190.

CHAPTER SEVEN

1. The following discussion on Jedediah Strutt is drawn from White 1836, 45–46.
2. Leavitt 1997.
3. White 1836, 88.
4. White 1836, 74.

5. R. C. Allen 1917; Weightman 2007.
6. Wengrow and Graeber 2015.
7. Lenski 1984; Miller and Tilley 1984; Nelson 2004.
8. Sahlins 1968.
9. Kohler and Smith 2018.
10. Graeber and Wengrow 2021, 150; see also Linklater 2015.
11. Graeber and Wengrow 2021, 52.
12. M. E. Smith, Kohler, and Feinman 2018, 12.
13. Trinkaus and Buzhilova 2018.
14. Graeber and Wengrow 2021.
15. Lemire 2018.
16. A. N. Greene 2009.
17. Peel 1880.
18. Conniff 2011.
19. Poitras 2020; on gun loopholes, see Sisson 2020.
20. Burton 2000.
21. Landes 2003, 41.
22. Hahn 2020.
23. Carlyle 1829, 442.
24. Carlyle 1829, 444.
25. Carlyle 1829, 444.
26. Fletcher 1941, 155.
27. The following discussion on Richard D'Oyly Carte is drawn from Williams 2021 unless otherwise noted.
28. *American Gas Light Journal* 1881, 276.
29. Schivelbusch 1995.
30. Barkas 1882.
31. *Telegraphic Journal and Electrical Review* 1889.
32. *Telegraphic Journal and Electrical Review* 1889.
33. *Telegraphic Journal and Electrical Review* 1889.
34. Stearns 2020, 103–86.
35. Freeberg 2013.
36. Schlereth 1991.
37. Rosen 2012.
38. Wrigley 2010.
39. Du Boff 1967.
40. Harford 2017.
41. Hounshell 1984, 288; Flink 1990 48, 241.
42. DeBisschop 2013.
43. The following on plastics is drawn from Freinkel 2011 and Meikle 1995 unless otherwise noted.
44. Quoted in Knight 2014.
45. Blomster and Chávez 2020.
46. Mossman 1994.
47. Freinkel 2011, 16–19, 248; Meikle 1995, 11.

NOTES TO CHAPTER EIGHT

48. Powers 1993.
49. Wolfe 2008.
50. Spivack 2012.
51. Crosley 2015.
52. Eschner 2017.
53. Ofgang 2019.
54. Cutlip 2015.
55. Quoted in Freinkel 2011, 6.
56. Clarke 1999.
57. Freinkel 2011, 7.
58. Powers 1995, 3.
59. UN Department of Economic Affairs 1952.
60. Gertner 2013; Molotch 2005; Mowery and Rosenberg 1998.

CHAPTER EIGHT

1. A. Davis 2020.
2. Spivack 2012.
3. *New York Times* 1942.
4. *New York Times* 1944.
5. *New York Times* 1946b.
6. *New York Times* 1996.
7. *New York Times* 1946a.
8. H. Allen 1988.
9. Quoted in DeGraaf 1997/1998, 55.
10. DeGraaf 1997/1998, 60.
11. DeGraaf 1997/1998, 63.
12. Cross and Proctor 2014, 161.
13. E. Thompson 1995, 138.
14. Fullerton 1988.
15. Peck 2005.
16. Glancey 2020, Nevett 1977.
17. Higgs 2014, 69.
18. McKendrick, Brewer, and Plumb 1982, 16.
19. Fullerton 1988, 120.
20. Bix 2014.
21. J. Hardy 2016.
22. Arons 2011.
23. Lipartito 2012, 227.
24. Handley 1999, 50.
25. Handley 1999, 51.
26. Handley 1999, 63.
27. Handley 1999, 53.
28. A. Davis 2020.
29. Phillips 2004, 98.

30. Galbraith 1998.
31. J. H. Davis 2004, 1189.
32. Beaudreau 1996, 11–28.
33. Bernays (1928) 2005, 84.
34. Gordon 2016, 18.
35. Galbraith 1998.
36. Kyrk 1923, 292; see also Hunnicutt 1988, 57.
37. Galbraith 1998, 125.
38. Galbraith 1998, 126.
39. Galbraith 1998, 127.
40. Leach 1993.
41. Marshall and Morreale 2018, 86.
42. Dutt 2008.
43. Dutt 2008, 536.
44. Hood 2019, ix–x.
45. Kettering 1929, 31.
46. Kettering 1929, 30.
47. Galbraith 1998, 153.
48. Jordan 1919, 146.
49. Anderson 1978, 5.
50. History 2020.
51. Veblen 1899.
52. Burrows 1995; Patton 2006.
53. Blaszczyk 2008, 87.
54. Packard 1959, 7.
55. Higgs 2014, 74.
56. Cross 2000.
57. Featherstone 2001; Kiron, Ackerman, and Goodwin 1997; D. Miller 1987; Murphy 2016; J. Liu 2022; Sassatelli 2007.
58. S. Miles 1998.
59. Lury 2011, 2.
60. Quoted in Coghlan 2009.
61. Stewart 2021.
62. Kasser and Kanner 2004.
63. Sodaro 2018, 191.
64. Douglas and Isherwood 1979; Mathur 2013.
65. Baudrillard 1998.
66. Bauman 2013.
67. Leach 1993, 3.
68. Townsend 2019.
69. King 2021.
70. FCN News 2021.
71. Wood 2021.
72. Heller 2017.
73. Calkins 2003, 130.

74. Calkins 2003, 131.
75. Calkins 2003, 131.
76. Calkins 2003, 132.
77. Slade 2006, 40.
78. Slade 2006, 72.
79. Quoted in Adamson 2003, 4.
80. Packard 1957.
81. Gantz 2014, 157.
82. Thomas 2019.
83. Morgan 2015.
84. Packard 1960, 39.
85. Krajewski 2014.
86. Gonen 2021, 131.
87. Sabbaghi et al. 2017.
88. *Life* 1955, 43.
89. Quoted in Goodheart 2012.
90. Segran 2019.
91. Tenenbaum 2019.
92. Laville and Taylor 2017.
93. Van Cauwenberghe and Janssen 2014.
94. Geyer, Jambeck, and Law 2017.
95. Denison 2021.

CHAPTER NINE

1. The following discussion on the Collyer brothers is drawn from Faber 1947b unless otherwise noted.
2. Faber 1947c.
3. Herring 2011.
4. McAllister 1995, 203.
5. Faber 1947a.
6. *New York Times* 1947b.
7. Goheen and Swihart 2003.
8. Bryce 2018.
9. Careau, Giroux, and Berteaux 2007, 2008; Samelius et al. 2007.
10. T. T. Holmes 2016; M. L. Miller 2017.
11. Vander Wall 1990.
12. Soley and Alvarado-Díaz 2011.
13. C. C. Smith and Reichman 1984.
14. Duenwald 2004.
15. Quoted in Brody 1991.
16. Andersson and Krebs 1978.
17. Vander Wall 1990, 224–25.
18. E. Brown 2017.
19. Waldron 2020.

20. Dupont 2017.
21. Locke 1821, 209–10, emphasis in the original.
22. Bobroff 2001.
23. Hood 2019, x.
24. Quoted in Zorich 2009.
25. Yohe and Bamforth 2013.
26. Quoted in Strickland 2009.
27. Luncz et al. 2019.
28. Sanz and Morgan 2007.
29. Carvalho et al. 2009.
30. Brauna et al. 2009; Potts 1991.
31. Dibble et al. 2017, 3, 13.
32. Potts 1984.
33. Carson 1959.
34. Fern, Dickinson, and Webster 2020.
35. Bradley 1990, 1996, 2017.
36. Cort 2009; Kal 1999; Kunen, Galindo, and Chase 2002.
37. Penzel 2014.
38. New International Version.
39. Collins 2013.
40. Penzel 2014.
41. Gogol (1842) 1996, 132.
42. Dickens 1853, 35, 176, 394.
43. Doyle 1893, 479.
44. Lobdell 2013, 7.
45. Lobdell 2013, 7.
46. Smail 2014, 110.
47. James 1887, 668.
48. Frost and Steketee 2011, 15; Herring 2011, 2.
49. Weiss 2010.
50. Lilienfeld and Arkowitz 2013.
51. Quoted in Agdari-Moghadam 2021, 75.
52. Cooperman 2019; Halliday 2018; Van Buskirk 2019.
53. Nakao and Kanba 2019.
54. Kuwano et al. 2020.
55. Frost and Steketee 2011, 21.
56. Frost and Steketee 2011, 20.
57. Frost and Steketee 2011, 15.
58. Winters 2015.
59. Frost and Steketee 2011, 42.
60. Frost and Steketee 2011, 15.
61. Frost and Steketee 2011.
62. Bates et al. 2020.
63. Arnold et al. 2012, 23.
64. Arnold et al. 2012, 44.

65. O'Brian 2015.
66. Hanson 2010.
67. Giles 2020.
68. Sanburn 2015.
69. Humes 2012, 4.
70. Center for Sustainable Systems 2021.
71. *New York Times* 1947a.
72. *New York Times* 1958.
73. Quoted in Gray 2002.
74. Hood 2019, x.

ON THE FUTURE OF THINGS

1. CBS News 2021.
2. Kasser 2003; Schlossberg 2019.
3. Currier 2015; Olsen 2010, 9.
4. Chin 2016.
5. Dixon 1995.
6. Dobbin 2012.
7. Morritt 2010, 92.
8. Gummere 1917, 405.
9. Galbraith (1958) 2011, 92.
10. McGregor 2020.
11. Becker 2020.
12. E. Scott 2020.
13. Becker 2020.
14. Becker 2018; Carver 2020; Millburn and Nicodemus 2011; Sasaki 2017; Seferian 2021.
15. Aguilar 2017; Jaquith 2017; Wimbush 2002.
16. Main 1913, 216.
17. New International Version.
18. Gethin 1998, 88.
19. Dass 2018, 22.
20. Thoreau (1854) 2004, 27.
21. Thoreau (1854) 2004, 134.
22. Robinson 2020.
23. Kaysen 2021.
24. Fagan 2021. See also Chayka 2020; and Tolentino 2020.
25. Cross 2000.
26. D. Miller 2008.
27. D. Miller 1998.
28. Eriksen 2017.
29. Eriksen 2017, 7.
30. Eriksen, Lebreton, et al. 2014.
31. EPA 2018.

32. Keep America Beautiful 1971, 0:45–0:50.
33. Dunaway 2017; Levere 2013; Strand 2008.
34. Quoted in Becker 2020.
35. Stahel 2016.
36. Eriksen 2017, 171.
37. Cottom 2019.
38. Chen 2021.
39. Stone 2021.
40. Behuria 2021; Owili 2022.
41. Ruiqi 2022.
42. Corvellec, Stowell, and Johansson 2021.
43. Larrinaga and Garcia-Torea 2022.
44. T. Zink and Geyer 2017.
45. Narberhaus and Mitschke-Collande 2017.
46. Mah 2021.
47. Barnett 2018.
48. Kalmykovaa, Sadagopan, and Rosado 2018.
49. Commoner 1971.
50. Eriksen, Mason, et al. 2013.
51. Zremski 2022.

REFERENCES

Adamson, Glenn. 2003. *Industrial Strength Design.* Milwaukee: Milwaukee Art Museum.

Agdari-Moghadam, Nassim. 2021. *Hoarding Disorder: A Practical Guide to an Interdisciplinary Treatment.* Cham, Switzerland: Springer.

Aguilar, Mario I. 2017. *The Way of the Hermit: Interfaith Encounters in Silence and Prayer.* London: Jessica Kingsley.

Aiello, Leslie C., N. Bates, and T. Joffe. 2001. "In Defense of the Extensive Tissue Hypothesis." In *External Anatomy of the Primate Cerebral Cortex,* edited by D. Falk and K. R. Gibson, 57–78. Cambridge: Cambridge University Press.

Aiello, Leslie C., and Peter Wheeler. 1995. "The Expensive-Tissue Hypothesis: The Brain and the Digestive System in Human and Primate Evolution." *Current Anthropology* 36 (2): 199–221.

Alemseged, Zeresenay. 2021. "Beyond the Cuts: Earliest Stone Tool Use in Hominins and the Significance of the Dikika Cutmarks." *CNRS éditions et l'Académie Pontificale des Sciences*: 101–38.

Alighieri, Dante. 1836. *The Comedy.* Translated by Odoardo Volpi. London: Edward Moxon.

Allen, Henry. 1988. "Their Stocking Feat." *Washington Post,* January 13. https://www.washingtonpost.com/archive/lifestyle/1988/01/13/their-stocking-feat/8aeffd17-c3e0-48e1-accb-e126c076e17e/.

Allen, Robert C. 1917. *The Industrial Revolution.* Oxford: Oxford University Press.

Allington-Jones, Lu. 2015. "The Clacton Spear: The Last One Hundred Years." *The Archaeological Journal* 172 (2): 273–96.

Almécija, Sergio, Jeroen B. Smaers, and William L. Jungers. 2015. "The Evolution of Human and Ape Hand Proportions." *Nature Communications* 6 (7717). https://doi.org/10.1038/ncomms8717.

Almécija, Sergio, Ian J. Wallace, Stefan Judex, David M. Alba, and Salvador Moyà-Solà. 2015. "Comment on 'Human-Like Hand Use in *Australopithecus africanus*.'" *Science* 348 (6239): 1101.

Ambrosino, Brandon. 2019. "How and Why Did Religion Evolve?" BBC, April 18.

https://www.bbc.com/future/article/20190418-how-and-why-did-religion-evolve.

American Gas Light Journal. 1881. "The Electric Lighting of the Savoy Theater." December 16, 275–76.

Anderson, Susan H. 1978. *The Most Splendid Carpet.* Washington, DC: National Park Service.

Andersson, M., and J. Krebs. 1978. "On the Evolution of Hoarding Behaviour." *Animal Behaviour* 26:707–11.

Arnold, Jeanne E., Anthony P. Graesch, Enzo Ragazzini, and Elinor Ochs. 2012. *Life at Home in the Twenty-First Century.* Los Angeles: Cotsen Institute of Archaeology Press.

Arons, Marc de Swaan. 2011. "How Brands Were Born: A Brief History of Modern Marketing." *Atlantic,* October 3. https://www.theatlantic.com/business/archive/2011/10/how-brands-were-born-a-brief-history-of-modern-marketing/246012/.

Arthur, W. Brian. 2009. *The Nature of Technology: What It Is and How It Evolves.* New York: Free Press.

Aubert, M., R. Lebe, A. A. Oktaviana, M. Tang, B. Burhan, Hamrullah, and A. Jusdi, et al. 2019. "Earliest Hunting Scene in Prehistoric Art." *Nature* 576 (7787):442–45. https://doi.org/10.1098/rsos.17133910.1038/s41586-019-1806-y.

Backwell, Lucinda, Francesco d'Errico, and Lyn Wadley. 2008. "Middle Stone Age Bone Tools from the Howiesons Poort Layers, Sibudu Cave, South Africa." *Journal of Archaeological Science* 35 (6): 1566–80.

Bahn, Paul, and Michel Lorblanchet. 2017. *The First Artists: In Search of the World's Oldest Art.* London: Thames & Hudson.

Bahn, Paul G., and Jean Vertut. 1997. *Journey through the Ice Age.* Berkeley: University of California Press.

Bailey, D. H., and D. C. Geary. 2009. "Hominid Brain Structure: Testing Climatic, Ecological and Social Competition Models." *Human Nature* 20:67–79.

Ball, Eve, Nora Henn, and Lynda A. Sánchez. 1973. *Indeh: An Apache Odyssey.* Norman: University of Oklahoma Press.

Balter, Michael. 2000. "Paintings in Italian Cave May Be Oldest Yet." *Science* 290 (5491): 419–21.

———. 2014. "How Sheep Became Livestock." *Science,* April 29. https://www.sciencemag.org/news/2014/04/how-sheep-became-livestock.

———. 2015. "World's Oldest Stone Tools Discovered in Kenya." *Science,* April 14. https://www.sciencemag.org/news/2015/04/world-s-oldest-stone-tools-discovered-kenya.

Balzeau, A., E. Gilissen, R. L. Holloway, S. Prima, and D. Grimaud-Herve. 2014. "Variations in Size, Shape and Asymmetries of the Third Frontal Convolution in Hominids: Paleoneurological Implications for Hominin Evolution and the Origin of Language." *Journal of Human Evolution* 76:116–28.

Barham, Lawrence S. 2002. "Systematic Pigment Use in the Middle Pleistocene of South-Central Africa." *Current Anthropology* 43 (1): 181–90.

Barkas, T. P. 1882. "Electricity and Electric Lighting: Concluding Paper." *English Household Magazine* 3 (1): 270–71.

Barker, James. 1868. *Narrative of a Journey to Shoa and of an Attempt to Visit Harrar.* Bombay: Education Society's Press.

Barnett, Zach. 2018. "No Free Lunch: The Significance of Tiny Contributions." *Analysis* 78 (1): 3–13.

Barsky, Deborah. 2009. "An Overview of Some African and Eurasian Oldowan Sites: Evaluation of Hominin Cognition Levels, Technological Advancement and Adaptive Skills." In *Interdisciplinary Approaches to the Oldowan*, edited by E. Hovers and D. R. Braun, 39–47. Dordrecht, Netherlands: Springer.

Barth, Alison L. 2018. "Tool Use Can Instantly Rewire the Brain." In *Think Tank: Forty Neuroscientists Explore the Biological Roots of Human Experience*, edited by D. J. Linden, 60–65. New Haven, CT: Yale University Press.

Bataille, Georges. 1955. *Lascaux: Or, The Birth of Art: Prehistoric Painting.* Lausanne: Skira.

Bates, Sage, Andrew J. De Leonardis, Patrick W. Corrigan, and Gregory S. Chasson. 2020. "Buried in Stigma: Experimental Investigation of the Impact of Hoarding Depictions in Reality Television on Public Perception." *Journal of Obsessive-Compulsive and Related Disorders* 26:100538.

Baudrillard, Jean. 1998. *The Consumer Society: Myths and Structures.* London: Sage Publications.

Bauman, Zygmunt. 2013. *Consuming Life.* Malden, MA: Wiley.

BBC. 2000. "Earliest Evidence of Art Found." May 2. http://news.bbc.co.uk/2/hi/sci/tech/733747.stm.

———. 2012. "Anyone for Sphairistiké?" April 18. https://www.bbc.co.uk/blogs/wales/entries/d4437526-3b92-32f4-89a6-bd3c29f296f0.

Beach, Alfred. 1877a. "The Talking Phonograph." *Scientific American* 37 (25): 384.

———. 1877b. "A Wonderful Invention.—Speech Capable of Indefinite Repetition from Automatic Records." *Scientific American* 37 (20): 304.

Beaudreau, Bernard C. 1996. *Mass Production, the Stock Market Crash, and the Great Depression.* Westport, CT: Greenwood Press.

Becker, Joshua. 2018. *The More of Less: Finding the Life You Want under Everything You Own.* New York: WaterBrook.

———. 2020. "The Ultimate Guide to a No-Buy Year." *Forbes*, October 29. https://www.forbes.com/sites/joshuabecker/2020/10/29/the-ultimate-guide-to-a-no-buy-year/?sh=6092e3af244f.

Bednarik, Robert G. 1995. "Towards a Better Understanding of the Origins of Body Decoration." *Anthropologie* 33 (3): 201–12.

Beecher, Henry Ward. 1868. *Norwood: Or, Village Life in New England.* New York: Charles Scribner & Company.

Behuria, Pritish. 2021. "Ban the (Plastic) Bag? Explaining Variation in the Implementation of Plastic Bag Bans in Rwanda, Kenya and Uganda." *Environment and Planning C: Politics and Space* 39 (8): 1791–808.

Belk, Russell W. 1988. "Possessions and the Extended Self." *Journal of Consumer Research* 15 (2): 139–68.

Benazzi, S., V. Slon, S. Talamo, F. Negrino, M. Peresani, S. E. Bailey, S. Sawyer, et al. 2015. "Archaeology: The Makers of the Protoaurignacian and Implications for Neandertal Extinction." *Science* 348 (6236): 793–96.

Bennett, Jane. 2010. *Vibrant Matter: A Political Ecology of Things*. Durham, NC: Duke University Press.

Bentley-Condit, Vicki K., and E. O. Smith. 2010. "Animal Tool Use: Current Definitions and an Updated Comprehensive Catalog." *Behaviour* 147 (2): 185–221.

Berger, Daniel, Jeffrey S. Soles, Alessandra R. Giumlia-Mair, Gerhard Brügmann, Ehud Galili, Nicole Lockhoff, and Ernst Pernicka. 2019. "Isotope Systematics and Chemical Composition of Tin Ingots from Mochlos (Crete) and Other Late Bronze Age Sites in the Eastern Mediterranean Sea: An Ultimate Key to Tin Provenance?" *PLoS One* 14 (6): e0218326.

Berger, Lee R., John Hawks, Darryl J. de Ruiter, Steven E. Churchill, Peter Schmid, Lucas K. Delezene, Tracy L. Kivell, et al. 2015. "*Homo naledi*, a New Species of the Genus *Homo* from the Dinaledi Chamber, South Africa." *eLife* 4:e09560.

Bernays, Edward. (1928) 2005. *Propaganda*. Brooklyn: IG Publishing.

Biggio, Monica, Ambra Bisio, Laura Avanzino, Piero Ruggeri, and Marco Bove. 2017. "This Racket Is Not Mine: The Influence of the Tool-Use on Peripersonal Space." *Neuropsychologia* 103:54–58.

Bix, Cynthia Overbeck. 2014. *Spending Spree: The History of American Shopping*. Minneapolis: Twenty-First Century Books.

Blasco, R., J. Rosell, M. Arilla, D. Villalba, A. Gopher, and R. Barkai. 2019. "Bone Marrow Storage and Delayed Consumption at Middle Pleistocene Qesem Cave, Israel (420 to 200 ka)." *Science Advances* 5 (10):eaav9822.

Blaszczyk, Regina Lee. 2008. "Designing Synthetics, Promoting Brands: Dorothy Liebes, DuPont Fibres and Post-war American Interiors." *Journal of Design History* 21 (1): 75–99.

Blaxland, Beth. 2020. "Hominid and Hominin: What's the Difference?" Australian Museum. https://australian.museum/learn/science/human-evolution/hominid-and-hominin-whats-the-difference/.

Blomster, Jeffrey P., and Víctor E. Salazar Chávez. 2020. "Origins of the Mesoamerican Ballgame: Earliest Ballcourt from the Highlands Found at Etlatongo, Oaxaca, Mexico." *Science Advances* 6 (11). https://doi.org/10.1126/sciadv.aay6964.

Blum, Dani, and Jaspal Riyait. 2021. "What Loss/ Love/ Grief/ Memory/ Mourning Looks Like." *New York Times*, April 6. https://www.nytimes.com/interactive/2021/well/covid-death-grief-loss.html.

Bobroff, Kenneth H. 2001. "Retelling Allotment: Indian Property Rights and the Myth of Common Ownership." *Vanderbilt Law Review* 54 (4): 1559–623.

Boesch, Christophe, and Hedwige Boesch. 1982. "Optimization of Nut-Cracking with Natural Hammers by Wild Chimpanzees." *Behaviour* 83 (3/4): 265–86.

Boethius, Adam. 2016. "Something Rotten in Scandinavia: The World's Earliest Evidence of Fermentation." *Journal of Archaeological Science* 66:169–80.

Botigué, Laura R., Shiya Song, Amelie Scheu, Shyamalika Gopalan, Amanda L.

Pendleton, Matthew Oetjens, Angela M. Taravella, et al. 2017. "Ancient European Dog Genomes Reveal Continuity Since the Early Neolithic." *Nature Communications* 8:16082.

Bouzouggar, Abdeljalil, Nick Barton, Marian Vanhaeren, Francesco d'Errico, Simon Collcutt, Tom Higham, Edward Hodge, et al. 2007. "82,000-Year-Old Shell Beads from North Africa and Implications for the Origins of Modern Human Behavior." *Proceedings of the National Academy of Science* 104 (24): 9964–69.

Bowles, Samuel, and Jung-Kyoo Choi. 2019. "The Neolithic Agricultural Revolution and the Origins of Private Property." *Journal of Political Economy* 127 (5): 2186–228.

Boyd, Robert, and Peter J. Richerson. 2005. *The Origin and Evolution of Culture*. Oxford: Oxford University Press.

Bradley, Richard. 1990. *The Passage of Arms: An Archaeological Analysis of Prehistoric Hoards and Votive Deposits*. Cambridge: Cambridge University Press.

———. 1996. "Hoards and Hoarding." In *The Oxford Companion to Archaeology*, edited by B. M. Fagan, 305–7. Oxford: Oxford University Press.

———. 2017. *A Geography of Offerings: Deposits of Valuables in the Landscapes of Ancient Europe*. Oxford: Oxbow Books.

Brahic, Catherine. 2014. "Shell 'Art' Made 300,000 Years before Humans Evolved." *New Scientist*, December 3. https://www.newscientist.com/article/mg22429983-200-shell-art-made-300000-years-before-humans-evolved/#ixzz6FqvJpatx.

Bratley, Jesse H. 1932. "Autobiography of Jesse Hastings Bratley." Archives of the Denver Museum of Nature & Science.

Braun, David R., Vera Aldeias, Will Archer, J. Ramon Arrowsmith, Niguss Baraki, Christopher J. Campisano, Alan L. Deino, et al. 2019. "Earliest Known Oldowan Artifacts at >2.58 Ma from Ledi-Geraru, Ethiopia, Highlight Early Technological Diversity." *Proceedings of the National Academy of Science* 116 (24): 11712–17.

Brauna, David R., Thomas Plummer, Joseph V. Ferraro, Peter Ditchfield, and Laura C. Bishop. 2009. "Raw Material Quality and Oldowan Hominin Toolstone Preferences: Evidence from Kanjera South, Kenya." *Journal of Archaeological Science* 36 (7): 1605–14.

Bretas, Rafael Vieira, Yumiko Yamazaki, and Atsushi Iriki. 2020. "Phase Transitions of Brain Evolution That Produced Human Language and Beyond." *Neuroscience Research* 161:1–7.

British Listed Buildings. 2020. "Nantclwyd Hall." https://britishlistedbuildings.co.uk/300000765-nantclwyd-hall-llanelidan#.X8uoL7NlCUk.

Broderick, Carol. 2018. "Fossil Finders: Kamoya Kimeu." Leakey Foundation. https://leakeyfoundation.org/fossil-finders-kamoya-kimeu/.

———. 2019a. "Fossil Finders: Heselon Mukiri." Leakey Foundation. https://leakeyfoundation.org/fossil-finders-heselon-mukiri/.

———. 2019b. "Fossil Finders: The Hominid Gang." Leakey Foundation. https://leakeyfoundation.org/fossil-finders-hominid-gang/.

Brody, Jane E. 1991. "A Hoarder's Life: Filling the Cache—and Finding It." *New York Times*, November 19. https://www.nytimes.com/1991/11/19/health/a-hoarder-s-life-filling-the-cache-and-finding-it.html.

Brooks, William R. 1988. "The Influence of the Location and Abundance of the Sea

Anemone *Calliactis tricolor* (Le Sueur) in Protecting Hermit Crabs from Octopus Predators." *Journal of Experimental Marine Biology and Ecology* 116 (1): 15–21.

Brown, Eric. 2017. "Plato's Ethics and Politics in *The Republic*." In *The Stanford Encyclopedia of Philosophy*, edited by Edward N. Zalta. https://plato.stanford.edu/entries/plato-ethics-politics/.

Brown, Kyle S., Curtis W. Marean, Zenobia Jacobs, Benjamin J. Schoville, Simen Oestmo, Erich C. Fisher, Jocelyn Bernatchez, et al. 2012. "An Early and Enduring Advanced Technology Originating 71,000 Years Ago in South Africa." *Nature* 491 (7425): 590–93.

Brumm, Adam, Adhi Agus Oktaviana, Basran Burhan, Budianto Hakim, Rustan Lebe, Jian-xin Zhao, Priyatno Hadi Sulistyarto, et al. 2021. "Oldest Cave Art Found in Sulawesi." *Science Advances* 7 (3): eabd4648.

Bryce, Emma. 2018. "How Do Squirrels Remember Where They Buried Their Nuts?" *Live Science*, November 17. https://www.livescience.com/64104-how-do-squirrels-find-buried-nuts.html.

Burrows, John. 1995. "Good Old-Fashioned Wall-to-Wall?" *Old-House Interiors* 1 (2): 22–24.

Burton, Anthony. 2000. *Richard Trevithick: Giant of Steam*. London: Aurum Press.

Calkins, Earnest Elmo. 2003. "What Consumer Engineering Really Is." In *The Industrial Design Reader*, edited by C. Gorman, 129–32. New York: Allworth Press.

Call, Josep. 2013. "Three Ingredients for Becoming a Creative Tool User." In *Tool Use in Animals: Cognition and Ecology*, edited by C. M. Sanz, J. Call, and C. Boesch, 129–32. Cambridge: Cambridge University Press.

Callaway, Ewen. 2014. "*Homo erectus* Made World's Oldest Doodle 500,000 Years Ago." *Nature*, December 3. https://www.nature.com/news/homo-erectus-made-world-s-oldest-doodle-500-000-years-ago-1.16477.

Careau, Vincent, Jean-François Gauthier, and Dominique Berteaux. 2007. "Cache and Carry: Hoarding Behavior of Arctic Fox." *Behavioral Ecology and Sociobiology* 62:87–96.

———. 2008. "Surviving on Cached Foods—the Energetics of Egg-Caching by Arctic Foxes." *Canadian Journal of Zoology* 86 (10). https://doi.org/10.1139/Z08-102.

Carlin, George. 1986. "Comic Relief." https://www.youtube.com/watch?v=MvgN5gCuLac.

Carlson, Thomas A., George Alvarez, Daw-an Wu, and Frans A. J. Verstraten. 2010. "Rapid Assimilation of External Objects into the Body Schema." *Psychological Science* 21 (7): 1000–1005.

Carlyle, Thomas. 1829. "Signs of the Times." *Edinburgh Review* 98:439–59.

———. 1885. *The Works of Thomas Carlyle*. New York: John B. Alden.

Caron, F., F. d'Errico, P. Del Moral, F. Santos, and J. Zilhao. 2011. "The Reality of Neandertal Symbolic Behavior at the Grotte du Renne, Arcy-sur-Cure, France." *PLoS One* 6 (6): e21545.

Carson, R. A. G. 1959. "The Bredgar Treasure of Roman Coins." *Numismatic Chronicle* 19:17–22.

Carvalho, Susana, Dora Biro, William C. McGrew, and Tetsuro Matsuzawa. 2009.

"Tool-Composite Reuse in Wild Chimpanzees (Pan troglodytes): Archaeologically Invisible Steps in the Technological Evolution of Early Hominins?" *Animal Cognition* 12 (suppl. 1): S103–S114.

Carver, Courtney. 2020. *Project 333: The Minimalist Fashion Challenge That Proves Less Really Is So Much More*. New York: TarcherPerigee.

CBS News. 2021. "Fast Fashion in the U.S. Is Fueling an Environmental Disaster in Ghana." https://www.cbsnews.com/news/ghana-fast-fashion-environmental-disaster/.

Center for Sustainable Systems. 2021. *Municipal Solid Waste Factsheet*. Pub. No. CSS04-15. Ann Arbor: Center for Sustainable Systems, University of Michigan.

Chatfield, Tom. 2020. "Technology in Deep Time: How It Evolves Alongside Us." BBC, December 25. https://www.bbc.com/future/article/20190207-technology-in-deep-time-how-it-evolves-alongside-us.

Chavaillon, J. 1976. "Evidence for the Technical Practices of Early Pleistocene Hominids, Shungura Formation, Lower Omo Valley, Ethiopia." In *Earliest Man and Environments in the Lake Rudolf Basin*, edited by Y. Coppens, F. C. Howell, G. L. Isaac, and R.E.F. Leakey, 565–73. Chicago: University of Chicago Press.

Chayka, Kyle. 2020. *The Longing for Less: Living with Minimalism*. New York: Bloomsbury.

Chen, Brian X. 2021. "Why You Should Care about Your Right to Repair Gadgets." *New York Times*, July 14. https://www.nytimes.com/2021/07/14/technology/personaltech/right-to-repair-iphones-android.html?action=click&module=In%20Other%20News&pgtype=Homepage.

Chin, Elizabeth J. 2016. *My Life with Things: The Consumer Diaries*. Durham, NC: Duke University Press.

Chua, Liana, and Mark Elliott, eds. 2013. *Distributed Objects: Meaning and Mattering after Alfred Gell*. Oxford: Berghahn.

Clarke, Alison J. 1999. *Tupperware: The Promise of Plastic in 1950s America*. Washington, DC: Smithsonian Institution.

Clayton, Ewan. 2019. "Where Did Writing Begin?" British Library. https://www.bl.uk/history-of-writing/articles/where-did-writing-begin.

Clottes, Jean, and David Lewis-Williams. 1998. *The Shamans of Prehistory: Trance and Magic in the Painted Caves*. New York: Harry N. Abrams.

Coghlan, Andy. 2009. "Consumerism Is 'Eating the Future.'" *New Scientist*, August 7. https://www.newscientist.com/article/dn17569-consumerism-is-eating-the-future/.

Collard, Mark, Lia Tarle, Dennis Sandgathe, and Alexander Allan. 2016. "Faunal Evidence for a Difference in Clothing Use Between Neanderthals and Early Modern Humans in Europe." *Journal of Anthropological Archaeology* 44 (B): 235–46.

Collins, Michelle. 2013. "Pharaoh's Tomb or Hoarder's Apartment." *Vanity Fair*, March 20. https://www.vanityfair.com/news/2013/03/quiz-pharaohs-tomb-hoarders-apartment.

Colwell, Chip. 2022. "A Palimpsest Theory of Objects." *Current Anthropology* 63 (2): 129–57.

Commoner, Barry. 1971. *The Closing Circle: Nature, Man, and Technology*. New York: Knopf.
Conner, Steven. 2011. *A Philosophy of Sport*. London: Reaktion Books.
Conniff, Richard. 2011. "What the Luddites Really Fought Against." *Smithsonian Magazine*. https://www.smithsonianmag.com/history/what-the-luddites-really-fought-against-264412/.
Cook, Jill. 2017. "The Lion Man: An Ice Age Masterpiece." British Museum (blog post). https://blog.britishmuseum.org/the-lion-man-an-ice-age-masterpiece/.
Cooperman, Jeannette. 2019. "What's Causing the Rise of Hoarding Disorder?" *JSTOR Daily*, January 16. https://daily.jstor.org/whats-causing-the-rise-of-hoarding-disorder/.
Corbey, Raymond. 2012. "'*Homo habilis*'s Humanness: Phillip Tobias as a Philosopher." *History and Philosophy of the Life Sciences* 34 (1/2): 103–16.
Cort, John. 2009. *Framing the Jina: Narratives of Icons and Idols in Jain History*. Oxford: Oxford University Press.
Corvellec, Hervé, Alison F. Stowell, and Nils Johansson. 2021. "Critiques of the Circular Economy." *Journal of Industrial Ecology* 26 (2): 421–32.
Cottom, Theresa. 2019. "UPS and TerraCycle Partner to Close the Loop." *Recycling Today*, January 25. https://www.recyclingtoday.com/article/ups-terracycle-partner-loop-packaging-e-commerce/.
Coulson, Sheila, Sigrid Staurset, and Nick Walker. 2011. "Ritualized Behavior in the Middle Stone Age: Evidence from Rhino Cave, Tsodilo Hills, Botswana." *Paleo-Anthropology*, 18–61.
Cowen, Robert C. 1981. "Were Ancient Hominids Meat-Eaters? What Old Bones Can Tell Us." *Christian Science Monitor*, July 15. https://www.csmonitor.com/1981/0715/071533.html.
Cowgill, George L. 2004. "Origins and Development of Urbanism: Archaeological Perspectives." *Annual Review of Anthropology* 33:525–49.
Cranmer, Barb, Andrea Sanborn, and Leslie Logan. 2006. *Kwakwaka'wakw People: Ways of Living, Ways of Giving*. Washington, DC: National Museum of the American Indian.
Crosley, Sloane. 2015. "Why Nylon's Run Is Over." *Smithsonian Magazine*. https://www.smithsonianmag.com/arts-culture/why-nylon-run-over-180954954/.
Cross, Gary. 2000. *An All-Consuming Century: Why Commercialism Won in Modern America*. New York: Columbia University Press.
Cross, Gary S., and Robert N. Proctor. 2014. *Packaged Pleasures: How Technology and Marketing Revolutionized Desire*. Chicago: University of Chicago Press.
Crossley, Nick. 2001. "The Phenomenological Habitus and Its Construction." *Theory and Society* 30 (1): 81–120.
Csikszentmihalyi, Mihaly, and Eugene Halton. 1981. *The Meaning of Things: Domestic Symbols and the Self*. Cambridge: Cambridge University Press.
Currie, Gregory. 2009. "Art of the Paleolithic." In *A Companion to Aesthetics*, edited by S. Davis, K. M. Higgins, R. Hopkins, R. Stecker, and D.E. Cooper, 1–9. Malden, MA: Wiley-Blackwell.

Currier, Richard L. 2015. *Unbound: How Eight Technologies Made Us Human, Transformed Society, and Brought Our World to the Brink*. New York: Arcade.
Curry, Andrew. 2008. "Gobekli Tepe: The World's First Temple?" *Smithsonian Magazine*. https://www.smithsonianmag.com/history/gobekli-tepe-the-worlds-first-temple-83613665/.
Curtis, Gregory. 2007. *The Cave Painters*. New York: Anchor.
Cutlip, Kimbra. 2015. "How Nylon Stockings Changed the World." *Smithsonian Magazine*. https://www.smithsonianmag.com/smithsonian-institution/how-nylon-stockings-changed-world-180955219/.
D'Avella, Matt, dir. 2021. *The Minimalists: Less Is Now*. Booklight Productions. 53 mins.
d'Errico, Francesco, and April Nowell. 2000. "A New Look at the Berekhat Ram Figurine: Implications for the Origins of Symbolism." *Cambridge Archaeological Journal* 10 (1): 123–67.
Dass, Baba Hari. 2018. *The Yellow Book*. 4th ed. Santa Cruz, CA: Sri Rama Publishing.
Davidson, I., and W. Noble. 1993. "Tools, Language, and Cognition in Human Evolution." In *Tools, Language, and Cognition in Human Evolution*, edited by K. Gibson and T. Ingold, 363–88. Cambridge: Cambridge University Press.
Davies, Glyn. 2002. *A History of Money*. 3rd ed. Cardiff: University of Wales Press.
Davies, Stephen. 2013. *The Artful Species: Aesthetics, Art, and Evolution*. Oxford: Oxford University Press.
Davis, Austin. 2020. "'Pity the Poor Working Girl': Nylons, Work, Class, Ideology, and Politics in Pittsburgh, Pennsylvania, 1945–46." *Tortoise*, Spring. https://tortoise.princeton.edu/2020/05/11/pity-the-poor-working-girl-nylons-work-class-ideology-and-politics-in-pittsburgh-pennsylvania-1945-46/.
Davis, Joseph H. 2004. "An Annual Index of U.S. Industrial Production, 1790–1915." *Quarterly Journal of Economics* 119 (4): 1177–215.
Davis, Watson. 1950. "Pigeons Play Ping-Pong." *Science News Letter* 57 (24): 370–71.
de Heinzelin, Jean, J. Desmond Clark, Tim White, William Hart, Paul Renne, Giday WoldeGabriel, Yonas Beyene, et al. 1999. "Environment and Behavior of 2.5-Million-Year-Old Bouri Hominids." *Science* 284 (5414): 625–29.
de la Torre, Ignacio. 2019. "Searching for the Emergence of Stone Tool Making in Eastern Africa." *Proceedings of the National Academy of Science USA* 116 (24): 11567–69.
de la Torre, Ignacio, and Satoshi Hirata. 2015. "Percussive Technology in Human Evolution: An Introduction to a Comparative Approach in Fossil and Living Primates." *Philosophical Transactions B* 370 (1682):20140346.
de Waal, Frans. 2014. *The Bonobo and the Atheist: In Search of Humanism among the Primates*. New York: W. W. Norton.
Dean, Sam. 2013. "15 Raw Meat Dishes from around the World." *Bon Appétit*, May 20 https://www.bonappetit.com/trends/article/15-raw-meat-dishes-from-around-the-world.
DeBisschop, Dorothy. 2013. "Adeline Gray's Historic Leap." Patch, updated May 16. https://patch.com/connecticut/oxford-ct/adeline-grays-historic-leap.
DeGraaf, Leonard. 1997/1998. "Thomas Edison and the Origins of the Entertainment Phonograph." *NARAS Journal* 8 (1): 43–70.

Denison, Dave. 2021. "Exploding Plastic Inevitable." *Baffler* 60. https://thebaffler.com/salvos/exploding-plastic-inevitable-denison.

Dewey, A. T., and W. B. Ewer. 1878. "Thomas Edison and the Phonograph." *Pacific Rural Press*, May 25.

Dibble, Harold, Simon J. Holdaway, Sam C. Lin, David R. Braun, Matthew J. Douglass, Radu Iovita, Shannon P. McPherron, Deborah I. Olszewski, and Dennis Sandgathe. 2017. "Major Fallacies Surrounding Stone Artifacts and Assemblages." *Journal of Archaeological Method and Theory* 24 (3): 813–51.

Dickens, Charles. 1853. *Bleak House*. London: Bradbury & Evans.

Diez-Martín, F., P. Sánchez Yustos, D. Uribelarrea, E. Baquedano, D. F. Mark, A. Mabulla, C. Fraile, et al. 2015. "The Origin of the Acheulean: The 1.7 Million-Year-Old Site of FLK West, Olduvai Gorge (Tanzania)." *Scientific Reports* 5:17839.

Dixon, Donald F. 1995. "Retailing in Classical Athens: Gleanings from Contemporary Literature and Art." *Journal of Macromarketing* 15 (1): 74–85.

Dobbin, Robert. 2012. *The Cynic Philosophers: From Diogenes to Julian*. New York: Penguin Classics.

Doughton, Sandi. 2008. "Lucy on Display with Controversy." *Seattle Times*, October 2. https://www.seattletimes.com/seattle-news/lucy-on-display-with-controversy/.

Douglas, Mary, and Baron C. Isherwood. 1979. *The World of Goods: Towards an Anthropology of Consumption*. London: Allen Lane.

Doyle, A. Conan. 1893. "The Adventure of the Musgrave Ritual." *Strand Magazine* 5:479–89.

Du Boff, Richard B. 1967. "The Introduction of Electric Power in American Manufacturing." *The Economic History Review* 20 (3): 509–18.

Duenwald, Mary. 2004. "The Psychology of . . . Hoarding." *Discover*, January 19. https://www.discovermagazine.com/mind/the-psychology-of-hoarding.

Dunaway, Finis. 2017. "The 'Crying Indian' Ad That Fooled the Environmental Movement." *Chicago Tribune*, November 21. https://www.chicagotribune.com/opinion/commentary/ct-perspec-indian-crying-environment-ads-pollution-1123-20171113-story.html.

Dunbar, R. I. M. 2020. "Religion, the Social Brain and the Mystical Stance." *Archive for the Psychology of Religion* 42 (1): 46–62.

Dupont, Brandon. 2017. *The History of Economic Ideas: Economic Thought in Contemporary Context*. London: Routledge.

Dutt, Amitava Krishna. 2008. "The Dependence Effect, Consumption and Happiness: Galbraith Revisited." *Review of Political Economy* 20 (4): 527–50.

Earle, Rebecca. 2021. "Why Spanish Colonial Officials Feared the Power of Clothing." Psyche. https://psyche.co/ideas/why-spanish-colonial-officials-feared-the-power-of-clothing.

Earle, Timothy. 1997. *How Chiefs Come to Power: The Political Economy in Prehistory*. Palo Alto, CA: Stanford University Press.

Egeland, Charles P., Manuel Domínguez-Rodrigo, Travis Rayne Pickering, Colin G. Menter, and Jason L. Heaton. 2018. "Hominin Skeletal Part Abundances and Claims of Deliberate Disposal of Corpses in the Middle Pleistocene." *PNAS* 115 (18): 4601–6.

REFERENCES

Ehrsson, H. Henrik, Charles Spence, and Richard E. Passingham. 2004. "That's My Hand! Activity in Premotor Cortex Reflects Feeling of Ownership of a Limb." *Science* 305 (5685): 875–77.
Elbert, T., C. Pantev, C. Wienbruch, B. Rockstroh, and E. Taub. 1995. "Increased Cortical Representation of the Fingers of the Left Hand in String Players." *Science* 270 (5234): 305–7.
EPA. 2018. "Plastics: Material-Specific Data." https://www.epa.gov/facts-and-figures-about-materials-waste-and-recycling/plastics-material-specific-data.
Epstein, Robert, and Samuel D. Medalie. 1983. "The Spontaneous Use of a Tool by a Pigeon." *Behaviour Analysis Letters* 3:241–47.
Eren, Metin I., Stephen J. Lycett, and Masaki Tomonaga. 2020. "Underestimating Kanzi? Exploring Kanzi-Oldowan Comparisons in Light of Recent Human Stone Tool Replication." *Evolutionary Anthropology* 29 (6): 310–16.
Eriksen, Marcus. 2017. *Junk Raft: An Ocean Voyage and a Rising Tide of Activism to Fight Plastic Pollution*. Boston: Beacon Press.
Eriksen, Marcus, Laurent C. M. Lebreton, Henry S. Carson, Martin Thiel, Charles J. Moore, Jose C. Borerro, Francois Galgani, Peter G. Ryan, and Julia Reisser. 2014. "Plastic Pollution in the World's Oceans: More than 5 Trillion Plastic Pieces Weighing over 250,000 Tons Afloat at Sea." *PLoS One* 9 (12): e111913.
Eriksen, Marcus, Sherri Mason, Stiv Wilson, Carolyn Box, Ann Zellers, William Edwards, Hannah Farley, and Stephen Amato. 2013. "Microplastic Pollution in the Surface Waters of the Laurentian Great Lakes." *Marine Pollution Bulletin* 77:177–82.
Eschner, Kat. 2017. "Meet the Daredevil Parachutist Who Tested the First Nylon Parachute 75 Years Ago." *Smithsonian Magazine*. https://www.smithsonianmag.com/smart-news/meet-daredevil-parachutist-who-tested-duponts-first-nylon-parachute-180963527/.
Express. 2013. "Heirlooms? We'd Rather Save the TV." https://www.express.co.uk/news/uk/422352/Heirlooms-We-d-rather-save-the-TV.
Express Digest. 2020. "73 Qs with Roger Federer." https://expressdigest.com/roger-federer-used-to-mix-up-his-identical-twins/.
Faber, Harold. 1947a. "Body of Collyer in Found Near Where Brother Died." *New York Times*, April 9.
———. 1947b. "Homer Collyer, Harlem Recluse, Found Dead at 70." *New York Times*, March 22.
———. 1947c. "Police Fail to Find Collyer in House." *New York Times*, March 25.
Fagan, Chelsea. 2021. "Minimalism: Another Boring Product Wealthy People Can Buy." *Financial Diet*, January 20. https://thefinancialdiet.com/minimalism-just-another-boring-product-wealthy-people-can-buy/.
Faisal, Aldo, Dietrich Stout, Jan Apel, and Bruce Bradley. 2010. "The Manipulative Complexity of Lower Paleolithic Stone Toolmaking." *PLoS One* 5 (11): e13718.
Farago, Jason. 2018. "Was Australopithecus an Artist?" *New York Times*, February 1. https://www.nytimes.com/2018/02/01/arts/design/nasher-sculpture-center-dallas-first-sculpture-review.html.

FCN News. 2021. "Residential Carpet Sales Up 10%." https://www.fcnews.net/2021/02/residential-carpet-sales-up-10/.

Featherstone, Mike. 2001. "Consumer Culture." In *International Encyclopedia of the Social & Behavioral Sciences*, edited by N. J. Smelser and P. B. Baltes, 2662–69. Oxford: Elsevier.

Fellers, Joan H., and Gary M. Fellers. 1976. "Tool Use in a Social Insect and Its Implications for Competitive Interactions." *Science* 192 (4234): 70–72.

Fellman, Bruce. 1994. "Finding the First Farmers." *Yale Alumni Magazine*, October. http://archives.yalealumnimagazine.com/issues/94_10/agriculture.html.

Ferguson, T. J., and Wilfred Eriacho. 1990. "Ahayu:da: Zuni War Gods." *Native Peoples* 4 (1): 6–12.

Fern, Chris, Tania Dickinson, and Leslie Webster, eds. 2020. *The Staffordshire Hoard: An Anglo-Saxon Treasure*. London: Society of Antiquaries of London.

Fletcher, Edward Garland. 1941. "Electricity at the Savoy." *Studies in English* 21:154–61.

Flink, James J. 1990. *The Automobile Age*. Cambridge, MA: MIT Press.

Flinn, Mark V., David C. Geary, and Carol V. Ward. 2005. "Ecological Dominance, Social Competition and Coalitionary Arms Races: Why Humans Evolved Extraordinary Intelligence." *Evolution and Human Behavior* 26 (1): 10–46.

Fowler, Brenda. 2000. *Iceman: Uncovering the Life and Times of a Prehistoric Man Found in an Alpine Glacier*. New York: Random House.

Fox, Douglas. 2018. "How Human Smarts Evolved." *Sapiens*, July 27. https://www.sapiens.org/biology/primate-intelligence/.

Frazer, James George. 1922. *The Golden Bough: A Study in Magic and Religion*. New York: Macmillan.

Freeberg, Ernest. 2013. *The Age of Edison: Electric Light and the Invention of Modern America*. New York: Penguin.

Freinkel, Susan. 2011. *Plastic: A Toxic Love Story*. Boston: Houghton Mifflin Harcourt.

Frost, Randy O., and Gail Steketee. 2011. *Stuff: Compulsive Hoarding and the Meaning of Things*. Boston: Mariner Books.

Fruth, Barbara, and Gottfried Hohmann. 2018. "Food Sharing across Borders: First Observation of Intercommunity Meat Sharing by Bonobos at LuiKotale, DRC." *Human Nature* 29:91–103.

Fuentes, Agustín. 2017. *The Creative Spark: How Imagination Made Humans Exceptional*. New York: Dutton.

———. 2019. *Why We Believe: Evolution and the Human Way of Being*. New Haven, CT: Yale University Press.

———. 2020. "How Did Belief Evolve." *Sapiens*, February 26. https://www.sapiens.org/biology/religion-origins/.

Fujita, Masaki, Shinji Yamasaki, Chiaki Katagiri, Itsuro Oshiro, Katsuhiro Sano, Taiji Kurozumi, Hiroshi Sugawara, et al. 2016. "Advanced Maritime Adaptation in the Western Pacific Coastal Region Extends Back to 35,000–30,000 Years before Present." *Proceedings of the National Academy of Science* 113 (40): 11184–89.

Fullerton, Ronald A. 1988. "How Modern Is Modern Marketing? Marketing's Evolution and the Myth of the 'Production Era.'" *Journal of Marketing* 52 (1): 108–25.

Furness, Dyllan. 2017. "Do Animals Appreciate Art?" Vice, June 30. https://www.vice.com/en_us/article/d38zwz/animals-appreciate-art.

Galbraith, John Kenneth. (1958) 2011. "How Much Should a Country Consume?" In *Perspectives on Conservation: Essays on America's Natural Resources*, edited by H. Jarrett, 89–99. New York: RFF Press.

———. 1998. *The Affluent Society: Fortieth Anniversary Edition*. New York: Houghton Mifflin.

———. 1999. "The Affluent Society." Speech at Harvard University, August 19. https://www.famous-speeches-and-speech-topics.info/famous-speeches/j-k-galbraith-speech-the-affluent-society.htm

Gantz, Carroll. 2014. *Founders of American Industrial Design*. Jefferson, NC: McFarland.

Gardner, Colton. 2019. "Self Storage Industry Statistics." *Neighbor Blog*, August 15. https://www.neighbor.com/storage-blog/self-storage-industry-statistics/.

Gell, Alfred. 1998. *Art and Agency: An Anthropological Theory*. New York: Clarendon Press.

Gertner, Jon. 2013. *The Idea Factory: Bell Labs and the Great Age of American Innovation*. New York: Penguin.

Gethin, Rupert. 1998. *The Foundations of Buddhism*. Oxford: Oxford University Press.

Geyer, Roland, Jenna R. Jambeck, and Kara Lavender Law. 2017. "Production, Use, and Fate of All Plastics Ever Made." *Science Advances* 3 (7). https://doi.org/10.1126/sciadv.1700782.

Gibbons, Ann. 2010. "Lucy's Toolkit? Old Bones May Show Earliest Evidence of Tool Use." *Science* 329 (5993): 738–39.

———. 2011. "Who Was *Homo habilis*—and Was It Really *Homo*?" *Science* 332 (6063): 1370–71.

Gibson, K. R. 1993. "Tool Use, Language and Social Behavior in Relationship to Information Processing Capacities." In *Tools, Language and Cognition in Human Evolution*, edited by K. R. Gibson and T. Ingold, 251–69. Cambridge: Cambridge University Press.

Gibson, Margaret. 2008. *Objects of the Dead: Mourning and Memory in Everyday Life*. Melbourne: Melbourne University Publishing.

Giles, Anna. 2020. "8,000 Pounds of Trash Removed from Fairfield Home after Months-Long Battle by Police." CBS News Sacramento, February 12. https://sacramento.cbslocal.com/2020/02/12/8000-lbs-trash-fairfield-home-police-battle/.

Gilligan, Ian. 2019. *Climate, Clothing, and Agriculture in Prehistory: Linking Evidence, Causes, and Effects*. Cambridge: Cambridge University Press.

Glancey, Jonathan. 2020. "A History of the Department Store." BBC Culture, March 26. https://www.bbc.com/culture/bespoke/story/20150326-a-history-of-the-department-store/index.html.

Gogol, Nikolai. (1842) 1996. *Dead Souls*. Translated by R. Pevear and L. Volokhonsky. New York: Alfred A. Knopf.

Goheen, Jacob R., and Robert K. Swihart. 2003. "Food-Hoarding Behavior of Gray Squirrels and North American Red Squirrels in the Central Hardwoods Region: Implications for Forest Regeneration." *Canadian Journal of Zoology* 81 (9): 1636–39.

Gonen, Ron. 2021. *The Waste-Free World: How the Circular Economy Will Take Less, Make More, and Save the Planet*. New York: Portfolio/Penguin.

Goodall, Jane. 1964. "Tool-Using and Aimed Throwing in a Community of Free-Living Chimpanzees." *Nature* 201:1264–66.

———. 2002. *My Life with the Chimpanzees: The Fascinating Story of One of the World's Most Celebrated Naturalists*. New York: Aladdin.

———. 2010a. *Jane Goodall: 50 Years at Gombe*. New York: Stewart, Tabori & Chang.

———. 2010b. *Through a Window: My Thirty Years with the Chimpanzees of Gombe*. Boston: Mariner Books.

———. 2011. "Waterfall Displays." Dr. Jane Goodall & the Jane Goodall Institute USA, video, 2 min., 40 sec. https://www.youtube.com/watch?v=jjQCZClpaaY.

Goodheart, Eugene. 2012. "Our Consuming Problem." *Society* 49. https://doi.org/10.1007/s12115-012-9533-0.

Gordon, Robert J. 2016. *The Rise and Fall of American Growth: The U.S. Standard of Living since the Civil War*. Princeton, NJ: Princeton University Press.

Gotthardt, Alexxa. 2019. "Why Prehistoric Venus Figurines Still Mystify Experts." Artsy, July 3. https://www.artsy.net/article/artsy-editorial-prehistoric-venus-figurines-mystify-experts.

Graeber, David. 2012. *Debt: The First 5,000 Years*. Brooklyn, NY: Melville House.

Graeber, David, and David Wengrow. 2021. *The Dawn of Everything: A New History of Humanity*. New York: Farrar, Straus and Giroux.

Gray, Christopher. 2002. "Streetscapes/128th St. and Fifth Ave., Former Site of the Harlem House Where the Collyer Brothers Kept All That Stuff; Wondering Whether a Park Should Keep Its Name." *New York Times*, June 23. https://www.nytimes.com/2002/06/23/realestate/streetscapes-128th-st-fifth-ave-former-site-harlem-house-where-collyer-brothers.html.

Green, Adam S. 2020. "Debt and Inequality: Comparing the 'Means of Specification' in the Early Cities of Mesopotamia and the Indus civilization." *Journal of Anthropological Archaeology* 60:101232.

Greenberg, Richard. 2003. *The Dazzle*. New York: Dramatists Play Service.

Greene, Ann Norton. 2009. *Horses at Work: Harnessing Power in Industrial America*. Cambridge, MA: Harvard University Press.

Greene, Candace S., and Russell Thornton. 2007. *The Year the Stars Fell: Lakota Winter Counts at the Smithsonian*. Washington, DC: Smithsonian.

Gregory, Bateson. 1972. *Steps to an Ecology of Mind: Collected Essays in Anthropology, Psychiatry, Evolution, and Epistemology*. Chicago: University of Chicago Press.

Grobsmith, Elizabeth S. 1981. "The Changing Role of the Giveaway Ceremony in Contemporary Lakota Life." *Plains Anthropologist* 26 (91): 75–79.

Gummere, Richard M. 1917. *Seneca: Ad Lucilium Epistulae Morales*. London: William Heinemann.

Guthrie, R. Dale. 2005. *The Nature of Paleolithic Art*. Chicago: University of Chicago Press.

Guthrie, Stewart. 1993. *Faces in the Clouds: A New Theory of Religion*. New York: Oxford University Press.

Hahn, Barbara. 2020. *Technology in the Industrial Revolution.* Cambridge: Cambridge University Press.

Haidle, Miriam Noël. 2010. "Working-Memory Capacity and the Evolution of Modern Cognitive Potential: Implications from Animal and Early Human Tool Use." *Current Anthropology* 51 (Suppl. 1): 149–66.

Hailmann, William N. 1896. "Report of the Superintendent of Indian Schools." In *Annual Report of the Commissioner of Indian Affairs.* Washington, DC: Government Printing Office.

Hallemann, Caroline. 2016. "Why You Won't See Jackie Kennedy's Iconic Pink Suit on Display in a Museum." *Town & Country,* October 11. https://www.townandcountrymag.com/society/tradition/news/a8174/jackie-kennedy-pink-suit/.

Hallett, Emily Y., Curtis W. Marean, Teresa E. Steele, Esteban Álvarez-Fernández, Zenobia Jacobs, Jacopo Niccolò Cerasoni, Vera Aldeias, et al. 2021. "A Worked Bone Assemblage from 120,000–90,000 Year Old Deposits at Contrebandiers Cave, Atlantic Coast, Morocco." *iScience* 24 (9): 102988.

Halliday, Josh. 2018. "'It Looks Like You're a Lazy Idiot': Hoarders Welcome Medical Classification." *Guardian,* August 18. https://www.theguardian.com/society/2018/aug/18/it-looks-like-youre-a-lazy-idiot-hoarders-welcome-medical-classification.

Handley, Susannah. 1999. *Nylon: The Story of a Fashion Revolution.* Baltimore, MD: Johns Hopkins University Press.

Hanson, Michele. 2010. "How to Conquer the Clutter." *Guardian,* February 15. https://www.theguardian.com/lifeandstyle/2010/feb/15/how-to-conquer-clutter-homes.

Harari, Yuval Noah. 2015. *Sapiens: A Brief History of Humankind.* New York: Harper.

Hardy, Bruce. 2022. "Did Neanderthals Make Art?" *Sapiens,* August 11. https://www.sapiens.org/archaeology/did-neanderthals-make-art/.

Hardy, James. 2016. "The History of Marketing: From Trade to Tech." History Cooperative, September 14. https://historycooperative.org/the-evolution-of-marketing-from-trade-to-tech/.

Harford, Tim. 2017. "Why Didn't Electricity Immediately Change Manufacturing." BBC, August 21. https://www.bbc.com/news/business-40673694.

Harmand, Sonia, Jason E. Lewis, Craig S. Feibel, Christopher J. Lepre, Sandrine Prat, Arnaud Lenoble, Xavier Boës, et al. 2015. "3.3-Million-Year-Old Stone Tools from Lomekwi 3, West Turkana, Kenya." *Nature* 521:310–15.

Harrison, Rodney, Sarah Byrne, and Anne Clarke, eds. 2013. *Reassembling the Collection: Ethnographic Museums and Indigenous Agency.* Santa Fe: School for Advanced Research Press.

Hart, Donna, and Robert W. Sussman. 2018. *Man the Hunted: Primates, Predators, and Human Evolution.* New York: Routledge.

Hartenberger, Ursula. 2011. "Why Buildings Matter." *Guardian,* July 1. https://www.theguardian.com/sustainable-business/sustainable-building.

Harvey, Peter. 1990. *An Introduction to Buddhism: Teachings, History and Practices.* Cambridge: Cambridge University Press.

Hassett, Brenna. 2017. *Built on Bones: 15,000 Years of Urban Life and Death.* London: Bloomsbury Sigma.

Hawks, John, and Lee Berger. 2020. "On *Homo naledi* and Its Significance in Evolutionary Anthropology." In *Theology and Evolutionary Anthropology*, edited by C. Deane-Drummond and A. Fuentes, 51–68. New York: Routledge.

Hearn, Kelly. 2008. "Oldest Urban Site in the Americas Found, Experts Claim." http://news.nationalgeographic.com/news/2008/02/080226-peru-oldest.html.

Hecht, E. E., D. A. Gutman, N. Khreisheh, S.V. Taylor, J. Kilner, and A.A. Faisal. 2015. "Acquisition of Paleolithic Toolmaking Abilities Involves Structural Remodelling to Inferior Frontoparietal Regions." *Brain Structure and Function* 220 (4): 2315–31.

Heller, Steven. 2017. "Earnest Elmo Calkins: Founder of Modern Advertising and a Designer You Probably Don't Know." *Design Observer*. https://designobserver.com/feature/earnest-elmo-calkins/39651.

Henshilwood, Christopher S., Francesco d'Errico, and Ian Watts. 2009. "Engraved Ochres from the Middle Stone Age Levels at Blombos Cave, South Africa." *Journal of Human Evolution* 57 (1): 27–47.

Herring, Scott. 2011. "Collyer Curiosa: A Brief History of Hoarding." *Criticism* 53 (2): 159–88.

Higgs, Kerryn. 2014. *Collision Course: Endless Growth on a Finite Planet*. Cambridge, MA: MIT Press.

History. 2020. "Floor of the Floor." https://history.house.gov/Blog/2020/January/1-21-carpet/.

Hodder, Ian, and Arkadiusz Marciniak, eds. 2015. *Assembling Çatalhöyük*. New York: Routledge.

Hodgson, Derek, and Paul Pettitt. 2018a. "The Origins of Iconic Depictions: A Falsifiable Model Derived from the Visual Science of Paleolithic Cave Art and World Rock Art." *Cambridge Archaeological Journal* 28 (4): 591–612.

———. 2018b. "Warning Signs: How Early Humans First Began to Paint Animals." *The Conversation*, May 4. https://theconversation.com/warning-signs-how-early-humans-first-began-to-paint-animals-95597.

Hoffmann, D. L., D. E. Angelucci, V. Villaverde, J. Zapata, and J. Zilhao. 2018. "Symbolic Use of Marine Shells and Mineral Pigments by Iberian Neandertals 115,000 Years Ago." *Scientific Advances* 4 (2): eaar5255.

Hoffmann, D. L., C. D. Standish, M. Garcia-Diez, P. B. Pettitt, J. A. Milton, J. Zilhao, J. J. Alcolea-Gonzalez, et al. 2018. "U-Th Dating of Carbonate Crusts Reveals Neandertal Origin of Iberian Cave Art." *Science* 359 (6378): 912–15.

Hogenboom, Melissa. 2016. "We Did Not Invent Clothes Simply to Stay Warm." BBC Earth. http://www.bbc.com/earth/story/20160919-the-real-origin-of-clothes.

Holmes, Nicholas P., and Charles Spence. 2004. "The Body Schema and the Multisensory Representation(s) of Peripersonal Space." *Cognitive Processing* 5 (2): 94–105.

Holmes, Tao Tao. 2016. "Acorn Woodpeckers Hoard Thousands of Acorns in a Single Tree." *Atlas Obscura*, May 16. https://www.atlasobscura.com/articles/acorn-woodpeckers-hoard-thousands-of-acorns-in-a-single-tree.

Hood, Bruce. 2019. *Possessed: Why We Want More Than We Need*. Oxford: Oxford University Press.

Horton, Sarah J. 2007. *Living Buddhist Statues in Early Medieval and Modern Japan*. New York: Palgrave.

Hoskins, Janet. 2013. Agency, Biography, and Objects. In *Handbook of Material Culture*, edited by C. Tilley, W. Keane, S. Küechler, Mike Rowlands, and Patricia Spyer, 74–84. Los Angeles: Sage.

Hounshell, David A. 1984. *From the American System to Mass Production, 1800–1932: The Development of Manufacturing Technology in the United States*. Baltimore, MD: Johns Hopkins University Press.

Hublin, J. J., F. Spoor, M. Braun, F. Zonneveld, and S. Condemi. 1996. "A Late Neanderthal Associated with Upper Paleolithic Artefacts." *Nature* 381 (6579): 224–26.

Humes, Edward. 2012. *Garbology: Our Dirty Love Affair with Trash*. New York: Avery.

Hunnicutt, Benjamin Kline. 1988. *Work without End: Abandoning Shorter Hours for the Right to Work*. Philadelphia: Temple University Press.

Hunt, Gavin R., Russell D. Gray, and Alex H. Taylor. 2013. "Three Ingredients for Becoming a Creative Tool User." In *Tool Use in Animals: Cognition and Ecology*, edited by C. M. Sanz, J. Call and C. Boesch, 3–20. Cambridge: Cambridge University Press.

Hutchinson, Elizabeth. 2009. *The Indian Craze: Primitivism, Modernism, and Transculturation in American Art, 1890–1915*. Durham, NC: Duke University Press.

Ihde, Don, and Lambros Malafouris. 2019. "*Homo faber* Revisited: Postphenomenology and Material Engagement Theory." *Philosophy & Technology* 32 (2): 195–214.

Isler, Karin, and Carel P. van Schaik. 2012. "How Our Ancestors Broke through the Gray Ceiling: Comparative Evidence for Cooperative Breeding in Early *Homo*." *Current Anthropology* 53 (S6): 453–65.

Jacob, Sandra. 2010. "Scientists Discover Oldest Evidence of Human Stone Tool Use and Meat-Eating." EureakAlert!, August 12. https://www.eurekalert.org/pub_releases/2010-08/m-sdo081210.php.

Jacobs, Tom. 2014. "Why Original Artworks Move Us More Than Reproductions." *Pacific Standard*, September 18. https://psmag.com/social-justice/original-artworks-move-us-reproductions-90869.

James, William. 1887. "Some Human Instincts." *Popular Science Monthly*, September, 666–81.

Jaquith, Sterling. 2017. *Not of This World: A Catholic Guide to Minimalism*. Boise, ID: Ever Catholic.

Johanson, Donald, and Kate Wong. 2009. *Lucy's Legacy: The Quest for Human Origins*. New York: Three Rivers Press.

Joordens, J. C., F. d'Errico, F. P. Wesselingh, S. Munro, J. de Vos, J. Wallinga, C. Ankjaergaard, et al. 2015. "*Homo erectus* at Trinil on Java Used Shells for Tool Production and Engraving." *Nature* 518 (7538): 228–31.

Jordan, John W. 1919. *The Pennsylvania Magazine of History and Biography Vol. XLIII*. Philadelphia: Historical Society of Pennsylvania.

Joseph, Robert. 2005. "Introduction: An Elder's Perspective." In *Listening to Our Ancestors: The Art of Native Life along the North Pacific Coast*, edited by R. Joseph, 9–13. Washington, DC: Smithsonian Institution Press.

Jurmain, Robert, Lynn Kilgrove, Wenda Trevathan, and Russell L. Ciochon. 2012. *Introduction to Physical Anthropology*. 13th ed. Belmont, CA: Wadsworth.

Kaas, Jon H. 2004. "Evolution of Somatosensory and Motor Cortex in Primates." *Anatomical Record* 281A (1): 1148–56.

———. 2009. "Evolution of the Somatosensory System in Mammals." In *Encyclopedia of Neuroscience*, edited by M. D. Binder, N. Hirowaka, and U. Windhorst. Berlin: Springer. https://link.springer.com/referenceworkentry/10.1007%2F978-3-540-29678-2_3169.

Kal, Wilhelmina, ed. 1999. *Precious Metals in Early Southeast Asia*. Amsterdam: Royal Tropical Institute.

Kalmykovaa, Yuliya, Madumita Sadagopan, and Leonardo Rosado. 2018. "Circular Economy—from Review of Theories and Practices to Development of Implementation Tools." *Resources, Conservation and Recycling* 135 (August): 190–201.

Kaneda, Toshiko, and Carl Haub. 2021. "How Many People Have Ever Lived on Earth?" Population Reference Bureau. https://www.prb.org/articles/how-many-people-have-ever-lived-on-earth/.

Kappelman, John, Richard A. Ketcham, Stephen Pearce, Lawrence Todd, Wiley Akins, Matthew W. Colbert, Mulugeta Feseha, Jessica A. Maisano, and Adrienne Witzel. 2016. "Perimortem Fractures in Lucy Suggest Mortality from Fall Out of Tall Tree." *Nature* 537:503–7.

Karetzky, Patricia Eichenbaum. 2014. *Chinese Religious Art*. Lanham, MD: Lexington Books.

Kasser, Tim. 2003. *The High Price of Materialism*. Cambridge, MA: MIT Press.

Kasser, Tim, and Allen D. Kanner, eds. 2004. *Psychology and Consumer Culture: The Struggle for a Good Life in a Materialistic World*. Washington, DC: American Psychological Association.

Kaufman, Michael T. 1972. "A Stubborn Search." *New York Times*, October 2. https://www.nytimes.com/1972/10/02/archives/a-stubborn-search.html.

Kaysen, Ronda. 2021. "Inside the World of Buy Nothing, Where Dryer Lint Is a Hot Commodity." *New York Times*, October 22. https://www.nytimes.com/2021/10/22/realestate/buy-nothing-facebook-group.html.

Kaza, Silpa, Lisa C. Yao, Perinaz Bhada-Tata, and Frank Van Woerden. 2020. *What a Waste 2.0: A Global Snapshot of Solid Waste Management to 2050*. Washington, DC: World Bank, Urban Development.

Keep America Beautiful. 1971. "'Crying Indian' PSA, 1971. 'People Start Pollution. People Can Stop It.'" https://www.youtube.com/watch?v=lR06-RP3n0Q. 1 min.

Kelly, Robert L. 2019. *The Fifth Beginning: What Six Million Years of Human History Can Tell Us about Our Future*. Berkeley: University of California Press.

Kemeny, Richard. 2019. "Fat, Not Meat, May Have Led to Bigger Hominin Brains." *Sapiens*, March 28. https://www.sapiens.org/biology/brain-evolution-fat/.

Kettering, Charles F. 1929. "Keep the Consumer Dissatisfied." *Nation's Business* 17 (1): 30–31, 79.

Key, Alastair J. M., Ivan Jarić, and David L. Roberts. 2021. "Modelling the End of the Acheulean at Global and Continental Levels Suggests Widespread Persistence into the Middle Palaeolithic." *Humanities and Social Sciences Communications* 8 (55). https://doi.org/10.1057/s41599-021-00735-8.

Kimbel, William, R. C. Walter, Donald Johanson, Kaye Reed, J. L. Aronson, Z. Assefa, Curtis Marean, et al. 1996. "Late Pliocene Homo and Oldowan Tools from the Hadar Formation (Kada Hadar Member), Ethiopia." *Journal of Human Evolution* 31:549–61.

King, Amy Swanson. 2021. "Comfy Carpet, Once Dismissed as Out-of-Date, Is Back in Vogue." *Seattle Times*, updated May 24. https://www.seattletimes.com/explore/at-home/comfy-carpet-once-dismissed-as-out-of-date-is-back-in-vogue/.

Kiron, David, Frank Ackerman, and Neva R. Goodwin, eds. 1997. *The Consumer Society*. Washington, DC: Island Press.

Kissel, Marc, and Agustín Fuentes. 2017. "WISDOM Database." https://marckissel.shinyapps.io/wisdom_march28/.

——. 2018. "'Behavioral Modernity' as a Process, not an Event, in the Human Niche." *Time and Mind* 11 (2): 163–83.

Kivell, Tracy L. 2015. "Evidence in Hand: Recent Discoveries and the Early Evolution of Human Manual Manipulation." *Philosophical Transactions of the Royal Society B* 370. https://doi.org/10.1098/rstb.2015.0105.

Klein, Richard G. 2009. *The Human Career: Human Biological and Cultural Origins*. 3rd ed. Chicago: University of Chicago Press.

Knight, Laurence. 2014. "A Brief History of Plastics, Natural and Synthetic." BBC, May 17. https://www.bbc.com/news/magazine-27442625.

Kohler, Timothy A., and Michael E. Smith, eds. 2018. *Ten Thousand Years of Inequality: The Archaeology of Wealth Differences*. Tucson: University of Arizona Press.

Köhler, Wolfgang. (1925) 2019. *The Mentality of Apes*. Translated by E. Winter. New York: Routledge.

Kohn, Marek, and Steven Mithen. 1999. "Handaxes: Products of Sexual Selection?" *Antiquity* 73 (281): 518–26.

Kouwenhoven, Arlette P. 1997. "World's Oldest Spears." *Archaeology Archive* 50 (3). https://archive.archaeology.org/9705/newsbriefs/spears.html.

Krajewski, Markus. 2014. "The Great Lightbulb Conspiracy." *IEEE Spectrum*, September 24. https://spectrum.ieee.org/the-great-lightbulb-conspiracy.

Krause, Johannes, and Thomas Trappe. 2021. *A Short History of Humanity: A New History of Old Europe*. New York: Random House.

Krmnicek, Stefan, ed. 2019. *A Cultural History of Money in Antiquity*. London: Bloomsbury Academic.

Kronenberger, Louis. 1973. "Tennysse Major Wingfield's Invention." *New York Times*, May 6. https://www.nytimes.com/1973/05/06/archives/major-wingfields-invention-tennysse-although-lawn-tennis-is-only.html.

Krützen, Michael, Janet Mann, Michael R. Heithaus, Richard C. Connor, Lars Bejder, and William B. Sherwin. 2005. "Cultural Transmission of Tool Use in Bottlenose Dolphins." *Proceedings of the National Academy of Science* 102 (25): 8939–43.

Kunen, Julie L., Mary Jo Galindo, and Erin Chase. 2002. "Identifying Maya Ritual Behavior in the Archaeological Record." *Ancient Mesoamerica* 13 (2): 197–211.

Kuwano, Masumi, Tomohiro Nakao, Koji Yonemoto, Satoshi Yamada, Keitaro Murayama, Kayo Okada, Shinichi Honda, et al. 2020. "Clinical Characteristics of Hoarding Disorder in Japanese Patients." *Heliyon* 6 (3): e03527.

Kvavadze, Eliso, Ofer Bar-Yosef, Anna Belfer-Cohen, Elisabetta Boaretto, Nino Jakeli,

Zinovi Matskevich, and Tengiz Meshveliani. 2009. "30,000-Year-Old Wild Flax Fibers." *Science* 325 (5946): 1359.

Kyrk, Hazel. 1923. *A Theory of Consumption*. Boston: Houghton Mifflin.

Laferrière, Daniel. 1978. *Sign and Subject: Semiotic and Psychoanalytic Investigations into Poetry*. Lisse, Netherlands: Peter de Ridder Press.

Landes, David S. 2003. *The Unbound Prometheus: Technological Change and Industrial Development in Western Europe from 1750 to the Present*. 2nd ed. Cambridge: Cambridge University Press.

Larrinaga, Carlos, and Nicholas Garcia-Torea. 2022. "An Ecological Critique of Accounting: The Circular Economy and COVID-19." *Critical Perspectives on Accounting* 82. https://doi.org/10.1016/j.cpa.2021.102320.

Latour, Bruno. 1999. *Pandora's Hope: Essays on the Reality of Science Studies*. Cambridge, MA: Harvard University Press.

Laville, Sandra, and Matthew Taylor. 2017. "A Million Bottles a Minute." *Guardian*, June 28. https://www.theguardian.com/environment/2017/jun/28/a-million-a-minute-worlds-plastic-bottle-binge-as-dangerous-as-climate-change.

Leach, William. 1993. *Land of Desire: Merchants, Power, and the Rise of a New American Culture*. New York: Vintage Books.

Leakey, L. S. B. 1936. *Stone Age Africa: An Outline of Prehistory in Africa*. London: Oxford University Press.

Leakey, L. S. B., Arthur T. Hopwood, and Hans Reck. 1931. "New Yields from the Oldoway Bone Beds, Tanganyika Territory." *Nature* 128 (3243): 1075.

Leakey, L. S. B., P. V. Tobias, and J. R. Napier. 1964. "A New Species of Genus *Homo* from Olduvai Gorge." *Nature* 202:7–9.

Leakey, Richard. 1994. *The Origin of Humankind*. New York: Basic Books.

Leavitt, Sarah. 1997. *Slater Mill*. Dover, NH: Arcadia.

Lemire, Beverly. 2018. *Global Trade and the Transformation of Consumer Cultures: The Material World Remade, c.1500–1820*. Cambridge: Cambridge University Press.

Lenski, Gerhard E. 1984. *Power and Privilege: A Theory of Social Stratification*. Chapel Hill: University of North Carolina Press.

Levere, Jane L. 2013. "After the 'Crying Indian,' Keep America Beautiful Starts a New Campaign." *New York Times*, July 16. https://www.nytimes.com/2013/07/17/business/media/decades-after-a-memorable-campaign-keep-america-beautiful-returns.html.

Levine, Philippa. 2008. "States of Undress: Nakedness and the Colonial Imagination." *Victorian Studies* 50 (2): 189–219.

Lewin, Roger. 2002. "The Old Man of Olduvai Gorge." *Smithsonian Magazine*. https://www.smithsonianmag.com/history/the-old-man-of-olduvai-gorge-69246530/.

Lewis, Jason E., and Sonia Harmand. 2016. "An Earlier Origin for Stone Tool Making: Implications for Cognitive Evolution and the Transition to Homo." *Philosophical Transactions: Biological Sciences* 371 (1968): 1–8.

Library of Congress. 2020. "History of the Cylinder Phonograph." https://www.loc.gov/collections/edison-company-motion-pictures-and-sound-recordings/articles-and-essays/history-of-edison-sound-recordings/history-of-the-cylinder-phonograph/.

Life. 1955. "Throwaway Living." Vol. 39 (5): 43–44.

Lilienfeld, Scott O., and Hal Arkowitz. 2013. "Clutter, Clutter Everywhere." *Scientific American Mind* 24 (4): 68–69.

Lillios, Katina T. 1999. "Objects of Memory: The Ethnography and Archaeology of Heirlooms." *Journal of Archaeological Method and Theory* 6 (3): 235–62.

Linklater, Andro. 2015. *Owning the Earth: The Transforming History of Land Ownership*. New York: Bloomsbury.

Lipartito, Kenneth. 2012. "Subliminal Seduction: The Politics of Consumer Research in Post-World War II America." In *The Rise of Marketing and Market Research*, edited by H. Berghoff, P. Scranton, and U. Spiekermann, 215–36. New York: Palgrave Macmillan.

Liu, Jianguo. 2022. "Consumption Patterns and Biodiversity." Royal Society. https://royalsociety.org/topics-policy/projects/biodiversity/.

Liu, Lucen, and P. David Howe. 2012. "Phenomenology and Embodiment in Crosscultural Sporting Contexts: A Case of Chinese Female Students." *Asia Pacific Journal of Sport and Social Science* 1 (2–3): 169–85.

Lobdell, Nicole Catherine. 2013. "'The Hoarding Sense': Hoarding in Austin, Tennyson, Dickens, and Nineteenth-Century Culture." PhD diss., University of Georgia, Athens.

Locke, John. 1821. *Two Treatises of Government*. London: Whitmore and Fenn.

Lombard, Marlize, and Laurel Phillipson. 2010. "Indications of Bow and Stone-Tipped Arrow Use 64,000 Years Ago in KwaZulu-Natal, South Africa." *Antiquity* 84 (325): 635–48.

Loo, Tina. 1992. "Dan Cranmer's Potlatch: Law as Coercion, Symbol, and Rhetoric in British Columbia, 1884–1951." *Canadian Historical Review* 73 (2): 125–65.

Lu, Houyuan, Jianping Zhang, Kam-biu Liu, Naiqin Wu, Yumei Li, Kunshu Zhou, Maolin Ye, et al. 2009. "Earliest Domestication of Common Millet (*Panicum miliaceum*) in East Asia Extended to 10,000 Years Ago." *Proceedings of the National Academy of Science* 106 (18): 7367–72.

Luncz, Lydia V., Mike Gill, Tomos Proffitt, Magdalena S. Svensson, Lars Kulik, and Suchinda Malaivijitnond. 2019. "Group-Specific Archaeological Signatures of Stone Tool Use in Wild Macaques." *eLife* 8:e46961.

Lury, Celia. 2011. *Consumer Culture*. Cambridge: Polity.

Lycett, Stephen J., and John A. J. Gowlett. 2008. "On Questions Surrounding the Acheulean 'Tradition.'" *World Archaeology* 40 (3): 295–315.

Lycett, Stephen J., Kerstin Schillinger, Metin I. Eren, Noreenvon Cramon-Taubadel, and Alex Mesoudi. 2016. "Factors Affecting Acheulean Handaxe Variation: Experimental Insights, Microevolutionary Processes, and Macroevolutionary Outcomes." *Quaternary International* 411 (Part B): 386–401.

MacVean, Mary. 2014. "For Many People, Gathering Possessions Is Just the Stuff of Life." *Los Angeles Times*, March 21. https://www.latimes.com/health/la-xpm-2014-mar-21-la-he-keeping-stuff-20140322-story.html.

Maestro, Betsy. 1993. *The Story of Money*. Boston: Houghton Mifflin.

Mah, Alice. 2021. "Future-Proofing Capitalism: The Paradox of the Circular Economy for Plastics." *Global Environmental Politics* 21 (2): 121–42.

Main, John. 1913. *Religious Chastity: An Ethnological Study*. New York: Macaulay.

Manoharan, Christopher, and Dimitris Xygalatas. 2019. "How Hearts Align in a Muslim Ritual." *Sapiens*, August 15. https://www.sapiens.org/biology/sufi-ritual-istanbul/.

Marks, Jonathan. 2015. *Tales of the Ex-apes: How We Think About Human Evolution*. Berkeley: University of California Press.

Marris, Emma. 2016. "Iconic Fossil Assigned Probable Cause of Death: A Big Fall." *Sapiens*, August 26. https://www.sapiens.org/biology/arboreal-human-ancestors-lucy/.

Marshall, P. David, and Joanne Morreale. 2018. *Advertising and Promotional Culture: Case Histories*. New York: Palgrave Macmillan.

Martel, Marie, Lucilla Cardinali, Alice C. Roy, and Alessandro Farnè. 2016. "Tool-Use: An Open Window into Body Representation and Its Plasticity." *Cognitive Neuropsychology* 33 (1–2): 82–101.

Martland, Peter. 2012. *Recording History: The British Record Industry, 1888–1931*. Lanham, MD: Scarecrow Press.

Marzke, Mary W. 2013. "Tool Making, Hand Morphology and Fossil Hominins." *Philosophical Transactions of the Royal Society B* 368. https://doi.org/10.1098/rstb.2012.0414.

Mathur, Nita, ed. 2013. *Consumer Culture, Modernity and Identity*. Thousand Oaks, CA: Sage Publications.

Mauss, Marcel. 1950. *The Gift: The Form and Reason for Exchange in Archaic Societies*. Glencoe: Free Press.

Mayer, Daniella E. Bar-Yosef, Iris Groman-Yaroslavski, Ofer Bar-Yosef, Israel Hershkovitz, Astrid Kampen-Hasday, Bernard Vandermeersch, Yossi Zaidner, and Mina Weinstein-Evron. 2020. "On Holes and Strings: Earliest Displays of Human Adornment in the Middle Paleolithic." *PLoS One* 15 (7): e0234924.

McAllister, Jackie. 1995. "The Collyer Brothers." *Grand Street* 54:203–11.

McGregor, Kate. 2020. "Can You Fit Eight Years of Trash Into a Mason Jar? Lauren Singer Can." Yahoo News, April 21. https://news.yahoo.com/fit-eight-years-trash-mason-134500826.html.

McKee, Jeffrey K., Frank E. Poirier, and W. Scott McGraw. 2016. *Understanding Human Evolution*. 5th ed. London: Routledge.

McKendrick, Neil, John Brewer, and J. H. Plumb. 1982. *The Birth of a Consumer Society: The Commercialization of Eighteenth-Century England*. Bloomington: Indiana University Press.

McPherron, Shannon P. 2013. "Perspectives on Stone Tools and Cognition in the Early Paleolithic Record." In *Tool Use in Animals: Cognition and Ecology*, edited by C. M. Sanz, J. Call, and C. Boesch, 286–309. Cambridge: Cambridge University Press.

McPherron, Shannon P., Zeresenay Alemseged, Curtis W. Marean, Jonathan G. Wynn, Denné Reed, Denis Geraads, René Bobe, and Hamdallah A. Béarat. 2010. "Evidence for Stone-Tool-Assisted Consumption of Animal Tissues before 3.39 Million Years Ago at Dikika, Ethiopia." *Nature* 466:857–60.

Mead, John S. 2017. "The 'Sciencing' of *Homo naledi*." *Education Blog*, National Geo-

REFERENCES

graphic. https://blog.education.nationalgeographic.org/2017/10/19/the-sciencing-of-homo-naledi/.

Meikle, Jeffrey L. 1995. *American Plastic: A Cultural History*. New Brunswick, NJ: Rutgers University Press.

Merleau-Ponty, Maurice. (1945) 1962. *Phenomenology of Perception*. Translated by C. Smith. London: Routledge.

Mesoudi, Alex, and Alex Thornton. 2018. "What Is Cumulative Cultural Evolution?" *Proceedings of the Royal Society B: Biological Sciences* 285:20180712.

Mhatre, Natasha, Robert Malkin, Rohini Balakrishnan, and Daniel Robert. 2017. "Tree Crickets Optimize the Acoustics of Baffles to Exaggerate Their Mate-Attraction Signal." *eLife* 6:32763.

Michel, Henri. 1967. *Scientific Instruments in Art and History*. New York: Viking Books.

Miles, Steven. 1998. *Consumerism: As a Way of Life*. London: Sage Publications.

Miles, Tiya. 2021. *All That She Carried: The Journey of Ashley's Sack, a Black Family Keepsake*. New York: Random House.

Millburn, Joshua Fields, and Ryan Nicodemus. 2011. *Minimalism: Live a Meaningful Life*. Missoula, MT: Asymmetrical Press.

Miller, Daniel. 1987. *Material Culture and Mass Consumption*. Oxford: Blackwell Press.

———. 1998. *A Theory of Shopping*. Ithaca, NY: Cornell University Press.

———. 2008. *The Comfort of Things*. Cambridge: Polity.

Miller, Daniel, and Christopher Tilley, eds. 1984. *Ideology, Power and Prehistory*. Cambridge: Cambridge University Press.

Miller, George. 2000. *The Mating Mind: How Sexual Choice Shaped the Evolution of Human Nature*. New York: Doubleday.

Miller, Luke E., Cécile Fabio, Valeria Ravenda, Salam Bahmad, Eric Koun, Romeo Salemme, Jacques Luauté, et al. 2019. "Somatosensory Cortex Efficiently Processes Touch Located Beyond the Body." *Current Biology* 29 (4): 4276–83.

Miller, Matthew L. 2017. "Acorn Woodpecker: The Fascinating Life of the Master Hoarder." *Cool Green Science* (blog), April 24. Nature Conservancy. https://blog.nature.org/science/2017/04/24/acorn-woodpecker-the-fascinating-life-of-the-master-hoarder/.

Minter, Adam. 2017. "We've Been Buying Stuff for a Generation." *Bloomberg*, August 28. https://www.bloomberg.com/opinion/articles/2017-08-28/the-self-storage-business-is-booming-here-s-why.

Molotch, Harvey. 2005. *Where Stuff Comes From: How Toasters, Toilets, Cars, Computers and Many Other Things Come to Be as They Are*. New York: Routledge.

Montgomery, Lindsay M., and Chip Colwell. 2019. *Objects of Survivance: A Material History of the American Indian School Experience*. Louisville: University Press of Colorado.

Moore, Mark W., and Yinika Perston. 2016. "Experimental Insights into the Cognitive Significance of Early Stone Tools." *PLoS One* 11 (7): e0158803.

Morell, Virginia. 2011. *Ancestral Passions: The Leaky Family and the Quest for Humankind's Beginnings*. New York: Simon & Schuster.

Morgan, Maybelle. 2015. "Throwaway Fashion." *Daily Mail*, June 9. https://www.dailymail.co.uk/femail/article-3116962/Throwaway-fashion-Women-adopted

-wear-culture-binning-clothes-wears-aren-t-pictured-outfit-twice-social-media.html.

Morin, Brandi. 2021. "These Indigenous Children Died Far Away More Than a Century Ago. Here's How They Finally Got Home." *National Geographic*, August 6. https://www.nationalgeographic.com/history/article/these-indigenous-children-died-far-away-more-than-a-century-ago-heres-how-they-finally-got-home.

Morriss-Kay, G. M. 2010. "The Evolution of Human Artistic Creativity." *Journal of Anatomy* 216 (2): 158–76.

Morritt, Robert D. 2010. *Echoes from the Greek Bronze Age: An Anthology of Greek Thought in the Classical Age*. Newcastle Upon Tyne: Cambridge Scholars Publishing.

Mossman, Susan. 1994. "Parkesine and Celluloid." In *The Development of Plastics*, edited by S. T. I. Mossman and P. J. T. Morris, 10–25. Cambridge: Royal Society of Chemistry.

Mowery, David C., and Nathan Rosenberg. 1998. *Paths of Innovation: Technological Change in 20th-Century America*. Cambridge: Cambridge University Press.

Moyer, Michael. 2009. "Recorded Music." *Scientific American*, September 1. https://www.scientificamerican.com/article/recorded-music/.

Mruczek, Ryan E. B., Isabell S. von Loga, and Sabine Kastner. 2013. "The Representation of Tool and Non-tool Object Information in the Human Intraparietal Sulcus." *Journal of Neurophysiology* 109 (12): 2883–96.

Murphy, Wendy Wiedenhoft. 2016. *Consumer Culture and Society*. Thousand Oaks, CA: Sage Publications.

Musgrave, Stephanie, David Morgan, Elizabeth Lonsdorf, Roger Mundry, and Crickette Sanz. 2016. "Tool Transfers Are a Form of Teaching among Chimpanzees." *Scientific Reports* 6:34783.

Muskett, Georgina. 2018. *Archaeology Hotspot France: Unearthing the Past for Armchair Archaeologists*. Lanham, MD: Rowan & Littlefield.

Nakao, Tomohiro, and Shigenobu Kanba. 2019. "Pathophysiology and Treatment of Hoarding Disorder." *PCN Frontier Review* 73 (7): 370–75.

Narberhaus, Micha, and Joséphine von Mitschke-Collande. 2017. "Circular Economy Isn't a Magical Fix for Our Environmental Woes." *Guardian*, July 14. https://www.theguardian.com/sustainable-business/2017/jul/14/circular-economy-not-magical-fix-environmental-woes-global-corporations.

Nelson, Sarah Milledge, ed. 2004. *Gender in Archaeology: Analyzing Power and Prestige*. 2nd ed. Walnut Creek, CA: AltaMira Press.

Nevett, Terry. 1977. "London's Early Advertising Agents." *Journal of Advertising History* 1:15–17.

Newman, George E., Gil Diesendruck, and Paul Bloom. 2011. "Celebrity Contagion and the Value of Objects." *Journal of Consumer Research* 38 (2): 215–28.

New York Times. 1942. "Stocking Exchange a Near Riot." November 7.

———. 1944. "Nylon Hose to Be Plentiful as Soon as Peace Comes." April 22.

———. 1946a. "5,000 Mother's Darlings Mob Nylon Sale." May 6.

———. 1946b. "25,000 Mob Store to Buy Nylon Stockings." January 23.

———. 1947a. "200 Bid Spiritedly for Collyer Items." June 11.

REFERENCES

———. 1947b. "Razing of Collyer Home Is Considered by City." May 10.
———. 1958. "Harlem Children Clearing Collyer Lot for Flowers." September 25.
———. 1996. "1946: A Nylon Run." Editorial, April 13. https://www.nytimes.com/1996/04/13/opinion/IHT-1946-a-nylon-run-in-our-pages100-75-and-50-years-ago.html.
Nilles, Billy. 2019. "How an Obsession with Organizing Built an Empire: Inside Marie Kondo's Controversially Tidy World." E! News, January 24. https://www.eonline.com/news/1007829/how-an-obsession-with-organizing-built-an-empire-inside-marie-kondo-s-controversially-tidy-world.
Nollet, Abbé. 1769. *Memoir I: On the Curious Application of Certain Electrical Phenomenon.* Paris: Royal Academy of Sciences.
Nordling, Linda. 2021. "Raising Up African Paleoanthropologists." *Sapiens,* September 28. https://www.sapiens.org/biology/african-paleoanthropologists/.
Nowell, April, and Melanie L. Chang. 2014. "Science, the Media, and Interpretations of Upper Paleolithic Figurines." *American Anthropologist* 116 (3): 562–77.
Oakley, Kenneth P. 1956. *Man the Tool-Maker.* London: Trustees of the British Museum.
O'Brian, Jane. 2015. "The Stuff Paradox: Dealing with Clutter in the US." BBC, February 6. https://www.bbc.com/news/magazine-31051632.
Ofgang, Erik. 2019. "How a Connecticut Company's Parachutes Helped Launch D-Day." *Connecticut Magazine,* May 22. https://www.connecticutmag.com/history/how-a-connecticut-company-s-parachutes-helped-launch-d-day/article_0b628ae0-77f1-11e9-a3b2-8390e8ec8a6c.html.
Olsen, Bjørnar. 2010. *In Defense of Things: Archaeology and the Ontology of Objects.* Lanham, MD: AltaMira Press.
Osiurak, François. 2020. *The Tool Instinct.* Hoboken, NJ: John Wiley & Sons.
Owili, Ronald. 2022. "Kenya Urged to Expand Single Use Plastics Ban Ahead of Treaty." KBC. https://www.kbc.co.ke/kenya-urged-to-expand-single-use-plastics-ban-ahead-of-treaty/.
Packard, Vance. 1957. *The Hidden Persuaders.* New York: Pocket Books.
———. 1959. *The Status Seekers.* New York: D. McKay.
———. 1960. *The Waste Makers.* New York: D. McKay.
Palmer, David A., Martin M. H. Tse, and Chip Colwell. 2019. "Guanyin's Limbo: Icons as Demi-persons and Dividuating Objects." *American Anthropologist* 121 (4): 897–910.
Park, Ji Kyung, and Deborah Roedder John. 2010. "Got to Get You into My Life: Do Brand Personalities Rub Off on Consumers?" *Journal of Consumer Research* 37 (4): 655–69.
Patton, Randall. 2006. "A History of the U.S. Carpet Industry." EH.net. http://eh.net/encyclopedia/a-history-of-the-u-s-carpet-industry/.
Pearson, Mike Parker. 2013. *Stonehenge: A New Understanding.* New York: The Experiment.
Peck, Linda Levy. 2005. *Consuming Splendor: Society and Culture in Seventeenth-Century England.* Cambridge: Cambridge University Press.
Peel, Frank. 1880. *The Risings of the Luddites.* Heckmondwike, UK: T. W. Senior.

Penzel, Fred. 2014. "Hoarding in History." In *The Oxford Handbook of Hoarding and Acquiring*, edited by R. O. Frost and G. Steketee. Oxford: Oxford Handbooks Online. http://doi.org/10.1093/oxfordhb/9780199937783.013.001.

Peterson, Dale. 2006. *Jane Goodall: The Woman Who Redefined Man*. Boston: Houghton Mifflin.

Phillips, Stephen. 2004. "Plastics." In *Cold War Hothouses: Inventing Postwar Culture, from Cockpit to Playboy*, edited by B. Colomina, A. Brennan, and J. Kim, 91–123. New York: Princeton Architectural Press.

Phys.org. 2011. "U.S. Shuttle, the Most Complex Flying Machine Ever Built." July 20. https://phys.org/news/2011-07-shuttle-complex-machine-built.html.

Pickering, Kathleen Ann. 2000. *Lakota Culture, World Economy*. Lincoln: University of Nebraska Press.

Pinsker, Joe. 2019. "Why Are American Homes So Big?" *Atlantic*, September 12. https://www.theatlantic.com/family/archive/2019/09/american-houses-big/597811/.

Plummer, Thomas. 2004. "Flaked Stones and Old Bones: Biological and Cultural Evolution at the Dawn of Technology." *American Journal of Physical Anthropology* suppl 39:118–64.

Pobiner, Brianna. 2013. "Evidence for Meat-Eating by Early Humans." *Nature Education Knowledge* 4 (6): 1.

Poitras, Geoffrey. 2020. "The Luddite Trials: Radical Suppression and the Administration of Criminal Justice." *Journal for the Study of Radicalism* 14 (1): 121–66.

Pontzer, Herman. 2012. "Overview of Hominin Evolution." *Nature Education Knowledge* 3 (10): 8.

Potts, Richard. 1984. "Home Bases and Early Hominids." *American Scientist* 72 (4).

———. 1991. "Why the Oldowan? Plio-Pleistocene Toolmaking and the Transport of Resources." *Journal of Anthropological Research* 47 (2): 153–76.

Powers, Vivian. 1993. *The Bakelizer*. Washington, DC: American Chemical Society.

———. 1995. *The First Nylon Plant*. Washington, DC: American Chemical Society.

Pratt, Richard H. 1973. "The Advantages of Mingling Indians with Whites." In *Americanizing the American Indians: Writings by the "Friends of the Indian" 1880–1900*, edited by F. P. Prucha, 260–71. Cambridge, MA: Harvard University Press.

———. 2004. *Battlefield and Classroom: An Autobiography*. Norman: University of Oklahoma.

Preucel, Robert W. 2006. *Archaeological Semiotics*. Malden: Blackwell.

———. 2021. "The Predicament of Ontology." *Cambridge Archaeological Journal* 31 (3).

Priddey, M. W. 1977. "Blackbird Using Tool." *British Birds* 70:262.

Prum, Richard O. 2017. *The Evolution of Beauty: How Darwin's Forgotten Theory of Mate Choice Shapes the Animal World*. New York: Doubleday.

Putt, Shelby, Sobanawartiny Wijeakumar, Robert G. Franciscus, and John P. Spencer. 2017. "The Functional Brain Networks That Underlie Early Stone Age Tool Manufacture." *Human Nature Behavior* 1 (0102). https://doi.org/10.1038/s41562-017-0102.

Py-Lieberman, Beth. 2007. "Smithsonian Says No to 'Lucy.'" *Smithsonian Maga-*

zine, September 4. https://www.smithsonianmag.com/smithsonian-institution/smithsonian-says-no-to-lucy-21338295/.

Racquets. 2020. "Early Lawn Tennis: Walter Clopton Wingfield." https://racquets.tennisfame.com/lawn-tennis/walter-clopton-wingfield.

Radivojević, Miljana, Thilo Rehren, Shahina Farid, Ernst Pernicka, Duygu Camurcuoğlu, Th. Rehren M. Radivojević, S. Farid, E. Pernicka, and D. Camurcuoğlu. 2017. "Repealing the Çatalhöyük Extractive Metallurgy: The Green, the Fire and the 'Slag.'" *Journal of Archaeological Science* 86:101–22.

Radovčić, D., A. O. Sršen, J. Radovčić, and D. W. Frayer. 2015. "Evidence for Neandertal Jewelry: Modified White-Tailed Eagle Claws at Krapina." *PLoS One* 10 (3): e0119802.

Ramirez, Ainissa. 2020. *The Alchemy of Us: How Humans and Matter Transformed One Another*. Cambridge, MA: MIT Press.

Ramos, Pedro A. Saura. 1999. *Cave of AltaMira*. New York: Harry N. Abrams.

Ranere, Anthony J., Dolores R. Piperno, Irene Holst, Ruth Dickau, and José Iriarte. 2009. "The Cultural and Chronological Context of Early Holocene Maize and Squash Domestication in the Central Balsas River Valley, Mexico." *PNAS* 106 (13): 5014–18.

Rappaport, Roy A. 1999. *Ritual and Religion in the Making of Humanity*. Cambridge: Cambridge University Press.

Reuell, Peter. 2016. "Big Gains in Better Chewing." *Harvard Gazette*, March 20. https://news.harvard.edu/gazette/story/2016/03/big-gains-in-better-chewing/.

Rendu, William, Cédric Beauval, Isabelle Crevecoeur, Priscilla Bayle, Antoine Balzeau, Thierry Bismuth, Laurence Bourguignon, et al. 2014. "Evidence Supporting an Intentional Neandertal Burial at La Chapelle-aux-Saints." *Proceedings of the National Academy of Science USA* 111 (1): 81–86.

Rising Starr Middle School Chorus. 2017. "Evolution of Music in Recording." August 4. https://rsmschorus.org/2017/08/04/193/.

Robinson, Britany. 2020. "It's Not That Hard to Buy Nothing." *New York Times*, December 28. https://www.nytimes.com/2020/12/28/style/self-care/how-to-buy-less.html.

Roche, H., A. Delagnes, J.-P. Brugal, C. Feibel, M. Kibunjia, V. Mourre, and J. Texier. 1999. "Early Hominid Stone Tool Production and Technical Skill 2.34 Myr Ago in West Turkana, Kenya." *Nature* 399:57–60.

Rodríguez-Vidal, Joaquín, Francesco d'Errico, Francisco Giles Pacheco, Ruth Blasco, Jordi Rosell, Richard P. Jennings, Alain Queffelec, et al. 2014. "A Rock Engraving Made by Neanderthals in Gibraltar." *PNAS* 111 (37): 13301–6.

Rognini, Giulio, Francesco Maria Petrini, Stanisa Raspopovic, Giacomo Valle, Giuseppe Granata, Ivo Strauss, Marco Solcà, et al. 2019. "Multisensory Bionic Limb to Achieve Prosthesis Embodiment and Reduce Distorted Phantom Limb Perceptions." *Journal of Neurology, Neurosurgery & Psychiatry* 90 (7): 833–36.

Rosen, William. 2012. *The Most Powerful Idea in the World: A Story of Steam, Industry, and Invention*. Chicago: University of Chicago Press.

Rosenheim, Jay A. 1987. "Nesting Behavior and Bionomics of a Solitary Ground-

Nesting Wasp, *Ammophila dysmica* (Hymenoptera: Sphecidae): Influence of Parasite Pressure." *Annals of the Entomological Society of America* 80 (6): 739–49.

Rowan, John, Patricia Princehouse, Rahab N. Kinyanjui, and Kevin T. Uno. 2022. "Isaiah Odhiambo Nengo (1961–2022)." *Nature Ecology & Evolution* 6 (659). https://doi.org/10.1038/s41559-022-01741-y.

Ruiqi, Rachel Teng. 2022. "In World First, Chile to Ban Single-Use Food and Beverage Products Over Three Years." Mongabay, August 1. https://news.mongabay.com/2022/08/in-world-first-chile-to-ban-single-use-fb-products-over-three-years/.

Sabbaghi, Mostafa, Willie Cade, Sara Behdad, and Ann M Bisantz. 2017. "The Current Status of the Consumer Electronics Repair Industry in the U.S.: A Survey-Based Study." *Resources Conservation and Recycling* 116 (7): 137–51.

Sahlins, Marshall. 1968. "Notes on the Original Affluent Society." In *Man the Hunter*, edited by R. B. Lee and I. DeVore, 85–89. New York: Aldine Publishing.

———. 1972. *Stone Age Economics*. Chicago: Aldine-Atherton.

Sahnouni, Mohamed, Josep M. Parés, Mathieu Duval, Isabel Cáceres, Zoheir Harichane, Jan van der Made, Alfredo Pérez-González, et al. 2018. "1.9-Million- and 2.4-Million-Year-Old Artifacts and Stone Tool-Cutmarked Bones from Ain Boucherit, Algeria." *Science* 362 (6420): 1297–1301.

Samelius, Gustaf, Ray T. Alisauskas, Keith A. Hobson, and Serge Larivière. 2007. "Prolonging the Arctic Pulse: Long-Term Exploitation of Cached Eggs by Arctic Foxes When Lemmings Are Scarce." *Journal of Animal Ecology* 76 (5): 873–80.

Samuelsson, Marcus. 2020. *The Rise: Black Cooks and the Soul of American Food*. New York: Little, Brown.

Sanburn, Josh. 2015. "America's Clutter Problem." *Time*, March 12. https://time.com/3741849/americas-clutter-problem/.

Sandgathe, Dennis, and Harold L. Dibble. 2016. "Who Started the First Fire?" *Sapiens*, January 26. https://www.sapiens.org/archaeology/neanderthal-fire/.

Sanz, Crickette M., and David B. Morgan. 2007. "Chimpanzee Tool Technology in the Goualougo Triangle, Republic of Congo." *Journal of Human Evolution* 52 (4): 420–33.

Sartre, Jean-Paul. 1943. *Being and Nothingness: A Phenomenological Essay on Ontology*. New York: Philosophical Library.

Sasaki, Fumio. 2017. *Goodbye, Things: The New Japanese Minimalism*. New York: W. W. Norton.

Sassatelli, Roberta. 2007. *Consumer Culture: History, Theory and Politics*. Los Angeles: Sage Publications.

Schaik, Carel P. van, Gauri R. Pradhan, and Claudio Tennie. 2019. "Teaching and Curiosity: Sequential Drivers of Cumulative Cultural Evolution in the Hominin Lineage." *Behavioral Ecology and Sociobiology* 73 (2). https://doi.org/10.1007/s00265-018-2610-7.

Schettler, Aubrie, Vicente Raja, and Michael L. Anderson. 2019. "The Embodiment of Objects: Review, Analysis, and Future Directions." *Frontiers in Neuroscience* 13. https://doi.org/10.3389/fnins.2019.01332.

Schick, Kathy D., and Nicholas Toth. 1993. *Making Silent Stones Speak: Human Evolution and the Dawn of Technology*. New York: Touchstone.

———. 2003. "The Origin of the Genie." In *Living with the Genie: Essays on Technology and the Quest for Human Mastery*, edited by A. Lightman, D. Sarewitz, and C. Desser, 23–34. Washington, DC: Island Press.

Schick, Kathy D., Nicholas Toth, Gary Garufi, E. Sue Savage-Rumbaugh, Duane Rumbaugh, Rose Sevcik. 1999. "Continuing Investigations into the Stone Tool-Making and Tool-Using Capabilities of a Bonobo (*Pan paniscus*)." *Journal of Archaeological Science* 26 (7): 821–32.

Schindler, Bill. 2019. "Are We Designed to Eat Meat?" YouTube. https://www.youtube.com/watch?v=9VaUBGarZ2w.

Schivelbusch, Wolfgang. 1995. *Disenchanted Night: The Industrialization of Light in the Nineteenth Century*. Translated by A. Davies. Berkeley: University of California Press.

Schlereth, Thomas J. 1991. *Victorian America: Transformations in Everyday Life, 1876–1915*. New York: HarperPerennial.

Schlossberg, Tatiana. 2019. *Inconspicuous Consumption: The Environmental Impact You Don't Know You Have*. Boston: Grand Central Publishing.

Schomburg-Scherff, Sylvia M. 2000. "The Power of Images: New Approaches to the Anthropological Study of Images." *Anthropos* 95 (1): 189–99.

Schwarcz, H. P., R. Grün, B. Vandermeersch, O. Bar-Yosef, H. Valladas, and E. Tchernov. 1988. "ESR Dates for the Hominid Burial Site of Qafzeh in Israel." *Journal of Human Evolution* 17 (8): 733–37.

SciNews. 2015. "3.3-Million-Year-Old Stone Tools Unearthed in Kenya." http://www.sci-news.com/archaeology/science-lomekwi-3-oldest-stone-tools-02822.html.

Scott, Ellen. 2020. "Mum Who Did a 'No Buy' Challenge Shares How Her Family Saved £25,000 in a Year." *Metro*, March 25. https://metro.co.uk/2020/03/25/mum-no-buy-year-shares-family-saved-25000-not-spending-12454697/.

Scott, James C. 2018. *Against the Grain: A Deep History of the Earliest States*. New Haven, CT: Yale University Press.

Seaford, Richard. 2004. *Money and the Early Greek Mind: Homer, Philosophy, Tragedy*. Cambridge: Cambridge University Press.

Seferian, Stephanie Marie. 2021. *Sustainable Minimalism: Embrace Zero Waste, Build Sustainability Habits That Last, and Become a Minimalist without Sacrificing the Planet*. Coral Gables, FL: Mango Publishing.

Segran, Elizabeth. 2019. "Americans Toss 20 Billion Diapers Per Year." *Fast Company*. https://www.fastcompany.com/90420061/americans-toss-20-billion-diapers-per-year-a-radical-seaweed-redesign-could-change-that.

Seymour, Roger S. 2020. "How Smart Were Our Ancestors? Turns Out the Answer Isn't in Brain Size, but Blood Flow." *The Conversation*, January 26. https://theconversation.com/how-smart-were-our-ancestors-turns-out-the-answer-isnt-in-brain-size-but-blood-flow-130387.

Shelach-Lavi, Gideon. 2015. *The Archaeology of Early China: From Prehistory to the Han Dynasty*. Cambridge: Cambridge University Press.

Sherwood, Chet C., Francys Subiaul, and Tadeusz W. Zawidzki. 2008. "A Natural History of the Human Mind: Tracing Evolutionary Changes in Brain and Cognition." *Journal of Anatomy* 212 (4): 426–54.

Shinozuka, K., H. Ono, and S. Watanabe. 2013. "Reinforcing and Discriminative Stimulus Properties of Music in Goldfish." *Behavioural Processes* 99:26–33.

Shipman, Pat. 2002. *The Man Who Found the Missing Link: Eugène Dubois and His Lifelong Quest to Prove Darwin Right* Cambridge, MA: Harvard University Press.

Simmons, Alan H. 2011. *The Neolithic Revolution in the Near East: Transforming the Human Landscape*. Tucson: University of Arizona Press.

Sisson, Val. 2020. "Belper Mills." Picture the Past. https://picturethepast.org.uk/image-library/image-details/poster/dchq000806/posterid/dchq000806.html.

Skinner, Matthew M., Nicholas B. Stephens, Zewdi J. Tsegai, Alexandra C. Foote, N. Huynh Nguyen, Thomas Gross, Dieter H. Pahr, Jean-Jacques Hublin, and Tracy L. Kivell. 2015. "Human-like Hand Use in *Australopithecus africanus*." *Science* 347 (6220): 395–99.

Slack, Kevin. 2018. "A Foucauldian Study of Spanish Colonialism." *Latin Americanist* 62 (3): 433–57.

Slade, Giles. 2006. *Made to Break: Technology and Obsolescence in America*. Cambridge, MA: Harvard University Press.

Smail, Daniel Lord. 2014. "Neurohistory in Action: Hoarding and the Human Past." *Isis* 105 (1): 110–22.

Smith, C. C., and O. J. Reichman. 1984. "The Evolution of Food Caching by Birds and Mammals." *Annual Review of Ecology and Systematics* 15:329–51.

Smith, Michael E. 2013. *The Aztecs*. 3rd ed. Malden, MA: Wiley-Blackwell.

Smith, Michael E., Timothy A. Kohler, and Gary M. Feinman. 2018. "Studying Inequality's Deep Past." In *Ten Thousand Years of Inequality: The Archaeology of Wealth Differences*, edited by T. A. Kohler and M. E. Smith, 3–38. Tucson: University of Arizona Press.

Sodaro, Amy. 2018. *Exhibiting Atrocity: Memorial Museums and the Politics of Past Violence*. New Brunswick, NJ: Rutgers University Press.

Sokolowski, Alexandre. 2020. October 16, 1833: "The Day Walter Clopton Wingfield—the Man Who Invented Lawn Tennis—Was Born." Tennis Majors, October 16. https://www.tennismajors.com/our-features/on-this-day/october-16-1833-the-day-walter-clopton-winfield-the-man-who-invented-lawn-tennis-was-born-298750.html.

Solecki, Ralph S. 1971. *Shanidar: The First Flower People*. New York: Knopf.

Soley, Fernando G., and Isaías Alvarado-Díaz. 2011. "Prospective Thinking in a Mustelid? *Eira barbara* (Carnivora) Cache Unripe Fruits to Consume Them Once Ripened." *Naturwissenschaften* 98:693–98.

Spivack, Emily. 2012. "Stocking Series, Part 1: Wartime Rationing and Nylon Riots." *Smithsonian Magazine*, September 4. https://www.smithsonianmag.com/arts-culture/stocking-series-part-1-wartime-rationing-and-nylon-riots-25391066/.

Sposito, Ambra, Nadia Bolognini, Giuseppe Vallar, and Angelo Maravita. 2012. "Extension of Perceived Arm Length Following Tool-Use: Clues to Plasticity of Body Metrics." *Neuropsychologia* 50 (9): 2187–94.

Sprague, Donovin Arleigh. 2005. *Rosebud Sioux*. Charleston, SC: Arcadia.

St. Amant, R., and T. E. Horton. 2008. "Revisiting the Definition of Animal Tool Use." *Animal Behaviour* 75:1199–208.

REFERENCES

Stahel, Walter R. 2016. "The Circular Economy." *Nature* 531:425–38.
St Clair, James J. H., Barbara C. Klump, Shoko Sugasawa, Caitlin G. Higgott, Nick Colegrave, and Christian Rutz. 2018. "Hook Innovation Boosts Foraging Efficiency in Tool-Using Crows." *Nature Ecology & Evolution* 2:441–44.
Stearns, Peter N. 2020. *The Industrial Revolution in World History*. 5th ed. London: Routledge.
Stewart, Emily. 2021. "How 9/11 Convinced Americans to Buy, Buy, Buy." *Vox*, September 9. https://www.vox.com/the-goods/22662889/september-11-anniversary-bush-spend-economy.
Stone, Maddie. 2021. "Why France's New 'Repairability Index' Is a Big Deal." Grist, February 8. https://grist.org/climate/why-frances-new-repairability-index-is-a-big-deal/.
Stout, Dietrich. 2006. "Oldowan Toolmaking and Hominin Brain Evolution: Theory and Research Using Positron Emission Tomography (PET)." In *The Oldowan: Case Studies into the Earliest Stone Age*, edited by N. Toth and K. D. Schick, 267–305. Gosport, IN: Stone Age Institute Press.
Stout, Dietrich, Erin Hecht, Nada Khreisheh, Bruce Bradley, and Thierry Chaminade. 2015. "Cognitive Demands of Lower Paleolithic Toolmaking." *PLoS One* 10 (4): e0121804.
Strand, Ginger. 2008. "The Crying Indian." *Orion*. https://orionmagazine.org/article/the-crying-indian/.
Strickland, Eliza. 2009. "Bloodstained Tools from 13,000 Years Ago Found in a Suburban Backyard." *Discover*, February 26. https://www.discovermagazine.com/planet-earth/bloodstained-tools-from-13-000-years-ago-found-in-a-suburban-backyard.
Stringer, Chris. 2012. *Lone Survivor: How We Came to Be the Only Humans*. New York: Times Books.
Sweetlove, Lee. 2011. "Number of Species on Earth Tagged at 8.7 Million." *Nature*, August 23. https://www.nature.com/news/2011/110823/full/news.2011.498.html.
SWNS. 2020. "More Than 40% of Americans Have a Family Heirloom That's Over 50 Years Old." *New York Post*, July 10. https://nypost.com/2020/07/10/more-than-40-of-americans-have-a-family-heirloom-thats-over-50-years-old/.
Sykes, Rebecca Wragg. 2020. *Kindred: Neanderthal Life, Love, Death, and Art*. London: Bloomsbury Sigma.
Tattersall, Ian. 2008. *The World from Beginnings to 4000 BCE*. Oxford: Oxford University Press.
———. 2012. *Masters of the Planet: The Search for Our Human Origins*. New York: St. Martin's Press.
Taylor, Timothy. 2010. *The Artificial Ape: How Technology Changed the Course of Human Evolution*. New York: St. Martin's Press.
Telegraphic Journal and Electrical Review. 1889. "The Electric Lighting of the Savoy Hotel." September 27, 364.
Tenenbaum, Laura. 2019. "Plastic Cutlery Is Terrible for the Environment and We Don't Need to Have It Delivered." *Forbes*, July 16. https://www.forbes.com/sites/lauratenenbaum/2019/07/16/plastic-cutlery-is-terrible-for-the-environment-and-we-dont-need-to-have-it-delivered/?sh=44c954874019.

Tennie, Claudio, Josep Call, and Michael Tomasello. 2009. "Ratcheting Up the Ratchet: On the Evolution of Cumulative Culture." *Philosophical Transactions B* 364 (1528): 2405–15.

Tennie, Claudio, L. S. Premo, David R. Braun, and Shannon P. McPherron. 2017. "Early Stone Tools and Cultural Transmission: Resetting the Null Hypothesis." *Current Anthropology* 58 (5): 652–72.

Than, Ker. 2013. "Neanderthal Burials Confirmed as Ancient Ritual." *National Geographic*, December 16. https://www.nationalgeographic.com/news/2013/12/131216-la-chapelle-neanderthal-burials-graves/.

Thomas, Dana. 2019. "The High Price of Fast Fashion." *Wall Street Journal*, August 29. https://www.wsj.com/articles/the-high-price-of-fast-fashion-11567096637.

Thompson, Emily. 1995. "Machines, Music, and the Quest for Fidelity: Marketing the Edison Phonograph in America, 1877–1925." *Musical Quarterly* 79 (1): 131–71.

Thompson, Jessica C., Susana Carvalho, Curtis Marean, and Zeresenay Alemseged. 2019. "Origins of the Human Predatory Pattern: The Transition to Large-Animal Exploitation by Early Hominins." *Current Anthropology* 60 (1): 1–23.

Thoreau, Henry David. (1854) 2004. *Walden*. Boston: Houghton Mifflin.

Titmuss, Richard M. 1997. *The Gift Relationship: From Human Blood to Social Policy*. New York: The Free Press.

Titton, Stefania, Deborah Barsky, Amèlia Bargalló, Alexia Serrano-Ramos, Josep Maria Vergès, Isidro Toro-Moyano, Robert Sala-Ramos, José García Solano, and Juan Manuel Jimenez Arenas. 2020. "Subspheroids in the Lithic Assemblage of Barranco León (Spain): Recognizing the Late Oldowan in Europe." *PLoS One* 15 (1): e0228290.

Tolentino, Jia. 2020. "The Pitfalls and the Potential of the New Minimalism." *New Yorker*, January 27. https://www.newyorker.com/magazine/2020/02/03/the-pitfalls-and-the-potential-of-the-new-minimalism.

Tomasello, Michael. 1999. *The Cultural Origins of Human Cognition*. Cambridge, MA: Harvard University Press.

Toth, Nicholas. 1985. "The Oldowan Reassessed: A Close Look at Early Stone Artifacts." *Journal of Archaeological Science* 12 (2): 101–20.

Toth, Nick, and Kathy Diane Schick. 2006. *The Oldowan: Case Studies into the Earliest Stone Age*. Bloomington, IN: Stone Age Institute Press.

———. 2009. "The Oldowan: The Tool Making of Early Hominins and Chimpanzees Compared." *Annual Review of Anthropology* 38:289–305.

Toups, Melissa A., Andrew Kitchen, Jessica E. Light, and David L. Reed. 2011. "Origin of Clothing Lice Indicates Early Clothing Use by Anatomically Modern Humans in Africa." *Molecular Biology and Evolution* 28 (1): 29–32.

Townsend, Matthew. 2019. "'Big Carpet' Is Betting This New Floor Covering Will Get Americans to End Their Love of Hardwood." *Time*, June 6. https://time.com/5602251/carpet-industry-hardwood-floors/.

Trinkaus, Erik, and Alexandra P. Buzhilova. 2018. "Diversity and Differential Disposal of the Dead at Sunghir." *Antiquity* 92 (361): 7–21.

Tuan, Yi-Fu. 1980. "The Significance of the Artifact." *Geographical Review* 70 (4): 462–72.

Tythacott, Louise. 2011. *The Lives of Chinese Objects: Buddhism, Imperialism and Display*. New York: Berghahn.

UN Department of Economic Affairs. 1952. *World Economic Report, 1950–51*. New York: United Nations.

Vale, Gillian L., Sarah J. Davis, Susan P. Lambeth, Steven J. Schapiro, and Andrew Whiten. 2017. "Acquisition of a Socially Learned Tool Use Sequence in Chimpanzees: Implications for Cumulative Culture." *Evolution and Human Behavior* 38 (5): 635–44.

Van Buskirk, Eric. 2019. "A New Understanding of Hoarding Disorder." Open Forum, June 12. https://www.openforum.com.au/a-new-understanding-of-hoarding-disorder/.

Vander Wall, Stephen B. 1990. *Food Hoarding in Animals*. Chicago: University of Chicago Press.

Van Cauwenberghe, L., and C. Janssen. 2014. "Microplastics in Bivalves Cultured for Human Consumption." *Environmental Pollution* 193:65–70.

van Leeuwen, Edwin J. C., Katherine A. Cronin, and Daniel B. M. Haun. 2017. "Tool Use for Corpse Cleaning in Chimpanzees." *Scientific Reports* 7:44091.

Veblen, Thorstein. 1899. *The Theory of the Leisure Class: An Economic Study of Institutions*. New York: Macmillan.

Vidale, Massimo, Luca Bondioli, David W. Frayer, Marina Gallinaro, and Alessandro Vanzetti. 2016. "Ötzi the Iceman: Examining New Evidence from the Famous Copper Age Mummy." *Expedition Magazine* 58 (2): 13–17.

Villmoare, Brian, William H. Kimbel, Chalachew Seyoum, Christopher J. Campisano, Erin N. DiMaggio, John Rowan, David R. Braun, Ramón Arrowsmith, and Kaye E. Reed. 2015. "Early *Homo* at 2.8 Ma from Ledi-Geraru, Afar, Ethiopia." *Science* 347 (6228): 1352–55.

Waggoner, Josephine. 2013. *Witness: A Húŋkpapȟa Historian's Strong-Heart Song of the Lakotas*. Lincoln: University of Nebraska Press.

Waldron, Jeremy. 2020. "Property and Ownership." In *The Stanford Encyclopedia of Philosophy*, edited by Edward N. Zalta. https://plato.stanford.edu/entries/property/.

Wales, Nathan. 2012. "Modeling Neanderthal Clothing Using Ethnographic Analogues." *Journal of Human Evolution* 63 (6): 781–95.

Watanabe, S., J. Sakamoto, and M. Wakita. 1995. "Pigeons' Discrimination of Paintings by Monet and Picasso." *Journal of the Experimental Analysis of Behavior* 63 (2): 165–74.

Wayman, Erin. 2012a. "Becoming Human: The Evolution of Walking Upright." *Smithsonian Magazine*, August 6. https://www.smithsonianmag.com/science-nature/becoming-human-the-evolution-of-walking-upright-13837658/.

———. 2012b. "Louis Leakey: The Father of Hominid Hunting." *Smithsonian Magazine*, June 13. https://www.smithsonianmag.com/science-nature/louis-leakey-the-father-of-hominid-hunting-119543967/.

Weatherford, Jack. 1997. *The History of Money: From Sandstone to Cyberspace*. New York: Three Rivers Press.

Weightman, Gavin. 2007. *The Industrial Revolutionaries: The Making of the Modern World, 1776–1914*. New York: Grove Press.

Weiss, Kenneth J. 2010. "Hoarding, Hermitage, and the Law: Why We Love the Collyer Brothers." *Journal of the American Academy of Psychiatry and the Law Online* 38 (2): 251–57.

Wengrow, David, and David Graeber. 2015. "Farewell to the 'Childhood of Man': Ritual, Seasonality, and the Origins of Inequality." *Journal of the Royal Anthropological Institute* 21 (3): 597–619.

Wheeler, S. Christian, and Christopher J. Bechler. 2021. "Objects and Self-Identity." *Current Opinion in Psychology* 39:6–11.

White, George S. 1836. *Memoir of Samuel Slater, the Father of American Manufactures*. Philadelphia: No. 46 Carpenter Street.

Wierer, Ursula, Simona Arrighi, Stefano Bertola, Günther Kaufmann, Benno Baumgarten, Annaluisa Pedrotti, Patrizia Pernter, and Jacques Pelegrin. 2018. "The Iceman's Lithic Toolkit: Raw Material, Technology, Typology and Use." *PLoS One* 13 (6): e0198292.

Will, Manuel, Adrián Pablos, and Jay T. Stock. 2017. "Long-Term Patterns of Body Mass and Stature Evolution within the Hominin Lineage." *Royal Society Open Science* 4. https://doi.org/10.1098/rsos.171339.

Williams, Olivia. 2021. *The Secret Life of the Savoy: And the D'Oyly Carte Family*. Terra Alta, WV: Headline.

Wills, Ian. 2019. *Thomas Edison: Success and Innovation through Failure*. New York: Springer.

Wimbush, Vincent L., ed. 2002. *Asceticism*. Oxford: Oxford University Press.

Winters, Renee M. 2015. *The Hoarding Impulse: Suffocation of the Soul*. London: Routledge.

Wolfe, Audra J. 2008. "Nylon: A Revolution in Textiles." Distillations, October 2. Science History Institute. https://www.sciencehistory.org/distillations/nylon-a-revolution-in-textiles.

Wood, Laura. 2021. "Global Carpets and Rugs Market Report 2021." Business Wire, March 22. https://www.businesswire.com/news/home/20210322005505/en/Global-Carpets-and-Rugs-Market-Report-2021-Market-is-Projected-to-Exceed-41-Billion-by-2024---ResearchAndMarkets.com.

Wrangham, Richard. 2010. *Catching Fire: How Cooking Made Us Human*. New York: Basic Books.

Wright, Robert. 2009. *The Evolution of God*. New York: Little, Brown.

Wrigley, E. A. 2010. *Energy and the English Industrial Revolution*. Cambridge: Cambridge University Press.

Wu, Xiaohong, Chi Zhang, Paul Goldberg, David Cohen, Yan Pan, Trina Arpin, and Ofer Bar-Yosef. 2012. "Early Pottery at 20,000 Years Ago in Xianrendong Cave, China." *Science* 336 (6089): 1696–700.

Yohe, Robert M., II, and Douglas Bamforth. 2013. "Late Pleistocene Protein Residues from the Mahaffy Cache, Colorado." *Journal of Archaeological Science* 40 (5): 2337–43.

Young Bear, Severt, and R. D. Theisz. 1994. *Standing in the Light: A Lakota Way of Seeing*. Lincoln: University of Nebraska Press.

Yü, Chün-fang. 2001. *Kuan-yin: The Chinese Transformation of Avalokiteśvara*. New York: Columbia University Press.

Zaraska, Marta. 2016. *Meathooked: The History and Science of Our 2.5-Million-Year Obsession with Meat*. New York: Basic Books.

Zauzmer, Julie. 2017. "A Scientist's New Theory: Religion Was Key to Humans' Social Evolution." *Washington Post*, February 27. https://www.washingtonpost.com/news/acts-of-faith/wp/2017/02/27/a-scientists-new-theory-religion-was-key-to-humans-social-evolution/.

Zimmer, Carl. 2016a. "A 3.2-Million-Year-Old Mystery: Did Lucy Fall from a Tree?" *New York Times*, August 29. https://www.nytimes.com/2016/08/30/science/lucy-hominid-fossils-fall.html.

———. 2016b. "Unappetizing Experiment Explores Tools' Role in Humans' Bigger Brains." *New York Times*, March 9. https://www.nytimes.com/2016/03/09/science/evolution-meat-stone-tools-cooking-brains-hominins.html.

Zink, Katherine D., and Daniel E. Lieberman. 2016. "Impact of Meat and Lower Paleolithic Food Processing Techniques on Chewing in Food." *Nature* 531:500–503.

Zink, Trevor, and Roland Geyer. 2017. "Circular Economy Rebound." *Journal of Industrial Ecology* 21 (3): 593–602.

Zorich, Zach. 2009. "Caching In." *Archaeology Archive* 62 (3). https://archive.archaeology.org/0905/trenches/caching_in.html.

Zremski, Jerry. 2022. "Rep. Chris Jacobs Pushes Fight against Plastic in Great Lakes." *Buffalo News*, updated August 9. https://buffalonews.com/news/local/rep-chris-jacobs-pushes-fight-against-plastic-in-great-lakes/article_e508bdaa-7e1a-11ec-8309-23bd3f38976b.html.

IMAGE CREDITS

FIGURE 1.	A1797.1 © Denver Museum of Nature & Science
FIGURE 2.	Mike R / Wikimedia (CC BY-SA 3.0, https://creativecommons.org/licenses/by-sa/3.0/deed.en)
FIGURE 3.	H. Zell / Wikimedia (CC BY-SA 3.0, https://creativecommons.org/licenses/by-sa/3.0/deed.en)
FIGURE 4.	American Philosophical Society / Mss.B.K815
FIGURE 5.	Catherine Gilman
FIGURE 6.	Catherine Gilman
FIGURE 7.	Dietrich Stout / Catherine Gilman
FIGURE 8.	Catherine Gilman (based on Pontzer 2012)
FIGURE 9.	Catherine Gilman (based on Bretas, Yamazaki, and Iriki 2020)
FIGURE 10.	Neanderthal-Museum, Mettmann / Wikimedia (CC BY-SA 4.0, https://creativecommons.org/licenses/by-sa/4.0/deed.en)
FIGURE 11.	Catherine Gilman (based on Will, Pablos, and Stock 2017)
FIGURE 12.	The US National Archives
FIGURE 13.	Sohee Park / Body, Mind, Brain Lab at Vanderbilt University
FIGURE 14.	© South Tyrol Museum of Archaeology / Harald Wisthaler
FIGURE 15.	Still from *Iceman*, a feature film directed by Felix Randau, produced by Omnibus Entertainment; courtesy of Film Movement / Beta Cinema
FIGURE 16.	AN-1997-141.157 © Denver Museum of Nature & Science
FIGURE 17.	Catherine Gilman
FIGURE 18.	© National Museum of Slovenia, photo Tomaž Lauko
FIGURE 19.	Catherine Gilman
FIGURE 20.	Thomas Edison National Historical Park (National Park Service)
FIGURE 21.	Catherine Gilman
FIGURE 22.	AN-2018-87.1 © Denver Museum of Nature & Science
FIGURE 23.	Chip Colwell
FIGURE 24.	Henk Caspers / Naturalis / Wikimedia (digitally enhanced) (CC BY-SA 3.0, https://creativecommons.org/licenses/by-sa/3.0/)

FIGURE 25.	Image courtesy of Professor Christopher Henshilwood. Photo credit: Stephen Alvarez
FIGURE 26.	Jc Domenech / L'Anthropologie / Wikimedia (CC BY-SA 4.0, https://creativecommons.org/licenses/by-sa/4.0/)
FIGURE 27.	José-Manuel Benito / Wikimedia (public domain)
FIGURE 28.	Reproduced by permission from Rodríguez-Vidal et al. (2014, fig. 2A)
FIGURE 29.	Chip Colwell
FIGURE 30.	Animalparty / Wikimedia (CC BY-SA 4.0, https://creativecommons.org/licenses/by-sa/4.0/)
FIGURE 31.	Sheila Coulson, Department of Archaeology, University of Oslo, Norway
FIGURE 32.	Klaus-Peter Simon / Wikimedia (CC BY-SA 3.0, https://creativecommons.org/licenses/by-sa/3.0/)
FIGURE 33.	Dimitris Xygalatas / Catherine Gilman (based on Manoharan and Xygalatas 2019)
FIGURE 34.	Martin Tse
FIGURE 35.	BR61-378 © Denver Museum of Nature & Science
FIGURE 36.	Epiphanesnikophoros / Wikimedia (CC BY-SA 4.0, https://creativecommons.org/licenses/by-sa/4.0/)
FIGURE 37.	University of Washington / Wikimedia (public domain)
FIGURE 38.	Shameran81 (Middleton Place) / Wikimedia (CC BY-SA 4.0, https://creativecommons.org/licenses/by-sa/4.0/)
FIGURE 39.	BR61-346 © Denver Museum of Nature & Science
FIGURE 40.	AC.5676 © Denver Museum of Nature & Science
FIGURE 41.	Wesley Tingey / Unsplash
FIGURE 42.	Morio / Wikimedia (CC BY-SA 3.0, https://creativecommons.org/licenses/by-sa/3.0/)
FIGURE 43.	Charles Chipiez / Wikimedia (public domain)
FIGURE 44.	Oxyman / Wikimedia, photo by Hugh Llewelyn (CC BY-SA 2.0, https://creativecommons.org/licenses/by-sa/2.0/)
FIGURE 45.	Charles J. Phipps / Wikimedia (public domain)
FIGURE 46.	Oxford Historical Society, Oxford CT
FIGURE 47.	Catherine Gilman (based on Geyer, Jambeck, and Law 2017)
FIGURE 48.	Catherine Gilman
FIGURE 49.	NYPL b17041184
FIGURE 50.	Catherine Gilman (based on J. H. Davis 2004)
FIGURE 51.	Courtesy of Independence National Historical Park
FIGURE 52.	Catherine Gilman (based on J. Liu 2022)
FIGURE 53.	Edward Stojakovic / Flickr (CC BY 2.0, https://creativecommons.org/licenses/by/2.0/)
FIGURE 54.	Alden Jewell / Flickr (CC BY 2.0, https://creativecommons.org/licenses/by/2.0/)
FIGURE 55.	NYPL / Wikimedia
FIGURE 56.	Allan Hack / Flickr (CC BY-ND 2.0, https://creativecommons.org/licenses/by-nd/2.0/)

IMAGE CREDITS

FIGURE 57.   Arthur Iles / Wikimedia (public domain)
FIGURE 58.   alh1 / Flickr (CC BY-ND 2.0, https://creativecommons.org/licenses/by-nd/2.0/)
FIGURE 59.   Adam73 / Wikimedia (CC BY-SA 3.0, https://creativecommons.org/licenses/by-sa/3.0/)
FIGURE 60.   Chip Colwell

INDEX

Page numbers in italics refer to figures.

Acheulean tools, 7, *44*, 65–67, *65*, 92–94, 104, 251. *See also* tool use
acorn woodpecker, 209–10, *210*
advertising industry, 188–89, 191–93, 196, 199; changing styles in, 200; deflection of responsibility from corporations by, 241. *See also* consumerism; marketing; shopping
aesthetic sense: evolutionary basis for, 91–92, 111; instinct for art as, 91–97, 105, 150. *See also* art
Africa, 80, 132, 140, 166, 186, 243; West, 132
agriculture, 69, 77–80, 121, 131, 181; and clothing, 149–50; organized religion and, 121–22; and pastoralism, 79, 81–82, 159–60; rule of, 159; scientific approach to increasing productivity in, 162; and storage, 81–82, 218; tools of, 79–80. *See also* domesticated animals; Neolithic Revolution
Aldegani, Nico, 61–63
Alemseged, Zeray, 24–29, 36–37
Alighieri, Dante, 220
Almécija, Sergio, 48–49
Almy, William, 157–58
Altamira Cave (Spain), 99
American Numismatic Society (New York City), 131, 133
Americas, 166, 186
ant, 22
Anthropoid, 44
anthropomorphism, 114
Apple laptop, 204
Aquinas, Thomas, 212
archaeology, 4, 90, 93–97, 102–3, 109; discovery of world's oldest clothing, 148; discovery of world's oldest painted art, 88–89; excavations of Neanderthal graves, 111; hoards found, 8, 215–18; stories from material evidence of, 27–28
archerfish, 22
Archimedes, 168, 171
Ardipithecus, *40*, 49
Aristotle, 212
Arkowitz, Hal, 222
Arkwright, Richard, 155–56
Arkwright machine, 155–58, *156*, 166, 178, 251. *See also* Industrial Revolution; machinery

INDEX

arrowhead, 64, 68; flint, 82. *See also* tool use
art, 7, 69, 87–105, 232, 251; birth of visual, 90–91, 102; painted stones in cave as, 87–89, *89*; representational, 99–101; Stone Age, 97–102; stone tools as works of, 92–93. *See also* aesthetic sense; meaning; sculpture; symbolic thinking
Arthur, W. Brian, *The Nature of Technology*, 70–73
Asia, 34, 132, 166, 186
assembly line, 172. *See also* factories; Second Industrial Revolution
Athens, 232–33
Auman, Heidi, 240
Aurignacian tools, 69. *See also* tool use
Australia, 6, 222
Australopithecus, 25, *26*, 33, 40, 44, *44*, 47–49, *48*, 231, 251. *See also* Lucy
Austria, 62, 67
Austro-Hungarian Empire, 143
automobiles, 191, 193; changing styles in the design of, 201, 203; dynamic obsolescence in, 201. *See also* consumer society

Baba Hari Dass, 232, 235–36
Bach, J. S., 91
Baekeland, Leo, 174
Baha'i, 235. *See also* religion
Bamforth, Douglas, 215–16
Barker, James, 38
Barth, Alison L., 54
Beatty, Harry, 17
Bechler, Christopher J., 147
Beecher, Henry Ward, 144
beer, 132
behavioral innovation, 18–24, 29, 251. *See also* reasoning
behavioral specialization, 22, 28–29, 251
Behaviour, 19
Belk, Russell W., "Possessions and the Extended Self," 146–48
Bell, Alexander Graham, 72, 184
Bentley-Condit, Vicki, 19–20

Berekhat Ram, 100, *100*, 103
Berliner, Emile, 184
Bernays, Edward, *Propaganda*, 189–90
Bessemer, Henry, 165
Better Living, 189
Bird, Matthew, 199–200, 203–4
blank-canvas stage, 251. *See also* intelligence
Blombos Cave (South Africa), 96
body: assimilation of tools into the, 54–56; map of the, 53. *See also* radical embodiment
bonobo, 16, 36, 120
Borneo, 132
Boyd, Robert, 76
Bradley, Richard, 217–18
brain: energy that fuels the, 43–44, 46; primate, 45; size of the hominin, 44–45, 49–50, 54; smarter hominin, 45–46; and social competition, 44; "tool-specific" region of the human, 45–46. *See also* hominins
branded proposition, 182–88, 196, 251. *See also* marketing
Bratley, Jesse H., 127–30, 134–35, 140, 144–46, 151; photograph of children in front of Cantonment Indian Boarding School (Oklahoma) by, *129*; photograph of "Indian corner" in home of, 144–46, *145*, 148
Brazil, 178
Bredgar Hoard (Kent), 217
Broglio, Alberto, 88
bronze, 80; hoes and knives, 132
Brown, Smith, 157–58
Buddhism, 107–8, 112, 119, 122, 245; ascetic practices of, 235–36; statues and ritual objects of, 116. *See also* Guanyin (bodhisattva of compassion); religion
Burma, 132
Bush, George W., 196
Buy Nothing, 236–37

Calkins, Earnest Elmo, 199, 205; *Modern Advertising* (with Ralph Holden), 199;

"What Consumer Engineering Really Is," 199–200
Call, Josep, 21–22
Cambodia, 2, 79
Cambridge Archaeological Journal, 114
Canada, 6, 135
capitalism, 186, 196, 243; and global economy, 245. *See also* consumer society
Carlin, George, 1
Carlisle Indian Industrial School, 128–30, 134
Carlyle, Thomas, 17, 57; "Signs of the Times," 166–67
Carothers, Wallace H., 175
carpets, 194–96, *194*; manufacturing of, 194–95; wall-to-wall, 195–96, 198. *See also* consumer society
Carte, Richard D'Oyly, 168–69
Carter, Howard, 230
Çatalhöyük, 78–80
catalyst invention, 168–72, 231, 252. *See also* invention
Cavalcade (TV show), 188
Central America, 80
Chatfield, Tom, 74
Chatterjee, Anjan, *The Aesthetic Brain*, 92, 111
Chellean culture, 33
chemicals, 171–72, 174. *See also* plastics
Chevrolet, 201, *202*
chiefdoms, 142–43. *See also* heirlooms
child labor, 167, 178
Chile, 242
chimpanzee, 13–15, 17–18, 20, 22, *40*, 211; as behavioral innovator, 29; as creative tool user, *23*, 28, 35; cultural transmission, 76; feelings of spirituality, 113; reuse of tools, 216; ritualistic behaviors around the dead, 111
China, 2, 69, 74, 78, 80, 132, 178, 243; Guanyin in, 106; hoards in, 219; professional athletes in, 56; Song dynasty, 161; Stone Age engraved bones in, 103; Yellow River region of northeastern, 122. *See also* Hong Kong

Chipiez, Charles, *161*
Christianity, 107, 128, 213, 235; admonitions against greed in, 219; Protestant Reformation, 162; Roman Catholic Church, 161–62. *See also* religion
Churchill, Winston, 56
circular economy, 239–45, 252; criticism of, 242–43; as political and industrial sustainability strategy, 243
climate change, 149, 231. *See also* environment
clothing, 2, 7, 69, 237–38; complex, 149, 252; lice as source of information about, 148; meaning of, 150–51; Native American, 128, 151; needles and thread for the sewing of, 87; of Ötzi, 62–63, 150; of Spanish colonialists, 150–51; as symbol that shapes us, 128–29; throwaway, 230. *See also* fashion and clothing industry
collective consumption, 230. *See also* consumer society
Collyer Brothers Park, 225–27, *226*
Collyer mansion, 206–8, *207*, 225–27, *226*
colonialism, 135, 186, 252; European, 162, 166, 177; Spanish, 150; United States government, 151
Columbia Phonograph Company, 184
Commoner, Barry, *The Closing Circle*, 246
composite tool, 74–75, 252. *See also* tool use
Congo Republic, 13
Conner, Steven, *A Philosophy of Sport*, 52
conspicuous consumption, 194, 245; and minimalism, 238. *See also* consumerism
consumer engineering, 199–200
consumerism: and compulsive hoarding, 8, 208–9; global culture of, 178; ideology of, 182, 196, 200, 205, 220, 232–34, 238; shifts with values and taste, 198; sustainable, 199; and throwaway living, 205; total global spending, *197*; and values of liberty

and democracy, 196, 238. *See also* advertising industry; conspicuous consumption; consumer society; stuff
consumer society, 1–2, 5, 8–9, 208, 235, 247, 252; American change to, 205; as capitalist social progress, 196; culture of, 178, 190–93, 196–97; hoarding as strategy of, 219; manufacture of goods for, 8, 158, 182–93, *191*; mass consumption in, 196, 231; passive consumption in, 190; private sector and public sector in, 193; purposeful consumption in, 190–92; shopping mall as emblem of, 197. *See also* automobiles; capitalism; carpets; collective consumption; consumerism; hoarding; houses; marketing; shopping; stuff; waste
contagious magic, 143–44, 252
copper, 80, 132; rings, 132
cotton, 132; spinning by cotton mill, 156, 162–63, 178–79
Coulson, Sheila, 115
Cranmer, Dan, 135, 138
Cremaschi, Mauro, 88
Croatia, 97, 105
Crossley, Nick, 54
Csikszentmihalyi, Mihaly, 146, 148
Cummins, Anna, 241–42
cumulative culture, 76–77, 252. *See also* technology
Current Anthropology, 29, 49
Currie, Gregory, 93
Czech Republic, 103

DADS (Denver Arapahoe Disposal Site), 229–31
dagger, 64. *See also* tool use
Daoism, 119, 123. *See also* religion
Darwin, Charles, 48–49, 93
Davy, Humphry, 170
dead, burial of the, 103, 105, 109–12, 122
debt, 82, 132, 219
DeGraaf, Lenny, 182–83
de Martinville, Édouard-Léon Scott, 72

democracy, 196
Denver Arapahoe Disposal Site (DADS), 229–31
dependence effect, 188–93, 252
d'Errico, Francesco, 100
dhikr (collective trance), 121, *121*
Dickens, Charles, *Bleak House*, 221
digger wasp, 29
Dinknesh. *See* Lucy
Diogenes, 232–36, 245
disposophobia, 220–25. *See also* hoarding
division of labor, 79–80, 131, 159. *See also* social organization
Dollard, John, 187
dolphin: brain size, 45; cultural transmission, 76; ritualistic behaviors around the dead, 111
domesticated animals, 69, 78–79. *See also* agriculture
Doyle, Arthur Conan, "The Adventure of the Musgrave Ritual," 221
Dubois, Eugène, 17, 93–94
Dunbar, Robin, 121
DuPont Fiber Company, 175–76, 180–81, 187–89, 192; marketing of nylon, 188–89; synthetic carpeting, 195; Tupperware, 176. *See also* plastics
Durand, Peter, 165

Earle, Rebecca, 151
economies of scale, 166, 181. *See also* factories
Edelman, David, 95
Edison, Thomas, 37, 69–76, 73, 171, 183–84
Egypt, 79–80; pyramids, 120
Egyptian vulture, 22
El Castillo Cave (Spain), 114
electricity, 166, 183; as catalyst invention, 168–72; commercial, 171–72; incandescent lighting and increased demand for, 171; plant powered by methane from decomposing trash, 230; steam-powered generator of,

168. *See also* incandescent lightbulb; Second Industrial Revolution
electronics, personal use, 203
electrum, 133, *134*
elephants, 20; ritualistic behaviors around the dead, 111
energy, 8, 41; sources of, 43, 166
English light opera, 168
Enlightenment, 162
environment, 8, 234; extreme consumption and the, 231; as public good, 246. *See also* climate change; waste
Environmental Protection Agency, 240
Eriksen, Marcus, 239–42, 246–47
ethic of reuse, 236–37
Ethiopia, 6, 27, 36; ants guarding treasure in traditions of, 219; cuisine of, 38; Ledi-Geraru fossils in, 40–41, 64; northeastern, 24
Europe, 80, 99, 132, 177, 243; cold winter temperatures of, 148; northern, 142; rise of capitalism and colonialism in early modern, 186; southern, 80; transition from the Middle Ages to the Renaissance, 161; western, 34
evolution: biocultural, 42; braided stream of human, 102–5; scientific interpretations of, 33. *See also* hominins; techno-organic evolution; tool use
Exposition Universelle (Paris), 99

factories, 8; electric power in, 172; labor practices and low-quality goods produced by textile mills and, 164; mass production in, 172, 187, 189–90; maximizing production in, 166; steam power in, 172; women's labor in, 190. *See also* assembly line; economies of scale; Industrial Revolution; machinery
Fagan, Chelsea, 238, 245
Faraday disk, 165
Farago, Jason, 93

fashion and clothing industry, 203. *See also* clothing
feathers, 132
Federer, Roger, 52
Fertile Crescent, 77–78, 80, 121. *See also* Mesopotamia
fiber, 69
film, 189
fire, 39–41, 62–63, 87, 94, 170, 183. *See also* lighting
fishhooks, 69. *See also* tool use
foraging, 78; and hunting, 81. *See also* hunter-gatherer societies
Forbes, 234
Ford, Henry, 172, 201
France, 5, 103, 242; southern, 89, 110; southwestern, 97
Franklin, Benjamin, 17, 57
Frazer, James George, *The Golden Bough*, 143
freedom, 238; consumption as a symbol of, 245. *See also* liberty
Freinkel, Susan, *Plastic*, 176
Frost, Randy O., 222–23
Fuentes, Agustín, 103–5, 125
Fullerton, Ronald A., 186–87

Galbraith, John Kenneth, 188; *The Affluent Society*, 189–90, 192–93, 233
garbage patches, 231, 240–41. *See also* waste
Georgia, Republic of, 69
Germany, 5, 66–67, 69, 75, 103, 190; southern, 101
Ghana, 230
Gibson, Margaret, 142
gift-giving, 137–38, 232, 247
Gilbert, William: *HMS Pinafore*, 168; *The Sorcerer*, 168
Gilligan, Ian, *Climate, Clothing, and Agriculture in Prehistory*, 149
Gilliland, Ezra T., 184
Glass, Louis, 184
Göbekli Tepe (Turkey), 120–22, *120*, 125

Gogol, Nikolai, *Dead Souls*, 220
gold, 132; ingots, 132–33; rarity of, 133
Goodall, Jane, 13–18, 26, 31–32, 113
Goodyear, Charles, 165
Gordon, Robert J., 190
Gorham's Cave (Gibraltar), *104*
Grable, Betty, 180
Graeber, David, and David Wengrow, *The Dawn of Everything*, 9, 131–32, 159–60
Gray, Adeline, 172, *173*, 175–76, 180
Gray, Russell, 28
gray squirrel, 217
Great Depression, 190, 200–201
Greeks, ancient, 132, 155; mythology, 116–17, 219
green monkey, 211
Gregory I (pope), 219
Grotta di Fumane (Italy), 88–89, 96, 101
Grotte Chauvet (France), 89, 101
Grotte du Renne (France), 96–97
Guanyin (bodhisattva of compassion), *86*, 106–9, 112–13, 123–26, 252; abandoned statues of, *108*, 117; statues of, 116–19, 122–26, *124*. See also Buddhism
Gutenberg press, 74
Guthrie, Stewart, *Faces in the Clouds*, 113–14

Haidle, Miriam Noël, 29, 75
Halton, Eugene, 146, 148
hand ax, 7, *61*, 252; copper, 83; hominin manipulation of the, 46. See also Acheulean tools; tool use
Handley, Susannah, *Nylon*, 188
Harari, Yuval, *Sapiens*, 9
Harford, Tim, 172
Harmand, Sonia, 25–26
Hawaiian Islands, 142
Hayes, Rutherford B., 70
heirlooms, 139–44, *141*, 232. See also chiefdoms
Herculano-Houzel, Suzana, 45

Higgs, Kerryn, 186, 195
Hinduism, 112, 235. See also religion
Hoarders (TV show), 223–24
hoarding, 209–21, *210*, 225, 232; animal, 211; collecting as, 220; concept of ownership as foundation of human, 215; by *Homo sapiens*, 211–12; in industrial societies, 221; of metal items, 217–18, *218*; Paleolithic, 215–18; as psychological condition, 222–23; Scandinavian, 217–18; scatter hoarding strategy of early hominins, 217; wealth as, 219. See also consumer society; disposophobia; stuff; wealth
Hobbes, Thomas, 212–13
Hodgson, Derek, 114–15
Holden, Ralph, and Earnest Elmo Calkins, *Modern Advertising*, 199
hominins, 25, 252; cumulative culture of, 77; diet of, 40–43; experimentation with tools by, 58; family tree of, *26*; fossil remains of, 32; hands of, 47–49; height of, *50*; invention of clothing as help, 148; inventions of, 181; material world of, 67–68; painting bodies of, 96; skulls of, 32–33, 45; storage of tools by early, 216–17; teeth of, 40–41, *40*, 49; visuospatial and sensorimotor systems of, 54; working memory of, 29, 75. See also brain; evolution; tool use
Homo erectus, 7, 17, *40*, *44*, 58, 65–67, 92–96, 103, 252; toolmaking by, 104; zigzag pattern in mussel shell etched by, 94–96, *95*, 103, 105
Homo florensis, 58
Homo habilis, 33–35, 43–44, *44*, 50
Homo heidelbergensis, 66, 105
Homo naledi, 103, 109–10, 122, 125, 252
Homo neanderthalensis, 4, 7, 44, 67–68, 253; art of, 100–101; burial of the dead by, 103, 111; cave of, 87–88, *104*; clothing of, 148–49; hunters, 114; jewelry of, 97, 105
Homo sapiens, 2–3, 8, 14, 17, 20–22, *40*,

INDEX

44, *44*, *48*, 49, 67–69, 100–105, 110, 231, 252; burial of the dead by, 111; clothing of, 149; as *Homo faber*, 56–58; material world of, 67–69; in Neanderthal cave, 87–88; propensity for hoarding of, 211–12; symbolic thinking of, 150, 231. *See also* humanity; symbolic thinking

honeybee, 211

Hong Kong, 106–13, 117–19; Chi Lin Nunnery, 122–23; Sin Chai Buddhist-Daoist Hall, 123–25. *See also* China

Hood, Bruce, 192–93, 215, 227

House Beautiful (magazine), 189

houses, 1–2, 69; big, 5–6, 191, 193; clutter in, 224, *224*; storage in, 79. *See also* consumer society

humanity: creativity of, 3, 18; definition of the distinctiveness of, 18; material luxuries as hindrance to, 236. See also *Homo sapiens*

Hume, David, 212–13

Humes, Edward, *Garbology*, 225

Hung Hom Guanyin Temple (Hong Kong), 112–13, 117–18, 122–23

Hunt, Gavin, 28–29

Hunter, Rick, 109–10

hunter-gatherer societies, 7, 87, 131, 159–60, 252. *See also* foraging

Hurault, Paul, 97–99

Hyatt, John and Isaiah, 174

Ice Age, 69, 88, 98–99, 111, 149, 158–60; people of the, 114

Iceman (film), 63

identity, 8; Native American, 128–29; things as vehicles of, 147. *See also* self

Ihde, Don, 57

Inca Empire, 161

incandescent lightbulb, 170–71, 183, 203; as catalyst invention, 171. *See also* electricity; lighting

incorporative process, 146, 252

India, 2, 106, 178; griffins guarding treasure in ancient, 219; hoards in, 219

Indigenous peoples: Abelam, 117; Māori, 143, *214*; San, 116; Xingú, 117; Yoruba, 143. *See also* Native Americans

Indonesia, 101–2, 103, 105

Industrial Revolution, 8, 158, 162–67, 171–72, 177–79, 181, *182*, 232, 253; American, 178; chemists of, 174; marketing practices advanced by, 186; scientific advances, 162–63. *See also* Arkwright machine; factories; invention; machinery; steam power; water mill; Watt steam engine; weaving loom

inequality, 82; collective ownership as a way to avoid, 212; debt and, 193, 219; economic, 231; material, 159; origins of, 160. *See also* wealth

intelligence, 20–21, 24; brain size and, 45; innovative, 42; and stone technology, 46. *See also* blank-canvas stage; reasoning

invention: as intergenerational project, 75–76; moment of, 36; of phonograph, 70–75; of plastics, 174; of stone tools, 26, 30, 41, 57. *See also* catalyst invention; Industrial Revolution; machinery; plastics

iPhone, *154*

Iran, 80

Iraq, 80; northern, 111

iron, 132; hoes, 132; hot-blast technique for making, 165; mass production of, 171. *See also* steel

Islam, 112; Sufi, 121, 235. *See also* religion

Isler, Karin, 49

Israel, 178

Italy, 62; northern, 87

jade, 132

Jains, 218. *See also* religion

James, William, 222

Japan, 69, 106, 173, 178, 222

Jarvis, Lara Joanna, 234, 236

Java, 17, 93–94, 218

Joordens, Josephine, 94–95

Journal of Consumer Research, 146
Journal of Gas Lighting, 169
Judaism, 112, 235. *See also* religion

Kahlo, Frida, 92
Kalahari Desert (Botswana), 115; massive boulder as object of worship in, 115–16, *115*, 125
Kant, Immanuel, 213
Kappelman, John, 47
Kennedy, Jackie, 143
Kennedy, John, 144
Kenya, 6, 31–32, 104, 242. *See also* Lomekwi 3
Kettering, Charles, "Keep the Consumer Dissatisfied," 193
Kimeu, Kamoya, 34
Kissel, Marc, 103–5
Kivell, Tracy, 48
Kondo, Marie, 6, 237
Korea, 74
Kyrk, Hazel, 192

Landes, David S., 166
landfills. *See* waste
Lascaux Cave (France), 99
Latour, Bruno, 118
Laysan albatross, 240
Leach, William, *Land of Desire*, 197
lead, 132
Leakey, Louis, 14–18, 31–35, 43, 47
Leakey, Richard, 17
Lebow, Victor, 196
liberty, 196, 238. *See also* freedom
lice, 148
Lieberman, Daniel, 39
Life, 204–5
lighting, 168–71, 183–84. *See also* fire; incandescent lightbulb
Lilienfeld, Scott O., 222
Lillios, Katina T., 142–43
Lincoln, Abraham, 144
Lobdell, Nicole, 221
Locke, John, 213–14
Lomekwi 3, 25, 36, 253. *See also* Kenya

London, 165, 168–70, 186, 238
London, Bernard, 201
Los Angeles Times, 242
love, 239
Lucy, 25, 35, 44, 46–50, 63–64, 70, 73, 252. *See also Australopithecus*
Ludd, Ned, 164
Luddites, 163–64, 167, 253; concerns about labor practices and low-quality goods, 164; concerns about mechanization of humanity, 167; real, 247–48; riots, 164
Lydians, 133–34; invention of coins, 133–34, *133*

macaque, 22, 216
machinery, 163–67; age of, 166–67, 251; British legislation to prevent unions and protect, 164; replacement of human labor by, 166. *See also* Arkwright machine; factories; Industrial Revolution; invention; machining tools
machining tools, 171–72. *See also* machinery
Mah, Alice, 243
Malafouris, Lambros, 57
Malaysia, 106
Mali, 78; Kingdom of, 161
Manoharan, Christopher, 121
marketing, 8; mass, 187–88; modern, 186. *See also* advertising industry; branded proposition; consumer society
Marx, Karl, 213
Maurya Empire, 161
Mauss, Marcel, "The Gift," 137
Max Planck Institute for Evolutionary Anthropology (Leipzig), 25
Maya Empire, 161, 218
McCoy, J. W., 192
McPherron, Shannon, 25
meaning: of dress codes, 129; emergence of, 90; invention of, 7–8, 101–2; of objects, 151–52; process of the

development of, 103–5. *See also* art; money; religion; symbolism
Mediterranean region, 34, 132; coins in, 134; eastern, 80
Merfield, Fred, 17
Mesopotamia, 161. *See also* Fertile Crescent
Messner, Reinhold, 60–61
metal alphabet pieces, 74
metallurgy, 80
Mexico, 78–79, 151; Aztec Empire, 132
microbeads, 246–47
microplastics, 205, 231, 240. *See also* plastics
Middle East, 116, 132; hoards, 219
Midway Atoll, 239–40
Miles, Tiya, *All That She Carried*, 141–42
Miller, Daniel, 238
Miller, George, 91
minerals, 166. *See also* mining
minimalism, 4–5, 234–39, 245, 253; aesthetic of, 234, 238; criticism of, 238–39; reduction, 237. *See also* zero-waste lifestyle
Minimalists, The (film), 237
mining, 159; steam engines fueled by coal for, 172. *See also* minerals
mobile attention, 146, 253
Monet, Claude, 91
money, 7–8, 130–34, 232; invention of, 160; value in consumer culture, 197. *See also* meaning; symbolic thinking; wealth
Mongolia, 106
Moore, Charlie, 240
Morgan, David B., 216
Morocco, 68, 148
Morriss-Kay, Gillian M., 96, 100–101
Mousterian tools, 44, 67, 253. *See also* tool use
Mukiri, Heselon, 32
Munro, Stephen, 94
museums, 3–5, 135; American Museum of Natural History (New York), 48; Coryndon Museum (Nairobi), 14;

Denver Museum of Nature and Science, 107, 126–27; Houston Museum of Natural Science, 47; Museum of Natural History (University of Colorado, Boulder), 215; National Museum of African American History and Culture (Washington, DC), 140; National Museum of Ethiopia, 24, 47; National Museum of Natural History (Brazil), 4; National September 11 Memorial and Museum (New York City), 197, *198*; South Tyrol Museum of Archaeology (Italy), 61; U'mista Cultural Centre (Alert Bay), 138
musical instruments, 69; drum, 69; flute, 68, *68*, 103; rattle, 69

Napoleonic Wars, 163
NASA space shuttle, 75
National Academy of Sciences, 70
National Geographic, 18
National Phonograph Company, *185*
Native Americans, 4, 145–46; assimilation of, 127–28; defiance of, 151–52; Hopi, 112, 214–15; Kwakwa̱ka̱'wakw, 135, 137; Lakota, 130, 134–35, 139, *150*, 151–52; on ownership of property, 214; religious practices of, 112; S'Klallam, 127; Zuni, 117. *See also* Indigenous peoples; potlatches
Nature, 39, 47, 102
Neanderthals. See *Homo neanderthalensis*
Near East, 68, 103; decorated stone from the, 96
Neilson, James Beaumont, 165
Nengo, Isaiah, 34
Neolithic Revolution, 77–82, 253; storage of the, 81; trade, 131. *See also* agriculture; New Stone Age; sedentary lifestyle
New Caledonian crow, 21–22
New Stone Age, 77, 80. *See also* Neolithic Revolution
New York City, 157, 181–82, 204
New York Times, 93, 142

New Zealand, 6
Nextdoor, 236
Niagara Falls, 171
Nicol, Mary Douglas, 32
Niépce, Joseph Nicéphore, 165
North Africa, 34, 132
Nowell, April, 100
nylon stockings, 180–82, 188, 195, 203. *See also* plastics

obsessive-compulsive disorder (OCD), 222
obsolescence, 200–201; planned, 201, *202*, 203, 237, 242, 253; programming, 203; psychological, 203, 247; stylistic, 204
ochre, 69, 88, 96, 103; block engraved with zigzags of, *97*; body painting with, 99
octopus, 19–20
Oldowan toolkit, 6–7, 33–36, *34*, 40, *44*, 45–46, 253; refined stone tools made from the, 64; reuse of tools from, 216. *See also* tool use
Olduvai Gorge, 14, 16, 31–33, 232
olive oil, 132
orangutan, 22
ornamental beads, 87; copper, 80; shell worked into, 68
Ötzi, 62–64, *63*, 69, 77; clothing of, 62–63, 150; murder of, 82–83
oxen, 132

Pacific Phonograph Company, 184
Packard, Vance, 203; *The Hidden Persuaders*, 201; *The Status Seekers*, 195
paleoanthropology, 54
Paleoindian peoples, 215–16
Paleolithic era, 41, 97–102, 131, 253; bear sculpture from, 125; late, 101–2
paper, 74; factory-scale making of, 171
Parkes, Alexander, 174
Penda, King, 217
Peresani, Marco, 88–89, *89*, 101

Persian Empire, 161; painted reconstructed palace of Darius I, *161*
Peru, 122; Andes, 142
petroleum refining, 171
Pettitt, Paul, 114–15
Philippines, 178
phonograph, 70–72, *73*, 74–75, 183–84, 186; advertisement for, *185*; coin-operated, 184
photograph, 165
Picasso, Pablo, 91, 143, 147
pigeon, 21–22, 91
Pioneer Parachute Company, 175–76
Pithecanthropus erectus, 94
planned perseverance, 237, 247
plastics, 172–78, 220, 236, 246; age of, 251; Bakelite, 175; celluloid, 174–75; crisis of, 239–44; cumulative global production of, *177*, 205; in the ocean, 240, 247; Parkesine, 174; synthetic, 174–75; wartime production of, 176. *See also* chemicals; DuPont Fiber Company; invention; microplastics; nylon stockings; Third Industrial Revolution
Plato, *Republic*, 212
population, global explosion of, 80–81
potlatches, 125, 135–39, *136*, 219, 253; Canadian prohibition of, 135–38. *See also* Native Americans
pottery, fired clay, 69
Pradhan, Gauri R., 77
Pratt, Richard Henry, 128
print media, 189
private property, 212–15. *See also* stuff
problem-solution distance, 75, 254
Proconsul, 32
Prum, Richard, *The Evolution of Beauty*, 91

radical embodiment, 53–54, 254. *See also* body
radio, 189
railroads, 183, 186

Rappaport, Roy A., *Ritual and Religion in the Making of Humanity*, 124–25
ratchet effect, 76–77, *77*, 254
raw meat, 38–39
reasoning, 22, 24; learning and, 28. *See also* behavioral innovation; intelligence
red squirrel, 211
red-tailed hawk, 19, 29
reindeer, 132
religion, 7, 80, 232; and agriculture, 121–22; ascetic practices of, 235–36; belief in life after death, 112; birth of, 110–11; community of believers as hallmark of, 119–20; cooperation and empathy as foundation of, 120; material component of, 112, 124–25; religious things and religious belief, 116. *See also* Baha'i; Buddhism; Christianity; Daoism; Hinduism; Islam; Jains; Judaism; meaning; symbolic thinking
Rhode Island School of Design, 199
Richerson, Peter J., 76
Rising Star Cave (South Africa), 109–12, 125; Dinaledi Chamber, *110*
Roman Empire, 217–18
rook, 21
rubber, 165, 174
rubber-hand illusion, 55, *55*
Russia, 160
Rwanda, 242

salt, 132
Sanz, Crickette M., 216
Sanz de Sautuola, Marcelino, 99
Sartre, Jean-Paul, 146–47
Savoy Theater, 168–70, *169*
Scandinavia, 39
Schaik, Carel P. van, 49–50, 77
Schick, Kathy, 36, 41–43, 47, 50
Schindler, Bill, 41
Schwalbe, Gustav, 94
Science, 48
Scientific American, 70, 72, 76
sculpture: figurative, 69; representational, 100; Stone Age *Venus impudique*, 97–98, *98*. *See also* art
Second Industrial Revolution, 170–72, *182*, 186. *See also* assembly line; electricity; steel
sedentary lifestyle, 78, 159–60, 254. *See also* Neolithic Revolution
Seeley, Thomas D., 211
self: development of, 146; objects as extensions of, 144–48. *See also* identity
Sella, Andrea, 174
Shanidar (Iraq), 111
shell, 68; as currency, 132; engraved or painted, 92, 94–97, *95*, 99
shipping, 186
shopping: as act of love, 238–39; mail-order, 187; online, 187; as patriotism, 196; retail, 187, 232. *See also* advertising industry; consumer society
Siberia, 99, 132
silk, 173, 175–76
silver: ingots, 132–33; rarity of, 133
Simon, Helmut and Erika, 59–60, 62, 83
Singer, Lauren, 234, 237
Skinner, Matthew, 48
Slade, Giles, 201
Slater, Samuel, 156–58, 178
Sloan, Alfred P., Jr., 201, 203
Slovenia, 68
Smail, Daniel Lord, 221
Smith, Adam, *The Wealth of Nations*, 163
Smith, E. O., 19–20
Smith, Michael E., 160
social hierarchies, 80–82, 159
social organization, 103. *See also* division of labor
Solecki, Ralph, 111
South Africa, 68, 103, 109–12; cave painting in, 96
Soviet Union, 177
Spain, 97
squirrel monkey, 211
Staffordshire Hoard, 217
steam power, 164–65, 170; as catalyst invention, 172; in factories, 172. *See also*

Industrial Revolution; Watt steam engine
steam railway engine, 165, *165*
steel, 165; mass production of, 171, 176. *See also* iron; Second Industrial Revolution
Steketee, Gail, 222–23
Stevens, Brooks, "Planned Obsolescence," 201
Stonehenge, 120, 122
storage, 6, 81–82; surplus and, 81–82. *See also* stuff
Stravinsky, Igor, 91
Strutt, Jedediah, 155–56, 158
stuff, 1–5, 9, 244, 247, 254; human beings becoming social beings through, 83, 90; human desire for more, 232–33, 235–36; transition to settled life and dramatic increase in, 79; world overflowing with, 196, 232. *See also* consumerism; consumer society; hoarding; private property; storage; waste
Sudan, 78, 103; ancient, 132
Sullivan, Arthur: *HMS Pinafore*, 168; *The Sorcerer*, 168
Switzerland, 98
symbolic thinking, 97–102, 105, 150, 231–32, 254. *See also* art; *Homo sapiens*; money; religion
symbolism, 196. *See also* meaning
Syria, 78

Tanzania, 242; Geological Survey of, 31; Gombe National Park, 15, 31–32; Serengeti Plains, 31
Taylor, Alex, 28
tayra, 211
technology: advances in more sophisticated, 6–7, 36–37, 46, 75; chain to create novel, *71*; Clovis spearpoints as early stone, *12*; complex clothing, 149; complex stone, 46, 68–69; definition of, 19; discovery of novel, 73–74; of fermentation, 41; of fire, 41; first human, 7, 34–35; history of human, 71, 160–61; magic and power of, 17. *See also* cumulative culture; tool use
techno-organic evolution, 17, 41–42, 254. *See also* evolution
telegraph, 165, 183
television, 189, 196
Tell Abu Hureyra, 78
Tennie, Claudio, 77
tennis, 51–53, *52*
Terra Amata (France), 66; huts, *67*, 69
Third Industrial Revolution, 177, 181, *182*, 192. *See also* plastics
Thoreau, Henry David, 236
Times (London), 168
tin can, 165
Tomasello, Michael, 76
tool use, 2, 6–8, 20, 30, 254; bone, 69; evolutionary benefits of, 5, 19, 24, 41–42, 50, 92, 104; for food processing, 43, 50; human, 7, 16–18, 34–35, 68, 99, 231; nonhuman, 18–20, *20*, 35–36, 76, 231; secondary, 35; specialized, 80; stone, 16, 24–37, *30*, 40–43, 46–49, 54, 57, 63–69, 76, 88–93, 98, 104, 181, 215–16. *See also* Acheulean tools; arrowhead; Aurignacian tools; composite tool; dagger; evolution; fishhooks; hand ax; hominins; Mousterian tools; Oldowan toolkit; technology
Toth, Nicholas, 36, 41–43, 47, 50
Toungoo Empire, 161
trade, 80, 131; cotton, 139; networks facilitated by weighing piles of metal, 132–33; slave, 139–40
Tse, Martin, 107–8, 112–13, 117–19, 122–23
Tucker, Steven, 109–10
Turkey, 133, 194
Tut, King, 219, 230
typewriter, 165

Uganda, 242

Ukraine, 69
United Kingdom, 5, 157, 188, 190, 222
United States, 125–26, 157, 173–78, 190, 222, 230, 242–43; industrial index (1800–1914), *191*
urbanization, 80–81, 131, 159, 181, 186

Vale of York Hoard, *218*
Vander Wall, Stephen B., *Food Hoarding in Animals*, 211
Vanity Fair, 219
Veblen, Thorstein, 194

Waite, Tom, 211
Washington, George, 193–94, 196
waste, 6, 200; consumption and, 205, 225–27; landfills, 225, 227, 229–31, 236; plastic, 240–41. *See also* consumer society; environment; garbage patches; stuff
water buffalo, 132
water mill, 156–58, 171, 178. *See also* Industrial Revolution
Watt steam engine, 164–65. *See also* Industrial Revolution
wealth: accumulation of, 137, 160; ceremonial events as demonstrations of, 125; economic defensibility of, 160; as hoarding, 219; meaning of, 247; of nations, 158–63; as reason to be killed, 83. *See also* hoarding; inequality; money
Weatherford, Jack, 132, 134
weaving loom, 181, *182*. *See also* Industrial Revolution
Wengrow, David, and David Graeber, *The Dawn of Everything*, 9, 159–60
wheat, 132
Wheeler, S. Christian, 147
White, Randall, 101
wine-making presses, 74
Wingfield, Walter C., 51
Wolfgang Köhler Primate Research Center, 21
World Bank, 6, 177
World Economic Forum, 243
World War I, 172, 189
World War II, 170, 173, 175–77, 180, 187–88, 190, 195
writing, birth of, 80

Xygalatas, Dimitris, 121

Zambia, 66, 105
zero-waste lifestyle, 237. *See also* minimalism
Zinjanthropus boisei (*Paranthropus boisei*), 31–34
Zink, Katherine, 39